Two sisters from the Warm Springs Reservation ride their family's horse.

A Native American dancer performs a hoop dance in the Secret Slot Canyons of Arizona. Hoop dancing is a modern form of dance among Native tribes.

ENCYCLOPEDIA OF AMERICAN INDIAN HISTORY & CULTURE

STORIES, TIME LINES, MAPS, AND MORE

CYNTHIA O'BRIEN

NATIONAL GEOGRAPHIC
WASHINGTON, D.C.

CONTENTS

THE ARCTIC AND SUBARCTIC 14

THE NORTHEAST 42

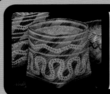

THE SOUTHEAST 78

THE PLAINS 100

THE SOUTHWEST 150

THE GREAT BASIN AND PLATEAU 180

THE NORTHWEST COAST 214

CALIFORNIA 248

HOW TO USE THIS BOOK

The *Encyclopedia of American Indian History and Culture* takes a tour of the United States and Canada, with a chapter for each of eight major regions of the area: the Arctic and subarctic, the Northeast, the Southeast, the Plains, the Southwest, the Great Basin and Plateau, the Northwest Coast, and California. You can read the book from cover to cover, or choose a region or tribe that interests you.

Each chapter begins with an introduction and a map of ancestral lands. You'll discover how people came to inhabit the region in the first place, and how they developed ways of life that depended on the natural resources available to them. You'll also learn about the impact that white settlers had on tribal life during the decades following first contact. These were turbulent times during which many Native people suffered from disease, brutality, and relocation. The introduction concludes with a short account of tribal life today, and the ways in which indigenous peoples have managed, in recent years, to right some of the past wrongs inflicted on them. The tribes included in each chapter are based on where those tribes live today. For this reason, not every tribe in each section appears on the map at the start of the chapter. The maps show ancestral lands to give readers a sense of how much area each tribe once occupied.

Following each chapter introduction is a time line with 15 to 20 key dates in the region's tribal histories. You can turn to this when reading about the tribes, to see how the major events unfolded in a particular region: Significant conflicts, acts of legislation, and cultural or political milestones are all listed here.

Next, from that region, the chapter tells the stories of tribes, from their origins thousands of years ago to the lifeways and achievements of their people in the present day. There is an emphasis on the traditions that have shaped the indigenous peoples of the United States and Canada—traditions that remain at the heart of their culture. You'll find the tribes organized alphabetically within each chapter, according to the names by which they are best known. While a given tribe might have lived in more than one region during the course of its history, each is featured in the chapter for the region in which the majority of its people live today.

Interspersed with the tribal stories, you'll find biographies of leading native figures past and present, and special features on many cultural aspects of tribal life, including clothing, transportation, ceremonies, and crafts. Turn to the end of each chapter for a traditional story from one of the region's tribes.

An introduction to each chapter tells the story of its people, including how environmental factors and historic events shaped their lives.

A map shows the tribes' ancestral lands. The larger the letters in the labels and the wider the spacing between them, the more land the tribe occupied.

A **time line** offers an instant history of the region. A short introduction summarizes the ways in which tribal life has changed over the centuries.

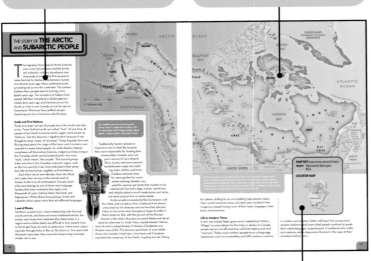

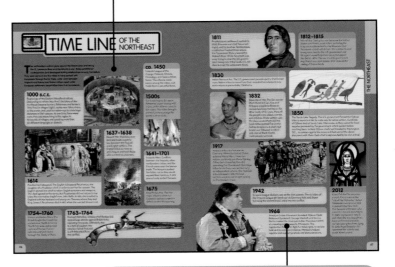

A **map key** shows the labeling used to identify each tribe on the regional map. A **locator map** shows where the region lies within North America.

Working from the earliest times to the present day, the **time line** highlights the dates and events that had the greatest impact on tribal life.

Special features and **In the Know** panels focus on cultural themes that are specific to a given tribe or to the tribes of the region as a whole.

The text is richly illustrated with photographs, illustrations, and paintings that capture the spirit of each tribe and its unique culture.

Key facts include a pronunciation guide for the tribe's name and information on its location both pre- and post-contact. A language guide includes tribal words for a greeting and "thank you." Most are written phonetically, and can be spoken just as they appear.

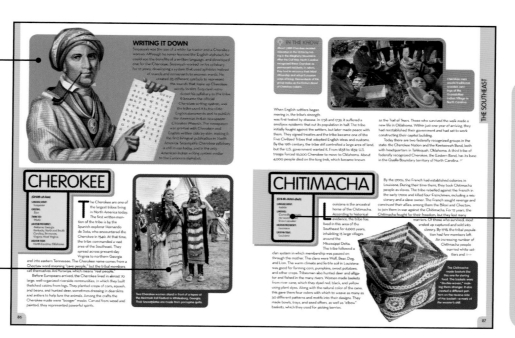

Each chapter includes a **Did You Know?** photo feature that focuses on one specific event or cultural theme.

All chapters end with a traditional story from one of the featured tribes. These stories have been passed down through many generations.

The photographs that accompany the stories reflect on the important role that nature continues to play in tribal culture.

With origins among the tribes of the Plains region, powwows are still a part of the lives of many North American tribes as a celebration of their culture. A Sioux powwow is pictured here.

PUBLISHER'S NOTE

The National Geographic *Encyclopedia of American Indian History and Culture* is an introduction to the rich histories and cultures of the native peoples of North America, featuring more than 160 tribes in the United States, and some of the First Nations, Inuit, and Métis indigenous peoples in Canada. Currently there are 573 federally recognized tribes in the United States. Having federal recognition means that a tribe may form its own government and that its land and various other rights are protected. In Canada, there are 634 First Nations groups and numerous groups of Inuit and Métis peoples. (Métis are those with both indigenous and European ancestry.) To see a listing and for more information about the native and indigenous peoples of the United States and Canada, please refer to the websites and listings at the back of this book.

The following terms and notes help provide critical context for readers of this encyclopedia.

Tribal Sovereignty

Before European settlement in what is now the United States and Canada, the indigenous people of this region had sovereignty, or the right of self-government.

As Europeans took over more territory, the Native populations began to decrease due to disease, conflict with settlers, and disruption of their traditional ways of life. At the time, tribes also lost their sovereignty, and many were forced to live on reservations.

Today, Native Americans in the United States are recognized by the federal government as "domestic dependent nations." This means Native American tribes have a unique sovereign status: Tribes have sovereignty to govern themselves, but federal law and the Constitution put limits on their ability to fully self-govern. Unlike any other minority group in the United States, indigenous communities have legal rights because of their sovereign status and special relationship to the federal government.

Naming Conventions

The encyclopedia uses Native, Native American, and American Indian interchangeably to refer to the indigenous peoples of the United States. The term Indian is used when referring to a proper name. As much as possible, the book uses the tribally-specific terminology

to refer to individual tribes. Canadian indigenous peoples are referred to as First Nations, Inuit, or Métis, based on the group to which they belong.

Edward Curtis Photos

Most available photography of Native American people between 1900 and 1930 is by Edward Curtis. Curtis photographed Native American life at the beginning of the 20th century after many Native Americans had been forcibly removed from their traditional homelands and were now living on reservations, adjusting to a way of life they neither understood nor wanted. Although Curtis captured beautiful and meaningful images of Native people, controversy surrounds his work. Some believe he romanticized his subjects, showing an idealized version of Native life that no longer existed.

Indian Removal Act

Readers will also find information on the Indian Removal Act of 1830. The law was created to authorize then U.S. president Andrew Jackson to remove Native Americans from their homelands. After the passage of the act, many Native people tried to resist, but their efforts were unsuccessful, and they were forcibly removed from their lands and made to walk west. During these removals, Native people suffered greatly

from starvation, disease, and exposure to harsh weather, and many lost their lives. The indefensible government removal policy formed the basis for continued European expansion onto Native lands for the remainder of the 19th century.

Native Americans Today

This encyclopedia shows different aspects of Native life, culture, and history. Readers will notice there are a variety of images of Native peoples in regalia as well as in contemporary, everyday clothing. Many Native peoples dress in regalia for certain festivals or other occasions, such as powwows, that are discussed and pictured in this book. Powwows are an important part of modern Native American life, in which tribes come together through dance, music, and song to honor their veterans, their families, and their cultures and traditions. In addition, though reservations still exist as established communities, Native peoples are no longer forced to live on them and most do not.

We hope readers find this encyclopedia to be an informative reference that acknowledges the significance of the history, culture, identities, and ways of self-governance of Native peoples. We also hope it helps readers to realize the impact that the history of settlement still has on Native peoples today.

INTRODUCTION

When the explorer Christopher Columbus first reached South and Central America in 1492, he had traveled there from Spain, in Europe. He and his men met people unknown to Europeans. Thinking he had reached India, Columbus called these people Indians, a name we Native peoples of the Americas share to this day.

The Truth About Native Peoples

The misnaming of Native people is but one of many misconceptions and misunderstandings about us. Another error that persists is to speak of "the" American Indians as though they are one collective people. In truth, with regard to language, clothes, crafts, traditions, and lifestyle, the Native peoples of the United States and Canada were, and still are, as different from one another as are the peoples of Europe. There were so many distinct groups in North America at the time of Columbus's first encounter that up to one hundred different languages were spoken in California alone. That is why an encyclopedia such as this one can only hope to feature a selection of the many tribes that represent the cultures and lifestyles to be found in the various geographical regions of the United States and Canada.

Another common misconception is that true Native Americans—those who practice ancient traditions—have vanished. In a sense Native Americans did vanish because, once settled on reservations in the late 19th century, they were largely forgotten about. They did not disappear, however, nor did their traditions, despite the efforts of the federal government, missionaries, and various organizations to force Native Americans to give up their languages and cultures to become part of mainstream society. Many Native cultures did change, but they were not destroyed. Threads of traditional life survived to be reawakened in the cultural resurgence of recent years. One of the most important factors in retaining traditional culture involves keeping the original language alive. This is why bilingual programs are so prominent in the Native community, with as many as 150 different indigenous languages being spoken across North America today. In reading this book you will discover that, instead of being a feature of the past, we Native Americans are still very much here and continue to cherish our traditional values, ceremonies, songs, and great love of the natural world.

The histories presented in this book are based on both Native and non-Native sources. Native peoples of this region did not have a written language. Their histories were not recorded in writing, but in pictures, or as the memories of tribal members. In many instances, their stories were passed down through a succession of specially trained individuals who were selected in their youth and given the responsibility of retaining their people's history. Over the centuries such stories have been recorded by others—in the diaries of the explorers who first encountered Native peoples, and by historians wanting to preserve a record of North America's past, for example.

Cultural Diversity

Whether called nations, tribes, or bands, the groups that occupied the United States and Canada presented a rich variety of lifestyles. From the Arctic to the Gulf of Mexico, and from the Atlantic Ocean to the Pacific Ocean, the differences between Native peoples were many and extreme. This makes sense considering that perhaps as many as six hundred different cultures shared North America before the Europeans first made contact more than five hundred years ago.

My people are the Northern Cheyenne. They lived on the Great Plains—a vast area that stretched from central Canada in the north to the Mexican border in the south, and was bounded on the west by the Rocky Mountains and on the east by the Missouri River. From the earliest times, the Plains territory was home to few tribes on a full-time basis because it was difficult for hunters to travel such vast distances on foot and with only dogs as pack animals. Most people living in the region were seminomadic, making occasional trips in search of buffalo and other large game to hunt, but also living in permanent camps

Children's dolls were often modeled on the adults of the tribe, as in this Cherokee example. The hair was often made from animal fur or was taken from the hair of a child's mother.

where they planted corn, beans, squash, and other crops. In the early 1500s, the Spanish introduced horses to Mexico and horse populations grew and spread across North America during the following centuries. Once my people and our neighbors the Lakota, Arapaho, Crow, and other Plains tribes had horses, we became full-time nomadic buffalo hunters. Over the years, the Plains tribes created a culture that came to symbolize all North American Indians for people of the world. To this day, no aspect of the American West has captured the imagination more universally than the image of our fiercely independent nomadic ancestors with their flashing eagle-feather war bonnets and painted ponies. Their distinctive lifestyle and militancy enabled Plains tribes to hold

European invaders at bay until well into the 19th century. Indeed, were it not for the loss of the buffalo and the inability of Plains tribes to put aside intertribal grievances and conflicts to unite against the invaders from the east, the U.S. Cavalry might well have been chasing them into the 20th century.

A Cultural Reawakening

Now, in the 21st century, I am pleased to report that the Native peoples of North America have not only survived their long ordeal, but are also reasserting their pride in themselves and their traditions. They continue to represent a minority in the United States, but their numbers are steadily growing, their landholdings are increasing, and they are building a professional class. Just a few decades ago, Native Americans were denied U.S. citizenship and were not allowed to vote in state or national elections. Today we not only vote, we can hold public office. I am a prime example of this remarkable transition. In 1987, the people of Colorado elected me to

Totem poles are associated with the tribes of the Northwest Coast region, particularly the Haida and the Tlingit. Painted in bright colors, the striking carvings represent aspects of a tribe's family history, such as which clan it belongs to. This totem pole was carved in honor of Tlingit Chief Johnson, in 1901.

During the 1800s several artists painted scenes of tribal life across North America, such as this Pikuni encampment near Fort McKenzie on the Musselshell River, Montana. The Pikuni were one of three main bands of the Blackfeet tribe.

the U.S. House of Representatives and then, in 1992, to the U.S. Senate. I am but one Native American to hold public office in cities and states across this great country. Moreover, despite the injustices American Indians have endured, we remain among the nation's most patriotic citizens. Native Americans have served in the armed forces of the United States in each of our nation's conflicts and today we serve at a higher rate than any other ethnic group. Why? In the past, we served to reaffirm treaty alliances with the United States or to honor the warrior tradition that is inherent to most Native American societies. Nowadays most, like me, who served in the Korean War, do so for sheer love of home and country.

Looking Forward

Because Native Americans straddle two societies—our own and that of the more mainstream United States—challenges and concerns remain. One such area is the future of our reservations. Even though the majority of Native Americans— perhaps 75 percent—now live off their reservations, they still consider them home. Reservations are viewed as havens from the stress and distractions of the outside world. Reservations are a place where tribal peoples can practice their traditional ceremonies and ways of living without interference from others. How long will the federal government continue to give reservations special status when they serve so few people? The Northern Cheyenne Reservation is in Montana, but I live in Colorado. Nonetheless, when I visit Lame Deer, the tribal headquarters, I feel like I have come home. I am surrounded by friends and relatives—people for whom my position in the white world is secondary to our shared ancestral roots.

Another concern is the survival of our cultures. Like all young people, our youths are distracted by the attractions of a world that places little value on tradition. Our challenge now is to ensure that the non-Native world knows our history and recognizes the need to preserve our homes, our cultures, and our religions so that future generations of Native Americans will hold firmly the legacy that has been ours since ancient times. That is why books like this one are so important. After reading it, dig deeper into the histories and cultures of American Indians. A good place to begin is in one of the many local museums that celebrate our lives, or at the National Museum of the American Indian in Washington, D.C. Here, you can see the artistic creations of Indian craftspeople from previous generations and can experience our songs and foods. Everyone is welcome.

Ben Nighthorse Campbell

Ben Nighthorse Campbell (Northern Cheyenne) served in the House and in the Senate, representing the state of Colorado for two terms. A rancher and trainer of quarter horses, he is an award-winning jewelry designer, having learned the skill from his father. In 1991, he led and won the effort to change the name of the Custer Battlefield Monument to the Little Bighorn Battlefield National Monument, legislation that honors American Indians who died in battle.

MAP OF
NATIVE AMERICAN AND FIRST NATION CANADIAN REGIONS

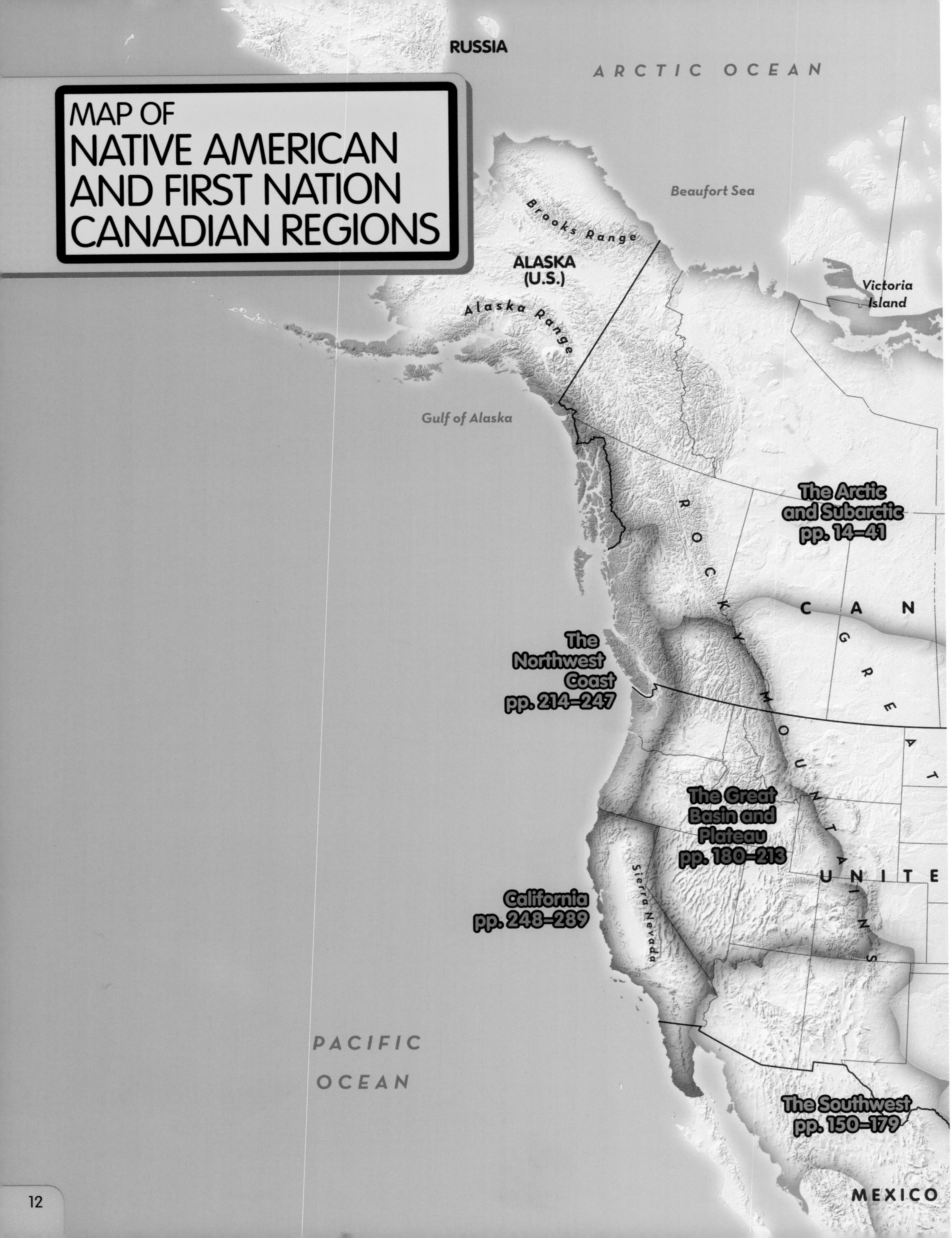

RUSSIA

ARCTIC OCEAN

Beaufort Sea

Brooks Range

ALASKA (U.S.)

Alaska Range

Victoria Island

Gulf of Alaska

R O C K Y   M O U N T A I N S

C A N

G R E

The Arctic and Subarctic pp. 14–41

The Northwest Coast pp. 214–247

The Great Basin and Plateau pp. 180–213

G R E A T

U N I T E

Sierra Nevada

California pp. 248–289

PACIFIC

OCEAN

The Southwest pp. 150–179

MEXICO

Ellesmere
Island

Iceland

Greenland

Baffin Bay

Baffin Island

Labrador
Sea

Hudson Bay

Island of
Newfoundland

A D A

ATLANTIC

OCEAN

The Plains
pp. 100–149

The Northeast
pp. 42–77

APPALACHIAN MOUNTAINS

D · STATES

The Southeast
pp. 78–99

0	miles	600

0	kilometers	600

Gulf of Mexico

A young Inupiat girl cuddles two puppies in the coastal village of Kotzebue, northwestern Alaska. She stands in front of a traditional shelter, covered with caribou skins. When they grow older, the dogs will likely be used for pulling sleds.

THE ARCTIC AND SUBARCTIC

The North American Arctic is an icy, treeless region with long, cold winters. Thousands of years ago people came here from Asia, crossing the Bering Strait into Alaska. Some of them stayed in the Arctic North, hunting caribou, musk ox, and seals. Others traveled south to the subarctic region. Even here, summers were short, but the forested land offered bountiful hunting and fishing grounds.

THE STORY OF **THE ARCTIC** AND **SUBARCTIC PEOPLE**

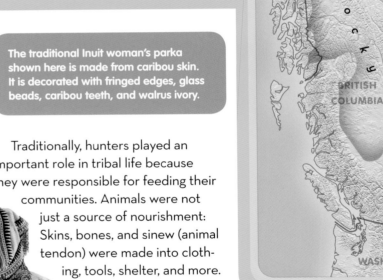

The migration from Asia to North America was a very slow process and the Arctic and subarctic cultures developed over thousands of years. The first people to make the trek to Alaska came between 15,000 and 20,000 years ago. Many continued south, spreading out across the continent. The earliest Eskimo-Aleut people started arriving some 8,000 years ago. The ancestors of today's Inuit people left their homeland in Alaska approximately 800 years ago and traveled across the North to what is now Canada and as far east as Greenland. Wherever they settled, people found ways to live in harmony with the land.

Inuits and First Nations

Today, two major groups of people live in the Arctic and subarctic. Those farthest north are called "Inuit." At one time, all people of the North American Arctic region were known as "Eskimos," but this became a negative term because it was thought to mean "eater of raw meat." Today, linguists have conflicting ideas about the origin of the term, and it remains unacceptable to some tribal people. So, while Alaskan Natives sometimes call themselves Eskimos, indigenous tribes living in the Canadian Arctic and Greenland prefer the word "Inuit," which means "the people." The second group—tribes who live in the Canadian subarctic region, such as the Innu and Oji-Cree—have individual tribal names but refer to themselves together as First Nations.

Each tribe has its own identity—from the Aleut, who make their homes on the islands west of Alaska, to the Innu of northeastern Canada. Each tribe also belongs to one of three main language families that have evolved in this region over thousands of years: Eskimo-Aleut, Na-Dené, and Algonquian. Within these three groups, Arctic and subarctic tribes speak more than 40 different languages.

Land of Plenty

Northern people have a close relationship with the land and its animals, and there are many traditional stories, festivities, and rituals that celebrate this relationship. In a region where edible plants are difficult to find, people hunt or fish to get food. As early as 4500 B.C.E., tribes were capturing seals through holes in the ice. By 1000 C.E., five and a half thousand years later, they were also harpooning bowhead whales out at sea.

The traditional Inuit woman's parka shown here is made from caribou skin. It is decorated with fringed edges, glass beads, caribou teeth, and walrus ivory.

Traditionally, hunters played an important role in tribal life because they were responsible for feeding their communities. Animals were not just a source of nourishment: Skins, bones, and sinew (animal tendon) were made into clothing, tools, shelter, and more. Caribou and polar bear fur were perfect for warm winter clothing. Sealskin was used for summer garments that needed to be waterproof. Furs from dogs, wolves, wolverines, and rabbits added warmth inside boots and socks, and were used as trim on parka hoods.

Arctic people encountered few Europeans until the 1700s, and carried on their traditional lives almost untouched by the diseases and warfare that affected tribes to the south when Europeans began to settle in North America. But, with the growth of the Russian Empire in the 1700s, Russians occupied Alaska and developed an extensive fur trade. Many coastal Alaskan Natives were forced to adopt Russian Orthodox Christianity and Russian ways of life. The Russians punished—or even killed—those who resisted. Much later, Americans and Canadians exploited the resources of the North, trapping animals, fishing

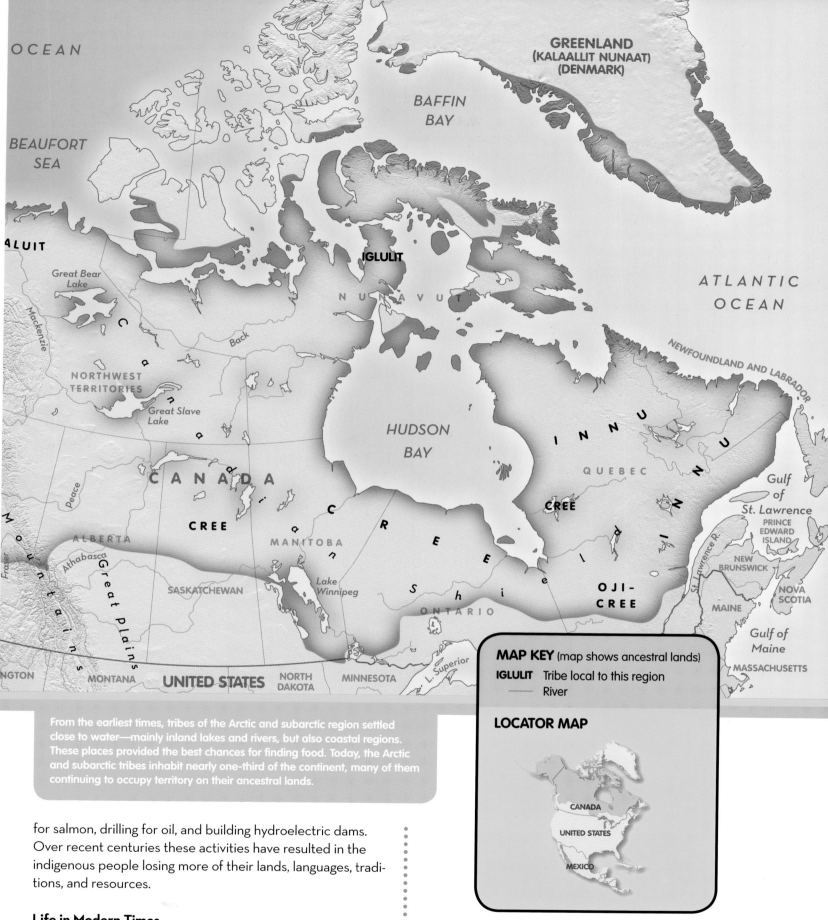

OCEAN

BEAUFORT
SEA

LUIT

Great Bear
Lake

Mackenzie

NORTHWEST
TERRITORIES

Great Slave
Lake

Back

GREENLAND
(KALAALLIT NUNAAT)
(DENMARK)

BAFFIN
BAY

IGLULIT

N U N A V U T

ATLANTIC
OCEAN

NEWFOUNDLAND AND LABRADOR

HUDSON
BAY

CANADA

CREE

Peace

ALBERTA

Athabasca

Great Plains

Fraser

SASKATCHEWAN

MANITOBA

Lake
Winnipeg

ONTARIO

C R E E

S h i e l d

C a n a d i a n

QUEBEC

INNU

CREE

INNU

OJI-
CREE

Gulf
of
St. Lawrence

St. Lawrence R.

PRINCE
EDWARD
ISLAND

NEW
BRUNSWICK

NOVA
SCOTIA

MAINE

Gulf of
Maine

MASSACHUSETTS

Mountains

NGTON

MONTANA

UNITED STATES

NORTH
DAKOTA

MINNESOTA

L. Superior

MAP KEY (map shows ancestral lands)

IGLULIT   Tribe local to this region
———   River

LOCATOR MAP

CANADA

UNITED STATES

MEXICO

From the earliest times, tribes of the Arctic and subarctic region settled close to water—mainly inland lakes and rivers, but also coastal regions. These places provided the best chances for finding food. Today, the Arctic and subarctic tribes inhabit nearly one-third of the continent, many of them continuing to occupy territory on their ancestral lands.

for salmon, drilling for oil, and building hydroelectric dams. Over recent centuries these activities have resulted in the indigenous people losing more of their lands, languages, traditions, and resources.

Life in Modern Times
In 1971, the United States government established "Native Villages" as reservations for the tribes in Alaska. In Canada, people live on and off what they call First Nations and Inuit "reserves." Today, most northern people have cutting-edge equipment, such as snowmobiles and GPS receivers, and live in modern communities. Elders still teach the young about ancient traditions, and many tribal people continue to speak their native languages; to participate in traditional arts, crafts, and customs; and to depend on the land in the ways of their ancestors before them.

TIME LINE OF THE ARCTIC AND SUBARCTIC

Early Arctic cultures included Dorset and Thule. These tribes were defined by the tools they used and their methods of survival. Different languages and customs evolved. From the 1700s, the Arctic tribes endured slavery, deadly disease, and colonization. Residential, or boarding, schools forced families apart and tried to erase languages and traditions. In spite of this, land-claims agreements and political acts have helped to regain lost land and hunting and fishing rights. The indigenous people survived, and many languages and customs endured.

20,000 B.C.E.

People migrate across the land bridge between Asia and North America. Ice sheets across the North forced sea levels to lower, revealing the large area known as the Bering Land Bridge. Many people probably lived in this area for thousands of years. When sea levels rose again, people made their way across in boats.

1000–1400 C.E.

Vikings arrive. Vikings traveling across the North Atlantic from Norway to Iceland reached Greenland in around 1000 C.E. Explorer Eric the Red established a colony that lasted for 400 years. His son, Leif Eriksson, explored farther west and discovered an area of what is now northern Newfoundland. The Norse met and traded with the Dorsets and their Thule successors.

4500 B.C.E.–1400 C.E.

The Palaeoeskimo peoples of the Pre-Dorset and Dorset cultures live throughout the region. Hunters of the Dorset culture developed new types of harpoons (pictured right). They captured seals through breathing holes in the ice and walruses at the ice's edge. The Dorsets created ivory and soapstone carvings of animals and people.

1000 C.E.

The Thule culture begins. Thule hunters utilized large, open, skin boats called *umiaks* for capturing sea mammals such as bowhead whales. They used boats to travel during the summer, while dogsleds were used for winter trade and transport.

1576–1578

Martin Frobisher (left) arrives from England. The search for a Northwest Passage to China brought Frobisher to southeastern Baffin Island, where he mined for gold. The project failed after three expeditions, when the "gold" was found to be worthless black rock.

1607–1610

Henry Hudson explores the Arctic region. Hudson's expeditions brought the British and the Dutch to the Arctic.

1745

Russians enslave Aleut people. In the mid-1700s, the Russians began their fur trade in western Alaska, forcing the Aleut to hunt for them. In 1762, the Aleuts rebelled and killed a group of Russians. The Russians retaliated, killing Aleut, Yup'ik, and other tribal people over several years.

1799–1867

Russian-American Company establishes 14 forts in Alaska and California. During this time, Russian missionaries converted many people to the Orthodox Church. In 1804, the Russians established their first permanent settlement at Sitka and continued their hold on the area for over 40 more years. Pictured is St. Michael's Russian Orthodox Cathedral, built in Sitka in the 1840s and still standing today.

1867

The United States buys Alaska. The Russian-American Treaty was signed on March 30. The Americans purchased Alaska for $7.2 million, and the official land transfer took place October 18, now Alaska Day.

1880s

Indigenous children attend residential schools. From the early 1900s, the U.S. and Canadian governments expanded the residential, or boarding, school system. The schools were far away from families and communities, taught in English, and banned native culture.

1912

Alaska Native Brotherhood founded. This organization, and the Sisterhood, founded three years later, fights for civil and land rights for the Native peoples of this region.

1921

Canadian government signs Treaty 11. The treaty was signed with 21 First Nations of the Northwest Territories following the discovery of oil on their land. The treaty assigned reserves to the indigenous people in exchange for land.

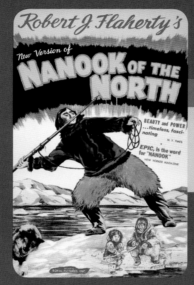

1922

Nanook of the North film is released. Robert Flaherty's film, the first full-length documentary, introduced the Inuit culture to a wider audience.

1936

Alaska Native villages receive federal recognition. The U.S. government offered funding to villages that adopted a western, city-style government.

1959

Alaska officially becomes the 49th state. On January 3, President Eisenhower signed the proclamation creating the state of Alaska.

1971

Alaska Native Claims Settlement Act. The act gave 220 Native Villages rights to 44 million acres (18 million ha) of land and $962 million.

1975

James Bay and Northern Quebec Agreement. This agreement paved the way for the government of Quebec, Canada, to complete the James Bay hydroelectric project in exchange for special land, cultural, and other rights for the Cree and Inuit people.

1976

The Tobeluk Consent Decree. When students sued the Alaska state government for failing to provide high schools in Native Villages, the government signed a decree agreeing to build some. Above, students learn native crafts at a Yup'ik village high school in Akiak, Alaska.

1979

Greenland Home Rule Act. Under Danish rule since 1953, Greenland gained many rights from the Danish government. Denmark kept control of foreign policy and defense.

1999

Nunavut made a Canadian territory. On April 1, 1999, Nunavut separated from Canada's Northwest Territories, gaining its own government. Most of its people are Inuit. Pictured right is Pangnirtung, Nunavut.

2001

Alaskan tribes sign the Millennium Agreement with the state of Alaska. The agreement provided a government-to-government relationship between more than 80 tribes and the state. The agreement established greater recognition and respect for the tribes and their culture, and allowed them to self-govern, but with aid and support from the state government.

AHTNA

(OTT-nah)

LANGUAGE GROUP:
Athabascan

GREETING:
Nts'e dit'ae? (How
are you?)

THANK YOU:
Tsin'aen

LOCATION PRECONTACT:
Copper River Basin, Alaska

LOCATION TODAY:
Copper River Basin, Alaska

The people known as Athabascan were once a single group, but are now fragmented into many different tribes living across the subarctic regions of the United States and Canada. One of these groups, the Ahtna, or "ice people," settled along the Copper River in southeast Alaska. These people were hunters, gatherers, and traders who lived in three separate groups, each with its own chief.

Their subarctic location made it easy to find food, from salmon, moose, and caribou to berries and herbs. In their villages, they built winter homes partially underground, using a wooden framework that they then covered in bark. Summer homes were more temporary wooden structures, with animal-hide or bark covering. To help transport equipment between camps, women and girls used a tumpline—a cloth or animal-skin sling. Braced across the forehead or chest, the sling supported a load on the back. The Ahtna traded furs and copper with neighboring tribes, such as the Tlingit to the south.

Two Ahtna girls carry burdens on their backs, using tumplines to help support their loads. They are likely walking from summer camp back to their winter village.

When Russian traders arrived in the late 1700s to explore the Copper River, they found themselves outnumbered by the local tribes. The Ahtna forced the Russians to close their only trading post on the river and to retreat, leaving the tribe to continue its traditional way of life for another century. When the United States purchased Alaska from the Russians in 1867, the U.S. government sent its own explorers to the Copper River. They met an Ahtna chief, called Nicolai, who helped them to survive in the harsh conditions. He also pointed the way to rich copper deposits. By the early 1900s, the establishment of the Northwestern Railway and copper mines near the village of Chitina had attracted more outsiders to the area.

The mines closed in the 1930s, but the Ahtna people continued to live here, fishing and hunting for food as they had in the past. In the 1970s, the Ahtna gained control of more than one million acres (405,000 ha) of land. This was possible through the Alaska Native Claims Settlement Act of 1971, which allowed Native tribes to establish businesses on areas of designated land. The tribe lives on this land today in seven villages in the Copper River Basin and one called Cantwell, northwest of the river. ✒

Ahtna men of higher standing wear "chief coats" at ceremonies to signify their status. The beaded designs are often purely decorative.

ALEUT

(a-LYOOT)

LANGUAGE GROUP:
Eskimo-Aleut

GREETING:
Aang

THANK YOU:
Qa aasakung

LOCATION PRECONTACT:
Alaska

LOCATION TODAY:
Alaska

The Aleutian Islands are a chain of around 100 islands that extends 1,300 miles (2,000 km) west from mainland Alaska. The Aleutian people have lived on these rugged islands for thousands of years, and their lives have always been bound to the sea and a few inland rivers. They call themselves Unangan, meaning "original people."

Traditionally, Aleutian men used *baidarkas*, a type of kayak covered with animal skins, to hunt sea mammals, such as seals, whales, and sea otters, for food, hides, and fur. Women fished for salmon, hunted birds, and foraged. The tribe used animal skins for clothing and made tools and utensils from animal bones and ivory. The women also wove fine baskets from rye grass, which grew on the beaches. The Aleut people built their sod-covered dwellings, called *ulax*, partially underground. The entrance was through the home's grass-covered roof. The heat from the surrounding earth helped to keep the houses warm.

Life changed for the Aleut with the arrival of Russian traders in the 1700s. The Russians established trading posts on the islands and coerced skilled Aleut hunters into supplying them with sea otter furs. At times, the Aleut resisted the Russians. Many were killed, while others were forced to hunt with them, traveling to the Kuril Islands in Russia, Fort Ross in California, and other locations. By the time the United States purchased the Russian colonial territories in North America (also known as Russian America) in 1867, the sea otter population was dangerously low and the fur trade was in huge decline. The

In this painting, an Aleut hunter heads out into the Bering Sea in his *baidarka*, a type of kayak. There are many seals for him to hunt close to the shore. In the distance is a Russian merchant ship.

Americans also forced the Aleut people to help them hunt for sea otters, until the animals almost became extinct.

The Aleut tribe faced further trouble when the Japanese bombed Unalaska Island and occupied Kiska and Attu during World War II. For their own safety, U.S. troops forced the Aleut to abandon their remaining villages, which were destroyed while they were gone. It wasn't until after the war that the Aleut were able to return and rebuild their communities. More recently, they have received government support. Today, five of the Aleutian Islands make up a national wildlife refuge.

Elsewhere, Aleut people share land on three other islands, in communities that include Dutch Harbor, Adak Village, and Nikolski. Some continue to speak their native language and have revitalized some of their crafting and hunter-gatherer traditions.

The Aleut wore hunting hats made from wood. Decorated with ivory amulets, the hats had long bird-like visors and were said to please the spirits of their animal prey. Each sea lion bristle extending out from the back of the hat signifies a successful hunt.

IN THE KNOW

Aleut men wore coats, called *kamleika*, made from seal intestines. They provided a waterproof layer over a warm parka. The tradition no longer continues, but the skill is not lost. Such coats are sometimes made for museums or ceremonial purposes.

MEETING THE OUTSIDERS

While Norse, or Viking, sailors arrived in the Arctic around 1000 C.E., the frozen landscape did not appeal to the European explorers who arrived several hundred years later. Instead, they saw the North as providing a possible route to China and spent 300 years looking for the Northwest Passage. Some of the explorers, such as Martin Frobisher, captured Inuit and took them back to Europe as proof of the new land. Others traded with the Arctic people they met, paving the way for whalers, fur traders, and ivory traders to expand their businesses. In the 1700s, Russian fur traders (pictured) set up trading posts and colonies in Alaska. Northern tribes acquired guns, cloth, and metal from the Europeans, but the newcomers also brought disease, including a smallpox epidemic that lasted from 1836 to 1840.

ALUTIIT

(a-LOO-tiit)

LANGUAGE GROUP:
Eskimo-Aleut

GREETING:
Cama'i

THANK YOU:
Quyanaa

LOCATION PRECONTACT:
Alaska

LOCATION TODAY:
Alaska

The Alutiit (singular Alutiiq) live on the Kodiak Archipelago—a group of islands south of mainland Alaska—and the nearby peninsulas. Like other coastal people, the Alutiit have always relied heavily on the sea for their survival. In spring, they caught octopus and shellfish during low tides, while summer brought calmer seas and the tribe hunted whales and sea lions on the open water. In fall, they collected wild plants and berries; they also caught salmon in the rivers and preserved some of it for the winter months, either by smoking or drying the fish. In winter, the tribe hunted land animals, such as foxes and otters. Living in large village communities, the tribe held celebrations during the winter months, in which dancing played an important role. Accompanied by the steady beat of drumming, men reenacted scenes from the hunt and women danced in honor of the tribe's ancestors.

There were about 10,000 Alutiit people living on the islands before Russian fur traders arrived in the late 1700s. In 1784, armed Russians attacked a group of Alutiit at a place known as

Refuge Rock, near what is now Old Harbor, killing 500 of them. The Russian-American Company then used Alutiit men to hunt sea otters for its fur industry and forced many to convert to the Russian Orthodox religion. In the early 1800s, the Russians established a city at St. Paul Harbor—now the modern city of Kodiak—which became a major fur-trading center. The Russians

Covered in ice and snow for most of the year, Mount Katmai volcano has a large lake-filled caldera (pictured). The volcano was cone-shaped before it erupted in 1912. Its peak collapsed during the blast, causing the sides to crumble.

☀ IN THE KNOW

The Alaskan state flag was designed by Benny Benson, a 13-year-old of Alutiit descent, in 1927. His flag—dark blue for the Alaskan sky—includes the North Star and the seven smaller stars of the Big Dipper constellation.

An Alutiiq girl wears a traditional beaded headdress to the Alaska State Fair in Palmer, Alaska. Her face is painted to represent tattoos, a sign of status.

occupied Kodiak well into the 1900s. Today, a Russian Orthodox church, built in 1945, remains a reminder of their influence.

The Alutiit endured two major natural disasters during the 20th century. The first, in June 1912, was the eruption of Mount Katmai on the Alaska Peninsula. More devastating than that was the severe "Good Friday" earthquake of 1964. Huge tsunamis followed the quake, sweeping away homes, businesses, and boats and killing 119 people.

Today, the Alutiit still rely on the sea for their livelihood. Many people work in the fishing industries at Ouzinkie, Old Harbor, and other Alutiit villages. They also work to preserve, honor, and celebrate the language and culture of their ancestors. In 1995, the Alutiiq Museum opened in Kodiak. 🖋

CREE

(CREE, to rhyme with see)

LANGUAGE GROUP:
Algonquian

GREETING:
Tân'si

THANK YOU:
Tiniki

LOCATION PRECONTACT:
Northwest Territories, Alberta, Saskatchewan, Manitoba, Ontario, Quebec (Canada)

LOCATION TODAY:
Northwest Territories, Alberta, Saskatchewan, Manitoba, Ontario, Quebec (Canada)

The Cree are a large group that includes 150 First Nations communities living across central and northern Canada, as well as the Plains Cree groups in Montana and North Dakota. The tribe inhabited such a wide area that its various bands adapted differently to the environments in which they lived. For example, many Cree bands enjoyed the rich natural resources of the pine forests of Canada's subarctic region.

Also, the area's lakes and rivers provided freshwater fish, while the land was home to many different animals and plants. In this homeland, the Cree moved around to hunt and gather according to the seasons. Traveling in small groups, they lived in cone-shaped tepees, covered in animal skins in warmer weather. In winter, they built sturdy wooden lodges, which they covered with bark or turf for extra warmth. Different groups gathered together to celebrate feasts in summer. With an emphasis on the sharing of food, such feasts continue today. They are held in honor of the animals that give their lives to ensure Cree survival.

In the early 1600s, Europeans began exploring in Cree territory. Cree played a key role in the ➡

☀ IN THE KNOW

The Cree developed close relationships with French settlers. Many Frenchmen married Cree women and the two cultures merged. The children of these French and indigenous marriages, and their descendants, are called Métis. They speak their own language, called Michif.

Traditionally made of wood, with hide bindings, snowshoes offered a practical solution when crossing deep snow on foot. This pair of Cree snowshoes dates from the 1920s and features detailed patterns in the woven sections.

booming fur trade—not only as trappers, but also as guides. By the 1700s, the Europeans had built a number of trading posts and the Cree settled in villages nearby. European missionaries converted many Cree to Christianity. Constant contact with Europeans led to tragic losses for the Cree. In the 1800s, smallpox swept through Cree camps, killing large numbers of people. From the late 1800s onward, the Cree also lost their homelands through various treaties that forced them to give up their lands. Although many Cree died of European diseases, with determination they rebuilt their communities. Today, the Cree language is spoken across the different bands and, although not all Cree people live on reserves, many continue to hunt and fish to keep their ancient traditions alive. The Cree are active in Canadian politics, too. In 2013, Chief Theresa Spence gained fame as a leader of the Idle No More movement that fights for the rights of First Nations people. 🖋

An Idle No More protest in Toronto. Idle No More is a movement started by the First Nations people of Canada to bring awareness to violations of treaty rights of indigenous Canadians.

FINDING FOOD

The Arctic region is teeming with an amazing variety of fish and sea and land mammals. In the past, tribes in the North hunted and fished year-round. They had great knowledge of animal species and their behavior. Understanding migration patterns meant that hunters could track caribou, capturing great numbers in spring and fall, when the herds were on the move. Arctic people were experts at using hunting tools such as harpoons (pictured). They were also skilled at fishing for salmon and Arctic char with different kinds of spears, hooks, and traps. Hunters would wait patiently beside breathing holes in the ice to catch seals, and they went out to sea in kayaks to hunt whales. At hunting camps, tribal people shared their knowledge, skills, and food with each other. This sharing culture enabled entire communities to survive through the seasons in this harsh environment.

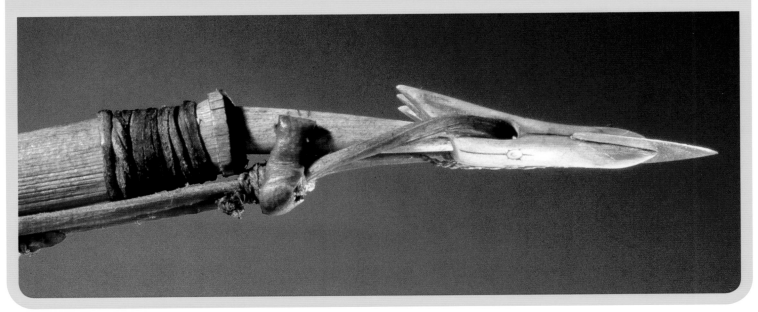

DENA'INA

(deh-NY-nah)

LANGUAGE GROUP:
Athabascan

GREETING:
Dunilggux

THANK YOU:
Chin'an

LOCATION PRECONTACT:
Alaska

LOCATION TODAY:
Alaska

The Dena'ina have lived in the lands surrounding Cook Inlet, Alaska, for more than 1,000 years. Alaska's capital, Anchorage, sits on Dena'ina homelands—in the past, many Dena'ina had summer fishing camps there. In those days, the tribe built temporary summer dwellings, which they also used for smoking the fish they caught. During the year, the tribe moved from place to place, but in winter they established more settled villages, with families living together in large houses: Built partially underground, these houses had log walls covered with earth and grass.

Like the Ahtna, the Dena'ina are an Athabascan people. They are the only northern Athabascan people to live by the sea. On the coast, hunters captured harbor seals, shellfish, and other sea creatures. Inland, they snared bears, bighorn sheep, and smaller animals. In order to become a *qeshqa*, or leader of the tribe, a man had to prove himself through his hunting skills. The *qeshqa* arranged trade with members of other indigenous groups and made sure that the tribe's hunters supplied enough food for their people.

The Dena'ina had no contact with white settlers until the late 1700s, when the Russians built trading posts in their territory. Interaction with the newcomers led to problems for the Dena'ina, including the smallpox epidemic of 1836–1840 that killed many people. Russian missionaries arrived in the mid-1800s and converted survivors to the Russian Orthodox religion. Although the Dena'ina adapted to the Russian presence, they clung to their traditional belief system, particularly the idea that all natural things—animals, rivers, plants, and rocks—had supernatural power.

The late 1800s brought gold prospectors to the region, followed by more settlers. In 1915, a railroad was built through Dena'ina land, bringing even more people to Anchorage. The city continued to grow in the 1940s, when it became the site of a military base, and in the 1950s, following the discovery of oil. Today, the Dena'ina live in Eklutna Native Village, which sits on almost 125,000 acres (50,500 ha) of ancestral land northeast of Anchorage. The village cemetery has small, brightly colored "spirit houses" containing mementoes of the deceased—a tradition that has roots in the Russian Orthodox religion.

IN THE KNOW

Dena'ina people kept track of their age using a string calendar, made from lengths of sinew (animal tendon) tied to the waist. For each day a person lived, they tied a knot in the sinew—sometimes also adding a bead. On reaching the end of one string, they set it aside and started another.

Dena'ina men and women wore outfits like this for summer ceremonies. It includes an animal-hide shirt, oversleeves, booted leggings, and gloves.

EYAK

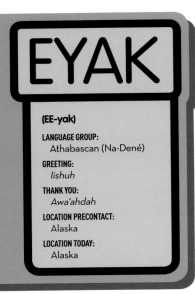

(EE-yak)

LANGUAGE GROUP:
Athabascan (Na-Dené)

GREETING:
Iishuh

THANK YOU:
Awa'ahdah

LOCATION PRECONTACT:
Alaska

LOCATION TODAY:
Alaska

The Eyak people inhabit a small part of their traditional homelands in southeastern Alaska. Originally, the tribe lived in four major villages in the Copper River delta between the larger Chugach and Tlingit tribes. In each Eyak village, tribe members built two potlatch houses in which feasts were held—one with a post topped with a raven, the other with an eagle. These represented the two family groups, known as clans, that made up Eyak society. Each group fished, hunted, and harvested plants in its own area. Food from seals, ptarmigan, bears, and mountain goats was plentiful, and the tribe used snares, traps, and bows and arrows to hunt the animals. The Eyak's primary food source was the abundant salmon. The fish swim up the Copper River to spawn in spring, so during spring each year, the Eyak left their winter villages to fish. They built summer camps upstream and preserved the salmon they caught by drying or smoking it. In the fall, men hunted duck, lynx, and beaver. The communities had plenty to eat during the long winter.

Being a small tribe, the Eyak were targets for slave raids by other tribes. They survived the raids, but contact with the Russians brought them close to disaster. In the late 1700s, the Russians traded with the Eyak, but they also tried to force their own culture and religion on the Alaskan people. At different times, groups of Eyak rebelled and, on one occasion, they

The last full-blooded Eyak, Marie Smith Jones (right), was also the last speaker of the tribe's language. She died in 2008. Since that time, the tribe has begun to revive its language using video and audio recordings and transcripts of ancestral stories.

helped the Tlingit tribe attack the Russian post in the town of Yakutat. The Russians retreated, but a smallpox epidemic between 1837 and 1838 brought devastation to the Eyak. By the late 1800s, the survivors were living in just the one village—Orca. In the early 1900s, the oil industry, railroads, and canneries continued to threaten the tribe's way of life. The fishing industry destroyed the salmon population and forced the Eyak off the land to find work in the canning factories or elsewhere.

Today, many members live in Eyak Native Village, now part of Cordova, Alaska, where they continue to preserve their culture. Together with local environmental groups, they work to protect their ancestral homelands and the animals they share the land with, including the salmon—their most important food source for many generations. ✎

The moose is an important staple for the Eyak tribe. Members of the tribe are working with rangers from the Chugach National Forest, Eyak Corporation, and Alaska Fish and Game to help stabilize the moose's winter foraging habitat.

💡 IN THE KNOW

The potlatch feast is unique to the tribes of northwest Canada, Alaska, and the U.S.'s northwest coast. To celebrate a family event, hosts give away possessions as a demonstration of their wealth.

ARTS OF THE NORTH

Arctic people have created carvings with strong spiritual meanings. In the 1800s, indigenous people started trading ivory sculptures with European sailors and whalers. Soapstone became a popular material, too. This is a soft stone with a smooth surface that is easier to carve than ivory. Soapstone sculptures were in high demand by the mid-1900s. Printmaking, the craft shown here, started around the same time and has become a specialized Inuit art. Other arts include basket weaving, which the Aleut perfected, Yup'ik masks, and beautifully beaded and embroidered clothing and boots made by Athabascan tribes, such as the Eyak. Themes include flowers in the beadwork and animals in sculptures and printed works, reflecting the tribes' deep respect for the land and its creatures.

GWICH'IN

(GWITCH-inn)

LANGUAGE GROUP:
Athabascan

GREETING:
Nakhwal'in shoo ihłii

THANK YOU:
Mahsi'

LOCATION PRECONTACT:
Northern Alaska;
the Yukon Territory,
the Mackenzie River
Valley (Canada)

LOCATION TODAY:
Alaska (U.S.); Northwest
Territories, Yukon
(Canada)

Gwich'in homelands once covered a large area across northern Alaska and the Yukon Territory of Canada and into the Mackenzie River Valley. By the 1800s, there were nine bands of Gwich'in people living across this territory. They traded goods with each other and joined together for feasts. The Scottish explorer Alexander Mackenzie met the Gwich'in tribe in 1789 and was the first European to write about it. In his journals, he mentions visiting the tribe's fishing camps.

The Gwich'in tribe began trading with European fur traders in the early 1800s. By the middle of the century, the British Hudson's Bay Company had established trading posts at Fort Yukon and Fort McPherson. The company had been set up to trade goods with the tribe for fur. At the time, there was a great demand for animal fur in Britain.

Traditionally, the Gwich'in were seminomadic, moving around in small family groups, surviving mostly by hunting caribou and fishing. They built domed dwellings, which they made by stitching caribou skins together and draping them over a curved-pole framework. By the 20th century, the tribe had established permanent villages in both Alaska and Canada and they live in these communities today. This tribe is well known for its storytelling—an oral tradition that has passed from ➤➤➤

Gwich'in Paul Josie sits beneath numerous fillets of locally caught salmon. He is smoking the fish, which, traditionally, would have fed the tribe through winter, when caribou were scarce.

generation to generation—with Gwich'in stories recounted in their native language. The tribe has used a written language since the late 1800s. Lively music is at the heart of many celebrations. Over the years, the tribe adopted the fiddle as part of its culture and fiddlers play music as Gwich'in dancers perform high-tempo jigs that include the Duck Dance and the Rabbit Dance.

The caribou is central to Gwich'in culture, with creation stories telling how the tribe is bound to the animal because each has a piece of the other's heart. The caribou was the main food source for the tribe, who also hunted smaller animals and fished for salmon. The animals provided skins for boots, bags, and summer shelters. For centuries, the caribou have migrated north in summer, along ancient paths, and the Gwich'in people built their camps on the migration routes. The tribe still hunts these animals and, in 1988, established a committee to protect the Porcupine caribou birthing grounds from oil drilling.

 **IN THE KNOW**

Porcupine caribou—named for the area near the Porcupine River where they give birth—travel 1,500 miles (2,500 km) each year, from their winter grounds to their spring birthing grounds.

A Gwich'in man takes part in the opening event at the annual Denver March Powwow. He wears an impressive wolf mask. The wolf is featured in a Gwich'in story, where it leads a hungry hunter to caribou.

FAMILY LIFE IN THE ARCTIC

In the Arctic, groups of families moved around and camped together to hunt and fish, but the core family of parents and children always stayed together. In the subarctic, some tribes built villages in which large extended families or clans lived. Gwich'in family groups comprised brothers and sisters and their children. Pictured is a Yup'ik elder with her grandchildren. In Yup'ik villages, men and older boys once lived in a separate house from women and young children (see p. 38 for more on the Yup'ik). In all tribes, children were very important and adoption was common within Inuit communities. It is still part of Inuit culture today.

HOLIKACHUK

(hol-EEK-a-chuck)

LANGUAGE GROUP:
Athabascan

LANGUAGE:
Dormant; last known speaker, Wilson "Tiny" Deacon, died in 2012

LOCATION PRECONTACT:
Alaska

LOCATION TODAY:
Alaska

Originally, the Holikachuk lived in Alaska—along the upper part of the Innoko River, a 500-mile (800-km)-long tributary of the Yukon River. Holikachuk was the name of the tribe's main village on the river. During winter, this small tribe lived in subterranean, or partly underground, earthen homes that had a central fire pit. In the spring, the tribe went on caribou hunts. The animal was an important food source, and also provided skins for clothing and blankets. The tribe hunted other animals living in Holikachuk territory, such as lynx and bears.

The Holikachuk were traders who exchanged their caribou skins for beads, tobacco, and dentalia (cone-shaped seashells). Tribal members also obtained Inuit clothing during these trading trips. Many coastal people, including the Inuit, made clothes from sea-mammal skins. When other tribes obtained cloth from white traders, the Holikachuk traded for this as well. Eventually, cloth and sea-mammal clothes replaced the tribe's traditional caribou-skin clothing.

During the spring and summer months, the Holikachuk traveled far from their territory to trade and to fish for salmon on the Yukon River. They set up fishing camps there in summer, living in brush shelters. Once dried, the fish they caught kept the tribe fed through the long winter. One of the most important ceremonies during this time was the potlatch—a great feast that the Holikachuk held every December in honor of the dead.

The Holikachuk had little contact with white settlers and traders during the 1800s, although missionaries came to the area toward the end of the century, converting most of the tribe to Christianity. Between 1962 and 1963, the Holikachuk moved their village to Grayling, on the lower Yukon River. The tiny Holikachuk tribe lives here today, mostly surviving by hunting and fishing. Although the Holikachuk no longer live in their ancestral homelands, today, the Innoko National Wildlife Refuge protects the animals and plants on millions of acres of land that lie between the Yukon and Innoko Rivers.

IN THE KNOW

The Holikachuk received government aid to build homes in their village at Grayling. Trees cut down in local forests were floated downriver to Grayling and the people built the houses themselves.

The Iditarod Trail dogsled race takes place in March, with teams of eight dogs taking 8 to 15 days to cross the frozen Alaskan landscape. The Iditarod name comes from the Holikachuk word *hidedhod*, which means "distant place."

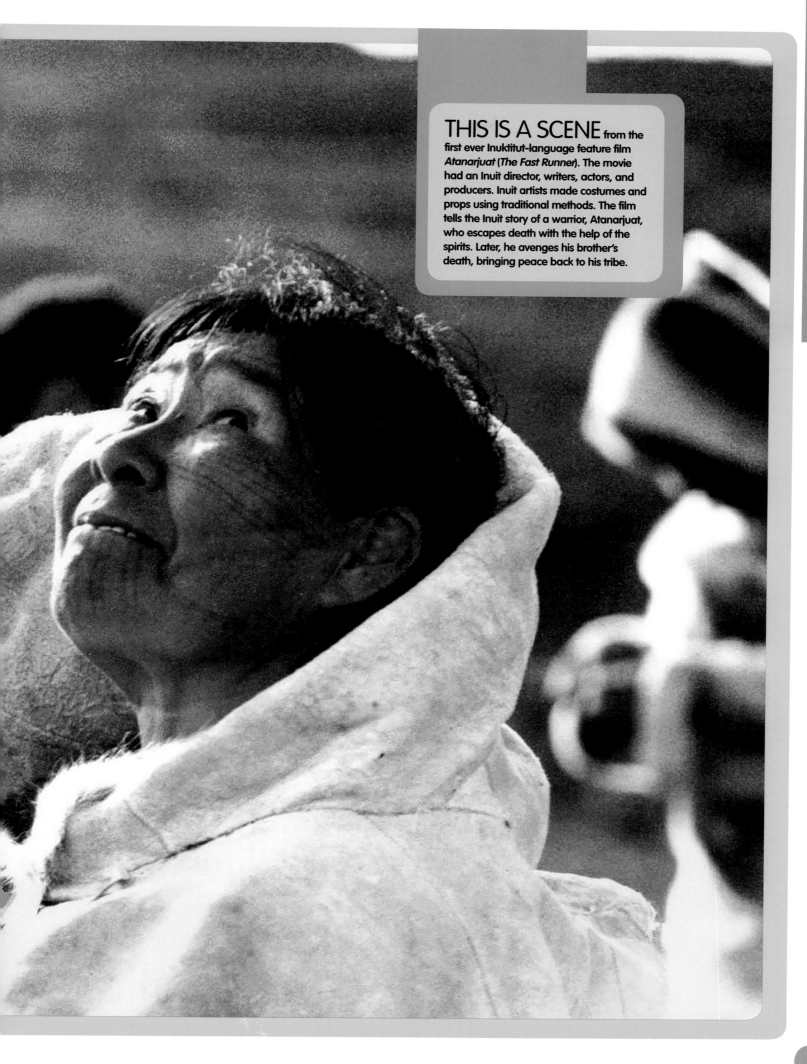

THIS IS A SCENE from the first ever Inuktitut-language feature film *Atanarjuat* (*The Fast Runner*). The movie had an Inuit director, writers, actors, and producers. Inuit artists made costumes and props using traditional methods. The film tells the Inuit story of a warrior, Atanarjuat, who escapes death with the help of the spirits. Later, he avenges his brother's death, bringing peace back to his tribe.

IGLULIT

(ig-LOO-lit)

LANGUAGE GROUP:
Inuktitut

GREETING:
Aingai

THANK YOU:
Nakurmiik

LOCATION PRECONTACT:
Nunavut (Canada)

LOCATION TODAY:
Western Baffin Island,
Melville Peninsula
(Nunavut, Canada)

The Iglulit people live on their ancestral lands on the western side of Baffin Island and the Melville Peninsula in Nunavut, Canada—an area that is also home to many caribou, seals, and walruses. The name Iglulit means "there is a house there." "Igloolik," a word that has the same meaning, is the name of a large town in the area.

In the past, the Iglulit hunted seals through holes in the ice at their two main winter camps. In the early summer, the tribe would move south to the Melville Peninsula to hunt caribou. The tribe's movements were informed by the teachings of the elders about the changing seasons, stars, and animal movements. Using their knowledge, and relocating every three years, the Iglulit lived without harming the land or endangering its wildlife. Today, although the Iglulit live in modern communities, they still hunt seals and catch salmon. Traditionally, men hunted and women stayed behind, but today women hunt, too. The tribe refers to the food the hunters catch as "country food," and communities share it, just as they did in the past.

The Iglulit lived an isolated life until the 1800s. Before this time, they traded only with neighboring groups, sometimes traveling farther afield to trade with whalers. By the end of the 1930s, the Hudson's Bay Company had set up a trading post on the island of Igloolik in Nunavut. Missionaries and scientists soon followed. During the 1950s and 1960s, the Canadian government wanted the Iglulit people to adopt a less nomadic lifestyle, like that of Canadians to the south. The government placed children in residential boarding schools away from their homes, in a bid to lessen the influence of their indigenous culture. It took many years for the Iglulit to have schools of their own, with Iglulit teachers. Eventually, the Iglulit people settled into their present-day communities in Nunavut, where they balance modern ways with their ancient traditions. 🖋

This *inuksuk* (stone marker) is located in the town of Igloolik. Stone markers were built as signposts for future travelers. They may have marked a trail to follow or a good spot for fishing or hunting game.

DRESSING FOR THE COLD

The Arctic and subarctic people came up with ingenious ideas for surviving the cold, dressing in layers of clothing made from animal skins and furs, such as caribou. Such coverings trap air between the animal hairs or fibers, creating natural insulation and a layer of warmth against the cold. While an inner parka had fur on the inside, a top parka had fur on the outside. People also used sealskin and sea-mammal guts to make waterproof coats and boots. Animal sinew, used for thread, expanded when it was wet and kept water from seeping through the seams. Today, although people may wear traditional clothing for a ceremony, daily clothes are made from synthetic, or man-made, materials, such as Gore-Tex.

INNU

(in-YOU)

LANGUAGE GROUP:
Algonquian

GREETING:
Pushu

GOODBYE:
Iame

LOCATION PRECONTACT:
Labrador, Quebec
(Canada)

LOCATION TODAY:
Labrador, Quebec
(Canada)

The Innu were once a widespread tribe that fell into two main groups. The northern Innu, also known as the Naskapi, lived in the subarctic areas of what is now eastern Quebec and Labrador, Canada. The southern Innu, or Montagnais, lived farther south. Both groups have lived in these areas for at least 2,000 years.

Living in a colder climate, the northern Innu traveled around using snowshoes and pulling toboggans. They depended on fishing and hunting caribou for food, clothing, and shelter. They lived in small groups, sharing large lodge homes that were covered in caribou skins. They also used caribou skins to make warm clothes to protect themselves from the harsh climate. The southern Innu lived in a warmer area and wore lighter clothing. They traveled mostly by birchbark canoe. They tracked and caught moose for food and covered their homes in bark.

Innu people living on the coast and around the Gulf of St. Lawrence first met European fishermen in the 1500s.

In the early 1600s, the French established permanent settlements along the St. Lawrence River. Members of the southern Innu became guides and trappers for the French and fought with them against the Iroquois tribes. Once the British took over the area in the 1760s, the southern Innu stayed closer to the trading posts along the St. Lawrence River, but continued to support themselves by hunting and fishing. In the mid-1900s, the Canadian government constructed huge reservoirs and dams inland and ⟫⟫

This coat belonged to a Naskapi Innu man. Dating from the 1840s, it is made of caribou skin, stitched together using sinew (animal tendon). The patterns are carefully painted on by hand.

forced the Innu to move into settled communities. Today, while most Innu live in Quebec, there are two settlements in Labrador. They call their vast homeland *nitassinan* ("our land") and work hard to keep their culture alive. One project they have developed involves an online database of ancestral place-names, such as Ushkan-shipiss (Bone River) and Atiku-neiau (Caribou Point), along with details of their meanings and origins. ✎

Children take turns swinging around a wooden pole at an Innu camp on the western shores of Mistastin Lake in Labrador, Canada. The Innu word for the swing is *ueuepeshun*.

INUIT COUNTRY

Most people who live in Greenland are Kalaallit, an Inuit people, and they call their land Kalaallit Nunaat, which means "land of the people." For centuries, Denmark claimed Greenland, the world's largest island, as part of its kingdom, but in 1979, Greenland gained the right to take more control in areas that included taxes, education, and cultural affairs. In 2008, Greenlanders voted for self-government, transferring even more control from Denmark. The island now has its own parliament and prime minister. The official language was Danish until 2009, when it changed to the native Kalaallisut. The island culture continues to practice ancient traditions, such as ice fishing, dogsled racing, and welcoming the winter sun after months of darkness. Pictured is the settlement of Ittoqqortoormiit.

INUPIAT

(IN-yoop-yat)

LANGUAGE GROUP:
Eskimo-Aleut

GREETING:
Qaimarutin

THANK YOU:
Quyanaq

LOCATION PRECONTACT:
Alaska

LOCATION TODAY:
Alaska

The Inupiat of northern Alaska descend from the people of the Thule culture that developed around 1000 C.E. This nomadic society emerged in the Bering Strait and its people spread across the Arctic region. Surrounded by icy ocean and frozen land, the Inupiat hunted large sea mammals, such as walruses and bowhead and gray whales, as well as caribou, birds, and fish. The Inupiat have deep respect for the ocean and its creatures—particularly whales—and were expert whalers. They built large, skin-covered boats from which they could harpoon huge baleen whales. They got enough meat, bones, blubber, and baleen for an entire community from just one carcass. In winter, the Inupiat on the coast used driftwood and sod to build homes that were partly underground. Inland, people made homes from poles covered with skins or sod. At their hunting and fishing camps, the Inupiat made simple driftwood shelters or lived in skin-covered tents. They used soapstone lamps and pots that burned sea-mammal oil, and women sewed animal hides into socks, boots, and parkas.

For many centuries, the Inupiat met few outsiders apart from Siberian Yupik and Chukchi people and a few European explorers. In the 1800s, however, explorers, traders, and missionaries began to arrive more regularly. The American whaling industry hurt the walrus and whale population, and today whales are protected by international law. Inupiat people hunt whales under an exemption to that law for Native peoples.

WILLIAM HENSLEY

William Hensley's Inupiat name was Iggiagruk, which means "little mountain." He was born in a small community in northwestern Alaska. After graduating from George Washington University in Washington, D.C., Hensley returned to Alaska, where he championed the rights of the Alaskan people. He helped to found the Alaska Federation of Natives and fought tirelessly for Native land rights and payment. In 1971, Hensley's efforts helped secure 44 million acres (18 million ha) and $1 billion.

They do not kill more whales than they need. Today, the tribe maintains a number of its cultural traditions. Every spring, it holds a festival to honor the whale and its importance within Inupiat culture. Whale meat, blubber, and skin are distributed among all who attend. There is much singing and dancing, accompanied by drums made from whale skin. The festival ends in prayer. The Inupiat Heritage Center, in Barrow, Alaska, opened in 1999 and exhibits traditional arts. People can learn the crafts of their ancestors, such as constructing or repairing whaling boats and making tools. ☞

This Inupiat seal was carved from walrus ivory in around 1870. A good-luck charm for hunting, its simple shape comes to life with the addition of glass beads for eyes and bird-quill whiskers.

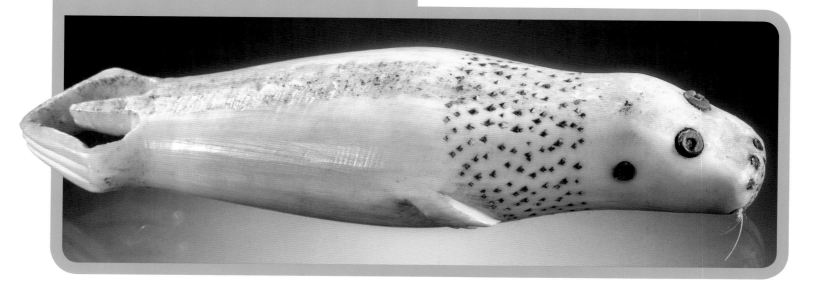

INUVIALUIT

(in-oo-vee-ah-LOO-it)

LANGUAGE GROUP:
Eskimo-Aleut

GREETING:
Atitu

THANK YOU:
Quyanainni

LOCATION PRECONTACT:
Canadian Arctic

LOCATION TODAY:
Canadian Arctic

The western Canadian Arctic is home to the Inuvialuit people, who are closely related to the Inuit and Inupiat. Originating from the Alaskan Thule cultures, they have lived around the mouth of the Mackenzie River and on the shores of the Beaufort Sea for 1,000 years. The Inuvialuit moved from place to place to hunt and fish. In the winter, hunters caught seals through their breathing holes in the ice; in summer, they hunted beluga whales, and in fall, caribou and musk ox. The Inuvialuit people changed their homes according to the season, living in warm earthen houses in winter and caribou-skin tents in summer.

Before European settlers arrived, the Inuvialuit had established a trade route along the coast to Alaska. They traded goods such as ivory and copper with other indigenous groups, including the Inupiat farther west. In the late 1700s, Europeans explored the western Arctic looking for furs to trade, and by the mid-1800s, the fur trade had reached Inuvialuit territory. Inuvialuit hunters traded white fox and muskrat furs. Then American whaling companies followed, although this industry was short-lived.

At the same time, missionaries worked among the Inuvialuit people and converted many to Christianity. Unfortunately, all of this interaction with outsiders brought deadly diseases, such as measles, to the Inuvialuit. By the 20th century, just a few hundred Inuvialuit people survived. By this time, many Inuvialuit were living in communities on the western edge of the Mackenzie Delta. In the late 1950s, the Canadian government built Inuvik, a planned town for the tribe. Other changes came in the 1960s and 1970s, as oil and gas companies came to the Arctic. Although many Inuvialuit worked in these industries, they also worried about their impact on the environment and their traditional way of life. In 1984, the Inuvialuit signed an agreement with the Canadian government that provides an area of land—the Inuvialuit Settlement Region (ISR)—rights, and a promise to protect the environment and traditional Inuvialuit culture. Today, thousands of Inuvialuit live in the six major communities of the ISR. ✒

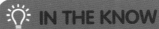

IN THE KNOW
The Inuvialuit have developed a cell phone app so that younger people can learn their native language.

An Inuvialuit girl wears a modern-day parka decorated with traditional braid designs and trimmed with a sunburst ruff of fur.

This Inuvialuit knife is carved from animal bone and has an iron blade. The handle is wrapped in a piece of animal hide for extra grip.

BOARDING SCHOOLS

From the late 1800s, the American and Canadian governments banned indigenous languages and ceremonies in order to force tribal people to fit into white society. Missionary and government schools educated children in English, white customs, and white history, and boarding schools took this assimilation even further. These schools took tribal children—some as young as five years old—hundreds of miles from their families. At school, children lost their traditions and if they tried to speak their language, they were punished severely. Cruel treatment was common. The trauma experienced by those who survived living in these schools is still felt today. Now, reservations have their own schools and children live at home.

OJI-CREE & JAMES BAY CREE

(OH-gee CREE)

LANGUAGE GROUP:
Algonquian

GREETING:
Waachiye
(James Bay Cree)

THANK YOU:
Miikwehch
(James Bay Cree)

LOCATION PRECONTACT:
Manitoba, Ontario
(Canada)

LOCATION TODAY:
Manitoba, Ontario
(Canada)

Centuries ago, Cree and Ojibwe people married. Their descendants—the Oji-Cree—developed their own identity and traditions, making their home around western Hudson Bay. Their relatives, the James Bay Cree, lived to the east.

The Oji-Cree moved between seasonal hunting grounds, snaring hare, caribou, and other animals. The large bay provided beluga whales, seals, and fish—even in the winter, when tribal members fished through the ice. During the summer, people traveled by canoe, but in the winter, they wore snowshoes to haul their belongings across frozen waters on wooden toboggans. Life continued in this way until 1668, when the Hudson's Bay Company established its first fur trading post. More posts followed, and the Oji-Cree began trading furs for European goods such as cloth. French missionaries worked among the tribe, converting many to Catholicism.

In 1975, an agreement signed by the James Bay Cree gave up land around James Bay to make way for hydroelectric dams. The dams caused flooding and mercury contaminated water supplies, killing fish and caribou. The damage forced thousands of tribal people to move far from their homes. Today, the Oji-Cree live in several scattered communities in northern Ontario and Manitoba, Canada. Most places are remote and reached only by plane or boat. ➡

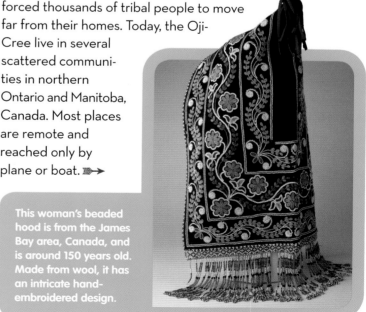

This woman's beaded hood is from the James Bay area, Canada, and is around 150 years old. Made from wool, it has an intricate hand-embroidered design.

An elderly James Bay Cree woman prepares a fire for cooking inside a traditional Cree shelter, or *sabtuan*. An opening in the top of the shelter allows smoke from the fire to escape.

ELIJAH HARPER

The Oji-Cree chief Elijah Harper was the first member of the Manitoba provincial parliament from the Canadian First Nations. In 1990, he made a stand against the province of Quebec joining the Canadian constitution because it did not guarantee the rights of the First Nations.

The tribe continues to fight for its rights and to preserve its language and traditions. Elders, language phrase books, and educational courses help younger tribal members to learn the language of their ancestors. The Ojibwe and Cree Cultural Centre contains a library and resource center, while the Cree Cultural Institute, which opened in the town of Oujé-Bougoumou, Quebec, in 2011, is a showcase of the tribal history and culture of the James Bay Cree. 🖋

YUP'IK

(YOO-peek)

LANGUAGE GROUP:
Eskimo-Aleut

GREETING:
Cama-i

THANK YOU:
Quyana

LOCATION PRECONTACT:
Alaska

LOCATION TODAY:
Alaska (U.S.); Russia

Numbering some 25,000 people, the Yup'ik form the largest group of Alaskan Native people. As many as 10,000 of them speak their ancestral language.

Traditionally, tribal members moved according to the seasons: In winter, they lived in villages and in summer, they traveled to fishing camps. On the coast, they hunted walruses and seals, while inland, they caught fish, birds, bears, and other land animals. The best hunters often became village leaders. The Yup'ik were skilled craftspeople. They carved figures from ivory and decorated their baskets with geometric motifs. Almost all of their clothes, tools, food vessels, and baskets were ornamented in some way, whether carved with intricate designs, woven with geometric patterns, or embellished with fur and feathers.

In many Yup'ik groups, the men lived separately from the women, who resided in small community homes, called *ena*, with their children and other female members of the family. Yup'ik men still lived in their large community houses called *qasgiq* up until the 1970s. The *qasgiq* operated like a

Yup'ik men scan the flat tundra landscape from a traditional wooden lookout. Their ancestors used such structures for hunting prey. They allowed the men to see far into the distance in all directions as they looked for animals to hunt.

GAME TIME

The indigenous people of the far North still play traditional games that have been around for centuries. These include the knuckle hop and the blanket toss. The knuckle hop tests skill and toughness. Men and women compete against each other by hopping forward on just their knuckles and toes. A more playful game is the blanket toss (pictured), in which people hold a blanket tight and raise it up and down to throw another person into the air. The aim is to be able to land on the blanket without losing balance. People also do twists and flips midair. Traditionally, the blanket was made from sealskin, but today people use canvas.

modern-day community center, with all members of the tribe gathering there regularly for ceremonies, singing, and dancing. Ceremonies are still held throughout the year and remain an important link between the tribe's past and the present. During the early 1800s, the Russians tried to establish fur-trading centers on the Yukon and Kuskokwim Rivers, but these were not as successful as their centers in Aleut and Alutiiq territories. Contact with the Russians caused devastation among the Yup'ik people when a smallpox epidemic swept through the region in 1837.

Today, the Bristol Bay area is home to one of the world's largest wild salmon runs. Yup'ik people work in the fishing industry and also hunt and fish for themselves. In recent years, climate change has become a threat to the Arctic way of life. The permafrost—a frozen layer just beneath Earth's surface—is melting and the land is eroding under villages. Yup'ik people in the isolated village of Newtock became the first Americans to relocate because of climate change. Other coastal villages may have to do the same in years to come. ☛

IN THE KNOW

Eskimos and Inuit rub noses when greeting family members and close friends. The word for the exchange is *kunik*.

The Yup'ik carved masks to wear at ritual dances. This example bears walrus tusks and whiskers and would probably have been made and worn to ensure a successful hunt for its wearer.

RAVEN'S GREAT ADVENTURE

The Raven in Alaska was no ordinary bird. He had remarkable powers and could change into whatever form he wished. He could change from a bird to a man, and he could not only fly and walk, but he could also swim under the water as fast as any fish.

One day Raven took the form of a little, bent-over old man so that he could walk through a forest. He wore a long, white beard and walked slowly. After a while, Raven felt hungry. As he thought about this, he came to the edge of a forest, near a village on the beach. There, many people were fishing for halibut.

In a flash, Raven thought of a scheme. He dived into the sea and swam to the spot where the fishermen dangled their hooks. Raven gobbled their bait, swimming from one hook to another. Each time Raven stole bait, a fisherman felt a tug on his line. When all the lines were pulled in, they had neither fish nor bait.

But Raven worked his trick once too often. When Houskana, an expert fisherman, felt a tug, he jerked his line quickly, hooking something heavy. Raven's jaw had caught on the hook. While Houskana tugged on his line, Raven pulled in the opposite direction. Then Raven grabbed hold of some rocks at the bottom of the sea and called, "Oh rocks, please help me!" But the rocks paid no attention.

Because of the great pain he felt, Raven said to his jaw, "Break off, oh jaw, for I am too tired." His jaw obeyed, and it broke off.

Houskana pulled in his line immediately. On his hook was the old man's jaw with a long white beard! It looked horrible enough to scare anyone. Houskana and the other fishermen were very frightened because they thought the jaw might belong to some evil spirit. They picked up their feet and ran as fast as they could to the chief's house.

Raven, still disguised as an old man, came out of the water and followed the fishermen. Though he was in great pain for lack of his jaw, no one noticed anything wrong because he covered the lower part of his face with his blanket.

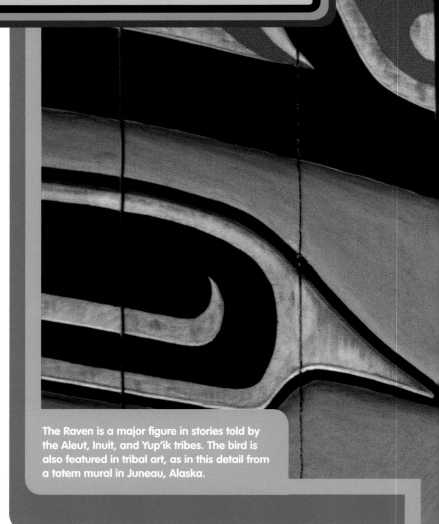

The Raven is a major figure in stories told by the Aleut, Inuit, and Yup'ik tribes. The bird is also featured in tribal art, as in this detail from a totem mural in Juneau, Alaska.

The chief and the people examined the jaw hanging on the halibut hook. It was handed from one to another and finally to Raven, who said, "Oh, this is a wonder to behold!" With this, he threw back his blanket and replaced his jaw. Raven performed his magic so quickly that no one had time to see what had happened. As soon as Raven's jaw was firmly in place again, he turned himself into a bird and flew out through the smoke hole of the chief's house. Only then did the people begin to realize it was the trickster Raven who had stolen their bait and been hooked on Houskana's fishing line.

On one Inuit totem pole, Raven was carved without his beak—a reminder of his great adventure.

An Eskimo (Inuit) story

THE NORTHEAST

People arrived in the Northeast thousands of years ago. Family groups traveled south from Alaska, then east to the woodlands around the Great Lakes and on to the Atlantic coast. They built their communities near lakes, rivers, and streams. The rivers and lakes connected one village to the next and established important routes for trapping and trading. Tribal peoples navigated the waterways in canoes made from birchbark or hollowed-out logs.

THE STORY OF **THE NORTHEASTERN PEOPLE**

The traditional lands of the northeastern tribes stretched from west of the Great Lakes to the Atlantic Ocean. Dense forests, thousands of lakes and rivers, and plentiful wildlife provided a rich existence for the people who lived here. They built their homes and canoes from the trees and used animal skins for clothing. People gathered wild food such as fruit and nuts, and their elders taught them to fish, farm, and hunt. Coastal tribes fished for cod and collected shellfish, while those around the western Great Lakes harvested wild rice. Beginning about nine hundred years ago, some tribes grew crops of corn, beans, and squash.

The Ancestors

Tribes spread across the entire northeastern region and developed their own cultures and languages. Most can trace their ancestors back to one of three large language groups, in which the languages are passed down through the generations, but differ from tribe to tribe. The language groups are Algonquian, Iroquoian, and Siouan.

All northeastern tribes followed a clan system, in which every tribal member belonged to a group of relatives that was represented by a type of animal, bird, or fish. In most Algonquian and Siouan tribes, a child belonged to the clan of its father, while an Iroquoian child belonged to the clan of its mother. Clans established social and political systems, and leaders made decisions for their people. Clan rules and traditions differed from one tribe to the next and changed over time.

Relationships among the different tribes varied, too. Tribes traded with one another, but they also fought over territory. In order to establish peace—or to achieve more power—some tribes formed confederacies (political unions) in which they established trading agreements and pledged to support each other in times of hardship. The most powerful of these unions, known as the Iroquois League among French settlers and as the Haudenosaunee Confederacy among Native peoples, was formed hundreds of years before Europeans arrived. The union included the Cayuga, Mohawk, Oneida, Onondaga, and Seneca tribes. (Another tribe, the Tuscarora, joined in 1722.) Belonging to this larger group made each of these tribes stronger, because they supported one another.

Times of Change

Europeans began to arrive in the Northeast in the early 1600s. On seeing the wild game, timber, and other natural resources of the tribal lands, the newcomers decided to build permanent settlements there, establishing trading posts and forcing Native people to live elsewhere. Some tribes moved in agreement with the Europeans and signed treaties with them, while other tribes were forced to leave against their will. Several tribes fought against the Europeans in a bid to save their lands, but they were rarely successful. Contact with the Europeans brought other problems, too, including new diseases, such as smallpox, measles, and mumps, which killed large numbers of tribal members and often left their communities struggling to survive.

Reservations

The treaties that the tribes made with the Europeans often allocated an area of land to the tribes, on which they could live. This land—literally "reserved" for their use—became known as a reservation. Some reservations were part of a tribe's traditional homeland, but often they would be far away. They were almost always smaller than the land the tribe had inhabited before, and had poorer natural resources. While some tribes stayed in their new locations—and continue to live there today—others returned to their homelands in later years. Today, many tribal members choose to live on reservations. Membership is determined not by where a person lives, but through a process that considers family ties, clans, or adoption by American Indians.

This 1830s portrait depicts two Menominee men. Each of the eagle feathers on their headdresses has been earned through an act of bravery in war.

MANITOBA

NORTH DAKOTA

MINNESOTA

SOUTH DAKOTA

IOWA

MISS

ARKA

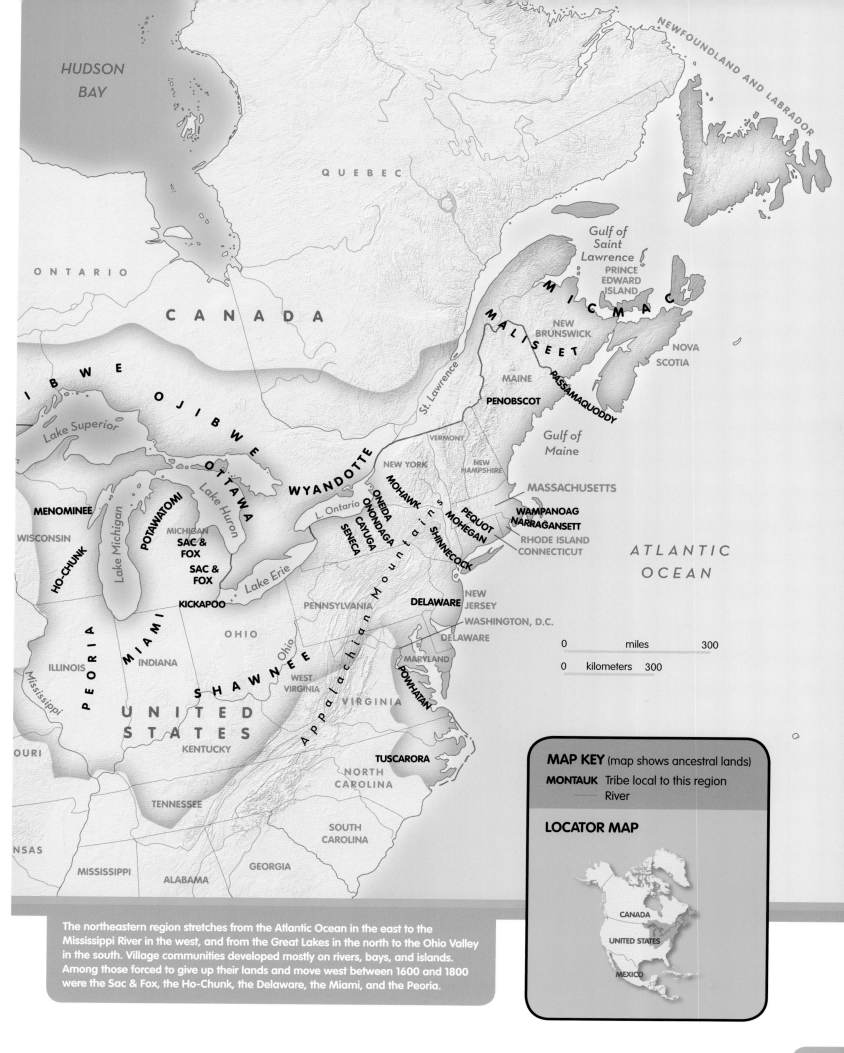

HUDSON
BAY

NEWFOUNDLAND AND LABRADOR

QUEBEC

ONTARIO

CANADA

Gulf of
Saint
Lawrence

PRINCE
EDWARD
ISLAND

M I C M A C

NOVA
SCOTIA

NEW
BRUNSWICK

MALISEET

St. Lawrence

MAINE

PASSAMAQUODDY

Lake Superior

I B W E

O J I B W E

VERMONT

PENOBSCOT

Gulf of
Maine

OTTAWA

NEW YORK

NEW
HAMPSHIRE

WYANDOTTE

MASSACHUSETTS

MENOMINEE

Lake Huron

MOHAWK

ONEIDA

ONONDAGA

CAYUGA

SENECA

L. Ontario

PEQUOT

MOHEGAN

WAMPANOAG

NARRAGANSETT

ATLANTIC
OCEAN

POTAWATOMI

Lake Michigan

MICHIGAN

SAC &
FOX

WISCONSIN

HO-CHUNK

SAC &
FOX

SHINNECOCK

RHODE ISLAND

CONNECTICUT

Lake Erie

KICKAPOO

PENNSYLVANIA

DELAWARE

NEW
JERSEY

WASHINGTON, D.C.

MIAMI

OHIO

DELAWARE

0   miles   300

0   kilometers   300

PEORIA

INDIANA

MARYLAND

ILLINOIS

SHAWNEE

Ohio

WEST
VIRGINIA

Appalachian Mountains

VIRGINIA

POWHATAN

U N I T E D
S T A T E S

OURI

KENTUCKY

TUSCARORA

NSAS

TENNESSEE

NORTH
CAROLINA

Mississippi

MISSISSIPPI

ALABAMA

GEORGIA

SOUTH
CAROLINA

MAP KEY (map shows ancestral lands)

MONTAUK   Tribe local to this region
——   River

LOCATOR MAP

CANADA

UNITED STATES

MEXICO

The northeastern region stretches from the Atlantic Ocean in the east to the
Mississippi River in the west, and from the Great Lakes in the north to the Ohio Valley
in the south. Village communities developed mostly on rivers, bays, and islands.
Among those forced to give up their lands and move west between 1600 and 1800
were the Sac & Fox, the Ho-Chunk, the Delaware, the Miami, and the Peoria.

TIME LINE OF THE NORTHEAST

The northeastern culture grew around the Great Lakes and along the St. Lawrence River and the Atlantic Coast. Tribes established confederacies and developed trading relationships among themselves. They were some of the first tribes to have contact with Europeans through the fur trade. Later, wars between England and France tore Native nations apart while European settlement forced tribes from their homelands.

1000 B.C.E.
Beginnings of the Eastern Woodland culture. Depending on where they lived, the tribes of the Northeast became hunters, fishermen, and farmers. They lived in villages (right), mainly near lakes, rivers, or the ocean, and used the waterways to cross large distances in their canoes. At one time, there were more than 100 tribes living in this region, in thousands of villages, and speaking more than 50 different languages or dialects.

1614
Pocahontas kidnapped. The English kidnapped Pocahontas, the daughter of a Powhatan chief, in order to use her for ransom. The English wanted the chief to return English prisoners and weapons. The chief agreed to the terms, but Pocahontas did not return to her tribe. She married an Englishman, John Rolfe. In 1616, she traveled to England with her husband and young son, Thomas, where they met King James I. Pocahontas died in 1617, when she was just 21 years old.

1637–1638
Pequot War. Problems over land and trade caused a war between the Pequot and English settlers. The English killed as many as 400 Pequot and took those who survived as prisoners.

ca. 1450
Iroquois League of the Cayuga, Mohawk, Oneida, Onondaga, and Seneca tribes forms. This alliance made peace among the tribes, and made them a powerful force.

1500s
Fur trade begins. European fishermen began trading with tribes on the Atlantic coast in the 1500s. The tribes brought animal furs to exchange for goods such as cloth.

1641–1701
Iroquois Wars. Conflicts between the Iroquois, other northeastern tribes, and the French arose over the beaver trade. The Iroquois pushed the tribes out so they could expand their territory. A 1701 peace treaty ended the wars.

1675
King Philip's War. The last major effort to drive out European settlers ended in defeat for the Wampanoag.

1754–1760
French and Indian Wars. The British fought the French for control over North America. The British won, and gained control of former French colonies and land claims through the Treaty of Paris.

1763–1764
Pontiac's Rebellion. Ottawa chief Pontiac led several large attacks against British forts, capturing nine posts. Ultimately, due to a lack of support, the rebellion failed. Pictured is a British pistol from the conflict.

1811

Prophetstown settlement sacked. In 1808, Shawnee war chief Tecumseh (right), and his brother, Tenskwatawa, established Prophetstown where the Tippecanoe River crossed the Wabash River. While Tecumseh was away trying to stop the U.S. government taking over tribal lands, U.S. soldiers burned the settlement down.

1812–1815

War of 1812. During the war between the United States and Britain, most tribes—including the Iroquois and those led by the Shawnee chief Tecumseh—sided with Britain. Many tribes feared losing more land to the U.S. government and thought it would help their cause to support the British. After the war, the U.S. government negotiated over 200 treaties that involved the ceding of Native lands.

1830

Indian Removal Act. The U.S. government passed a policy that forced many Native tribes to move from their ancestral homelands to new reservations in present-day Oklahoma.

1832

Black Hawk War. The Sac warrior Black Hawk led Sac, Fox, and Kickapoo people to Illinois to reclaim land they had lost in the 1804 Treaty of St. Louis. Many of the people were elders, women, and children. White settlers saw the move as an attack and the local militia opened fire on the Native Americans. A short, but brutal, war followed, in which only 200 of Black Hawk's 1,500 people survived.

1850

The Sandy Lake Tragedy. The U.S. government forced the Ojibwe tribe to move in order to make way for white settlers. Hundreds of Ojibwe died at Sandy Lake, Minnesota, as they waited for food supplies promised by the government, which spoiled before reaching them. In 1849, Ojibwe chiefs had traveled to Washington, D.C., to petition against the move and had carried the above document with them. Each chief is represented by his clan animal.

1917

Iroquois tribes declare war on Germany. When the United States entered World War I, American Indians could only join those fighting if they had citizenship. Few did, provoking the Oneida and Onondaga tribes to declare a war on Germany as independent nations. The Mohawk tribe followed in 1918. Mohawk soldiers are pictured at right serving on the Western Front.

1942

Iroquois League declares war on the Axis powers. The six tribes of the Iroquois League declared war on Germany, Italy, and Japan following the United States' entry into the conflict.

2012

Kateri Tekakwitha becomes a saint. Also known as the "Lily of the Mohawks," Kateri Tekakwitha was born in 1656 in present-day New York. She became a Christian who cared for the sick and elderly. In 1680, she became very ill and died. She was thought to have performed a miracle, saving a young boy from dying. In 2012, Pope Benedict XVI approved the miracle and made Kateri a saint.

1968

American Indian Movement founded. Ojibwe Clyde Bellecourt (pictured), George Mitchell, and Dennis Banks created the American Indian Movement (AIM) at a meeting in Minneapolis, Minnesota. The organization formed to fight for tribal rights, to reclaim land, and to end discrimination. Members helped organize and support protests and demonstrations.

CAYUGA

(kai-YOO-ga)

LANGUAGE GROUP:
Iroquoian

GREETING:
Ské:no'

THANK YOU:
Nyá:węh

LOCATION PRECONTACT:
New York State

LOCATION TODAY:
New York (not federally recognized), Oklahoma (U.S.); Ontario (Canada)

The Cayuga are the "people of the great swamp." Originally, they lived in large communities near what is now Cayuga Lake in the Finger Lakes district of New York State. Like other northeastern tribes, the Cayuga were farmers. They grew large crops of corn, beans, and squash, which they called the "three sisters," because these plants grew well together. The corn stalks provided a place for the bean vines to grow, while the broad leaves of the squash shaded the soil, blocking weeds and slowing water evaporation. The Cayuga also gathered other foods, such as fruit, and the men hunted and fished.

The Cayuga belonged to the Iroquois League, which also included the Mohawk, Oneida, Onondaga, Seneca, and later, Tuscarora tribes. When attending ceremonies, the men in the league wore a *gustoweh*, or headdress—a fitted cap made of wood and decorated with small, curled turkey feathers. Each tribe could be identified by the number and position of additional eagle feathers. The Cayuga had just one eagle feather that trailed to the rear of the *gustoweh*, rather than standing upright.

Iroquois tribes were made up of family clans that still exist today. The Cayuga clans are the Turtle, Snipe, Bear, Heron, and Wolf; each one has a clan mother and a chief or subchief. Clan families lived together in a longhouse—a large, log- and pole-framed house covered in bark. Up to 100 feet (30 m) long, a longhouse was home to more than 100 people. Today, most Cayuga live in modern homes on and off Cayuga land, but they still belong to their clan families, no matter where they live.

During the American Revolution (1775–1783), some Cayuga fought alongside the British, and the American army destroyed many of their villages. After the war, the Treaty of Canandaigua forced the Cayuga to give most of their land to the U.S. government. Many of them moved to a Seneca-Cayuga reservation in Oklahoma or to the Six Nations of the Grand River reserve (reservation), in Canada. Today, only a small number live in the Northeast—on, or near, the Seneca Nation Reservation in New York.

This Cayuga elder is dressed in traditional clothing, including his tribe's headdress with its single trailing eagle feather to the rear. Behind him stands a replica of a bark-covered longhouse.

BROKEN PROMISES

Treaties are written agreements or contracts. Countries sign treaties to end wars, such as the Treaty of Paris, signed in 1783 to end the Revolutionary War. However, treaties between the Europeans, and later, the U.S. and Canadian governments, and North American tribes became a way to gain control over tribal lands. In return for the land, the treaties promised payments, protection, and reservations or reserves (in Canada). The terms of the treaties were often unclear to the tribal nations who signed them, because they did not understand the languages in which they were written. Other times, treaty promises were broken, leaving tribes with little land, money, or rights. Hundreds of treaties were signed in North America, until the U.S. Congress abolished them in 1871. In Canada, between 1871 and 1921, the Canadian government and First Nations signed 11 treaties.

KICKAPOO

(KICK-a-poo)

LANGUAGE GROUP:
Algonquian

GREETING:
Aho

THANK YOU:
Kepiihcihi

LOCATION PRECONTACT:
Michigan, Wisconsin, Illinois, Indiana

LOCATION TODAY:
Kansas, Oklahoma (U.S.); Mexico

The Kickapoo first lived in a large territory in the western Great Lakes region. They were seminomadic, moving around the area with the seasons. In the 1600s, the tribes of the Iroquois League fought the Kickapoo for their territory, forcing them to move west and south. Relocating became a pattern for the tribe for many years and their name is a reflection of this. It comes from *kiwigapawa*, which means "standing now here, now there."

Wherever they found themselves, the Kickapoo adapted to their new environment. In the eastern woodlands, they farmed in the summer, growing crops of beans, squash, and corn; in winter, they hunted game, such as deer, eating the meat and using the skins to make clothes and moccasins. As the tribe moved farther south, they also hunted buffalo. Unlike other northeastern tribes, and more like the tribes of the Plains, the Kickapoo used horses for hunting and traveling.

When the Europeans arrived, the Kickapoo initially avoided conflict by moving away, but this changed in the early 1800s, when the Shawnee chief, Tecumseh, urged several tribes to fight to keep their lands. The Kickapoo joined Tecumseh, and went on to fight alongside him when he sided with the British in the War of 1812. Tecumseh's reason for helping the British was to gain favor and save Shawnee land, but the battles ended in defeat for him and the Kickapoo. Having signed one treaty ⇒

A young Kickapoo woman enjoys riding a horse with a friend. In the backdrop is the resistance camp against the Dakota Access oil pipeline. Members of different tribes joined the protest, as did non-Native people.

in 1809, the Kickapoo signed another in 1819. Giving up their lands in Illinois and Indiana, they left for Missouri.

The Kickapoo did not recover from the wars and treaties of the early 1800s. Signing as many as 10 treaties with the U.S. government between 1795 and 1854, the tribe moved frequently and eventually broke apart. Many tribal members settled in Kansas and Oklahoma in the 1830s. Then, in 1852, a band of Kickapoo moved to Mexico. In 1883, the U.S. government promised the Kickapoo ownership of land in Oklahoma, but failed to honor its promise. Several years later, under the Dawes Act of 1887, the Oklahoma Kickapoo finally agreed to something known as the allotment scheme, which meant each tribal member received a small parcel of land.

This lifelike portrait of a Kickapoo man with a painted face and wearing ceremonial dress was painted by the artist Elbridge Ayer Burbank. Burbank painted as many as 1,200 Native American portraits at the turn of the 20th century.

IN THE KNOW

You have to listen carefully to the Kickapoo language because it is a tone language. This means that the pitch of a vowel—that is, whether it is a high or a low sound—changes the meaning of the word being spoken.

Today, the Kickapoo continue to exist as four bands: the Kansas Kickapoo, the Oklahoma Kickapoo, the Texas Band of Kickapoo, and the Mexican Kickapoo. The separate bands have strong cultural ties but each runs its own government.

BEADS THAT TELL A STORY

Specific to the people of the Northeast, *wampum* is the name for beads made from clam and whelk shells (pictured). Tribes on the Atlantic coast collected quahog clams and whelks in the summer. They ate the meat inside, then pounded and polished the shells to create tiny beads. Purple beads were especially prized because they were rare. Inland, tribes traded other goods, such as furs and food, in exchange for the wampum. The beads were also used to create belts to commemorate treaties between tribes.

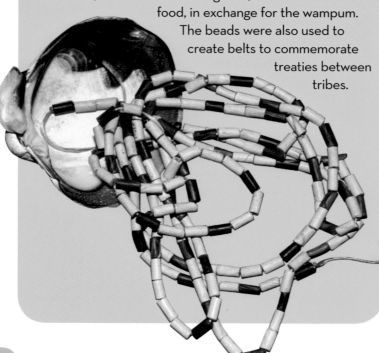

MALISEET

(MAL-uh-seet)

LANGUAGE GROUP:
Algonquian

GREETING:
Qey

THANK YOU:
Woliwon

LOCATION PRECONTACT:
Maine; New Brunswick (Canada)

LOCATION TODAY:
Maine (U.S.); New Brunswick, Quebec (Canada)

Present-day Maine, in the United States, and the Canadian provinces of New Brunswick and southern Quebec are the traditional homelands of the Maliseet people. Today, six communities live in Canada and one, the Houlton Band of Maliseet Indians, lives in Maine. The Maliseet call themselves Wolastoqiyik, meaning "of the beautiful river," for the St. John River that runs through their land. (They called the river Wolastoq.) They are close relatives of the Passamaquoddy and the two tribes speak similar languages.

The Maliseet were seminomadic people who fished for salmon in the St. John River and its tributaries, and hunted and gathered in the surrounding territory. They were excellent craftspeople and made everything necessary for the changing seasons, from birchbark canoes for summer travel to snowshoes and sleds to help them cross the snowy terrain in winter.

The patterns on this birchbark basket from around 1800 are made of dyed porcupine quills. The basket would likely have been used for storing personal items.

They also created beautiful beadwork and carvings and wove baskets with detailed designs. The Maliseet and their neighbors—the Penobscot, Micmac, Passamaquoddy, and Abenaki—formed the Wabanaki Confederacy. In times of need, their members met at a council fire to discuss issues such as war and trade.

The Maliseet traded furs with the French settlers who arrived in the 1600s to establish colonies on Maliseet land, but wars between French and English colonists created many problems. By the mid-1700s, the British had taken over the French colonies, and a few years later, the Revolutionary War (1775–1783) divided the Maliseet, with tribal members fighting on opposing sides.

The war created a border between the new United States and Britain's Canadian colony, which ran right through Maliseet territory. In 1794, the Jay Treaty granted tribal members the right to travel freely across this new border. Still, many Maliseet chose to move to Canada.

Today, the Houlton Band of Maliseet Indians remains the only Maliseet tribe within the United States, occupying an 850-acre (345-ha) reservation in Maine.

Two Canadian Maliseet men stand with the birchbark canoe they built.

IN THE KNOW

The Houlton Band of Maliseet Indians is working to protect the Meduxnekeag River watershed, a tributary of the St. John River that runs through their land. They hope to revive the river's fish and bald eagle populations.

MENOMINEE

(me-NOH-muh-nee)

LANGUAGE GROUP:
Algonquian

GREETING:
Posōh

THANK YOU:
Wāewāenen

LOCATION PRECONTACT:
Wisconsin, Upper Michigan

LOCATION TODAY:
Wisconsin

The central, puckered section of these deerskin moccasins from the 1830s is typical of Menominee moccasin style.

The Menominee have inhabited present-day Wisconsin for more than 10,000 years. Originally, the tribe also lived in northern Michigan. They call themselves Kyas-machatiwduk, meaning "ancient ones," or Mamaceqtaw, "the people."

The name Menominee comes from an Ojibwe word, *omanoominii*, which means "people of the wild rice." Wild rice is a grass that grows in shallow lakes and rivers, which the tribe harvested each fall, loading canoes with the kernels. The tribe also depended on freshwater fish, such as sturgeon. At one time, the tribe's territory spanned over 10 million acres (4 million ha), but it lost some of this land to neighboring tribes, such as the Fox. Once Europeans began to settle, the tribe lost more land through forced sales and treaties.

The French were the first colonists to move into Menominee land, establishing fur trading posts and trading with the tribe. After the Revolutionary War, the Menominee signed many treaties with the U.S. government and, in 1854, the tribe was forced onto a reservation in Wisconsin. The government expected the Menominee to farm the land but, instead, they built a sawmill and began a lumber industry. The business was very successful. By the 1950s, the tribe had $10 million in the bank.

Around the same time, the U.S. government introduced its "termination" policy. The idea was that Native Americans should give up their traditional ways of life and live more like "Americans." The process involved the removal of tribal status and tribes had to start paying taxes on their land. When "terminated" in 1961, the Menominee struggled to make enough money to survive. They had to sell some reservation land and closed their forestry program. It wasn't until 1973, following many protests from the tribe, that the government reinstated the Menominee. The tribe revived its forestry business and reestablished its tribal government. Today, the Menominee live on 235,000 acres (95,000 ha) of reservation land in Wisconsin.

Menominee children present the pelts of two raccoons trapped and skinned by their father, ca. 1970. The tribe once traded skins like these with European settlers.

IN THE KNOW

The Menominee developed one of the world's first sustainable forests. To keep the forest healthy, workers start harvesting just the mature trees at one end of the forest. By the time they reach the opposite end, the next wave of mature trees is ready for cutting at the first end, and so on.

SUMMER CAMPS

During the warmer weather, many tribes moved to camps near the coast or large lakes where they could fish. They needed shelter that was easy and quick to build. For short hunting trips, men made simple brush shelters from branches. At the summer camp, both men and women helped to make wigwams (pictured). These were small, domed homes for one family, so tribes made several in one camp. To build a wigwam, people gathered saplings, or young trees, and scraped the bark from them. Then they pushed the end of each flexible pole into a hole in the ground and bent the poles to make a rounded frame. Strips of bark held the poles together. People draped woven cattail mats over the top of the frame to make the walls. In fall, people left these camps and returned to their winter villages. They dismantled the temporary homes before leaving.

MICMAC

(MICK-mack)

LANGUAGE GROUP:
Algonquian

GREETING:
Pusùl

THANK YOU:
Welàlin

LOCATION PRECONTACT:
Maine; New Brunswick, Nova Scotia, Prince Edward Island, Newfoundland, Quebec (Canada)

LOCATION TODAY:
Maine, U.S. (Aroostook Band); Maritime Canada

The Micmac homelands stretch from Maine in the United States to the Canadian provinces of Newfoundland and Nova Scotia. The tribe probably moved farther north about 12,000 years ago and settled in the large territory they called Mi'kma'ki. The Micmac had an organized political system, dividing their land into seven districts. A chief from each district attended a Grand Council to manage important tribal business, such as building relationships with neighboring tribes. The Grand Council also oversaw the movement of Micmac families and the lands available to them.

For much of their history, the Micmac moved with the seasons. They built birchbark wigwams for their winter camps inland and moved to coastal villages in the spring and stayed through summer. The Micmac hunted moose, caribou, and porcupines. Besides eating the meat, the tribe used moose ➡

This is a birchbark wall-pocket from the 1880s. The decoration is made from dyed porcupine quills. The Micmac traded wall-pockets with white settlers, who put flowers in them.

Like many northeastern tribes, the Micmac used birchbark canoes for travel. They built their versions with especially high sides and ends, which made them sturdy enough for the open sea.

bones to make blades for their spears and dyed porcupine quills to use as decoration on clothing. They fished in the long St. John River and its many tributaries. Along the coast, the Micmac trawled the Atlantic Ocean for lobster, cod, and other seafood.

The Micmac welcomed the French colonists who arrived in the early 1600s, and French missionaries converted many tribal members to Catholicism. The most famous Micmac to convert was the grand chief—the first native leader to be baptized by the French. He took the name Henri Membertou. The Micmac's first treaty is recorded on a *wampum* belt that depicts both Catholic and Micmac symbols. The friendship between the Micmac and the French continued during the French and Indian Wars

(1754–1760), in which Micmac warriors fought alongside France. In the 1700s, the Micmac had joined other tribes to form the Wabanaki Confederacy to protect themselves against the Iroquois League. They also hoped to stop the increasing number of French and, later, English settlements. But even together the tribes were not successful in preventing the Europeans from taking more land. Most Micmac moved onto reserves in Canada.

Today, there are 28 Micmac communities in Canada and one, the Aroostook Band of Micmacs, in Maine, recognized by the U.S. government in 1991. Most tribal members live in Caribou, Presque Isle, and Houlton, Maine.

MOHAWK

(MOH-hawk)

LANGUAGE GROUP:
Iroquoian

GREETING:
Shé:kon

THANK YOU:
Niá:wen

LOCATION PRECONTACT:
New York

LOCATION TODAY:
New York (U.S.); Ontario, Quebec (Canada)

The Mohawk call themselves Kanienkehéka, or "people of the flint," and their territory Akwesasne, meaning "where the partridge drums." They made up the largest tribe within the Iroquois League when it was established. Their *gustoweh*, or headdress, is adorned with three upright eagle feathers. Of all the confederacy members, theirs was the land farthest east, in upper New York State—a location that led to early conflicts with French colonists arriving from Europe.

During the 1600s, the Mohawk and other tribes that belonged to the Iroquois League fought against the French and their Native allies, the Ojibwe and Potawatomi, in a series of wars known as the Iroquois Wars. The Mohawk competed in the fur trade as well as for territory, leading to decades of conflict with many losses on both sides. In 1701, the Mohawk and other Iroquois signed the Treaty of Montreal with the French, establishing a period of peace.

This headdress belongs to Chief Jake Swamp of the St. Regis Reservation. It was made by his son, Skahendowaneh, in 2009. It features peacock feathers as well as turkey feathers and has deer antlers on either side of a wooden, fabric-covered frame.

TRADING FURS

People living across North America belonged to vast trading networks long before Europeans came looking for furs. But in the 1500s, Native tribes began trading with European fishermen, who brought cloth, tools, and other goods to exchange for animal furs. Native tribes soon discovered that furs could make them a lot of money. By the early 1600s, the demand for fur, especially beaver fur, had skyrocketed. Felt hats, made from beaver fur, were the height of fashion in Europe. The French and the English established fur trading posts all over the Northeast territory, but fierce competition developed between the two European countries and among the Native tribes. Trade also brought settlers, merchants, and missionaries who cleared forests for farms, built towns, and made claims to tribal land.

During the Revolutionary War, the Mohawk became divided, some fighting with the Patriots (colonists opposed to British rule), and others supporting the British. After the war, tribal members settled in Canada, which was still under British control, but their territory was crossed by the border between Canada and the new United States. In 1794, the Jay Treaty allowed tribal members to cross the border freely. That same year, the Treaty of Canandaigua ceded most Mohawk land to the U.S. government.

Until this time, the tribe had lived from the land, building longhouses in villages on the northern banks of what is now the Mohawk River, where they hunted, fished, and trapped. Now, with so little land, this way of life could no longer support the tribe. Many of its men sought employment in the cities, working for the construction industry.

Today, several Mohawk communities remain in the Canadian provinces of Ontario and Quebec. There, and in the United States, the tribe actively works to keep its language and traditions alive. The tribe still has three clans, the Bear, the Turtle, and the Wolf. In 1979, the Mohawk opened the Akwesasne Freedom School, which immerses children in Mohawk culture, language, and traditional ancestral teachings. The St. Regis Mohawk Reservation in New York has steadily grown in numbers since its creation in 1896 and remains a vibrant community.

ꞏ☀ꞏ IN THE KNOW

In the late 1800s, Mohawk workers helped to build a bridge over the St. Lawrence River in Canada. Scaling the iron beams up high, they gained the nickname "skywalkers." The success of the project brought the ironworkers jobs in New York—where they helped build the Empire State Building and the Chrysler Building—and in Chicago and San Francisco.

One Mohawk community lives on the south shore of the St. Lawrence River in Quebec, Canada. Every July, the tribe holds a powwow featuring traditional tribal dances and drum music.

NORTHEASTERN tribes played lacrosse, a game known by various Native names, including the Ojibwe *bag-gataway* and Mohawk *tewaarathon*. Traditionally, men and boys played the game, using sticks with curved ends and nets. They scored points by throwing a ball into a goal area. In recent years, Native Americans have made their name in the sport again, playing for college teams.

MOHEGAN

(mo-HEE-gun)

LANGUAGE GROUP:
Algonquian

GREETING:
Aquy

THANK YOU:
Táput ni

LOCATION PRECONTACT:
Connecticut

LOCATION TODAY:
Connecticut

The Mohegan tribe originated as the Wolf clan of the ancient Lenni Lenape nation. Separating from the other clans, the Mohegan traveled to what is now upstate New York and then Connecticut. When European colonists arrived in North America, a dispute with the head chief resulted in a tribe member named Uncas leading a group to separate from the main tribe, now known as the Pequot. Taking back their old clan name, Uncas became the tribe's head chief, or sachem. The Mohegan occupied the territory along the Thames River in what is now Connecticut. They planted extensive fields of corn and other crops, and hunted and fished the local waterways in dugout canoes.

When English settlers arrived, the Mohegan became their allies, while the Pequot resisted the English. In 1637, the English launched an attack on the Pequot and, being English allies, the Mohegan were drawn into the conflict. Almost 40 years later, the Mohegan supported the English again in King Philip's War against the Wampanoag. Having lived near and among the English for many years, a good number of Mohegan converted to Christianity. In the 1700s, Samson Occum became one of the first Mohegan ordained ministers. He helped to raise funds for a Native school—an institution that later became Dartmouth College in New Hampshire.

Throughout the years of war and early contact with Europeans, battles and smallpox epidemics wiped out much of the Mohegan population, and the tribe struggled to maintain its culture, language, and traditions. The tribe lost much land to the English. To

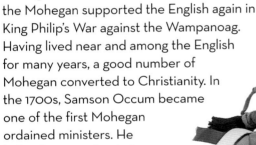

This doll made by Gladys Tantaquidgeon in around 1940 represents a male Mohegan in traditional clothing with embroidered details. Gladys also made dolls of female figures.

GLADYS TANTAQUIDGEON

Gladys Tantaquidgeon was born in 1899 and witnessed great change in her tribe's history. As a young girl, Gladys learned the stories of her elders and many tribal traditions, including a little of her tribe's language. She later studied anthropology (the study of humans and their communities) at the University of Pennsylvania. In 1931, Gladys helped found the Tantaquidgeon Museum—the oldest Native-owned museum in the United States. Gladys lived and worked among the Lakota Sioux and other tribes, supporting tribal culture, especially Native arts. After returning to her homeland and until her death in 2005, she worked to revive Mohegan spiritual beliefs and culture.

secure some land, the tribe built Mohegan Church in 1831. The reservation was almost gone by the late 1800s, except for that church in present-day Uncasville, Connecticut. In 1994, the U.S. government assigned official status to the Mohegan Tribe of Connecticut, allowing the tribe to repurchase some of its lands. Today, Mohegan people live on and off the reservation in Montville, Connecticut. The Mohegans are reviving their language, preserving tribal sites, and carrying on their ancient traditions, such as the Wigwam Festival, to celebrate the green corn. ✒

NARRAGANSETT

(nair-uh-GANN-set)

LANGUAGE GROUP:
Algonquian

LANGUAGE:
Limited number of words in current use; no dictionary available

LOCATION PRECONTACT:
Rhode Island

LOCATION TODAY:
Rhode Island

The Narragansett have lived in and around present-day Rhode Island for thousands of years. Their name comes from a word meaning "people of the small point." The tribe had an organized government divided into eight territories. Several sachems, or chiefs, controlled the different territories, but all answered to one head sachem.

In 1636, the Narragansett tribe allowed Englishman Roger Williams to found a settlement on its land. This later became the city of Providence, Rhode Island. Up until this time, the Narragansett had enjoyed a simple way of life, living from the land. They were excellent farmers who also hunted and fished for food. They inhabited villages in the winter, in which several families shared longhouses. In the summer, the tribe moved to temporary summer camps.

As their settlements grew, the English took over Narragansett lands and the tribe's way of life began to disappear. Worse still, the tribe became involved in a series of conflicts. The first major battle was the Pequot War, which started when the Pequot tribe resisted English settlement in its territory. The Narragansett and the Mohegans sided with the settlers and fought alongside them against the Pequot. The Pequot suffered tremendous losses and were no longer considered a threat to the English, but other tribes, such as the Wampanoag, still wanted to push the settlers out. Fearing that the Narragansett would support the tribes, the English organized an attack and killed 700 Narragansett people in what became known as the Great Swamp Massacre. The tribe took revenge by destroying Providence. By this time, they had lost many members in the wars, and also to disease, through such close contact with the European settlers. Some Narragansett moved away, while others were enslaved by the English. In 1682, the remaining Narragansett moved to a small reservation with the Niantic tribe at Charlestown, Rhode Island.

In 1934, the U.S. government passed the Indian Reorganization Act. Unlike the "termination" policy of the 1940s to 1960s, the Reorganization Act sought to encourage Native tribes to live traditionally, rather than become more like "Americans." Through a land-claim agreement with the U.S. government in 1978, the tribe acquired 1,943 acres (786 ha) of reservation land in Rhode Island. Their church, a small stone building, stands on three acres (1.2 ha) of ancestral land. The tribe did not receive federal recognition until 1983. 🪶

This Narragansett trumpet is made from a single cow horn. Northeastern tribes used horns like this to give a signal calling tribal people to attend an important meeting.

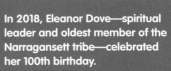

In 2018, Eleanor Dove—spiritual leader and oldest member of the Narragansett tribe—celebrated her 100th birthday.

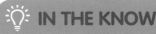

🔆 IN THE KNOW

The Narragansett term *sāchim* was used to describe the chief of the whole tribe. The English version of the word, "sachem," was commonly used for many tribal chiefs of the Northeast.

OJIBWE

(oh-JIB-wuh)

LANGUAGE GROUP:
Algonquian

GREETING:
Aaniin

THANK YOU:
Miigwech

LOCATION PRECONTACT:
Michigan, North Dakota

LOCATION TODAY:
Michigan, Minnesota, Montana, North Dakota, Wisconsin (U.S.); Manitoba, Ontario, Quebec, Saskatchewan (Canada)

The name Ojibwe comes from an Algonquian word meaning "puckered," possibly in reference to the style of moccasins that tribal members wore. Today, the tribe makes up one of the largest tribal groups in North America. They call themselves Anishinabe, which means "original people."

Some time before French colonists arrived in the 1600s, many Ojibwe moved west from the St. Lawrence River to the Great Lakes. They established towns around present-day Sault Ste. Marie, Michigan, and as far west as North Dakota. Rather than move around from season to season, the Ojibwe stayed in the same town year-round, living in wigwams. Early on, they began making birchbark canoes—a light and fast way to travel on waterways. The canoes were ideal for fishing, harvesting rice, and transporting fur.

The Ojibwe belong to the Three Fires Confederacy, which also includes the Ottawa and Potawatomi. This alliance helped the tribes develop a good trading relationship with the French. The confederacy also came together as a military unit to fight over territory against the Iroquois League to the east and the Dakota Sioux to the west. By the early 1700s, the Ojibwe had expanded their territory and become a powerful tribe, but their fortunes were very different a century later. Having fought alongside the British in the War of 1812, the tribe lost much land through treaties that they signed with the U.S. government. Still, the Ojibwe were not pushed out of their homelands altogether. Although the U.S. government acquired lands rich in timber, copper, and iron, the Ojibwe reservations had the largest lakes, enabling them to continue traditional ways of life—fishing, hunting, and farming. Today, thanks to the work of many Ojibwe activists, writers, politicians, and educators, the tribe continues to uphold its traditions and culture.

Like other Native tribes, the Ojibwe made drums from wood and deerskin. This example is painted with stylized animal figures.

☼ IN THE KNOW
The Ojibwe seasoned dishes with maple syrup. Each spring, women collected sap from sugar maple trees. They boiled it into a syrup and also made candies and maple sugar. Ojibwe people still make maple syrup in this way.

TRIBAL TRANSPORTATION

The Ojibwe invented the birchbark canoe approximately 3,000 years ago. They, and other northeastern tribes, such as the Ottawa, used this lightweight craft for travel and trade, and in warfare. Skilled oarsmen could weave the canoe swiftly through interconnected rivers and lakes, and over treacherous white-water rapids. The canoe weighed less than 300 pounds (136 kg), making it possible for people to carry it over land when necessary. To make a canoe, builders sewed bark onto a wooden frame using tree roots. Applying resin to the seams made them waterproof. The largest birchbark canoes were as long as 39 feet (12 m) and could carry more than 12 people, plus cargo. European explorers and traders abandoned their heavy boats in favor of the canoe, which was much more practical for traveling around on inland lakes and rivers.

CHIEF HOLE IN THE DAY

Hole in the Day was a powerful Ojibwe chief. He took the role over from his father, declaring himself head of several villages in central Minnesota. When the U.S. government tried to take Ojibwe land in the late 1800s, Hole in the Day negotiated treaties and demanded that the government make payments for land. Though admired by many, Hole in the Day also made enemies. In 1868, he traveled to Washington, D.C., to negotiate the terms of a treaty proposing the removal of the Ojibwe from their traditional homelands to the White Earth Reservation. While traveling, he was attacked and killed by a group of Ojibwe men hired by disgruntled traders.

ONEIDA

(oh-NYE-dah)

LANGUAGE GROUP:
Iroquoian

GREETING:
Shekú

THANK YOU:
Yawʌʔ

LOCATION PRECONTACT:
New York

LOCATION TODAY:
New York, Wisconsin (U.S.); Ontario (Canada)

According to tribal history, a stone always appeared to show the Oneida tribe the location of its next village, and the name Oneida translates as "people of the standing stone."

The Oneida tribe is one of the original five tribes belonging to the Iroquois League. A number of its chiefs continue to represent the tribe at the confederacy's Grand Council to this day. Each tribe in the Iroquois League can be identified by its *gustoweh*, or headdress, and the Oneida version has two eagle feathers that stand upright and one that trails to the side. Like the Mohawk, the tribe has just three clans: Bear, Wolf, and Turtle.

As part of the Iroquois League, the Oneida were drawn into the trading wars between the French and English, who were fighting over land and resources in North America. The Iroquois allied with their trading partners, the English, in the early 1800s, but their loyalties were divided when it came to fighting in the Revolutionary War. While most of the Iroquois tribes supported Britain, the Oneida and the Tuscarora tribes sided with the Patriots. The Oneida tribe fought in important battles, such as the Battle of Saratoga, in which the Patriots beat the British, marking a turning point in the war. ➤➤

Northeastern women carried their babies on their backs, strapped to a cradleboard. The hoop at the top protected the baby's head, in case the board fell. The carved block at the bottom served as a footrest.

61

Following the Revolutionary War, the Oneida signed several treaties with the U.S. government, resulting in the loss of most of their homeland. Originally, the tribe had occupied millions of acres in what is now central New York State. In 1794, the Treaty of Canandaigua, made between the U.S. government and the Iroquois League, promised the protection of this land and created a reservation of 300,000 acres (121,400 ha). Even so, settlers continued to take Oneida lands, and by the early 1900s the tribe owned just 32 acres (13 ha) of its homelands.

After years of court battles, the Oneida have reclaimed over 13,000 acres (5,260 ha). Today, there are four Oneida Nations. Many tribal members still live in New York, while others moved to communities in Green Bay, Wisconsin, and Ontario, Canada. In 1998, the Oneida Nation of New York took over the publication of *Indian Country Today*, the largest American Indian newspaper in the United States. It was founded in 1981 on the Lakota Tribe's Pine Ridge Reservation. Today, the paper delivers the news online and through social media networks.

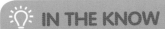 IN THE KNOW

During the Revolutionary War, the winter of 1777 was bitterly cold. George Washington's supplies were low. The Oneida chief Shenandoah sent bushels of corn to help feed the troops.

The Oneida chief Shikellamy is depicted here holding a flintlock rifle. His clothing is decorated with a turtle motif to represent his clan. Shikellamy was a negotiator between colonists and the tribes of the Iroquois League.

PEOPLE OF THE LONGHOUSE

The Cayuga, Mohawk, Oneida, Onondaga, and Seneca are the original members of the Iroquois League. Known as the Haudenosaunee (People of the Longhouse), these tribes built large bark-covered, pole-framed houses inhabited by several families that had their own area within the house. The longhouse became an important symbol for the Iroquois League.

Tribes are associated with their geographical location in relation to the other tribes in the league, and also to the layout of a longhouse. Those farthest east, the Mohawk, were the "keepers of the eastern door," for example. Those farthest west, the Seneca, were the "keepers of the western door." The Onondaga—geographically the most central of the tribes—were known as the "keepers of the central fire."

ONONDAGA

(ON-on-DAH-gah)

LANGUAGE GROUP:
Iroquoian

LANGUAGE:
Limited number of words in current use; no dictionary available

LOCATION PRECONTACT:
New York

LOCATION TODAY:
New York (U.S.); Ontario (Canada)

An Onondaga tribal member works on crafting a lacrosse stick at his workshop at the Onondaga Nation in New York.

The ancestral lands of the Onondaga—meaning "people of the hills"—make up about three million acres (1.2 million ha) of land around New York's Finger Lakes. Their villages were surrounded by hills, pine forests, lakes, and waterways that were full of natural resources. The tribe's location placed them at the center of the Iroquois League, with the Mohawk and Oneida to the east and the Cayuga and Seneca to the west. The tribal *gustoweh*, or headdress, has one upright and one trailing eagle feather.

Like their fellow Iroquois, the Onondaga are clan people. Each tribal member belongs to one of nine clans: Wolf, Turtle, Bear, Beaver, Snipe, Heron, Deer, Eel, or Hawk. Clan mothers have a vital role in the tribe's politics and culture. They select the 14 Onondaga chiefs and the head chief, known as *tadodaho*. They also ensure Onondaga customs and language continue through the generations by teaching children traditional ways of life. Faith keepers similarly have an important role in preserving and continuing sacred traditions. These men and women decide when important ceremonies should take place, such as Midwinter, a 21-day festival to celebrate the start of a new lunar year, and Green Corn, a ceremony that celebrates the beginning of the annual corn harvest.

During initial contact with Europeans, the Onondaga traded with the British. They remained neutral at the start of the Revolutionary War, but the Patriot army considered them to be British allies and, therefore, enemies. In 1779, the Patriots burned a long stretch of crops and settlements, including the principal Onondaga village. The tribe then sided with the British for the remainder of the war. In 1794, the Treaty of Canandaigua, which was made between the U.S. government and the Iroquois League, set aside some land for the Onondaga, but many tribal members left the U.S. to move to British territory in Canada. Today, the tribe has a reservation in New York State and two reserves in Ontario, Canada. ☛

A beaded necklace, created by Onondaga artist Helen Burning in 1988, features a mirror surrounded by five feather motifs made from tiny glass seed beads.

At Fort Stanwix in 1769, when selling their land to the founders of Pennsylvania, tribal chiefs of the Iroquois League used pictograms of their clan animals as signatures. The handwritten names beside the animals, which included turtles and snipes, were added later.

OTTAWA

(AH-ta-wa)

LANGUAGE GROUP:
Algonquian

LANGUAGE:
Limited number of words in current use; no dictionary available

LOCATION PRECONTACT:
Michigan; Ontario (Canada)

LOCATION TODAY:
Michigan, Oklahoma (U.S.); Ontario (Canada)

Ottawa lands stretched across the central and eastern Great Lakes region. In winter, tribal people traveled across their territory and much farther, hunting in forests and fishing in rivers and lakes. Like many other tribes of the Northeast, they also harvested wild rice in marshlands. The tribe's name comes from the Algonquian word *adawa*, which means "to trade." The tribe had a history of trading with other tribes long before they became involved in the fur trade with French settlers. They traded in tobacco, furs, cornmeal, sunflower oil, and mats.

The tribe's location, and its relationships with other tribes, made it an ideal trading partner for the French colonists, who arrived in the 1600s. The Ottawa acquired animal furs from other tribes and traded them with the French. Their business skills earned them the title "keepers of the trade" within the Three Fires Confederacy—an alliance with the Potawatomi and Ojibwe tribes. The confederacy developed a strong relationship with the French settlers and, as a result, joined the French in territory and trade wars against the British and their Iroquois allies. During such conflicts, the Iroquois—backed by British military power—pushed the Ottawa into present-day Wisconsin and farther west. The British defeated the French in the French and Indian War of 1754–1763, after which the British gained control of France's colonies. During the

PONTIAC

Pontiac was a powerful war chief. He aided the British during the French and Indian War, but felt that the British failed to show him the respect he deserved. So, in June 1763, Pontiac led a group of Ottawa, Potawatomi, and Ojibwe warriors in attacks against the British—now referred to as Pontiac's Rebellion. He and his men attacked and burned nine British forts. Six years later, a Peoria tribal member killed Pontiac in an act of vengeance, because he had stabbed and badly wounded a Peoria chief some years before. The assassination of Pontiac started a war between the Ottawa and Peoria tribes.

Revolutionary War, many Ottawa groups sided with the British and a number of them fled to Canada following the British defeat. In the 1800s, because of pressure from European encroachment, the Iroquois, and later the Indian Removal Act, the Ottawa were forced to relocate and lost most of their land. One group moved to Kansas in 1832, then relocated to Oklahoma in 1868. Their federal recognition was terminated by the U.S. government in 1955, and reinstated in 1978. Today, the Ottawa live in Oklahoma and have several reservations in Michigan and Ontario, Canada.

This pair of moccasins is from around 1830 and made from deer or moose hide. The decorative technique used on the top panel is called ribbonwork appliqué. The beaded cuffs at the back can be raised up over the ankles and held in place using the ribbon ties.

64

GAME TIME

Tribal children played many games. Young children had dolls (pictured) and bows and arrows. Children played bone and toggle, which involved a piece of leather punched with holes and an animal bone or sharpened stick. The leather was attached to the stick by a length of string. The idea was to toss the leather into the air and catch it by piercing the sharpened stick through one of the holes. In winter, older boys competed in a snowsnake game, which involved throwing a long, spear-like stick of wood down a mile-long (1.6 km) snow track. Players coated their sticks in wax to make them go faster. The winner was the boy whose stick traveled the farthest. In warmer weather, girls played doubleball, which was similar to the lacrosse played by boys. Their sticks had curved ends and the ball was made from two deerskin bags, joined and filled with sand. Players had to strike the opponent's goalpost with the ball to score.

PASSAMAQUODDY

(pass-uh-muh-KWAH-dee)

LANGUAGE GROUP:
Algonquian

GREETING:
Qey

THANK YOU:
Woliwon

LOCATION PRECONTACT:
Maine; New Brunswick (Canada)

LOCATION TODAY:
Maine (U.S.); New Brunswick (Canada)

Closely related to the Maliseet, the Passamaquoddy have lived in present-day Maine and parts of New Brunswick, Canada, for thousands of years. Like the Maliseet, they belonged to the Wabanaki Confederacy.

Traditionally, the tribe lived on the many resources around them, moving camp to take advantage of seasonal changes in fish and game populations. The tribe was particularly known for its craftsmanship, and produced fine wood carvings and jewelry as well as baskets from local plants.

In the 1600s, when the French began colonizing Maine and New Brunswick, their colonies became known collectively as Acadia. The Passamaquoddy became close to the French, and European missionaries converted many tribal members to Christianity. This friendship led to the tribe's involvement in land disputes between the British and the French, in which the

The lid of this birchbark box shows the image of a rabbit. The Passamaquoddy used boxes like this to store household items or food, and traded them with white settlers.

Passamaquoddy sided with the French Acadians. Following the British victory in the French and Indian War of 1754–1763, many French Acadians were deported, or forced to leave, while others fled. English settlers took their place, taking even more Passamaquoddy land away from the tribe. The Passamaquoddy fought against the British again when they sided with the Patriots in the Revolutionary War. In particular, the tribe helped to defend the Atlantic coast. When the British launched a ➤

naval attack on Machias, Maine, Chief Francis Joseph Neptune and his men helped to defeat them. In 1794, Chief Neptune signed a treaty allotting the tribe reservation land on what is now Passamaquoddy Bay, between Maine and Canada. Here, Pleasant Point Reservation has been the tribe's main village since 1770. Close by, Passamaquoddy people also live on the Indian Township Reservation—the largest reservation in Maine. There is also a Passamaquoddy community in New Brunswick, Canada.

In 1980, the Passamaquoddy bought back some of the land they had lost and now operate the Passamaquoddy Wild Blueberry Company, harvesting over 6,000 acres (2,400 ha) of blueberries a year.

IN THE KNOW

The Passamaquoddy name comes from their word *peskoto-muhkat,* which means "one who spears pollock." Pollock is a fish commonly found in the North Atlantic Ocean and was a long-time staple for the tribe.

The Passamaquoddy celebrate the opening of the Grand Falls fishway, which was dammed for 18 years following a dispute between the U.S. and Canada. The tribe now has access to local fish.

PENOBSCOT

(puh-NOB-scot)

LANGUAGE GROUP:
Algonquian

LANGUAGE:
Currently dormant; no record of last known speaker

LOCATION PRECONTACT:
Maine

LOCATION TODAY:
Maine

The Penobscot Nation received formal recognition from the U.S. government in 1980, but their history in Maine goes back many thousands of years. The tribe's name comes from the word *pan-awahpskek,* which means "where the rocks widen."

Their ancestral lands comprise a wide area along the length of the present-day Penobscot River, which was essential to the tribe's way of life. The river provided the most efficient travel routes across the tribe's territory, as well as access to bountiful fishing and hunting grounds. The Penobscot also used the resources of the surrounding land, growing crops such as corn and tapping maple trees for sap, which they boiled to make syrup. In winter, men tracked and hunted deer and bears in the forests. In summer, people traveled down the Penobscot River to the Atlantic Ocean, where they fished for crabs,

lobsters, and clams. The Penobscot were basketmakers and wove sturdy, functional baskets and fish traps from brown ash trees and sweet grass.

The Penobscot and their neighbors—the Passamaquoddy, Micmac, Abenaki, and Maliseet—form the Wabanaki Confederacy. This alliance of tribes fought to defend themselves against the tribes of the Iroquois League, particularly the Mohawk. The confederacy also formed a strong bond with French settlers and supported the French during the French and English wars. The many years of war and contact with

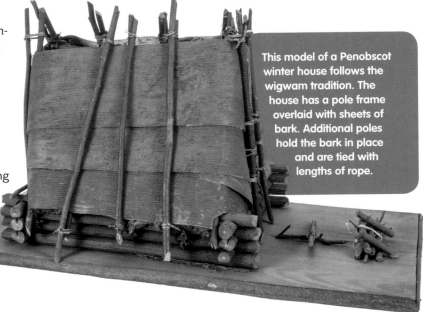

This model of a Penobscot winter house follows the wigwam tradition. The house has a pole frame overlaid with sheets of bark. Additional poles hold the bark in place and are tied with lengths of rope.

Europeans devastated the tribal population: Almost 90 percent of them died through warfare or from disease.

With headquarters on Indian Island Reservation, the tribe remains dedicated to preserving its cultural heritage. It is also active in the Penobscot River Restoration Project, launched in 2004. In June 2016, the project finished constructing a bypass, restoring a fish run for seagoing fish, such as the endangered wild Atlantic salmon. ✑

In this scene from the 5th Annual Indian Pageant of 1951, a Penobscot leader stretches his arms out as he greets representatives of the Passamaquoddy tribe. The two-day event was held on the Penobscots' Indian Island Reservation, Maine.

PEQUOT

(PEE-kwott)

LANGUAGE GROUP:
Algonquian

LANGUAGE:
Currently dormant; no record of last known speaker

LOCATION PRECONTACT:
Connecticut

LOCATION TODAY:
Connecticut

The Pequot lived a semi-nomadic life in what is now Connecticut. They built wigwams for homes in their communities, which they surrounded with palisades, or fences, to provide a defense against other tribes, particularly the Mohegan and Narragansett. Pequot lands were rich in natural resources. For example, the open land was very fertile and provided the perfect conditions in which to grow the traditional crops of corn, beans, and squash. The forests provided a source of wood for building canoes and wigwams. The Pequot also fished in the Atlantic Ocean and the numerous bays in their region.

When Dutch traders arrived in the early 1600s, the Pequot and the Dutch established a firm trading partnership: The tribe traded furs for European goods, such as metal pots and cloth. They also traded *wampum*, which the Dutch then used as currency to buy fur elsewhere. In 1636, the Pequot became involved in a conflict with English settlers to the north, when English militia burned two Pequot villages in revenge for a murder. The following year, the British declared war on the Pequot. The Mohegan and Narragansett joined the British, and attacks began on both sides. One such attack changed the Pequot ➡

💡 IN THE KNOW

Succotash is a traditional Native dish. Warming and nutritious, it is a stew made from beans and corn. All northeastern tribes, including the Pequot, had their own ways of cooking the dish. Many continue to make it today.

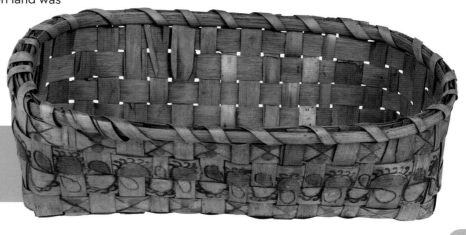

This shallow, rectangular Pequot basket was made by weaving woodsplints. The exterior surface was painted with a simple pattern, now faded.

forever. While Pequot warriors were away from their village, Mystic, in Connecticut, the British and their allies attacked, killing 300 to 400 women, children, and elderly men. This—and the Great Swamp Massacre at Fairfield, in which the tribe suffered more losses—ended the Pequot War. The members who survived were shipped as slaves to the West Indies or divided between the Mohegan and Narragansett tribes. After this, only about 500 members of the Pequot remained.

In recent years, some Pequot have returned to their ancestral lands and, today, the Mashantucket Pequot band occupy a reservation in Connecticut. The tribe finally regained federal recognition in 1983. The Pequot tribe runs successful businesses, and there is renewed interest in their history and culture. At the Mashantucket Pequot Museum and Research Center, visitors are transported back to the past via life-size walk-through dioramas and live demonstrations of contemporary arts and crafts. ☞

Mashantucket Pequot War Chief Stan Harris, Jr. (pictured left), and Pedro Johnson (right) carry the Mashantucket Eagle Staffs as they lead the Grand Entry at their annual Green Corn celebration. Only veterans can be members of the Honor Guard and carry the flags.

TOOLS AND WEAPONS

Northeastern tribes used their many natural resources to make a range of tools and weapons. Trees provided wood for bowls, spoons, farming tools, and many other useful items. People used an *adze*, a tool made from sharpened stone, to shape wood. Wooden weapons included war clubs, tomahawks, and bows and arrows. Arrows had flint (a very hard rock), bone, or copper arrowheads. Hunters and warriors also used long, wooden spears, topped with pointed bone or stone. A special tool called an *atlatl* was a hollowed-out pole that helped launch spears farther and faster. Tribal people sharpened stone, especially flint and chert, into knives and used large animal bones and antlers for farming hoes. They turned smaller bones into fishing hooks and awls for piercing hides and sewing.

POTAWATOMI

(poh-tuh-WAH-toh-mee)

LANGUAGE GROUP:
Algonquian

GREETING:
Bozho

THANK YOU:
Iwgwien

LOCATION PRECONTACT:
Michigan

LOCATION TODAY:
Michigan, Kansas, Oklahoma, Wisconsin (U.S); Ontario (Canada)

This Potawatomi doll dates from the early 1800s. It is a simple male figure that has been carved from wood and dressed in leggings made from woolen fabric.

Originally, the Potawatomi, whose name means "people of the place of fire," lived on lands around Lake Michigan. They hunted, gathered, and farmed in their villages, which were built around the lake. They also fished in Lake Michigan and in the many rivers that empty into it. They and their close relatives, the Ojibwe and Ottawa, formed the Three Fires Confederacy. Like their relatives, the tribe became involved in the fur trade in the 1600s, which caused them to spread into Illinois and Indiana.

During the French and Indian War, the Potawatomi supported the French and, following the British victory in 1763, some members joined in Pontiac's Rebellion against the British. When the rebellion failed, the tribe made peace with the British and began to trade with them.

The Potawatomi lost their traditional homelands following a series of treaties and other pressure from settlers. The Treaty of Greenville, signed in 1795, ceded most of present-day Ohio and much of Illinois, Indiana, and Michigan. The Treaty of Chicago, in 1833, forced the removal of all Native Americans living east of the Mississippi River and assigned a reservation in Kansas for the Potawatomi. In 1838, members of the tribe began their long walk across four states to Kansas. Many Potawatomi died on the journey and the move became known as the "Trail of Death." One band settled in Kansas—the Prairie Band Potawatomi Nation. Another band moved to Oklahoma and are now known as the Citizen Potawatomi Nation. The Pokagon and the Match-e-be-nash-she-wish bands stayed in Michigan in spite of government pressure to leave. Today, the Pokagon band continues to perform a good-will drum dance that the Potawatomi tribe developed—a ritual in which tribal members dance to the beat of a drum for several hours. 🖐

IN THE KNOW

Each of the three tribes in the Three Fires Confederacy had a title, based either on its name or a certain trait. The Potawatomi were "keepers of the sacred fire," the Ojibwe were the "keepers of the faith," and the Ottawa were the "keepers of the trade."

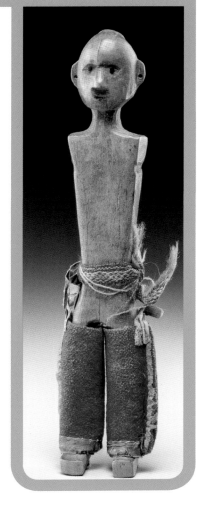

1838 THE POTAWATOMI TRAIL OF DEATH

Members of the Potawatomi tribe view an exhibit at the National Museum of the American Indian in Washington, D.C.

POWHATAN

(pow-HAT-un)

LANGUAGE GROUP:
Algonquian

LANGUAGE:
Currently dormant;
no record of last
known speaker

LOCATION PRECONTACT:
Virginia

LOCATION TODAY:
Virginia

Most often, the name "Powhatan" refers to a confederacy of nations, which included the Powhatan, the largest tribe, as well as 31 others. Each tribe within the confederacy had a leader, but by around 1600, their primary chief was Wahunsunacawh. The name Powhatan refers not only to the tribe, but also to Wahunsunacawh and to his village. He inherited the chiefdom of six tribes, including the Pamunkey and Mattaponi, and gained control of others as he expanded his empire. Tribes wishing to join his empire paid a kind of tax—either in goods or services—to Wahunsunacawh, as a symbol of their loyalty.

The Powhatan lived in what is now Virginia, in densely forested land surrounding the many rivers that run into the Chesapeake Bay. The people made good use of the waterways to travel between villages in dugout canoes and to trade. They farmed corn, beans, pumpkins, and other foods, and went into the forest to gather fruit and nuts, and to hunt.

When English settlers arrived in 1607, the Powhatan were a large and powerful group. Before long, conflicts arose between the settlers and the Powhatan. When the English expanded beyond their Jamestown colony and into Powhatan lands, the tribe resisted takeover, and several periods of conflict broke out. The first began in 1610 and led to the English capture of Pocahontas, Wahunsunacawh's daughter, whom the English kidnapped and held to ransom in exchange for stolen weapons. The second period of conflict, lasting from 1622 to 1632, brought death from war and disease to the Powhatan. Some tribal members fled north, while others became slaves in Virginia and elsewhere in the south.

In the 1980s, the Commonwealth of Virginia recognized eight Powhatan tribes. The Pamunkey and Mattaponi tribes have kept their reservations through a state agreement. The Pamunkey Tribe was formally recognized by the federal government in 2016. In all, there are now 11 state-recognized Powhatan tribes in Virginia.

A Powhatan Indian Village at Jamestown features models of reed-covered houses. Visitors can watch demonstrations of traditional cooking methods, tool- and pottery-making, and children's games.

POCAHONTAS

Pocahontas was the daughter of the Powhatan chief Wahunsunacawh. Her mother, also called Pocahontas, died in childbirth. As a child, Pocahontas was known as Matoaka, which means "bright stream between the hills." Captured by the British during a period of hostility, she was held for ransom. There are still questions today about the true nature of her treatment while in English custody. Some historians believe she may have been abused. Pocahontas married Englishman John Rolfe, possibly to bring peace. She later converted to Christianity. Pocahontas traveled to England for a state visit in 1616—this portrait of her in English clothing was painted at that time. Although she planned to return to her home in the United States, she became ill and died in England at the age of 21.

SENECA

(SEH-neh-kah)

LANGUAGE GROUP:
Iroquoian

GREETING:
Nya:wëh sgë:nö'

THANK YOU:
Nya:wëh

LOCATION PRECONTACT:
New York

LOCATION TODAY:
New York, Oklahoma
(U.S.); Ontario (Canada)

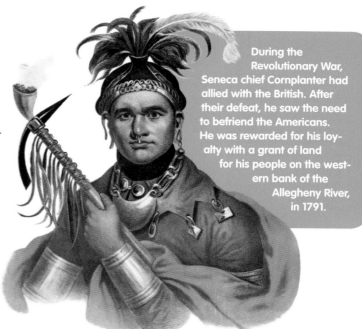

During the Revolutionary War, Seneca chief Cornplanter had allied with the British. After their defeat, he saw the need to befriend the Americans. He was rewarded for his loyalty with a grant of land for his people on the western bank of the Allegheny River, in 1791.

The Seneca are original members of the Iroquois League. Of all of the tribes in the confederacy, which also included the Cayuga, Mohawk, Oneida, Onondaga, and Tuscarora (who joined later), their homelands are the farthest west. The Seneca *gustoweh*, or headdress, bears a single, upright eagle feather. In their own language, the Seneca are called Onödowága, which means "people of the great hill." There are eight clans in the Seneca tribe: Turtle, Beaver, Bear, Wolf, Snipe, Heron, Deer, and Hawk.

Before Europeans arrived in America, the tribe controlled a large territory that stretched across 6.5 million acres (2.5 million ha) of western New York State along Lake Ontario and eastern Lake Erie. The land provided rich soil for crops, which included the "three sisters" of corn, beans, and squash. They also hunted game and fished in the lakes and rivers.

Initially, the Seneca were one of the largest tribes in the confederacy. They battled regularly with other tribes to the west, such as the Huron, Ottawa, and Ojibwe. During the Iroquois Wars of the 1600s, the Seneca fought to expand their hunting grounds and control of the fur trade. They also wanted to push out the French settlers but were not successful. In 1701, the Seneca and other Iroquois signed a peace treaty with the French called the Great Peace of Montreal.

From the mid-1700s, the Seneca became trade partners with the English, which led to the tribe allying themselves with the British during the Revolutionary War. The Seneca suffered major losses in the conflict. After the war, most Seneca remained in New York, and in 1794, they signed the Treaty of Canandaigua with the U.S. government, which established the tribe's right to land. Three Seneca bands live both on and off the reservations in New York, while others live in Oklahoma and Ontario, Canada. ✎

Zach Miller of the Seneca tribe (right) was the first member from any Iroquois tribe to play college lacrosse. Zach grew up on the Allegany Reservation in Steamburg, New York.

💡 IN THE KNOW

Salamanca, New York, is the only city in the United States to lie within an American Indian reservation. The city, on the Seneca's Allegany Indian Reservation, was once a major railroad town.

MUSIC AND CEREMONIES

Northeastern tribes marked many events—from the changing of the seasons to life events, such as births and deaths—with special ceremonies. The Midwinter ceremony was a New Year celebration among the tribes of the Iroquois League, such as the Mohawk and the Oneida. In the summer, the Green Corn ceremony welcomed the year's first ripe corn and was a time for giving thanks. Songs and dances were central to many ceremonies, and the tribes used rattles, drums, and flutes to accompany the singers and dancers. Early rattles were made from hickory bark, whereas later versions were made from horn. Many tribes, including the Powhatan, made water drums from hollowed-out wood and animal skin. By pouring a different volume of water into each drum, they were able to achieve a range of different drumming sounds.

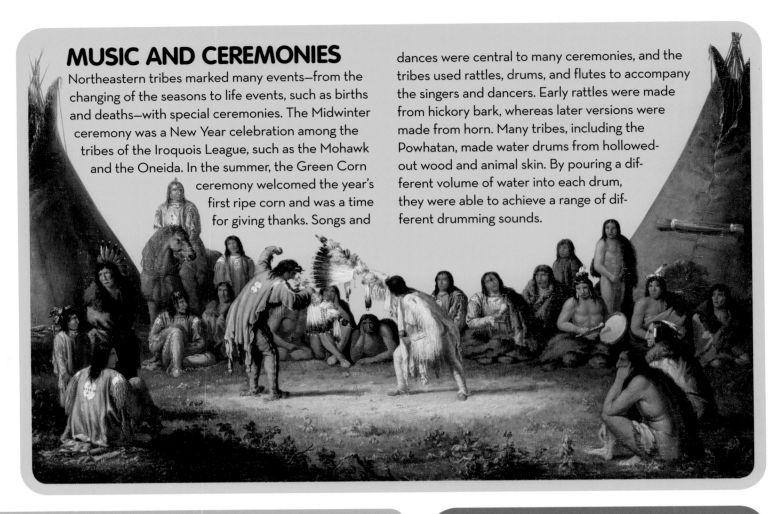

SHINNECOCK

(SHIN-nuh-kock)

LANGUAGE GROUP:
Algonquian

GREETING:
Aquay

GOODBYE:
Kunawush (see you later)

LOCATION PRECONTACT:
Long Island, New York

LOCATION TODAY:
Long Island, New York

The Shinnecock, the "people of the shore," have lived on Long Island for more than 10,000 years. They are close relatives of the Pequot and Mohegan, and all three tribes share a common language. The Shinnecock homelands border the Atlantic Ocean in eastern Long Island, and the tribe enjoyed all the benefits of the ocean: They braved the ocean waters in sturdy dugout canoes to catch whales and saltwater fish, and they collected clams and oysters from the rocky shores. The Shinnecock turned quahog shells into *wampum*, and traded the beads with tribes to the west. Shinnecock women grew traditional crops of corn, beans, and squash.

The Shinnecock way of life began to change after English settlers arrived in 1640. The tribe continued to fish and trade, but many members became ill from European diseases such as smallpox and measles. Others lost their lives in the Pequot War and King Philip's War involving the Wampanoag. By the 1800s,

A Shinnecock tribal member sings during an annual powwow in Long Island, New York.

Entitled "The Last of the Shinnecock Indians," this photograph was taken in 1884. At the time, the Shinnecock tribe's population had been on the decline ever since the arrival of the first European settlers more than 200 years earlier.

the Shinnecock on Long Island had become Christian, and some tribal members later married into the African-American community. Today, the tribe has a small reservation near Southampton, New York. Tribal members are working to revive the Shinnecock language, which had been close to extinction. The Shinnecock celebrate their culture and traditions at their annual August–September powwow—one of the largest in the eastern United States—with thousands of people attending the four-day event each year. People compete in dance ceremonies and competitions, and hold demonstrations of American Indian crafts. In 2010, the Shinnecock received formal recognition of their tribal status as the Shinnecock Indian Nation.

TUSCARORA

(tuh-skuh-ROAR-uh)

LANGUAGE GROUP:
Iroquoian

GREETING:
J'wan

THANK YOU:
Nyeah-weh

LOCATION PRECONTACT:
North Carolina

LOCATION TODAY:
New York

This 1870s Tuscarora bag has a floral pattern made from tiny glass beads stitched on with cotton thread.

The Tuscarora originally lived across a large territory in North Carolina, in communities along the Roanoke, Tar, and other rivers. The tribe used these waterways for fishing and as hunting and trading routes. During the early 1700s, the Tuscarora suffered many losses from diseases introduced by European settlers. They also found their land and their way of life under threat from the settlers, who took over traditional hunting lands. Tribal members were sometimes kidnapped and sold into slavery. This series of events led to warfare between the tribe and the European settlers. The Tuscarora War lasted from 1711 to 1715, with attacks on both sides bringing terrible losses. The final attack on the Tuscarora devastated the tribe and most of the survivors fled north, to New York or Pennsylvania.

In 1722, the Tuscarora who had moved north joined the Iroquois League, the alliance that already included the Cayuga, Mohawk, Oneida, Onondaga, and Seneca tribes, and which ➤

then became known as the League of Six Nations. The Tuscarora tribe has clans, just like the other confederacy members—Bear, Turtle, Wolf, Beaver, Eel, Deer, and Snipe. Its *gustoweh*, or headdress, has turkey feathers but no eagle feathers.

The Tuscarora Nation has maintained its traditions and language, but years of movement and population loss have taken their toll. The Revolutionary War divided the tribe, with some members supporting the British. These Tuscarora moved to Ontario, Canada, with other Iroquois at the end of the war. Other Tuscarora stayed in Virginia with the Monacan people. One band of Tuscarora remains in the North Carolina homeland. Although it does not have federal recognition, this band is loosely affiliated with a group that calls itself the Tuscarora One Fire Council. The Tuscarora Nation of New York is recognized by the U.S. government, and lives on and off the reservation at Niagara Landing.

This hair comb was made in 1968–1969 by Duffy Wilson, a sculptor from the Tuscarora Reservation. Carved from animal bone, it is decorated with a beaver design.

·ᜫ· IN THE KNOW
The name Tuscarora comes from a word that means "hemp gatherers." Hemp is a plant, and like cotton, it produces strong fibers. The Tuscarora used hemp to make such things as rope, cloth, and nets. They wore shirts made of hemp, too.

WORKING THE LAND

Farming tribes planted crops of corn, squash, and beans, nutritious foods that they made into stews, breads, and other dishes. These crops grew well together and the beans helped nourish the soil. Rotating the plantings around their land kept the soil rich year after year. Tribes such as the Wampanoag showed European settlers how to use their farming methods.

Farming started in the spring when men cleared the fields. They used stone axes to strip the bark and cut down trees and fire to clear the brush. The women then used stone or bone hoes to prepare mounds of soil for planting seeds. Children helped, too, and worked to keep the birds and animals away from the growing plants. At the fall harvest, there was enough food to trade or to store for the winter.

WAMPANOAG

(wamp-a-NO-ag)

LANGUAGE GROUP:
Algonquian

LANGUAGE:
Currently being revived; no dictionary or word lists available

LOCATION PRECONTACT:
Massachusetts, Rhode Island

LOCATION TODAY:
Massachusetts

The Wampanoag, or "people of the first light," lived in several towns across present-day Massachusetts and Rhode Island. They were skilled farmers who relied on a healthy diet of squash, corn, and beans. Wampanoag men hunted and fished for food, while women tended and harvested the crops, looked after the homes, and made most of the meals. The tribe held women in high regard; women participated in tribal government and were allowed to become chief, unlike women in many other tribes. In the warmer weather, Wampanoag families lived in a *wetu*, or wigwam. At the end of the growing season, the tribe held a harvest celebration.

When the Puritans—members of a religious group from England—arrived, the Wampanoag chief Massasoit signed a treaty giving them 12,000 acres (4,800 ha) of Wampanoag land. The tribe taught the Puritans how to rotate their crops to keep the soil healthy. Many members of the tribe were killed by settlers, either through warfare or disease. The weakened tribe could not defend itself against the stronger Narragansett and it lost territory. In 1675, three Wampanoag men were murdered by the English and the tribe took action. Chief Massasoit had died by this time and his son, Metacom, also known as Philip, led attacks on 90 English settlements, burning 42 of them. The conflict, later known as King Philip's War, was devastating to the Wampanoag, who lost most of their tribe, including Metacom.

In the years that followed, the Wampanoag struggled to survive. Three communities remained in 1800. The largest of these was the Aquinnah community. The people there organized themselves as the Wampanoag Tribal Council of Gay Head, which received federal recognition in 1987. Another community, the Mashpee Wampanoag Tribe, received recognition later, in 2007. 🪶

IN THE KNOW

Built in 1684 and moved to its present site in Mashpee in 1741, the Wampanoag's Old Indian Meeting House is the oldest Native American church in America. The Puritans converted many Wampanoag to Christianity.

A Wampanoag woman reenacts shellfish gathering. She is part of the Wampanoag Homesite "living exhibit" at Plimouth Plantation, Massachusetts.

Drummers at Plymouth, Massachusetts, participate in a National Day of Mourning event on Thanksgiving Day. The annual event honors Native ancestors and strives to bring awareness to the struggle for survival still faced by Native Americans today.

THE WOMAN WHO FELL FROM THE SKY

Up above the world, which was made only of water, the Sky World was quite different. Human-type beings lived there with many kinds of plants and animals to enjoy. Here was a Tree of Life that was very special to the people. They knew it grew at the entrance to the world below and forbade anyone to touch the Tree. One woman, who was soon to give birth, was curious about the Tree and convinced her brother to uproot it.

Under the Tree was a big hole. The woman peered from the edge into the hole and suddenly fell. As she was falling, she clutched some earth from the Sky World in her hand.

As she fell, the birds of the world below were disturbed and saw her distress. Many birds came together to break her fall and cradle her. They took her to the back of a giant sea turtle. The water creatures decided that she needed some land to live on, so many of them dived to the bottom of the world to get her some. Only the muskrat was able to do it. He put a bit of earth on the turtle's back, and the land began to grow there.

Sky Woman soon gave birth to a daughter on Turtle Island. The daughter grew very fast. There were no man-beings, but the West Wind came and married the daughter.

Soon the daughter of Sky Woman gave birth to twins. One was born the natural way and was called the Right-Handed Twin. The other came out under his mother's arm, which caused her to die. He was called the Left-Handed Twin. When the mother died, the twins' grandmother, Sky Woman, placed the fistful of earth that she had grabbed from the Sky World on top of her daughter's grave. Special seeds grew there from the body of the daughter: the sacred Tobacco, Strawberry, and Sweetgrass. These are called Kionhekwa, the Life Givers.

Many creation stories center on the idea that there can only be peace and harmony in the natural world if there is also chaos and conflict.

The twins had special powers. The Right-Handed Twin created gentle hills, beautiful flowers, quiet brooks, butterflies, and many animals, plants, and earth formations. The Left-Handed Twin made snakes, thorns, and thunder and lightning. Together they created man. The Right-Handed Twin believed in diplomacy and peaceful resolution to conflicts. The Left-Handed Twin enjoyed conflict. They were different, but everything they made is part of Earth's creation.

When their grandmother Sky Woman died, the Twins fought over her body and pulled it apart, throwing her head into the Sky World. She still shines there as Grandmother Moon. The Twins could not live together without fighting, so they agreed to live in different realms. The Right-Handed Twin rules the daylight, and the Left-Handed Twin rules at night. Between them, they keep the Earth in balance.

An Iroquois story, contributed by Karenne Wood, Monacan

A Seminole infant watches her mother feed a bottle of milk to a fawn on their Florida reservation. In the past, deer provided food and hides for making clothes and moccasins. The deer also represents one of eight Seminole clans.

THE SOUTHEAST

T he varied landscape of America's Southeast ranges from coastal plains to lush river valleys and grasslands. The region stretches from the Appalachian Mountains in the north to the Florida Everglades in the south and includes the coastal plains of the Atlantic Ocean and the Gulf of Mexico. For thousands of years, these diverse environments created loose, natural boundaries for the tribes that formed across the Southeast, and the people prospered in this land of plenty.

THE STORY OF **THE SOUTHEASTERN PEOPLE**

People have lived in the Southeast for at least 18,000 years. Their hunter-gatherer lifestyle changed when tribes began planting corn, first cultivated in Mexico more than 7,000 years ago. Gradually, Southeasterners became the settled farmers of the Mississippian culture that thrived between the 9th and 16th centuries. In addition to farming, the tribes of the Mississippian culture were mound builders: Large earthen mounds with flat tops were central to their communities. Tribes used them as burial places or when gathering for ceremonies. On some, they built temples or homes for their leaders.

During the 1500s, people began to spread out from the Mississippi Delta area and across the Southeast. They established large communities and developed their own languages and cultures. Most can trace their ancestors back to one of three language groups: Iroquoian, Muscogean, and Siouan. By the time the Spanish arrived in the mid-1500s, the Southeast was home to many thousands of Native people. Large populations lived close together, making it easy for diseases to spread. As in the Northeast, the Europeans brought smallpox, measles, and other diseases. It is thought that 95 percent of the Native population perished at this time.

The Struggle for Control

European settlers started to push tribes out of their ancestral homelands. The Spanish, English, and French all wanted to claim territory. Many thousands of Native people were captured by European slave traders, who swept through the region.

In 1715, the Yamasee and a confederation of other tribes, including the Creek, revolted against the white settlers in present-day South Carolina in response to this enslavement. A two-year war followed, which saw one of the largest tribes of the region, the Cherokee, allying with the European settlers. At the end of the war, and then again following the Creek Civil War 100 years later, the surviving Natives—many of them Creek—fled to Florida, where they became known as the Seminole, which means "free people" or "runaway."

The Five Civilized Tribes

After the Revolutionary War (1775–1783), George Washington's new U.S. government was determined to gain more control, and to "civilize" the larger southeastern tribes. The Cherokee, Creek, Choctaw, Chickasaw, and Seminole all adopted elements of European government, clothing, and farming methods. These tribes became known as the "Five Civilized Tribes."

In the 1830s, the U.S. government began to relocate Native Americans to what the government called "Indian Territory." This was an area of land in present-day Oklahoma that had been set aside for Natives who had been forced off their ancestral lands. Some tribal people left their lands willingly, while others tried to resist moving by signing treaties or rebelling. A few managed to avoid capture altogether, but many were forced to leave.

The Five Civilized Tribes were among those driven out of the Southeast. In Florida, the Seminole revolted against removal, but after years of fighting most agreed to move west. During the harsh winter of 1838, U.S. troops drove 16,000 Cherokee to leave the Southeast in what became known as the Trail of Tears. Of the Five Civilized Tribes, four of them still have reservations in the Southeast today, as well as in Oklahoma. The Chickasaw tribe is the only one to have lost all of its ancestral lands in the Southeast.

Looking to the Future

After years of devastating loss through disease, warfare, and relocation, the southeastern tribes that remain have gradually been rebuilding their communities. Many face difficulties over environmental issues, employment, education, and day-to-day living. Yet they are free to celebrate their ancestral, spiritual, and cultural traditions once more. A growing number of tribal members are involved in successful modern-day businesses and careers, both on and off their reservations. The tribes are looking forward to a promising future while acknowledging the injustices of the past.

Some southeastern tribes, such as the Miccosukee and the Seminole, made shirts (pictured) and dresses by stitching together strips of bright-colored fabric.

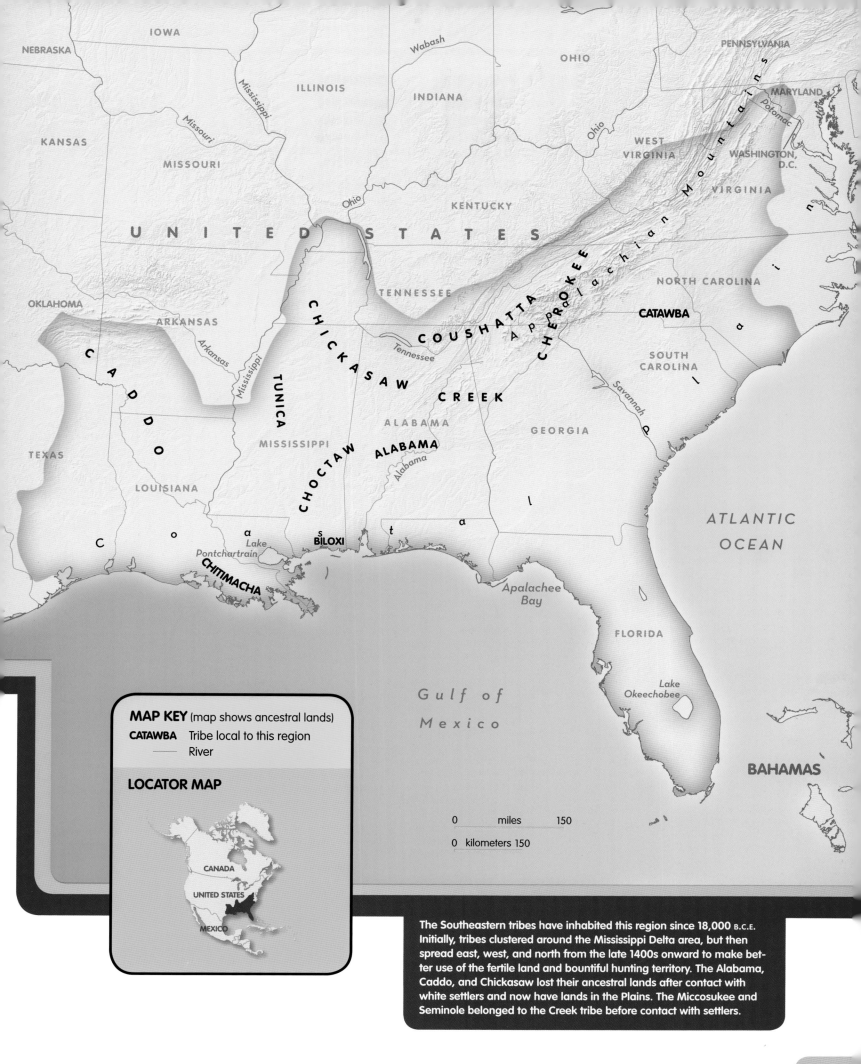

IOWA

NEBRASKA

ILLINOIS

Wabash

OHIO

PENNSYLVANIA

MARYLAND

Mississippi

INDIANA

Ohio

WEST VIRGINIA

WASHINGTON, D.C.

Potomac

KANSAS

Missouri

MISSOURI

VIRGINIA

OKLAHOMA

Ohio

KENTUCKY

U N I T E D   S T A T E S

NORTH CAROLINA

ARKANSAS

TENNESSEE

Arkansas

Tennessee

COUSHATTA

CHEROKEE

Appalachian Mountains

CATAWBA

SOUTH CAROLINA

C A D D O

Mississippi

CHICKASAW

TUNICA

CREEK

Savannah

TEXAS

ALABAMA

GEORGIA

MISSISSIPPI

CHOCTAW

ALABAMA

Alabama

LOUISIANA

ATLANTIC OCEAN

Lake Pontchartrain

BILOXI

CHITIMACHA

Apalachee Bay

FLORIDA

Gulf of Mexico

Lake Okeechobee

BAHAMAS

MAP KEY (map shows ancestral lands)

CATAWBA   Tribe local to this region
———   River

LOCATOR MAP

CANADA

UNITED STATES

MEXICO

0   miles   150

0   kilometers 150

The Southeastern tribes have inhabited this region since 18,000 B.C.E. Initially, tribes clustered around the Mississippi Delta area, but then spread east, west, and north from the late 1400s onward to make better use of the fertile land and bountiful hunting territory. The Alabama, Caddo, and Chickasaw lost their ancestral lands after contact with white settlers and now have lands in the Plains. The Miccosukee and Seminole belonged to the Creek tribe before contact with settlers.

The warm climate and plentiful resources of the Southeast allowed great cultures to develop. The mound-building culture lasted for many centuries before the Europeans came. European arrival marked the beginning of great change. The Europeans brought disease and conflict among Native tribes. Later, the U.S. government set its sights on taking over lands in the Southeast. With the army's help, the government forced thousands of Native peoples out of their homelands.

18,000 B.C.E.

People inhabit the Southeast. The first people of the Southeast were nomadic hunters.

800–1500s

Mississippian mound-building culture. People in the Southeast built huge earthen mounds (pictured) for ceremonies and other purposes. Communities developed surrounding the mounds. The largest was Moundville in present-day Alabama.

1540–1541

Hernando de Soto expedition. The arrival of Spanish explorers in the Southeast brought brutal violence to the Native population. They introduced diseases that wiped out 95 percent of the Mississippi mound-building culture.

1550s

Creek Confederacy forms. This political alliance brought together a number of tribes, including the Creek, Hitchiti, and Alabama, who agreed to support each other when challenged by other Native tribes and white settlers.

1715–1717

Yamasee War. The Yamasee and their Native allies rebelled against English colonists and slave traders in South Carolina. The Cherokee came to the aid of the English militia, and these forces pushed the Yamasee south into Florida. Pictured is a Cherokee tomahawk.

1779–1811

Five Civilized Tribes. During the late 1700s, the Cherokee, Creek, Chickasaw, Choctaw, and Seminole became known as the Five Civilized Tribes. The tribes adopted many aspects of European culture.

1813–1814

Creek Civil War. Fighting broke out between Lower (southern) Creeks and Upper (northern) Creeks, with the U.S. Army supporting the Lower Creeks. The war saw the Upper Creeks defeated at the Battle of Horseshoe Bend. The survivors fled to join the Seminole in Florida.

1817

Start of the Seminole Wars. General Andrew Jackson led the U.S. Army in the first attack against the Seminole tribe. Pictured is the capture of two Seminole chiefs in Florida. The Seminole moved farther south.

1831–1838

Trail of Tears. With the Removal Act, the government drove many tribes west. In 1831, the U.S. government forced the Choctaw to move to Indian Territory. The Creek followed in 1834. In the winter of 1838, the U.S. Army and militia rounded up 16,000 Cherokee to make the 1,000-mile (1,600-km) walk. Over 4,000 Cherokee and 2,000 black slaves died on the journey. The Cherokee called it the "trail where they cried" because of the devastation that it brought to their tribe.

1858

Seminole Wars end. A small number of Seminoles had signed a treaty in 1832, ceding their land, but most of the tribe fiercely resisted. When the U.S. Army tried to force the move, the Seminoles fought back. Two wars followed (1835–1842 and 1855–1858), costing the U.S. government millions of dollars. By 1855, however, most Seminole people had moved to Oklahoma. A small band remained in Florida.

1821

Sequoyah's syllabary introduced. Sequoyah, whose mother was a Cherokee, developed a writing system for his tribe. He created 85 characters to represent Cherokee sounds.

1830

Indian Removal Act. President Andrew Jackson signed the Indian Removal Act into law on May 30. The purpose of the act was to move tribes from the Southeast to "Indian Territory," or lands west of the Mississippi River. This opened up vast areas in the Southeast for white settlers. In the following years, the U.S. government signed almost 70 removal treaties and succeeded in forcing nearly 50,000 people to move to present-day Oklahoma.

1918

Code talkers. During World War I, 19 Choctaw U.S. Army soldiers used their language as a code to transfer important information. Since the Germans did not know the language, they could not break the code.

1981

Seminole win landmark court case. In 1979, the Florida Seminole opened a bingo business, which local police tried to shut down. The matter went to court, and was decided in the tribe's favor. This paved the way for similar businesses across the country. Such sources of income can be crucial to a tribe's survival.

1987

Wilma Mankiller elected. After standing in as principal chief from 1985, the Cherokee Nation elected Wilma Mankiller to the position in 1987. She was the first female principal chief ever elected. Mankiller was reelected in 1991.

2006

Nanih Waiya returned to the Choctaw. Nanih Waiya means "leaning hill" in Choctaw. It is a sacred mound for the tribe. The U.S. government took the mound from the Choctaw in 1830 under the Treaty of Dancing Rabbit Creek. Until its return to the Choctaw, the mound was part of a state park in Mississippi.

BILOXI

(bil-OCK-see)

LANGUAGE GROUP:
Siouan

LANGUAGE:
Dormant; last known speaker, Emma Dorsey Jackson, recorded in 1934

LOCATION PRECONTACT:
Mississippi, Louisiana, Texas

LOCATION TODAY:
Louisiana

With a name thought to mean "first people," the Biloxi tribe originally lived on lands along the coast of the Gulf of Mexico. The mighty Mississippi River flowed through their land, making it very fertile, and the Biloxi were settled, farming people. They also hunted bear, deer, and buffalo, and food was usually plentiful year-round. Like many of the tribes in the Southeast, the Biloxi practiced "river-cane" crafts. Women harvested local plants, including the river cane—a type of bamboo—which they wove into rattles, baskets, and vessels for storing and carrying food.

The tribe's population was small and, although it had avoided contact with Europeans for many years, interactions with other tribes brought European diseases into the Biloxi villages—smallpox, measles, whooping cough, and others. Their population decreased rapidly. The tribe moved westward to avoid conflicts with other tribes and European settlers—especially the British. When the French and Indian War ended in 1763, the British gained control of much of North America, including Biloxi lands east of the Mississippi River. By the late 1700s, the Biloxi had moved west, into territory controlled by the Spanish. They established small settlements there.

In the 1780s, Spanish colonist Bernardo Vicente Apolinar de Gálvez reserved some land for another tribe with a decreasing population—the Tunica—near Marksville, Louisiana. Further weakened by disease, the Biloxi felt vulnerable and decided to join the Tunica there. Although the two tribes spoke different languages and had different cultures, the Biloxi believed that there was safety in numbers. Over time, the two tribes intermarried, and the Biloxi language began to fade out of use. In the 1920s, the two tribes united to pursue land rights and tribal status from the U.S. government. Louisiana granted state recognition to the Tunica-Biloxi Indian Tribe in 1976, and the tribe received federal recognition later, in 1981. ✑

IN THE KNOW

The last traditional Tunica-Biloxi chief was Joseph Pierite, Sr., who had both Tunica and Biloxi ancestors. He died in 1975. Recorded in 1934, his wife's mother, Emma Dorsey Jackson, was the last known speaker of the Siouan Biloxi language. After this time, the language faded out of use.

As part of its Culture Revitalization Program, the Tunica-Biloxi tribe holds an annual Intertribal Stickball Clinic and Exhibition. Tunica-Biloxi children are joined by children from other tribes, including the Alabama-Coushatta and Chitimacha.

CATAWBA

(cuh-TAW-buh)

LANGUAGE GROUP:
Siouan

LANGUAGE:
Currently dormant; last known speaker died in 1959

LOCATION PRECONTACT:
North and South Carolina

LOCATION TODAY:
South Carolina

The Catawba are the only federally recognized tribe in South Carolina. Living on a 1,000-acre (400-ha) reservation today, they once inhabited a number of villages in North and South Carolina, most of them in river valleys. The tribe calls itself Iswa, which means "people of the river." Families lived in round, bark homes and gathered in another, more elaborate structure for religious ceremonies. A wooden palisade, or fence, surrounded the village and at its center lay an open plaza where members gathered to play games or to dance.

The tribe grew crops of corn, squash, beans, and sunflowers; visitors to the Catawba Reservation can see an old Native garden planted in the traditional way. The tribe was known for its fine pottery: They fashioned round pots using stacks of coiled clay, which they smoothed over for a flat surface—tribal people still make pots in this way. Other tribes regarded the Catawba as fearsome. They fought often with the Iroquois and Cherokee. To prepare for battle, they wore ponytails and painted their faces with striking black-and-white designs.

In the mid-1600s, English settlers moved into Catawba territory. Villages became trading hubs, and the tribe exchanged deerskins, baskets, and pottery for knives, kettles, and cloth with the Europeans. The tribe allied with the English against the Spanish and French, but the English did not return this loyalty. Later that century, English traders captured Catawba women and children and sold them as slaves, and they killed many men. By 1760, the Catawba numbered just 400 people. In the same year, the Pine Tree Hill Treaty, made with the British, confined the Catawba to a 15-square-mile (40-sq-km) reservation near the Catawba River.

In 1840, the state of South Carolina failed to honor the Pine Tree Hill Treaty, and took the Catawba land. Over the next century, many tribal members moved away and joined other cultures. The U.S. government's "termination" policy of the 1950s led to the tribe's loss of tribal status and land rights in 1959. That same year, the last Catawba speaker died, and the language faded out. In 1973, the tribe challenged the government's policy, and following a 20-year struggle, Congress restored the Catawba status and awarded the tribe a $50 million land claim.

KING HAIGLER

Arataswa Haigler, also known as King Haigler, was a Catawba warrior. In 1751, he signed a peace treaty with longtime enemies, the Iroquois, and negotiated the Pine Tree Hill Treaty with the British in 1760, for Catawba reservation land. A group of Shawnee attacked the Catawba in 1762, killing King Haigler. In 2009, he became the only American-Indian inductee into the South Carolina Hall of Fame.

Sara Ayers was one of the Catawba tribe's best-known 20th-century potters. She made this pot in 1973. Many of her pieces feature the figure of a chief's head.

WRITING IT DOWN

Sequoyah was the son of a white fur trader and a Cherokee woman. Although he never learned the English alphabet, he could see the benefits of a written language, and developed one for the Cherokee. Sequoyah worked on his syllabary for 12 years, developing a system that used syllables instead of vowels and consonants to express words. He created 85 different symbols to represent the sounds that make up Cherokee words. In 1821, Sequoyah introduced his syllabary to the tribe. It became the official Cherokee writing system, and the tribe used it to translate English documents and to publish the American Indian newspaper *Cherokee Phoenix*. The newspaper was printed with Cherokee and English written side by side, making it the first bilingual publication in North America. Sequoyah's Cherokee syllabary is still in use today, and is the only American-Indian writing system similar to the European alphabet.

CHEROKEE

(CHAIR-uh-kee)

LANGUAGE GROUP:
Iroquoian

GREETING:
Siyo

THANK YOU:
Wado

LOCATION PRECONTACT:
Alabama, Georgia, Kentucky, North and South Carolina, Tennessee, Virginia, West Virginia

LOCATION TODAY:
North Carolina, Oklahoma

The Cherokee are one of the largest tribes living in North America today. The first written mention of the tribe is by the Spanish explorer Hernando de Soto, who encountered the Cherokee in 1540. At that time, the tribe commanded a vast area of the Southeast. They spread across present-day Virginia to northern Georgia and into eastern Tennessee. The Cherokee name comes from a Choctaw word meaning "cave people," but the tribal members call themselves Ani-Yunwiya, which means "real people."

Before Europeans arrived, the Cherokee lived in almost 70 large, well-organized riverside communities, in which they built thatched cabins from logs. They planted crops of corn, squash, and beans, and hunted deer, sometimes dressing in deerskins and antlers to help lure the animals. Among the crafts the Cherokee made were "booger" masks. Carved from wood and painted, they represented powerful spirits.

Two Cherokee women stand in front of a tepee at the McIntosh Fall Festival in Whitesburg, Georgia. Their breastplates are made from porcupine quills.

Cherokee men create traditional wooden carvings at the Oconaluftee Indian Village in North Carolina.

When English settlers began moving in, the tribe's strength was first tested by disease. In 1738 and 1739, it suffered a smallpox epidemic that cut its population in half. The tribe initially fought against the settlers, but later made peace with them. They signed treaties and the tribe became one of the Five Civilized Tribes that adopted English ideas and customs. By the 19th century, the tribe still controlled a large area of land, but the U.S. government wanted it. From 1838 to 1839, U.S. troops forced 16,000 Cherokee to move to Oklahoma. About 4,000 people died on the long trek, which became known as the Trail of Tears. Those who survived the walk made a new life in Oklahoma. Within just one year of arriving, they had reestablished their government and had set to work constructing their capitol building.

Today there are two federally recognized groups in the state: the Cherokee Nation and the Keetoowah Band, both with headquarters in Tahlequah, Oklahoma. A third tribe of federally recognized Cherokee, the Eastern Band, has its base in the Qualla Boundary territory of North Carolina.

CHITIMACHA

(CHI-tih-MAH-chuh)

LANGUAGE GROUP:
Isolate

LANGUAGE:
Currently dormant; no record of last known speaker

LOCATION PRECONTACT:
Louisiana

LOCATION TODAY:
Louisiana

Louisiana is the ancestral home of the Chitimacha. According to historical evidence, the tribe has lived in this area of the Southeast for 6,000 years, inhabiting 15 large villages around the Mississippi Delta. The tribe followed a clan system in which membership was passed on through the mother. The clans were Wolf, Bear, Dog, and Lion. The warm climate and fertile soil in Louisiana was good for farming corn, pumpkins, sweet potatoes, and other crops. Tribesmen also hunted deer and alligator and fished in the many rivers. Women made baskets from river cane, which they dyed red, black, and yellow using plant dyes. Along with the natural color of the cane, this gave them four colors with which to weave as many as 50 different patterns and motifs into their designs. They made bowls, trays, and seed sifters, as well as "elbow" baskets, which they used for picking berries.

By the 1700s, the French had established colonies in Louisiana. During their time there, they took Chitimacha people as slaves. The tribe rebelled against the French in the early 1700s and killed four Frenchmen, including a missionary and a slave owner. The French sought revenge and convinced their allies, among them the Biloxi and Choctaw, to join them in war against the Chitimacha. For 12 years, the Chitimacha fought for their freedom, but they lost many warriors. Of those who survived, most ended up captured and sold into slavery. By 1718, the tribal population had few members left. An increasing number of Chitimacha people married white settlers and

The Chitimacha made baskets like this one for storing food. The baskets were "double-woven," making them stronger. It also created a different pattern on the reverse side of the basket—a mark of the weaver's skill.

lost much of their language, culture, and traditions. At its lowest, the tribal population numbered 51 people.

By the 1900s, the Chitimacha owned very little land. Then, a wealthy white woman named Sarah Avery McIlhenney helped to change that. A friend of the tribe, her family had made its fortune producing Tabasco sauce. In 1914, she bought 400 acres (160 ha) of the tribe's ancestral lands and sold them to the U.S. government. The understanding was that the government would now allow the tribe to use this land as a reservation, which they did. Two years later, the federal government formally recognized the Chitimacha tribe as well. Today, the tribe numbers about 1,300 people. They rent out some of their reservation land for oil mining, but also depend on agriculture and other tribal-run industries. ✎

IN THE KNOW

Chitimacha men and women tattooed their legs and arms as marks of beauty. Warriors also had painted knees. Fellow male tribal members scratched the warriors' knees and then rubbed charcoal into the roughened skin.

A Native American woman holds a traditional turkey feather fan while attending a meeting of the Biloxi, Choctaw, and Chitimacha tribes.

TRAIL OF TEARS

In 1830, President Andrew Jackson signed the Indian Removal Act, a law that enabled the government to take over valuable tribal lands, especially in the Southeast. The aim was to move all the tribes to "Indian Territory," the area that is now Oklahoma. Starting with the Choctaw in 1831, the government began the forced relocation of tribal people from their ancestral lands to new and unfamiliar territory. Thousands of people died on the way. As pressure increased on the Cherokee, a Cherokee chief named John

Ross organized a petition with 15,000 signatures to protest the move. In response, the government sent 7,000 U.S. Army troops and militia to round up 16,000 Cherokee into holding camps. Between 1838 and 1839, they walked the 1,000 miles (1,600 km) to Oklahoma, with little food or shelter and in bitterly cold weather. Four thousand died on the difficult journey. In remembrance, the Cherokee called this route *nunahi-duna-dlo-hilu-I*, which means, "the trail where they cried," now more commonly known as the Trail of Tears.

CHOCTAW

(CHOCK-taw)

LANGUAGE GROUP:
Muscogean

GREETING:
Halito

THANK YOU:
Yakoke

LOCATION PRECONTACT:
Mississippi

LOCATION TODAY:
Mississippi, Oklahoma

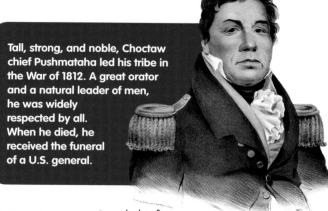

Tall, strong, and noble, Choctaw chief Pushmataha led his tribe in the War of 1812. A great orator and a natural leader of men, he was widely respected by all. When he died, he received the funeral of a U.S. general.

According to Choctaw history, the tribe began at Nanih Waiya, a sacred mound in Mississippi. The state controlled the site for many years, but returned it to the tribe in 2006. The Choctaw have lived in parts of what is now Louisiana, Mississippi, and Alabama for thousands of years. They are descended from the area's mound-building cultures.

Living in villages around the lower Mississippi River, the Choctaw were primarily farmers. Their lives revolved around the seasons for planting and harvesting crops of corn, beans, squash, melons, and sunflowers. While many southeastern tribal men shaved their heads, the Choctaw men wore their hair long. Like other southeastern tribes, the Choctaw played stickball. Village teams played against each other, sometimes in tournaments involving up to 700 players. By the 1600s, the large Choctaw tribe had divided into three groups, each with its own government and chief. All three actively traded with the French and, later, with the British. They supported the British during the Revolutionary War, but signed a peace treaty with the new U.S. government in 1786, at Hopewell, South Carolina. In the War of 1812, the Choctaw remained loyal to the new nation, fighting alongside U.S. troops against the British. Like the Cherokee, Creek, Chickasaw, and Seminole, the Choctaw were one of the Five Civilized Tribes that adopted a European way of life.

In 1820, the U.S. government forced its takeover of Choctaw land. By the early 1830s, the Choctaw had ceded almost 11 million acres (4.5 million ha). Most tribal members moved to lands west of the Mississippi River. Many made the horrific trip on the Trail of Tears to Indian Territory in present-day Oklahoma, with more than 2,500 dying on the way. In 1918, the U.S. government forced the few who remained in Mississippi onto a reservation. Today, both the Mississippi Band of Choctaw and the Choctaw Nation of Oklahoma practice their ancestral traditions and own and manage a number of successful businesses. 🖋

The Choctaw weave baskets from leaves of the palmetto tree. They cut dried leaves into strips, braid them, and stitch them into lengths for weaving.

💡 IN THE KNOW

The Choctaw hunted small game using weapons that included blow pipes with wooden darts and rabbit sticks. A rabbit stick was like a club with a long handle. When thrown sideways, it gained enough momentum to stun or kill a rabbit or squirrel.

THE STOMP DANCE

is part of the Green Corn ceremony that celebrates the harvest. Starting after dark, the dance continues until dawn the next day. A male elder sings while leading the dance. The men respond to his singing and the women shake rattles worn on their legs to set the rhythm. The line of people moves in a counterclockwise direction, around a fire. There are many tribes in Oklahoma and throughout the Southeast who perform the Stomp Dance.

COUSHATTA

(Koo-SHAH-tah)

LANGUAGE GROUP:
Muscogean

GREETING:
Boso!

THANK YOU:
Aliilamo

LOCATION PRECONTACT:
Alabama, Georgia

LOCATION TODAY:
Louisiana, Oklahoma, Texas

Living as widely spread as Louisiana, Texas, and Oklahoma today, the Coushatta have a vibrant culture featuring traditional ceremonies, arts, and language. Tribal artists produce baskets from long, coiled pine needles and woven cane, using techniques for which the tribe has long been known. Dancers perform at powwows, and compete against each other in such dances as the Women's Fancy Shawl Dance and the Men's Grass Dance. The tribe has also made great efforts to keep its language alive; many members speak Koasati, the language of their ancestors, as it was spoken centuries before.

The tribe's ancestral home was in northern Alabama, where people lived in towns near the Tennessee River and farmed corn, among other crops. They also hunted and fished, and traded with other southeastern tribes. Some time before the 1500s, the Coushatta moved farther south in Alabama and into Georgia. By the mid-1700s, the tribe was part of the Creek Confederacy, which included the Creek and the Alabama.

After the Revolutionary War, the Coushatta began to lose their lands to the U.S. government. In 1783, the tribe signed a treaty in which they ceded over 800 square miles (2,000 sq km) of land in Georgia. They were forced to move again. The tribe then spread west into Mississippi, Louisiana, and Texas, and after the Creek War in 1813, a group of Coushatta settled in Oklahoma. Although the U.S. government terminated their tribal status in 1953, the Coushatta regained federal recognition in 1973. Today, they run a rice farm, a woodworking business, and other industries. In Texas, the Coushatta share a reservation with the Alabama, on which they control the forestry and gas industries. Descendants of the southeastern Coushatta also formed an alliance with the Alabama tribe in Oklahoma and together they founded the federally recognized Alabama-Quassarte Tribal Town tribe. 🖎

IN THE KNOW

The Coushatta are a matrilineal society, which means that the children inherit their clan from their mother. The Coushatta have seven clans—Turkey, Deer, Panther, Bobcat, Bear, Beaver, and Cranefly. The tribe also selects young women to serve as royal representatives.

Many Native communities participate in intertribal powwows. Alabama Coushatta Gabe Bullock prepares for the Men's Fancy Dance at one. Originating in the 1920s, the dance kept traditional values alive at a time when Native religious dances were forbidden. Outfits are typically bright and colorful.

MOUNDVILLE

Between 800 and 1500 C.E., the Mississippi culture was a thriving society in the Southeast. The Mississippians were mound builders; they constructed villages and cities featuring numerous raised earthen platforms. The society used these mounds for nobles' homes, temples, and ceremonies. The most spectacular city was Moundville, in central Alabama, with at least 26 mounds. The tallest was almost 60 feet (18 m) high. A lively, wealthy community of about 1,000 people lived within the walled area of over 300 acres (120 ha), while another 10,000 people lived nearby, farming corn in the Black Warrior Valley. Corn was a main food, along with beans and deer meat. By the late 1400s, most people had moved out of Moundville and spread around the Southeast. The reasons for this are unclear, but may be due to a change in climate that made growing corn difficult.

CREEK

CREEK (to rhyme with seek)

LANGUAGE GROUP:
Muscogean

GREETING:
Hensci

THANK YOU:
Mvto

LOCATION PRECONTACT:
Georgia, Alabama, South Carolina

LOCATION TODAY:
Alabama, Oklahoma

The Creek, also known as the Muscogee, are descendants of the Mississippian mound builders who occupied a large area of flatland territory in what are now the states of Georgia and Alabama. The English first used the name Creek in relation to the people who lived near their trading post, Ochese Creek, in present-day South Carolina. The tribe's main towns in Georgia and Alabama were Coosa, Kasihta, Coweta, and Abihka, though there were many more smaller communities of the Creek tribe across the whole region.

Each town was distinct, with its own *mico*, or chief, but they each supported one another, especially in times of war. The tribe's living came mostly from farming, and crops included the three staples of corn, beans, and squash. Typically, the women farmed the land, while the men went out to hunt. Within their villages, the Creek built rectangular houses with pitched bark or thatched roofs. The walls were constructed from poles that were then covered with mud to form plaster. The houses were built around a plaza in which people gathered to take part in ceremonies, such as the midsummer Green Corn ceremony celebrating the fruits of that year's harvest.

The tribe roughly divided into Upper (northern) and Lower (southern) Creek groups.

Many tribal members died from the diseases introduced by the Europeans, but those who remained formed the Creek Confederacy in the mid-1500s. As the English, Spanish, and French battled for control over the Southeast, the Creeks tried to avoid conflict. ⇒

Tribal women made bandolier bags using cloth and glass beads traded with the Europeans. Men wore the bags diagonally across the body, traditionally as part of their elaborate ceremonial clothing.

They were more interested in protecting their profits from trading in slaves and deerskins with the English. Many thousands of deerskins exchanged hands every year. After the Revolutionary War, the Creek became one of the Five Civilized Tribes associated with George Washington's program to enforce European ways of life on the southeastern tribes. Most Creeks were open to the proposed ideas and adopted several of them, such as farming techniques, schooling their children, and housing.

A Creek civil war erupted during the War of 1812. The Upper Creeks were known as the Red Sticks. They joined the Shawnee chief Tecumseh in his support for the British. Ultimately, Tecumseh, and the tribes fighting alongside him, wanted to stop the U.S. government from taking over tribal lands. The Lower Creeks, known as the White Sticks, fought with U.S. troops to crush the Red Sticks. They ultimately succeeded at the Battle of Horseshoe Bend, in 1814. Following their defeat, the surviving Red Sticks joined the Seminole in Florida. During the next 20 years, the Creek ceded much of their vast lands in treaties. The Indian Removal Act of 1830 forced most remaining Creek to move to Oklahoma. Today, there are four federally recognized Creek groups in the state. The largest is the Creek Nation in Okmulgee. The Poarch Band of Creek Indians is a small band in Alabama. ✎

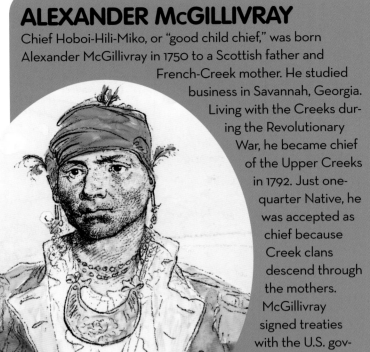

ALEXANDER McGILLIVRAY

Chief Hoboi-Hili-Miko, or "good child chief," was born Alexander McGillivray in 1750 to a Scottish father and French-Creek mother. He studied business in Savannah, Georgia. Living with the Creeks during the Revolutionary War, he became chief of the Upper Creeks in 1792. Just one-quarter Native, he was accepted as chief because Creek clans descend through the mothers. McGillivray signed treaties with the U.S. government and Spain, establishing Creek land boundaries and tribal sovereignty, respectively.

MICCOSUKEE

(mick-uh-SOO-kee)

LANGUAGE GROUP:
Muscogean

LANGUAGE:
Limited number of words in current use; no dictionary available

LOCATION PRECONTACT:
Georgia

LOCATION TODAY:
Florida

The Miccosukee tribe formed when a number of Creeks relocated to Spanish territory in Florida in the early 1700s. They settled in the Apalachee Bay area, south of present-day Tallahassee, where they farmed the land, growing corn and other crops.

It was not long before the tribe felt threatened by settlers and slave traders. To avoid conflict, they moved farther east and south. Even so, the tribe could not escape war altogether. Miccosukee warriors supported the Seminole in their rebellion against the U.S. government from 1817 to 1858. In 1819, Spain sold Florida to the United States and it became a U.S. territory three years later. The U.S. government wanted the land and forced the Miccosukee and the Seminole

to sign the Treaty of Moultrie. The treaty assigned a reservation in central Florida in return for all the remaining tribal land. During the 1830s, a number of Miccosukee avoided relocation under the Indian Removal Act by hiding in the Everglades. They built chickee houses here in order to cope with the swamplike territory. These houses were platforms raised up on poles. They had open sides and palmetto-thatched roofs. Growing traditional crops, such as corn, was difficult, but the Miccosukee found ways to survive in this new

🔅 IN THE KNOW
Visitors to the Miccosukee Indian Village can journey through the Everglades on an airboat to see a hammock-style Native camp that one Miccosukee family has owned for more than 100 years.

Miccosukee men wore cloth turbans with a decorative band (pictured) and, sometimes, bird feathers. Today, elders and spiritual leaders wear such turbans with ostrich plumes when celebrating the annual Green Corn ceremony.

environment. They learned to hunt and fish in the Everglades, which they knew as *kahayatle*, a word that describes its shimmering water. By the mid-1900s, Everglades National Park engulfed most of the Miccosukee lands. The Tamiami Trail highway, constructed in 1928, damaged the natural ecosystem, reducing fish and game populations. In spite of these difficulties, the Miccosukee fought for tribal status and for the land they had been living on. The U.S. government recognized the Miccosukee Tribe in 1962. The tribe continues to live in the Everglades, preserving its culture and protecting the land. 🖋

A Miccosukee man carves a traditional wooden spoon. The Miccosukee people continue many of their ancestral traditions. As well as woodcarving, they weave baskets and make dolls, patchwork, and beadwork.

MONACAN

The area around Bear Mountain, Virginia, has been home to the Monacans for thousands of years. A Siouan tribe, the Monacans formed a confederacy with a number of other Siouan-speaking tribes in the region. Primarily farmers, they planted the traditional crops of corn, squash, and beans, as well as sunflowers and fruit trees. The men hunted elk and deer, and the tribe mined copper, which they used for trade. In 1608, a conflict between the Monacans and European settlers led to a meeting between a wounded warrior, Amoroleck, and Captain John Smith. Amoroleck told Smith that his people believed the English had come to steal their world. The conversation remains the only record of speech from a Siouan-speaking Native person from this region for the whole of the 17th century. The Monacans avoided the English after this. Many moved away from the area, while some stayed in their homelands. In the 1990s, the Monacans purchased land on Bear Mountain. Today, the tribe is recognized by the state of Virginia and has more than 2,000 members.

SEMINOLE

(SEH-minn-ole)

LANGUAGE GROUP:
Muscogean

GREETING:
Ailkatesa

GOODBYE:
Ilcep-ah-non-es-tchah

LOCATION PRECONTACT:
Florida

LOCATION TODAY:
Florida, Oklahoma

The Seminole are descendants of tribal peoples, most of whom were Creeks who migrated to Florida from Georgia and Alabama in the 1700s and early 1800s. Although they spoke different languages and lived in independent towns, all the Florida Native peoples became known as "Seminoles." The name probably comes from the Spanish word *cimarrón*, which means "wild" or "runaway," but a more appropriate interpretation may be "free."

The Seminole lived in villages built on swampland and raised their houses on platforms to keep them dry, their open sides allowing the inhabitants to stay cool in summer. When the Creeks arrived, they brought their farming traditions with them, although crop-growing was less successful in this territory. Men fished the waterways from dug-out canoes, spearing fish and alligators.

Before the Creek Civil War of 1813–1814, the Seminole had been a small group. Afterward, the tribe's population grew to about 5,000. Living with the Seminole were many runaway slaves known as Black Seminoles. After defeating the Red Sticks (Upper Creeks) at the Battle of Horseshoe Bend in 1814, U.S. general Andrew Jackson led his troops to Florida to reclaim runaway slaves, burning Seminole villages and seizing Spanish towns in the process. The tribe succeeded in fighting back in what became known as the First Seminole War, but their victory was short-lived. After Spain ceded Florida to the United States, the Americans forced the Seminoles onto a reservation in central Florida. Then, in 1835, the U.S. government tried to relocate the Seminole to Oklahoma. Many refused to go, sparking the Second Seminole War, which lasted from 1835 until 1842. A third Seminole War followed (1855–1858). Many Seminole eventually relocated to Oklahoma, but a small group, 200 or so, avoided relocation by hiding in the Everglades. Today, they are the Seminoles of Florida. Having built on their agricultural past, they now run businesses that include citrus and cattle farms.

OSCEOLA

Osceola was a great resistance fighter. He moved to Florida after the Creek War and settled with the Seminole. When U.S. troops came to force the Seminole to move to Oklahoma, Osceola encouraged his people to fight back. In 1835, he and his warriors shot a U.S. Indian Agent who had taken power from the Seminole chiefs. (Indian Agents were employed by the U.S. government to communicate between Native peoples and government.) This started the Second Seminole War. Under Osceola, 4,000 Seminole fought alongside 1,500 black runaway slaves as they tried to defend their territory against 9,000 U.S. Army troops. The Seminole won several battles, but in 1837, U.S. troops captured and imprisoned Osceola. He died at Fort Moultrie in South Carolina just three months later, probably from malaria.

The Seminole carved dugout canoes up to 30 feet (9 m) in length from cypress trees. Traditionally, they placed hot embers on a log and used stone or shell tools to scrape out the charred wood, repeating the process to achieve the right thickness.

TUNICA

(TOO-nih-kah)

LANGUAGE GROUP:
Isolate

GREETING:
Heni

THANK YOU:
Tikahch

LOCATION PRECONTACT:
Mississippi, Arkansas

LOCATION TODAY:
Louisiana

Like their allies, the Biloxi, the Tunica are descendants of the ancient mound builders. Today, the two tribes share a reservation near present-day Marksville, Louisiana, and are united under a federally recognized name, the Tunica-Biloxi.

The early Tunica people lived in large villages in northern Mississippi and Arkansas with their capital at Quizquiz. When Spanish explorer Hernando de Soto first met them there in 1541, the Tunica were a large, powerful tribe. By the early 1700s—due to the spread of European diseases—the Tunica had dwindled in numbers and were less able to defend themselves against the Natchez tribe, with whom they had a history of conflict. In order to survive, the Tunica allied themselves with the French and fought with the Europeans in battles against the Natchez. The French and Tunica became firm trading partners, particularly in salt and horses. Even before European arrival, the tribe controlled the salt trade in the area and continued to hold that control.

After the French and Indian War, the Tunica moved into present-day Louisiana. At the time, the Spanish controlled the area and, in the 1780s, created a reservation for the tribe. The Biloxi joined the tribe, and together they fought for rights and recognition. The Tunica culture remained vibrant, but by the mid-1900s, few tribe members spoke their native language. Since 2010, the Tunica have been working with Tulane University on the Tunica Language Project, an initiative working to help restore and keep the ancestral language alive through children's books, recordings, camps, and many other projects.

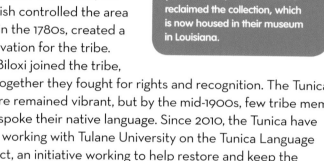

This is a model of the kind of trap the Tunica would have made for catching birds. To use it, they propped one side up using a stick. As a bird enters, it knocks the stick down, causing the trap to fall.

IN THE KNOW

The "Tunica Treasure" is a collection of artifacts discovered in a tribal burial ground. The discovery helped to fill gaps in our knowledge of the Tunica, but it also raised issues about ownership of tribal artifacts. After many years of work, the Tunica tribe reclaimed the collection, which is now housed in their museum in Louisiana.

This 1847 painting called "Louisiana Indians Walking Along a Bayou" is by Alfred Boisseau. Boisseau portrayed the lifeways of Native tribes at a time when their culture was rapidly disappearing.

THE JOURNEY OF THE CHOCTAW AND CHICKASAW

In ancient times, the ancestors of the Choctaws and the Chickasaws lived in a country far away in the west. They lived in two clans and were ruled by two brothers, whose names were Chahta and Chikasa.

As time passed, so many people were born that the land could no longer support them. There was not enough food to eat. The people looked to a great prophet for help. He told them: "We must leave this land and make our way to the east. There we will find a country with fertile soil and game of all kinds." The people prepared for the long journey, then set off by clan, with seven days' difference in their departing times. The great prophet marched at the head of Chahta's group, carrying a pole. When camp was made each night, the prophet planted the pole upright in front of the camp. "The pole will tell us which way to go," he said.

First the pole leaned north, and the people went in that direction. The journey led across streams, over mountains, through forest and barren prairies. Each day, the people followed the direction in which the pole pointed.

They had traveled a great distance when they came to the banks of O-kee-na-chitto, the great waterway (Mississippi River). They camped for the night and the prophet planted the pole. The next morning the pole leaned east, across the river. "We must build rafts and cross the great river," the prophet said. So the people felled trees and made a thousand rafts to cross on. On reaching the other side they found a beautiful country, with green forests and streams. There was game of every kind and abundant fruits and flowers. "This surely is the end of our journey," the prophet said. But the pole still leaned to the east.

At last the people came to a great mound and made camp beside it. The next morning they were awakened by the shouts of the prophet: "The pole stands straight. We

According to some versions of this story, it was the Chickasaw creator god Aba Binili who prompted their tribe to make its long journey from the west, and to cross the Mississippi River.

have found our country. This mound is the center of our land." The mound came to be known as Nanih Waiya.

As it so happened, the second clan, led by Chikasa, had crossed a creek further east and camped on its bank. During the night a great rain began to fall. It lasted several days and the creek flooded the low-lying land where Chikasa and his clan camped. When the rains stopped, Chahta sent a messenger to tell Chikasa that the long-sought land had been found. But the Chikasa clan had proceeded on their journey. The rain had washed away all trace of them. Chahta's messenger had to return with the news that his brother could not be found. Chikasa's group moved on to the Tombigbee River and eventually became a separate nation. In this way the Choctaws and the Chickasaws became two separate, though related, nations.

A Choctaw and Chickasaw story, contributed by Karenne Wood, Monacan

Two brothers of the Gros Ventre tribe are dressed in traditional tribal regalia. One wears a fox-fur headdress, the other a coyote headdress. Both have bone-beaded chokers around their necks and matching breastplates.

 THE PLAINS

The Plains span a vast area in the middle of North America. Very few people lived here before 1200 C.E. because the land was very dry. The climate changed over time, and increased rain and warm weather meant that more animals and plants could live and grow here. After this, people arrived to make the Great Plains their homeland. They traveled great distances, following herds of buffalo—the animal that became a source of food and enabled the Plains people to thrive.

For centuries, the buffalo gave the Plains people everything they needed—from food to shelter and clothing. Hunters never took more animals than they required, so the buffalo population stayed level. In addition to buffalo, the Plains territory was rich in antelope, bears, wolves, deer, and rabbits. Powerful tribes, such as the Blackfeet and Comanche, which numbered many thousands of people, controlled large hunting grounds. There were raids and battles over territory, but many tribes lived peacefully side by side or joined together to become larger groups.

Ways of Life

Some of the tribes who had migrated to the Plains from the north and east adapted their ways of life to suit their new environment. A few settled down to farm, while others became nomads, moving from place to place to follow the buffalo herds. When Plains tribes acquired horses from the Spanish in Mexico in the early to mid-1700s, they were able to travel farther. Horses also became a valuable trading item between tribes. Long before Spanish and French traders visited the area, tribal trading centers sprang up around the Missouri and Mississippi Rivers and their tributaries, the water highways of the region. People from all directions converged on these places to trade food, tools, and horses.

Many of the larger tribes tended to live in separate bands of related families. Each band might number several hundred people, all living in one village. The different bands would then gather together once or twice a year to celebrate a ritual, such as the Sun Dance, or to track buffalo as a group. Several Plains tribes were descendants of the Mississippi mound builders. Plains villages also featured raised mounds or platforms on which they built homes for the most important tribal members, such as their chiefs. Some villages were also enclosed within a palisade—a fence made from wooden posts. Smaller tribes, in particular, relied on such measures to deter hostile raiding parties from enemy tribes.

Times of Great Change

European colonists brought deadly epidemics that destroyed entire tribal communities, and many tribes struggled to survive. From the 1850s to the 1870s, the Plains Wars brought a series of conflicts as tribes fought against the United States over control of the region. Tribes lost their lands in treaties they made with the government. At the same time, white settlers began moving onto the Plains to farm and ranch. White hunters targeted the buffalo for their prized hides, killing them in the thousands. Others hunted the creatures for sport. The government did nothing to discourage the slaughter of the buffalo, believing that their eradication would threaten the Native way of life and persuade more tribes to give up their lands.

By 1880, most of the buffalo had been wiped out. The Plains people had lost their main source of survival and were forced to move to reservations. Most of them ended up in present-day Oklahoma. Others had to adjust to life on small reservations, turning to farming for survival and relying on government aid. At the end of the 19th century, the government passed the Dawes Act, an allotment scheme that divided Native land into parcels. Some parcels were allotted to tribal members, but many were given to white settlers. The Plains life that had existed for centuries had become extinct.

History, Language, and Traditions Today

During the 20th century, Plains tribes lost their tribal status and spent years fighting to regain it. Even today, the Plains people struggle over land rights and challenge broken treaties. There is great pride among the Plains communities. They have an eagerness to recover their history, languages, and traditions. In order to keep their ancestral past alive, they host events in celebration of their culture and have developed a wealth of creative online resources.

Sac & Fox chief Keokuk is depicted here, wearing a bear-claw necklace. His clan was the Fox and his name translates as "the watchful fox."

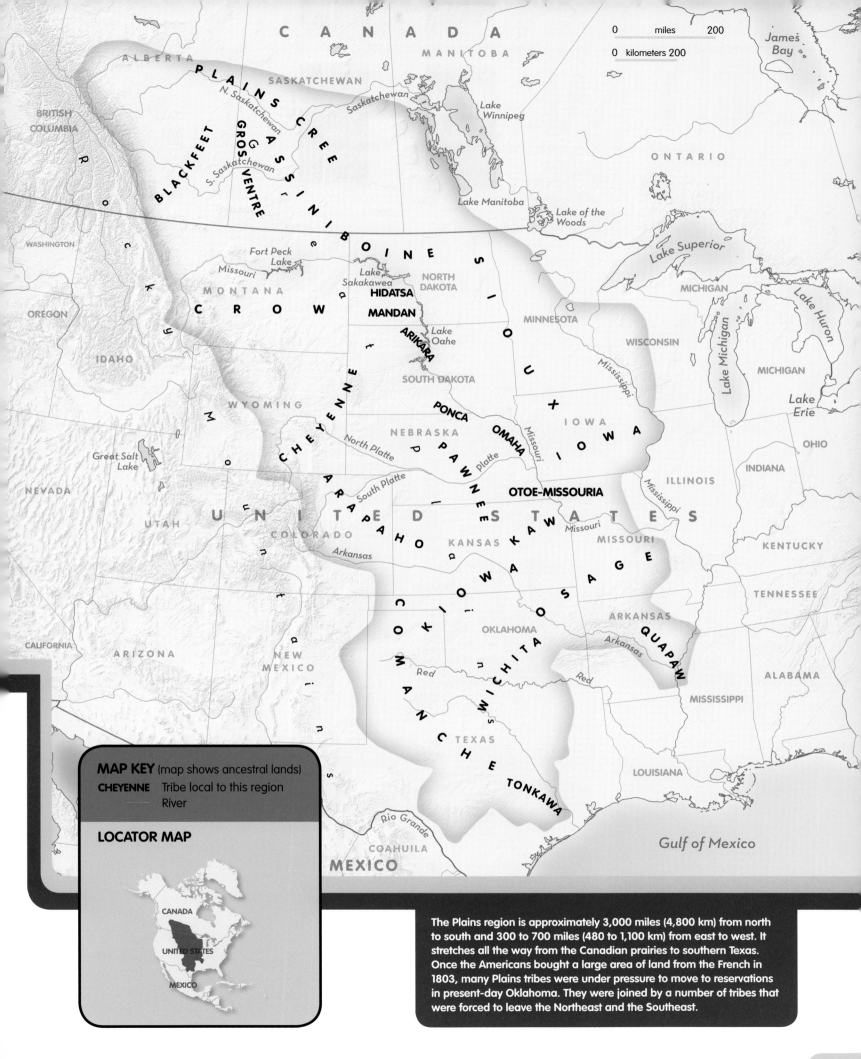

CANADA

ALBERTA

SASKATCHEWAN

MANITOBA

0   miles   200

0   kilometers 200

James Bay

PLAINS CREE

BRITISH COLUMBIA

BLACKFEET

GROS VENTRE

ASSINIBOINE

N. Saskatchewan

S. Saskatchewan

Saskatchewan

Lake Winnipeg

ONTARIO

WASHINGTON

R o c k y

Fort Peck Lake

Missouri

MONTANA

Lake Manitoba

Lake of the Woods

Lake Superior

OREGON

CROW

Lake Sakakawea

HIDATSA

MANDAN

NORTH DAKOTA

Lake Oahe

SIOUX

MINNESOTA

MICHIGAN

WISCONSIN

Lake Huron

IDAHO

ARIKARA

SOUTH DAKOTA

Mississippi

MICHIGAN

Lake Michigan

Lake Erie

M o u n t a i n s

WYOMING

CHEYENNE

PONCA

OMAHA

Missouri

IOWA

IOWA

OHIO

Great Salt Lake

North Platte

NEBRASKA

P a w n e e

Platte

ILLINOIS

INDIANA

NEVADA

CHEYENNE

ARAPAHO

South Platte

PAWNEE

OTOE-MISSOURIA

Mississippi

UNITED STATES

KENTUCKY

UTAH

COLORADO

Arkansas

KANSAS

KAW

o

Missouri

MISSOURI

CALIFORNIA

ARIZONA

NEW MEXICO

G r e a t

KIOWA

WICHITA

K i o w a

COMANCHE

OSAGE

OKLAHOMA

Arkansas

ARKANSAS

QUAPAW

TENNESSEE

ALABAMA

MISSISSIPPI

P l a i n s

Red

TEXAS

Red

m s

TONKAWA

LOUISIANA

Rio Grande

COAHUILA

MEXICO

Gulf of Mexico

MAP KEY (map shows ancestral lands)

CHEYENNE   Tribe local to this region

River

LOCATOR MAP

CANADA

UNITED STATES

MEXICO

The Plains region is approximately 3,000 miles (4,800 km) from north to south and 300 to 700 miles (480 to 1,100 km) from east to west. It stretches all the way from the Canadian prairies to southern Texas. Once the Americans bought a large area of land from the French in 1803, many Plains tribes were under pressure to move to reservations in present-day Oklahoma. They were joined by a number of tribes that were forced to leave the Northeast and the Southeast.

TIME LINE OF THE PLAINS

As the ice retreated from the Plains approximately 12,000 years ago, plants and animals took over. The first people moved into the area and spread out, creating various tribes that depended on the buffalo for their food, clothing, shelter, and tools. The people became expert horse breeders and riders. Tribes such as the Comanche and the Sioux became large and powerful. The 1800s brought European settlers and war to the Plains. The U.S. government forced tribes onto reservations, along with others from the Southeast and Northeast.

8000 B.C.E
People move into the Plains region. The bountiful resources on the Plains attracted tribes from all directions.

1000 C.E.
Central Plains Village tradition begins. The ancestors of Plains tribes, such as the Wichita and Pawnee, settled into villages, where they built their homes and farmed the land.

1600s
Plains tribes acquire horses. The Spanish introduced horses to Mexico in the late 1400s and populations of wild horses developed from that time. Horses made hunting, trading, and warfare easier.

1803
Louisiana Purchase: The U.S. purchase from the French of land that makes up the present-day states of Oklahoma, Nebraska, Louisiana, Kansas, South Dakota and parts of Montana, North Dakota, Wyoming, Colorado, Missouri, Arkansas, and Minnesota. This new land provided the government with an opportunity to move tribes west of the Mississippi River, allowing settlers to occupy territory to the east.

1803–1804
Lewis and Clark expedition. During their travels, Meriwether Lewis and William Clark met many Plains tribes.

1830
Indian Removal Act. The U.S. government forced Cherokee, Choctaw, Chickasaw, Creek, and Seminole people from the Southeast onto reservations in so-called Indian Territory, now present-day Oklahoma. The act brought 50,000 people to the Plains.

1851
First Treaty of Fort Laramie. The U.S. government acknowledged ancestral lands of the Arapaho, Cheyenne, Sioux, and other Plains tribes. In exchange for an annual fee, the tribes agreed to allow the safe passage of travelers and railroad workers through their land.

1862
Homestead Act. The act opened the West for settlement. Under the act, homesteaders claimed 270 million acres (109 million ha) of land. Most of the land was tribal.

1864
Sand Creek Massacre. On November 29, the U.S. Army killed 150 people in a surprise attack on the Cheyenne and Arapaho camp at Sand Creek, Colorado. Pictured is a U.S. Army Colt revolver.

1866–1868
Lakota wars. Conflict broke out when white settlers started moving through tribal hunting grounds. In 1866, Red Cloud and Crazy Horse of the Sioux tribe led warriors in a battle against the U.S. Army. War continued until Red Cloud signed the Second Treaty of Fort Laramie in 1868.

1868

Second Treaty of Fort Laramie. A treaty, signed on April 29, set aside the Black Hills of South Dakota for the Sioux. In 1874, prospectors found gold in the region and, within three years, the U.S. government had taken back the land. (Pictured is a Sioux camp at Fort Laramie.)

1876

Battle of the Little Bighorn. Sitting Bull and Crazy Horse led the Sioux and Cheyenne to resist the U.S. Army's invasion of the Black Hills. The short battle ended in a tribal victory.

1887

Dawes Act. The act broke reservation land into allotments, or parcels, of land. Under the act, individual tribal families received land for farming. The U.S. government took any leftover land to sell to white settlers. By the early 1930s, tribes had lost 90 million acres (36.5 million ha) of land.

1890

Ghost Dance movement begins. A new spiritual movement emerged in the Great Basin and Plateau regions, promoting a world free of white man's diseases and violence. Ceremonies began to spread to the Plains region, too. The U.S. government thought the new spiritual movement was a threat, and banned Native Americans from performing it.

1890

Wounded Knee Massacre. Though banned, the Ghost Dance continued to spread from tribe to tribe. Wanting to halt the movement, the U.S. government sent troops to Wounded Knee Creek in South Dakota. They attacked the camp there, killing or injuring as many as 300 men, women, and children.

1934

Indian Reorganization Act. This federal act aimed to increase tribal self-government. It also brought an end to the Dawes Act. Many Plains tribes adopted written constitutions, although the act still allowed the U.S. government to review decisions made by the new tribal governments.

1940s

Building of the Garrison Dam. The government-approved dam took 156,000 acres (63,000 ha) of the Mandan, Hidatsa, and Arikara reservation. The tribes suffered much flooding of their farmland.

1973

Occupation at Wounded Knee. On February 27, members of the American Indian Movement (AIM) led 200 Oglala Sioux to the village at Wounded Knee, South Dakota, to make a stand against broken treaty promises. The protestors stayed for 71 days. Eventually, the government agreed to investigate their claims. Pictured is a poster commemorating the event.

1980

United States v. Sioux Nation. The U.S. Supreme Court ruled that the Sioux should be paid $17.5 million plus interest dating back to 1877. The ruling recognized that the Black Hills had been taken from the Sioux unlawfully. Refusing the money, the Sioux continue to fight for the return of their land.

2016

Standing Rock Sioux oppose oil pipeline. In April, the Sioux began a protest against a 1,200-mile (1,900-km) oil pipeline from North Dakota to Iowa. Joined by U.S. veterans and other supporters, the Sioux protest continues.

ALABAMA

(al-uh-BAM-uh)

LANGUAGE GROUP:
Muscogean

GREETING:
Chíkmàa

THANK YOU:
Alíila

LOCATION PRECONTACT:
Louisiana, Alabama, Florida

LOCATION TODAY:
Oklahoma, Texas

The Alabama-Coushatta tribe of Texas has been working with the United States Department of Agriculture to restore the region's longleaf pine forests. The trees (pictured here) have long provided needles for the tribe's fine-woven baskets.

The ancestors of the Alabama were southeastern mound builders who lived in villages in present-day Louisiana, Alabama, and Florida, near the Gulf of Mexico. It is from this tribe that the state of Alabama takes its name.

The Alabama settled near the Gulf Coast and along inland rivers and lived by fishing, farming, and hunting. Traditionally, the men would hunt deer, turkey, and small game, while the women tended to the crops of corn, beans, and squash. The Alabama enclosed their villages within palisades. Inside the villages, and unlike many other Plains tribes, the Alabama lived in houses rather than tepees. They arranged their houses around a central square in which their temple stood. This was the heart of the community.

In 1539, the tribe met the Spanish explorer Hernando de Soto, in central Alabama. De Soto's expedition brought diseases to the Southeast that devastated many tribes, including the Alabama, who lost about 95 percent of their population in the decades that followed. The surviving Alabama and other tribes joined forces to form the Creek Confederacy, a union in which each tribe kept its own identity. The English, Spanish, and French who explored and settled in the Southeast treated the confederacy as one group, and the Creeks used this to their advantage. They became a powerful confederacy that traded with the Europeans and adopted some of their ways of life, including farming methods. At the same time, the Alabama and Coushatta tribes formed a close partnership of their own; members of these tribes married, bringing the two nations even closer together.

Wars between the French and the English in the 1700s drove the Alabama west to escape the conflict. In 1830, the U.S. government introduced the Indian Removal Act, forcing southeastern tribes to move to Indian Territory, west of the Mississippi River (in present-day Oklahoma). In the mid-1800s, a group of Alabama moved to Texas, where many Coushatta joined them. Later, another group of Alabama and Coushatta formed the Alabama-Quassarte Tribal Town in Oklahoma.

Today, the Alabama-Coushatta in Texas oversee forestry industries on their lands, and run campgrounds around Lake Tombigbee. Central to their spirituality is the idea of free will. To this day, the importance of an individual's freedom to choose between right and wrong lies at the heart of the elders' teaching.

Alabama men were known for the jewelry they made from silver. These disks were made for men to wear as ear ornaments. They have been stamped and punched with holes for decoration.

ARAPAHO

(uh-RAH-puh-hoe)

LANGUAGE GROUP:
Algonquian

GREETING:
Tous (f); *Héébee* (m)

THANK YOU:
Hohóú

LOCATION PRECONTACT:
Colorado, Wyoming

LOCATION TODAY:
Oklahoma, Wyoming

According to tribal history, the Arapaho were once one of the largest tribal groups inhabiting the Plains. They lived in what is now Colorado and Wyoming. In around 1700, the group realized that they were too large to continue living on their land without overusing its natural resources. One group, the Gros Ventre, moved to present-day Canada. The rest of the tribe stayed in the Plains but split into Northern and Southern Arapaho bands.

By the mid-1600s, both bands were making use of wild horses, which allowed them to travel and hunt buffalo. They followed buffalo herds as they migrated, moving their camps frequently. They lived in tepees made from buffalo skins, which were easy to put up, take down, and transport. Women decorated tribal clothing, tepees, and bags using beads and designs painted in colors made from vegetable dyes. The Arapaho traded and formed friendships with some tribes, such as the Comanche, but fought with others, such as the Lakota Sioux. In the 1800s, the warring tribes came together to defend the Plains from U.S. troops and white settlement.

During the 1849 gold rush,

This dress may have been worn at Arapaho dance ceremonies. It is made from animal hide, has a fringed skirt hem and sleeves, and the top has been stitched with beads to make geometric patterns.

 **IN THE KNOW**

Every year, the Northern and Southern Arapaho meet at the Wind River Reservation for the week-long Sun Dance, during which they pray and make sacrifices. The gathering is aimed at encouraging the natural cycle of Earth's seasons to continue.

thousands of gold-seekers and settlers traveled through Arapaho land on their way to California. Worried that they would lose their land, the Arapaho signed a treaty with the U.S. government assigning a reservation in Colorado for the Arapaho and the Cheyenne, and protecting this land from settlement by outsiders. By 1858, prospectors had found gold in Colorado. In spite of treaty promises, settlers moved onto Arapaho land, forcing the Northern Arapaho farther north into Wyoming. The U.S. government placed them on a reservation with the Shoshone and the tribe still lives on the Wind River Reservation today, farming and raising cattle. The Southern Arapaho tried, but failed, to keep their lands in Colorado. The Treaty of the Little Arkansas in 1865 forced them onto reservation land, which they shared with the Cheyenne tribe, in Indian Territory, now present-day Oklahoma. In 1891, the U.S. government took away most of this land, and the Southern Arapaho eventually settled around Concho, Oklahoma, also in Indian Territory.

This sculpture of Native American warriors stands at the Little Big Horn Battlefield National Monument in Montana.

ARIKARA

(uh-RIH-kuh-rah)

LANGUAGE GROUP:
Caddoan

GREETING:
Nawáh (f); *ĉiiRA* (m)

THANK YOU:
Asŝkawiitik

LOCATION PRECONTACT:
South Dakota, North
Dakota

LOCATION TODAY:
North Dakota

The Arikara call themselves Sahnish, which means "original people from whom all other tribes sprang." The Arikara were farmers, growing crops of corn, beans, and squash on land along the Missouri River in South Dakota. The tribe was particularly known for its corn and grew up to nine different types. The Arikara traded surplus corn with tribes such as the Sioux, who did not farm. In return they received buffalo skins and meat. With European traders, they exchanged corn for utensils and cloth. The tribe hunted buffalo and antelope in winter and used basket traps to catch fish in the river. At their peak, Arikara communities numbered thousands of people, living in homes made from wooden poles and packed earth.

By the time U.S. explorers Meriwether Lewis and William Clark met the tribe in 1804, many Arikara had died from diseases introduced by European settlers. The explorers recorded about 2,000 people living in just three villages. A smallpox epidemic in 1837 wiped out many more Arikara, forcing them to rely on neighboring tribes for survival. In 1851, the Fort Laramie

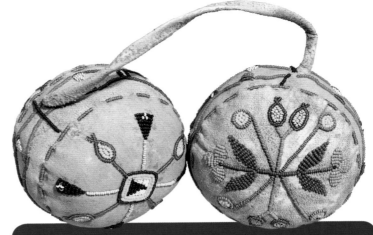

Beaded-hide balls, like these, featured in a game called double-ball, which was popular among Plains women. The object of the game was to pass the balls to team members, using sticks to hook the leather strip joining them, and to throw them over a goal post.

Treaty assigned land at Fort Berthold in North Dakota for the Arikara, the Hidatsa, and Mandan people, at which point they became known as the Three Affiliated Tribes.

The Fort Berthold Reservation covered more than 12 million acres (4.9 million ha) when the three tribes moved there. By 1887, this had been reduced to less than one million acres (405,000 ha) through the Dawes Act of 1887. The tribes continued to lose their land to flooding and unfair land deals. As their land rights diminished, the tribes were forced to move away from their soil-rich farmlands and onto higher, dry, and windy land, where they found it difficult to grow crops as successfully as they had done in the past.

Today, the Three Affiliated Tribes continue to live on the Fort Berthold Reservation. The Arikara language is endangered. Those with any knowledge of the language are age 65 and older, and no one is fluent. In 2014, the tribe started a project to revive its language through teaching programs in local schools and by developing learning tools for a more advanced use of the Arikara language. ✒

Arikara guide Dawn White and her daughter show visitors to the Fort Berthold Reservation how their ancestors used to live. Here, they wear fringed hide dresses and stand beside a garden planted with traditional crops, such as corn.

💡 IN THE KNOW

Actor Leonardo DiCaprio learned to speak some Arikara for his Oscar-winning performance in the movie *The Revenant*.

THE GIFT OF THE PLAINS

For Plains people, the buffalo, or bison, was key to survival. Tribes respected and honored the animal by paying tribute with dances, songs, and ceremonies. Buffalo meat provided food, but all parts were useful. People made soap from fat, bowstrings from tendons, clothing and shelter from hides, and tools from bones. At one time, more than 30 million buffalo lived on the Plains. Many tribes lived a nomadic lifestyle as they followed herds as they migrated. Hunting methods included driving the buffalo into a corral where they could spear them. Sometimes, they drove a herd off a low cliff. This killed or wounded a number, making them easier to capture. By the 1890s, with white settlers hunting the animals for sport and for hides, fewer than one thousand buffalo remained. Tribes had no choice but to change their traditional ways of living and to depend on the government. In recent years, buffalo herds have grown in number and there are now around 500,000 buffalo in North America. In 2016, President Obama signed the National Bison Legacy Act, making the buffalo the national mammal.

ASSINIBOINE

(ah-SIN-uh-boin)

LANGUAGE GROUP:
Siouan

LANGUAGE:
Limited number of words in current use

LOCATION PRECONTACT:
Montana; Alberta, Saskatchewan (Canada)

LOCATION TODAY:
Montana (U.S.); Saskatchewan (Canada)

Around 1600, a quarrel among the Nakota Sioux led a group within the tribe to break away and form the Assiniboine tribe. Its name comes from the Ojibwe word *asiniibwaan*, which means "stony Sioux," and may refer to the Assiniboine's method of using hot rocks to boil water.

As the tribe spread onto the Plains, it hunted over a territory stretching from Saskatchewan, in Canada, to the Missouri Valley in Montana. Family groups scattered across the region, living in temporary camps rather than in permanent villages. They used dogs to transport their belongings on a travois, a type of sled. For a time, the Assiniboine sought refuge with the Cree, who were enemies of the Nakota Sioux.

Because they were spread so widely, the Assiniboine adapted their ways of living to suit their environment. Those living near woodlands took up the fur trade in the late 1600s and early 1700s, exchanging beaver pelts for English guns, ➤

This headdress has a beaded headband that is further decorated with feathers and antelope horns. Such headdresses were considered emblems of power, valor, or reputation.

metal goods, and cloth. Those on the Plains traveled frequently to hunt and made buffalo-skin bags for storing and transporting food, rather than using hand-woven baskets. It was not unusual for women to accompany the men when hunting, to help butcher an animal once captured. Back at the camp, the women then prepared the buffalo skins for making clothes or tepees. They cut the buffalo meat and dried it for later use.

Contact with European settlers brought waves of new diseases during the late 1700s and early 1800s, causing many Assiniboine to die of smallpox, measles, and whooping cough. By the late 1800s, many bands of Assiniboine had lost land in treaties with the U.S. government, while the buffalo on which they depended had been almost wiped out by white hunters and soldiers. Landless and

This Assiniboine necklace is threaded with glass beads. Bone beads and ammunition cartridges are also decorative elements, and are threaded onto thin strips of animal hide.

starving, the Assiniboine moved to two reservations in Montana. Today, they share land with the Sioux at the Fort Peck Reservation, and a reservation at Fort Belknap with the Gros Ventre tribe. Other Assiniboine moved to reserves in Saskatchewan, Canada. Few people speak the Assiniboine language today and it is threatened with falling out of usage.

IN THE KNOW

As in many Plains tribes, women were usually responsible for taking down the camp when the Assiniboine moved to track a buffalo herd. The tepees were lightweight and easy to take down.

DANCING

Dancing is central to tribal culture, and is seen as a way to give thanks or to celebrate. Plains warriors performed the Grass Dance to celebrate a victory, for example. The Buffalo Dance (pictured below) honored the return of buffalo herds following their winter migration. The buffalos' return coincided with the willow tree being in full leaf. Men dressed in buffalo masks, and with willow boughs on their backs, danced in imitation of the buffalo. One of the most important dances for most Plains tribes was the Sun Dance, a spiritual ceremony of renewal. Held during midsummer, the Sun Dance drew different bands together each year. Dancers, who often fasted for the ceremony, moved around a central, sacred pole, while looking up at the sun. Many of these traditional dances remain important to tribal culture and are performed today.

BLACKFEET

(BLACK-feet)

LANGUAGE GROUP:
Algonquian

GREETING:
Óki

THANK YOU:
Sokápi

LOCATION PRECONTACT:
Montana; Alberta,
Saskatchewan (Canada)

LOCATION TODAY:
Montana (U.S.); Alberta
(Canada)

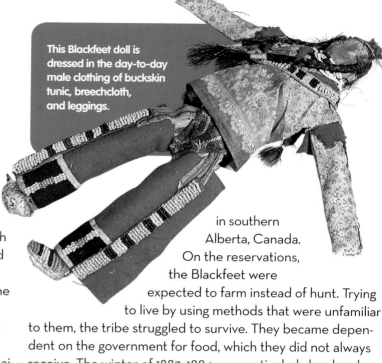

This Blackfeet doll is dressed in the day-to-day male clothing of buckskin tunic, breechcloth, and leggings.

The Blackfeet, an Algonquian-speaking tribe, once controlled large areas in present-day Alberta, east of the Rocky Mountains, and Saskatchewan—both now Canadian provinces—and in Montana. They probably migrated to the Plains from the Northeast. The tribe is a confederacy of three main bands that emerged many centuries ago: the Siksika, the Kainai, and the Pikuni. According to tribal stories, the Siksika and the Kainai are named after a particular characteristic. For example, Siksika refers to "those with black-dyed moccasins," from which this tribe's name comes, and Kainai means "bloods," as that band ate berries that stained their faces and hands red. The Blackfeet were hunters, who moved about the Plains using dogs and sleds to carry their loads. By the mid-1700s, the tribe had obtained horses from other tribes to the south and guns from European fur traders.

The Blackfeet hunted over a large territory, but the bands came together to trade and for important ceremonies, such as the sacred Sun Dance. The tribe followed this way of life for centuries, avoiding contact with settlers. In the 1850s, government treaties forced the Blackfeet to cede their lands. An 1855 treaty assigned the tribe a reservation in Montana—a parcel of land next to what later became Glacier National Park. Many Blackfeet people, especially descendants of the Southern Piegan band, moved there. Other bands went to reserves in southern Alberta, Canada. On the reservations, the Blackfeet were expected to farm instead of hunt. Trying to live by using methods that were unfamiliar to them, the tribe struggled to survive. They became dependent on the government for food, which they did not always receive. The winter of 1883–1884 was particularly hard and became known among the tribe as the "starvation winter."

Since that time, the Blackfeet have rebuilt their tribe and revived their language. They honor many traditions and maintain a deep respect for the land. Hunting and fishing regulations ensure that the animal populations continue to thrive. In 2014, they signed the Buffalo Treaty with other tribes, pledging to work together to restore wild buffalo to the Plains.

IN THE KNOW

The Blackfeet hunted bears and elk, among other animals. Women decorated their dresses with elk tusks, while men sometimes threaded a bear paw onto a necklace.

A member of the Blackfeet tribe makes a plant offering to Apistotoke, sometimes known in English as the Great Spirit. Apistotoke is this tribe's creator god.

CADDO

(CAD-oh)

LANGUAGE GROUP:
Caddoan

GREETING:
Haʔahat Haht'-ay'-baw'-sa?

THANK YOU:
Haw'-wih

LOCATION PRECONTACT:
Arkansas, Louisiana,
Oklahoma, Texas

LOCATION TODAY:
Oklahoma

The Caddo tribe is a confederation of many bands that lived in parts of Arkansas, Louisiana, Oklahoma, and Texas. Their ancestors had farmed the Red River Valley of East Texas for around 2,000 years. As well as corn, the Caddo grew watermelons, gathered nuts, such as walnuts and pecans, and made salt by boiling salty marshland water. The Caddo traded these goods with other tribes. Their main villages contained large, earthen mounds on which they built grass-covered temples for the tribe's spiritual leaders. They buried important people in other mounds. Family groups lived in pole-framed houses covered with grass thatch. Members followed a clan system in which children took the name of their mother's clan, such Panther or Wolf.

The Spanish explorer Hernando de Soto came across the Caddo in 1541. His invading forces fought the Tula band of Caddo and destroyed many of their villages. Like other tribes, the Caddo suffered many losses from diseases introduced by the Europeans. Then they began to lose their territory. American settlers moved into Caddo lands from the early 1800s, and in the 1830s, following the Indian Removal Act, the government began to force the Caddo out of their homelands. The Caddo settled on reservation land near Anadarko, Oklahoma, which was shared by Wichita and Delaware people.

The Caddo remain proud of their heritage. They have a National Heritage Museum and hold celebrations that include traditions such as the Turkey Dance, which used to mark the return of Caddo warriors from battle, traditionally taking place before sunset.

IN THE KNOW

Plains Native tribes spoke many different languages. In order to communicate with each other, the tribes developed a sign language, although this is no longer used. The sign for their own tribe involved passing the extended index finger, pointing under the nose, from right to left.

This ceramic bottle is at least 500 years old. The swirling pattern is incised, meaning it has been carved carefully into the surface using a sharpened stick or piece of bone.

This Caddo man is dressed in tribal regalia. Most striking, besides his black-and-white face paint, is his headdress. His impressive porcupine-hair roach is pierced with a calumet, or pipestem.

A PLACE TO LIVE

Most Plains tribes moved from one place to the next to hunt buffalo. This meant they needed shelters that were easy to put up and take down. Traditionally, women made cone-shaped tepees from long poles covered with buffalo hide; the door always faced east, toward sunrise. A hole in the top of the tepee let out the smoke from the fire inside, which was used to cook and keep warm. The Kiowa and Blackfeet painted designs on their tepees. The Mandan and Pawnee used tepees for hunting trips, but otherwise lived in lodges that were partially built underground. These farming cultures built circular framed lodges from timber and covered them in sod and grass. On the southern Plains, the Wichita and Caddo built dome-shaped grass lodges. The grass layer kept a lodge cool in summer and warm in winter.

CHEYENNE

(shy-ANN)

LANGUAGE GROUP:
Algonquian

GREETING:
Haaahe (m)

THANK YOU:
Né-á'eše!

LOCATION PRECONTACT:
Minnesota

LOCATION TODAY:
Oklahoma, Montana

The Cheyenne call themselves Tsethasetas, meaning "the people." They originated in Minnesota, where they had a farming culture, but some time before the 1700s, the tribe changed from living an agricultural life to following a more nomadic one on the Plains.

To some extent the move was inspired by the large numbers of buffalo living in the Plains area, but there was also pressure to move from their enemies, the Cree and Assiniboine. Instead of building earthen lodges in permanent villages, the tribe began to establish temporary camps, living in hide-covered tepees. As well as practicing their own version of the Sun Dance, the Cheyenne celebrated an Animal Dance that was to help hunters bring back enough food for the tribe.

By the 1730s, the Cheyenne were living in parts of modern-day Colorado and Wyoming and had split into two main bands—the Northern and the Southern Cheyenne. Cheyenne society included a number of peace chiefs—one for each band of Cheyenne—who got together to discuss and decide on important issues. As well as the peace chiefs, members from several bands formed groups known as "military" societies. These members were charged with leading hunts, directing battle, and enforcing discipline. One such society was the Hotamétaneo'o, "Dog Warrior Society," whose members were highly skilled Cheyenne warriors who played an important role in the Plains wars. Each of these military societies had its own paraphernalia, rituals, and dances. For example, ⮕

This pair of Cheyenne moccasins features a beaded sunburst pattern. The cuffs at the back could be turned down to stay cooler.

W. RICHARD WEST, JR.

W. Richard West, Jr., was the first director of the Smithsonian National Museum of the American Indian, which opened in 2004, in Washington, D.C. The museum took 15 years to develop and West over-saw its design, construction, and development during that time. The son of a Cheyenne father and Arapaho mother, West grew up in a log cabin in Muskogee, Oklahoma. His father was a respected Cheyenne artist. West studied American history at Harvard University and works hard to preserve and promote American Indian culture. Today he is a peace chief of the Southern Cheyenne, upholding a tribal tradition.

members of the Dog Warrior Society wore a whistle made from the bone of a bird's wing around their necks. They blew their whistles to give certain signals during combat.

The Cheyenne often fought to defend their lands. They won some battles but lost many against the much larger U.S. Army. One of the most tragic events in Cheyenne history took place in 1864, when more than 500 Southern Cheyenne, led by Chief Black Kettle, gathered for peace talks with the U.S. government. The Cheyenne, including women and children, camped at Sand Creek, Colorado, where Black Kettle flew an American flag and a white flag from his tepee to show that the tribe wanted peace. In spite of this, Colonel John Chivington led U.S. troops in a brutal attack against the encampment, killing around 150 innocent tribal members. Cheyenne warriors sought revenge and the conflicts continued until the U.S. Army forced the Southern Cheyenne to move to Oklahoma in 1877. Meanwhile, the Northern Cheyenne fought alongside other Native tribes against the U.S. government in the wars for the Black Hills.

Today, almost 5,000 people occupy the Northern Cheyenne Reservation in Montana, where many of them live by farming and ranching. The Southern Cheyenne share a reservation with the Arapaho in Oklahoma. The Cheyenne continue to practice a number of craft traditions, including pipe-carving, woodworking, quill embroidery, and leatherworking. ✐

CHICKASAW

(CHICK-uh-saw)

LANGUAGE GROUP:
Muscogean

GREETING:
Hallito

THANK YOU:
Chokma'shki

LOCATION PRECONTACT:
Alabama, Kentucky, Mississippi, Tennessee

LOCATION TODAY:
Oklahoma

Although the Chickasaw people have lived in Oklahoma since the 1830s, the tribe's ancestral homes are in Mississippi, Alabama, and other parts of the Southeast. In this fertile land, the Chickasaw established large villages, on high ground to avoid flooding when the Mississippi River overflowed. They built their pole-framed homes and dugout canoes from local hardwood trees. They established successful farms on the land surrounding their villages, growing corn, squash, beans, melons, and sunflowers. The men were also hunters and warriors. With access to three major rivers, the Mississippi, the Tombigbee, and the Tennessee, the tribe was able to travel great distances to become part of a wide trading network.

In 1540, the Chickasaw met Hernando de Soto and his men. The Chickasaw welcomed the Spanish, but de Soto executed two members for stealing pigs. When the British arrived in the 1600s, the tribe established a good trading relationship with them. During the French and Indian War (1754–1763), the Chickasaw fought with the British against the French. By the early 1800s, the Chickasaw and other southeastern tribes became interested in European customs and ideas, including government, farming techniques, and clothing. This impressed the new American government and, along with the Cherokee, Choctaw, Creek, and Seminole tribes of the Southeast, the Chickasaw became known as one of the Five Civilized Tribes.

These Chickasaw stickball players wear body paint to look handsome and impressive. Feathers and wings give the impression that they can move with speed and agility—like birds.

This beaded cap once belonged to a Chickasaw chief. His Native name was Tootemastubbe (1764–1839). He was also known as George Colbert. He gave the cap to an early white settler as an act of friendship.

IN THE KNOW

In 2002, John Bennett Herrington, a Chickasaw astronaut, became the first Native American to walk in space. With him, he carried sweet grass from his ancestral land and the Chickasaw Nation flag, which has on it six eagle feathers and two arrowheads. The eagle feathers represent honor and the arrowheads represent bravery.

When the U.S. government forced the Chickasaw to move to Indian Territory—now Oklahoma—the tribe faced a new life in a strange land. They fought attempts to make them share a reservation with the Choctaw tribe, settling on their own reservation in 1856. The Chickasaw tribe was the only one of the Five Civilized Tribes not to retain a reservation in its original southeastern homeland. Today, the Chickasaw Nation is one of the largest tribes in the United States, with its language still spoken by a significant number. It has a strong government and runs many businesses, as well as radio and television stations. The Chickasaw Cultural Center in Sulphur, Oklahoma, has a replica traditional village, art gallery, theater, and regular exhibits.

COMANCHE

(kuh-MAN-chee)

LANGUAGE GROUP:
Uto-Aztecan

GREETING:
Maruawe

THANK YOU:
Urako

LOCATION PRECONTACT:
Oklahoma, New Mexico, Texas, Colorado

LOCATION TODAY:
Oklahoma

At some point during the late 1600s, the Comanche split from their relatives, the Shoshone, and became one of the most powerful tribes on the Plains, expanding into large parts of Oklahoma, New Mexico, Texas, and Colorado. At the height of their power, the Comanche numbered more than 40,000 people spread across 12 bands. The people were nomadic hunters, who followed the buffalo herds, setting up their tepees in temporary camps and supplementing their diet with roots, nuts, and berries foraged by the women.

Because they moved frequently, the tribe made lightweight baskets and leather bags, rather than pottery, for carrying food and equipment. They carved utensils, ➡

A girl in a Comanche hide dress kisses a baby sibling in a cradleboard. The two vertical pieces with pointed tops are typical of Plains cradleboard design.

The warriors of the Comanche tribe were skilled horsemen. This painting captures the moment at which one warrior flings himself to one side of his horse, so that he can use the horse as a shield between himself and his enemy.

such as spoons, from buffalo horn. The tribe owned many thousands of horses, and raided and traded for even more, giving them an early advantage over some other Plains tribes. Both boys and girls learned to ride horses at a young age, so all tribal members became skillful riders and trainers.

During the 1700s, the Comanche held onto their large land base and way of life. For some time, their regular raids on other tribes and Europeans deterred outsiders from moving onto their lands. But this situation did not last. In the 1800s, the Comanche were forced to unite with the Kiowa and other Plains people to defend their land against U.S. Army troops and settlers. Yet they lost more people to disease than to warfare. By 1867, the tribal population had dropped to fewer than 3,000 people. That year, the Comanche signed a treaty ceding 38.5 million acres (15.5 million ha) of land in exchange for their own reservation, money, and a promise that white hunters would stop killing the buffalo. Quanah Parker, the son of a Comanche chief, led one last rebellion in 1874, but the U.S. Army forced Parker and his warriors to surrender in 1875.

Today, the Comanche, Kiowa, and Apache tribes share reservation land in Oklahoma. Each tribe lives in a different region of the reservation, with the Kiowa to the north, the Apache to the south, and the Comanche occupying the central territory between them. ✒

COUNTING COUP

Military societies, such as the Cheyenne Dog Warrior Society, were part of traditional tribal culture long before Europeans arrived and introduced large battles to the Plains. In Plains culture, raids and revenge killings were common, but a warrior did not need to kill to be honorable. In fact, he won the greatest praise when showing his courage by "counting coup." This tradition involved getting close enough to an enemy to be able to strike him with a weapon—such as the wooden club pictured—with the hand, or with a "coup stick." With each successful blow, a warrior would add a trophy, such as a feather, to his coup stick. The coup stick then became an outward sign of the warrior's daring in combat. The more feathers on his coup stick, the more respect a warrior earned for his bravery.

CROW

(CROW)

LANGUAGE GROUP:
Siouan

GREETING:
Kahé

THANK YOU:
Ahó·

LOCATION PRECONTACT:
Montana, Wyoming

LOCATION TODAY:
Montana

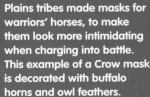

Plains tribes made masks for warriors' horses, to make them look more intimidating when charging into battle. This example of a Crow mask is decorated with buffalo horns and owl feathers.

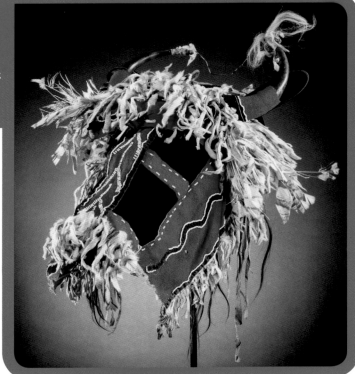

The Crow call themselves Apsáalooke— "children of the large-beaked bird." Early Crow people lived near Lake Erie, but the tribe moved west several times to avoid conflict with more powerful tribes. When the Cheyenne, Cree, and other Plains tribes forced them from Lake Winnipeg, Canada, the Crow moved south to what is now southern Montana and northern Wyoming. Like other Plains people, they were primarily hunters, living a nomadic life in temporary tepee camps, which they moved as they followed the buffalo. The tribe grew tobacco, which it traded along with buffalo hides. During a ceremony, a spiritual leader filled a pipe with tobacco and blessed it. He then passed the pipe from one participant to the next so that each could benefit from the blessing. Crow men grew their hair very long and both men and women wore colorful, beaded clothing. Within the tribal community, there was great emphasis on the fathers teaching their sons such survival skills as archery, and for the mothers to teach their daughters to cook and make clothes. By the mid-1700s, the Crow had horses and occupied a large territory along the Yellowstone River.

In 1851, the Crow signed the Treaty of Fort Laramie with the U.S. government, through which they gained 33 million acres (13.4 million ha) of reservation land, but this soon dwindled, as the tribe's traditional enemies, the Cheyenne and Lakota Sioux, hunted on the lands, forcing the Crow to move. A second treaty, signed in 1868, reduced the Crow Reservation to just eight million acres (3.25 million ha). Fearful for both their safety and their land, the Crow offered to help the U.S. Army by acting as scouts during the Plains Wars. Despite their service, the Crow lost more land. Their reservation currently consists of just two million acres (800,000 ha) in Montana.

Today, many Crow members continue to live on the reservation, the largest in the state, where the tribe depends on farming, gas, oil, and timber. There is a push to revitalize the tribal language and, each August, the tribe hosts the Crow Fair, one of North America's biggest American Indian events. Sometimes referred to as the "Tepee Capital of the World," because there may be as many as 1,000 tepees on display, the show provides Native families with an opportunity to gather together and celebrate their culture in a wide range of events, from rodeo to dancing and crafting. Each morning, there is a parade with floats as well as people on foot or on horseback, with many people dressed in traditional ceremonial regalia.

CROW CHIEFS

Chief Plenty Coups (far left) was born in 1848. In the early 1900s, he defended the tribe's rights to its ancestral land. After World War I, the U.S. government chose Plenty Coups to represent all American Indians at the dedication of the war memorial, the Tomb of the Unknown Indian.

Born in 1913, Joe Medicine Crow (left) was the last Crow war chief. He was awarded a Bronze Star for his achievements during World War II, when he is said to have worn war paint under his uniform. Raised when his people still hunted for survival, he was the first Crow to attend college and became a notable historian. In 2009, he received the Presidential Medal of Freedom from President Obama. He died in 2016.

DELAWARE

(DEL-a-ware)

LANGUAGE GROUP:
Algonquian

GREETING:
Hè

THANK YOU:
Wanishi

LOCATION PRECONTACT:
New York, New Jersey, Delaware, Pennsylvania

LOCATION TODAY:
Oklahoma (U.S.); Ontario (Canada)

Elaborately beaded shoulder bags, like this colorful example, were known as "bandolier bags." They were often presented to men as wedding gifts or ceremonial presents.

Delaware is the name that European colonists gave to the Lenni Lenape tribe—after the Delaware River. Originally, many of the tribal people occupied land near the Delaware River in present-day southern New York and northern New Jersey. Today, the tribal community in Oklahoma continues to use the Delaware name, while other groups use the name Lenape. The tribe is one of the oldest tribes of the Northeast—the name, Lenni Lenape, means "original people." Neighboring tribes recognized and respected the tribe's ancestry, calling them the "grandfathers."

At first, the Delaware welcomed European settlers, acting as scouts and soldiers for them in the early days of the United States. But, as more colonists moved into their territory, the tribe could not survive as a united group and scattered into many bands—some moving into present-day Pennsylvania, others into what is now Ohio. Once in these new areas, many Delaware bands merged with other tribes, often adopting their cultures.

Increasingly, members of the Delaware tribe who stayed in New Jersey and New York married non-Natives and, over time, many of them lost their culture and traditions.

In 1758, some 200 Delaware agreed to live on the Brotherton, the first reservation in New Jersey. In September 1778, the Delaware became the first tribe to sign a treaty with the U.S. government. The Treaty of Fort Pitt, also known as the Delaware Treaty, allowed U.S. troops and their allies to pass through Delaware land. Forced by treaties to cede their land, the Delaware struggled to become self-sufficient, and by the early 1800s, most of these Delaware had moved away.

One group settled in modern-day Missouri in 1793. Known as the Absentee Delaware, this group moved to Texas in 1820 and, finally, to Oklahoma in 1859. In Oklahoma, the tribe settled at the Wichita Reservation in 1890. At this time, the U.S. government enrolled them either as Caddo or Wichita Indians, stripping them of their true identity. From that time on, the community strived to rebuild its individual tribal status and culture. In 1977, the Absentee Delaware were finally recognized as the Delaware Tribe of Oklahoma and received joint ownership of lands with the Caddo and Wichita peoples.

IN THE KNOW

Delaware women sometimes dug large pits in the ground for storing food such as dried buffalo meat and corn through the winter. When lined with woven mats, these pits kept food dry and safe from rats or mice.

According to legend, the Delaware met William Penn in 1682, and each promised friendship. An Englishman, Penn (dressed in black, center) founded a colony that became the U.S. state of Pennsylvania.

GROS VENTRE

(grow VAUN-truh)

LANGUAGE GROUP:
Algonquian

LANGUAGE:
Limited number of words in current use; no dictionary available

LOCATION PRECONTACT:
Saskatchewan (Canada)

LOCATION TODAY:
Montana

No one is sure why the Gros Ventre have this name—French for "large belly." It may be that early French traders misunderstood the tribe's sign language. The tribe call themselves A'aninin, meaning "white clay people." According to Gros Ventre history, the creator made white clay people to keep him company.

Approximately 3,000 years ago, the Gros Ventre migrated from the coast of the Atlantic Ocean to the Great Lakes, and then to the eastern Plains, south of Lake Winnipeg, Canada. They lived a nomadic life, moving camp to hunt migrating buffalo for food and clothing. They excelled at making elaborate and beautiful beadwork and quillwork. At that time, the Gros Ventre and the Arapaho were one tribe, but in about 1700, the tribe split in two and the Arapaho moved south.

By the early 1800s, the Gros Ventre lived in Saskatchewan, Canada, but not peacefully. Cree and Assiniboine warriors, armed with guns, preyed on the tribe, while waves of European diseases reduced its population. With fewer people and no weapons, the tribe retreated south into Montana. In their new home, the Gros Ventre allied themselves with the Blackfeet. As settlers and miners moved west, hunting land began to disappear—as did the buffalo, killed for sport by white hunters and

Hawk feathers stand out on this Gros Ventre painted deer-hide shield cover. The hawk is a symbol of power for many tribes and its feathers invoke the bird's spiritual help.

targeted by government soldiers. As the buffalo died out, the Gros Ventre became dependent on food and clothing supplies from government forts. With much of their land taken over and their main food source gone, in 1888, the Assiniboine, Blackfeet, and Gros Ventre ceded more than 17 million acres (7 million ha) of land to the government and moved onto reservations.

Today the Gros Ventre share the Fort Belknap Reservation with the Assiniboine. Together, they form the Fort Belknap Indian Community Council, but each celebrates its separate culture independently. To earn income, the Gros Ventre tribe relies on agriculture, growing crops of wheat and barley, producing hay, and renting out land for ranching. There are few speakers of the tribe's native language, but it is now taught from primary age at school in order to keep it alive. Among the rituals still held by the tribe is the Ceremony of the Sacred Flat Pipe. Sacred pipes are significant religious objects for many Plains tribes, passing from one generation to the next. According to ancestral history, the Flat Pipe of the Gros Ventre was given to them when the world was created. Today, an annual ceremony serves to reinforce the tribe's link with its creator.

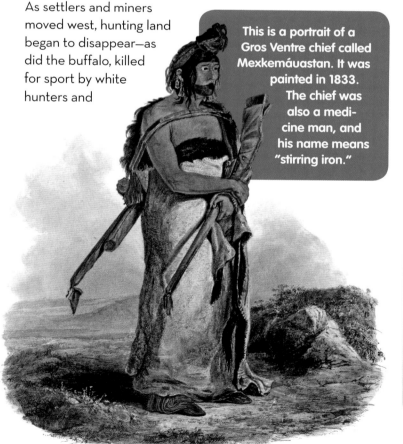

This is a portrait of a Gros Ventre chief called Mexkemáuastan. It was painted in 1833. The chief was also a medicine man, and his name means "stirring iron."

RUNNING FISHER

Before becoming chief of the Gros Ventre, Running Fisher was a warrior for his tribe, fighting in some 20 battles over 40 years. The first tribal chief of police at the Fort Belknap Reservation, Running Fisher also represented his tribe at the Little Big Horn Valley in 1909. This large gathering of chiefs from many tribes became known as the "last great Indian Council." Fisher was an accomplished military leader and believed that fasting gave him greater power in war.

HIDATSA

(hee-DOT-suh)

LANGUAGE GROUP:
Siouan

GREETING:
Dóosha?

THANK YOU:
Hahó

LOCATION PRECONTACT:
North Dakota

LOCATION TODAY:
North Dakota

The Hidatsa originated in Minnesota and moved several times before settling in villages along the Missouri River in North Dakota. In their new homeland, the tribe formed close friendships with its neighbors, the Arikara and Mandan, and became part of a thriving trading center on the river, exchanging crops for meat and hides with other tribes and with Europeans. They also hunted for their own meat. Hidatsa women built the tribe's homes—circular, earthen lodges made from wooden posts, packed earth, and grass. Unlike many of the nomadic Plains tribes, who made leather bags for the storage and transportation of their goods, the Hidatsa made pottery vessels.

A smallpox epidemic in 1830 devastated the Hidatsa, Mandan, and Arikara tribes. Seeking strength and protection in numbers, the Hidatsa joined the Mandan. The Arikara joined them 20 years later. Under Hidatsa chief Four Bears, the "Three Affiliated Tribes" formed a new village called Like-A-Fishhook. Treating the three tribes as one, the U.S. government assigned them a reservation, including Like-A-Fishhook Village, at Fort Berthold, North Dakota, in 1870. However, the government took more and more of this land and, in the 1940s, built the Garrison Dam, flooding tribal farmland and forcing many members of the three tribes onto higher land nearby. The tribal members who remain there today work hard to preserve their languages, crafts, and traditions—such as the use of the sweathouse. Like a modern-day sauna, this is a hut where water is poured over hot stones to create steam. Tribal members come here to pray and cleanse through sweating.

IN THE KNOW

At nearly one mile (1.6 km) long, the Four Bears Bridge over the Missouri River is the longest bridge in North Dakota. It is decorated with medallions representing different aspects of Hidatsa, Mandan, and Arikara heritage.

Hidatsa-Mandan Black Horse lights a pipe as he sits in the cottonwood, ash, and earth lodge he has built on his property on the Fort Berthold Reservation. Traditionally, earthen lodges are used for prayer and tribal ceremonies.

Following a successful raid, the Hidatsa tribe performed the victory Scalp Dance common to the Plains tribes. Women dressed as warriors held weapons and scalp trophies, while men beat out a rhythm on drums and with rattles. Scalping was also something practiced by white settlers.

HO-CHUNK

(HO-chunk)

LANGUAGE GROUP:
Siouan

GREETING:
Hinjkaragi

GOODBYE:
Žige hanjca kje

LOCATION PRECONTACT:
Wisconsin

LOCATION TODAY:
Trust lands in Wisconsin, Illinois

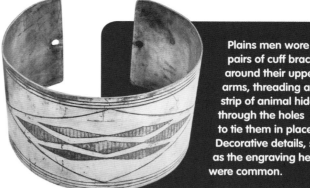

Plains men wore pairs of cuff bracelets around their upper arms, threading a strip of animal hide through the holes to tie them in place. Decorative details, such as the engraving here, were common.

Originally, the Ho-Chunk, or "people of the big voice," lived in large villages in northeastern Wisconsin, their numbers reaching many thousands. Farmers by tradition, the Ho-Chunk lived in villages with bark lodges and grew crops of beans, corn, and squash. They also hunted buffalo and speared fish. Neighboring Ojibwe tribes called the Ho-Chunk the Wiinibiigoo, which means "people of the muddy water," because they lived by Lake Winnebago. Algae grew in the lake in summer, causing the water's muddy appearance.

By the early 1700s, disease, starvation, and war had reduced the population to just 500. The U.S. government wanted to take over Ho-Chunk land, but this was more difficult than it expected: The tribe did not want to fight, but they were not willing to move, either. Gradually miners, traders, and others settled in the territory until, in 1837, the government introduced a treaty that gave the settlers rights over the entire area. This began years of movement for the Ho-Chunk that ended with the tribe becoming divided. Some Ho-Chunk moved to northern Wisconsin, while others were forced to move to Long Prairie, Minnesota, in 1846. Their new land was at the heart of a major conflict between the Ojibwe and the Dakota Sioux tribes and was constantly trampled over by the warring tribes. As a consequence, the tribe found it difficult to farm the land at Long Prairie, and the Ho-Chunk went on the move again, eventually settling in Nebraska.

Today, the Nebraska Ho-Chunk are known as the Winnebago tribe. Winnebago Village, the largest community on their reservation, is home to around one-third of its members. The tribe's annual "home-coming" powwow provides an opportunity for those living off the reservation to immerse themselves in Ho-Chunk culture. The other, larger, group of Ho-Chunk lives in Wisconsin. Although this community has no reservation, money earned from running a successful casino has enabled the tribe to buy back about 2,000 acres (800 ha) of its traditional territory. They have also invested in programs preserving their heritage—such as helping the Winnebago tribe to revitalize its native language. The Ho-Chunk have also reintroduced bison to the region.

Rick Cleveland, Jr. (right), of the Ho-Chunk Tribe of Wisconsin, has his face painted in preparation for a Washington, D.C., powwow celebrating the Smithsonian's National Museum of the American Indian.

IN THE KNOW

Ho-chunk lawyer Sharice Davids was elected to the United States Congress in November 2018, one of two Native American women elected that year. She is also the first openly gay member of Congress to represent Kansas.

IOWA

(I-ow-way)

LANGUAGE GROUP:
Siouan

GREETING:
Ahó

THANK YOU:
Aho/Ha

LOCATION PRECONTACT:
Iowa

LOCATION TODAY:
Kansas, Nebraska, Oklahoma

The Iowa tribe calls itself Báxoje, which means "people of the gray snow." The name may have come from the ash-covered snow on their winter homes. The ash came from the fire inside and was carried by the smoke through the hole in the roof. Like many Plains tribes, the Iowa came from the Northeast. Having separated from their Ho-Chunk relatives, they made their home in present-day Iowa. The tribe was seminomadic and people lived in villages for some of the time, while groups also moved around the tribe's territory between the Mississippi and Missouri Rivers. They farmed, hunted, and fished, using both the skills of their woodland ancestors and new ones learned from life on the Plains. Boys helped their fathers, who taught them to hunt deer, turkey, and raccoon from an early age. Girls helped their mothers and other women in the fields, or with food preparation—most meals involved roasting meat or fish, or making soups.

Iowa people painted their faces for different reasons. Warriors applied designs and colors that would protect and inspire them in battle, while others painted their faces for ceremonies. Women wore dresses made from deerskin, which they decorated with designs made from beads or porcupine quills. They wore their hair long, in braids. Men often wore nothing more than a breechcloth. For hundreds of years, the Iowa lived a good life on the Plains, holding on to their lands despite attempts from other tribes to take their land from them.

In the early 1800s, the U.S. government forced many southeastern tribes to move west of the Mississippi River, and it was not long before the government wanted Iowa territory for white settlers. During the 1820s and 1830s, the tribe signed several treaties ceding its territory, and many Iowa moved to a reservation on the Kansas–Nebraska border. This tribe became the Iowa Tribe of Kansas and Nebraska. Other members of the tribe went to Missouri to avoid living on this reservation, but the government relocated them to Oklahoma in 1883, to make room for more settlers.

Today the two communities are reviving their traditions. In recent years, the Iowa Tribe of Oklahoma received money from the federal government to build a number of traditional homes on its land. Using the basic tools of their ancestors, including an antler rake and a bison scapula, the people constructed longhouses and bark houses together. They also created an Iowa garden in which they planted crops of squash, corn, and beans. By returning to the methods of their ancestors, the Iowa have gained deeper insight into their traditional way of life.

Following the traditions of his ancestors, this Iowa man has a shaved head with just a single braid from the crown of the head, called a "scalp lock." He wears a roach headdress made from porcupine hair and has painted his face with a striking design.

Some Iowa men wore turbans made from otter fur. This example has beaded edges and decorative patches stitched down its length.

IN THE KNOW

An Iowa woman named Marie Dorion acted as a guide, an interpreter, and a bridge between Natives and white settlers during the Astor Expedition (1811–1812). The expedition attempted to expand the fur trade from Missouri to the Pacific coast. She was the only female member of the group.

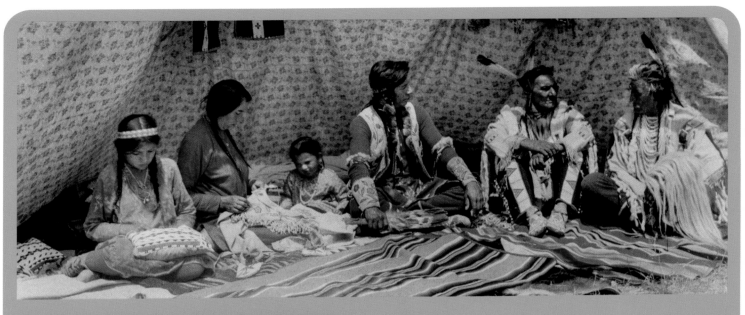

GROWING UP ON THE PLAINS

Parents and guardians play an important part in Plains family life. Children can have several fathers and mothers, since uncles and aunts take on these roles. In the same way, cousins are considered brothers and sisters. Children play, but also do chores, such as taking care of the dogs or helping with cooking. From a young age, they listen to stories told by the elders. Handed down through the generations, the tales teach tribal history and tell stories with moral lessons. In the past, male adults taught boys to hunt, while girls learned to make clothing from the women. Adults rewarded achievements with celebrations. A boy's first successful hunt and a girl's first well-prepared hide, which involved removing the hair and softening for use as clothing, were important milestones. Children learned their traditions and took on more responsibility as they grew older.

KAW

(KAH)

LANGUAGE GROUP:
Siouan

GREETING:
Hawé (f); *Ho* (m)

THANK YOU:
Wíblahaⁿ

LOCATION PRECONTACT:
Kansas, Iowa, Missouri, Nebraska

LOCATION TODAY:
Oklahoma

The Kaw people are the original people of Kansas. The tribal name, Kansa, means "people of the south wind." Kaw ancestors lived in the Ohio Valley, east of the Mississippi River, but moved to Kansas and parts of Iowa, Missouri, and Nebraska some time before the Europeans arrived. Kaw people lived in permanent villages along the Kansas River, in which they built earthen lodges. Once or twice a year the tribe would make hunting trips on the Plains, traveling great distances to catch buffalo. In winter, they hunted smaller game, including beavers, deer, and turkeys. Men often wore necklaces of animal claws or beads that they traded with other tribes.

Kaw warriors successfully protected their tribal homeland from raiding tribes, but in the early 1800s the U.S. government set its sights on it. In 1825, the Kaw signed a treaty giving up over ➡

Chief Monchousia was one of several Natives invited to meet President Monroe in the early 1820s. He was given the silver peace medallion he wears, bearing a portrait of the president.

Pipes, like this one, are smoked at the ceremonies of many Plains tribes. Pipe smoke rises upward, symbolizing a link between the earth and the sky.

In 1872, the U.S. government passed an act to remove the Kaw tribe from Kansas completely. The Kaw chief Allegawaho appealed to the U.S. government to allow the tribe to stay in its ancestral homeland, but his pleas did not work. The Kaw had to move to a reservation in present-day Oklahoma.

18 million acres (7 million ha) of land. Twenty years later, the tribe signed another treaty ceding two million more acres (800,000 ha). With their population diminished by disease, the remaining Kaw people moved to a small area of land near Council Grove, Kansas, while railroad companies and settlers moved onto the Kaw homelands.

Today, the Kaw tribe encourages its members to learn their native language, and released a language app in 2016. To honor Kaw history and culture, the tribe created the Allegawaho Memorial Heritage Park on the site of their ancestral village. The 168-acre (68-ha) park is home to the Kanza Monument, a 35-foot (10.5-m) tower built in honor of the tribe.

TRIBAL HISTORY

The elders say that Native peoples have lived in North America since "time immemorial," or for as long as anyone remembers. Ancestral histories from across North America explain how spirits created the Earth, animals, and people, and how everything is connected. For the Ojibwe, the Great Spirit, Kitchi Manitou, made the Earth and everything in it. In some Iroquois and Algonquian stories, the Earth began on the back of a giant turtle, creating "Turtle Island." Animals often play an important part in creation stories. The Pueblo, for example, tell a story of how the first people lived underground until the mole visited them and dug a tunnel back to the surface.

The coyote features in many Native stories. For many Plains tribes, the animal is often a trickster at the center of a cautionary tale. For the Mandan and Hidatsa tribes, Coyote is the form adopted by the First Creator, who, together with his cocreator, Lone Man, creates the world. For the Crow, Old Man Coyote is both a creator and a trickster. A Ute story tells the tale of Sinauf, a god who is half man and half wolf. Sinauf collects sticks and puts them into a magic bag, and the sticks turn into people. His brother, Coyote, cuts a hole in the bag and the people spread over the land. Stories like these are as important today as they were long ago. Tribal storytelling traditions pass on ancient wisdom and provide a special link between the past and the present.

KIOWA

(KYE-oh-wah)

LANGUAGE GROUP:
Kiowa-Tanoan

GREETING:
Háːcho

THANK YOU:
Aːhô

LOCATION PRECONTACT:
Oklahoma, Texas

LOCATION TODAY:
Oklahoma

The Kiowa language links this tribe to the Pueblo people of New Mexico. Records of Spanish exploration show that the Kiowa were living on the Plains by 1702. They were nomadic people, who moved around a large area of present-day Oklahoma and Texas. By the early 1800s, they had become allies with their neighbors, the Comanche.

Like the Comanche, the Kiowa bands traveled and hunted on horseback, following migrating buffalo herds. They built up substantial herds of horses, which they raided from Mexicans and enemy tribes. They trained some horses for their own use and traded others. The tribe was known not just for its horse trading, but also for the beautiful, beaded items made by Kiowa women, including moccasins, baby carriers, and clothes trimmed with shells. Beading traditions continue today. Using tiny seed beads and slightly larger pony beads, women stitch designs onto clothing to create geometric patterns—on a pair of moccasins, for example, or on a long fringe at the top of a legging.

Kiowa warriors were famously brave, often fighting tribes—such as the Osage, who tried to move into their territory—and opposing white settlers. The U.S. government negotiated peace among the warring tribes in the mid-1800s, but

CHRIS WONDOLOWSKI

Major League Soccer player Chris Wondolowski, aka Wondo, is a member of the Kiowa Nation. His Kiowa name is Bau Daigh, which means "warrior coming over the hill." The soccer forward, who plays for the San Jose Earthquakes, won the league's Most Valuable Player title in 2012, and was the first American Indian to play in the World Cup. Chris's brother Stephen Wondolowski also plays professional soccer.

European settlers continued to invade Kiowa lands. The Treaty of Medicine Lodge, in 1867, banned white hunters and promised benefits to the Kiowa if the tribe agreed to settle on a reservation. The government did not honor the treaty, however, and the Kiowa resorted to raiding in order to survive. Raids continued in Texas into 1870, and one of the most famous Kiowa warriors, Satanta, was imprisoned for his role in killing a number of men during a raid on a wagon train. He died in prison in 1878.

Today, the Kiowa live in Oklahoma near the Comanche and Apache tribes. As a way of earning income, they lease much of their land for ranching, farming, and oil drilling. ☞

Lone Wolf, also known as Guipago, was chief of the Kiowa tribe in the 1860s and 1870s. He led the tribe's warriors in raids against other tribes. He is pictured seated with his wife, Etla.

MANDAN

(MAN-dun)

LANGUAGE GROUP:
Siouan

GREETING:
Háu

THANK YOU:
Nátkashi

LOCATION PRECONTACT:
North Dakota

LOCATION TODAY:
North Dakota

Originally from the east or southern Great Lakes region, the Mandan tribe migrated and settled in villages along the Missouri River in around 1400. They grew crops of corn, squash, beans, and sunflowers, which they traded for fresh meat and supplies. Once a year, the tribe headed into the Plains to hunt buffalo, drying much of the meat to help them survive the winters. They made round boats, called bull boats, in which to ferry their catch across the Missouri River. Along with the Arikara and Hidatsa tribes, the Mandan established a busy trading center that attracted tribes from all over the Plains as well as European explorers and traders using the Missouri River. The explorers Lewis and Clark found the Mandan friendly and hospitable. For much of the year, the tribe lived

This 20th-century pitcher was made by Sadie Young Bear Mann, a Mandan potter at the Three Tribes Pottery and Stoneware Company established by the Mandan, Hidatsa, and Arikara tribes.

MATO'-TOPE

Mato'-Tope, or Chief Four Bears, was a famously brave warrior and Mandan leader in the early 1800s. His name, "Four Bears," is believed to be a reference to his strength when charging at the enemy. He is known for wearing a robe covered with illustrations depicting his battles. In 1837, Mato'-Tope died from smallpox, the disease that killed most of his tribe.

in villages where they built earthen lodges. These homes were partially underground and housed several related families. Mandan communities followed a clan system that was passed down through the mother.

A smallpox epidemic brought on by interaction with the Europeans swept through the Upper Missouri River area in 1837, killing almost all the Mandan people. The Hidatsa and Arikara suffered similar losses, so the three tribes moved close together for protection and support. In 1851, the U.S. government assigned a small area of land to the Mandan, Hidatsa, and Arikara, who then became known as the Three Affiliated Tribes. Twenty years later, their land became the Fort Berthold Reservation, and this was reduced even further in size when the U.S. government completed the Garrison Dam on the Missouri River in 1954. The Mandan still live on the Fort Berthold Reservation, with lands on both sides of the Missouri River. Some Mandan people live in New Town, North Dakota.

The Mandan built their bull boats from sticks of willow, bending the wood to make a circular frame. They stretched a buffalo hide over the frame, so that the fur acted as a waterproof layer.

MIAMI

(my-AM-ee)

LANGUAGE GROUP:
Algonquian

GREETING:
Aya

THANK YOU:
Neewe

LOCATION PRECONTACT:
Indiana, Illinois, Ohio, Wisconsin, Michigan

LOCATION TODAY:
Oklahoma

This Miami hand tool is actually the jaw of a deer, filled with the animal's original teeth. The tool would have been used for scraping the kernels from fresh ears of corn.

Originally, the Miami tribe's homelands extended over a large area of modern Indiana, Illinois, Ohio, Wisconsin, and Michigan. Several bands spread out across this territory, using the resources around them. They planted crops and hunted for food, and traveled frequently on the region's waterways in dugout canoes. During the spring and summer, women collected maple syrup, grew vegetables such as corn, and gathered berries. After the corn harvest, the tribe moved to winter grounds, where the men hunted buffalo and elk. In the early days of hunting, before the tribe had horses, Miami men would trap buffalo inside a ring of fire before shooting at them with their bows and arrows. Often, the women and children of the tribe would accompany the men on the hunt to prepare the hides and meat for transporting back to the village.

This life continued well into the 1600s, at which point the Miami formed close relationships with French explorers, traders, and missionaries. After 1763, the British took ownership of French territory in North America, and the Miami then began trading with them. During the Revolutionary War, the Miami fought alongside the British against the Patriots. When the British lost, the Miami continued to fight against the United States—and against white settlers encroaching on their territory.

The Miami tribe and its Native allies won several victories against U.S. troops in the 1700s, but they met with catastrophic defeat at the Battle of Fallen Timbers in 1794 and were forced to sign the Treaty of Greenville, along with other tribes. This treaty ceded all Miami lands to the government. In 1840, the Indian Removal Act forced the Miami to move to present-day Kansas and then to present-day Oklahoma in 1867. Some tribal members stayed behind in Kansas and are now known as the Miami Nation of Indiana.

Today, members of the Miami tribe live all over the United States, although the Miami Tribe of Oklahoma is the only Miami community to have federal recognition. On their reservation they raise cattle and look after pecan groves on 1,000 acres (400 ha) of land. The tribe practices and teaches its language and arts across the country.

In 2001, the tribe started the Myaamia Project, now the Myaamia Center, an educational and research organization working with the University of Miami in Oxford, Ohio.

This Miami chief wears a turban-style headdress. In one hand he holds a spear, possibly used for dancing or warfare; in the other, he clutches a war club.

IN THE KNOW

The Miami tribe publishes its own newspaper, *Atotankiki Myaamiaki*, which translates as "What the Miami Are Talking About." Printed four times a year, the paper is mailed to each tribal household.

THE PLAINS

CLOTHING

Women made clothes for their families from tanned buffalo, deer, and antelope hides. Men wore shirts or tunics (pictured) and women wore dresses. Both wore leggings and buffalo robes, a cross between a blanket and a cloak. On their feet, they wore moccasins made from pieces of hide sewn together. Women decorated clothes and moccasins with quills and, later, beads. Tanning was another job for women. It was a long and difficult process of cleaning, stretching, scraping, and soaking hides to make them soft enough to fashion into clothes.

Plains peoples wore many types of headdresses, including woven basketry hats and porcupine roaches. The best-known style—frequently worn today at powwows—was the eagle-feather headdress, or warbonnet, on which each eagle feather represented a success in battle for the warrior.

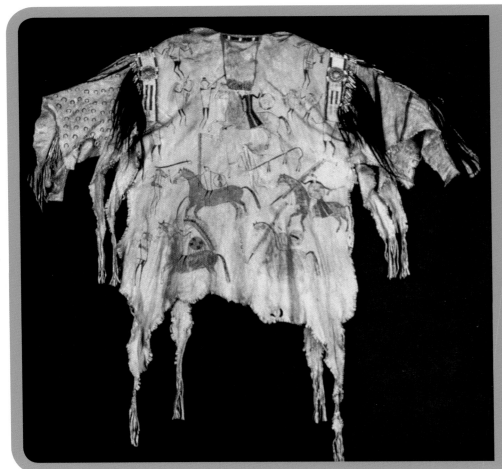

MODOC

(MO-dock)

LANGUAGE GROUP:
Penutian

GREETING:
Waq lis ?i

THANK YOU:
Sepk'eec'a

LOCATION PRECONTACT:
California, Oregon

LOCATION TODAY:
Oklahoma

The Modoc lived on about 5,000 square miles (13,000 sq km) of mountains, forests, flatlands, and lava beds in what is now southern Oregon and northern California.

Seminomadic, the small tribe moved between the best fishing, foraging, and hunting grounds and defended their land against raiding tribes such as the Klamath, to the south. There were three bands within the tribe: the Gumbatwa, the "people of the west"; the Paskanwa, the "river people"; and the Kokiwa, the "people of the far out country." They worked with European fur traders and later befriended settlers and ranchers. Finding the ways of the newcomers appealing, the Modoc began wearing European-style clothes and taking non-Native names. One chief, Kientpoos, became known as Captain Jack.

As more white settlers moved onto Modoc lands, the U.S. government forced the peaceful tribe to sign a treaty in 1864 that ceded their lands. The government assigned reservation land for the Modoc and the Klamath, who had also given up their land. The reservation did not have nearly enough resources for both tribes and, when tensions arose, Captain Jack decided to lead a small band of Modoc back to their ancestral land by the Lost River in northern California. The government sent troops to return the group to the reservation,

This Modoc bow and arrow may have been used for ceremonial purposes. The bow is carved from wood and wrapped in cotton cloth. The geometric patterning on its surface is made using tiny glass beads.

Toby Riddle (standing center), also known as Kaitchkana, married a white settler, Frank Riddle (top left). She was an interpreter and peacemaker during the Modoc War.

and this led to the Modoc War in 1872. The small group fought off the U.S. Army for eight months, but surrendered in 1873. The government hanged the leaders, including Captain Jack, and sent the remaining Modoc to Oklahoma. In 1891, just 68 tribal members remained, and in the 1950s the Modoc lost their tribal status as a result of the government's "termination" policy. It was restored in 1978. Today, the small but proud Modoc Tribe of Oklahoma guards its heritage. In recent years, Modoc ranchers have reintroduced buffalo to their 600-acre (240-ha) Modoc Reservation.

OMAHA

(OH-muh-hah)

LANGUAGE GROUP:
Siouan

GREETING:
Hó

THANK YOU:
Hó

LOCATION PRECONTACT:
Iowa, Nebraska

LOCATION TODAY:
Nebraska

The Omaha, Kansa, Osage, Ponca, and Quapaw were once one people. Separating from the group in around 1600, the Omaha moved to an area in what is now northwestern Iowa, where they developed their own language and culture. There were two groups within the tribe: the Insta'shunda, "Sky People," and the Hon'gashenu, "Earth People." The Sky People looked after the tribe's spiritual needs while the Earth People took care of their physical needs, such as food and shelter. In Iowa they built winter villages. Families lived together in earthen houses arranged in a circle around a central plaza.

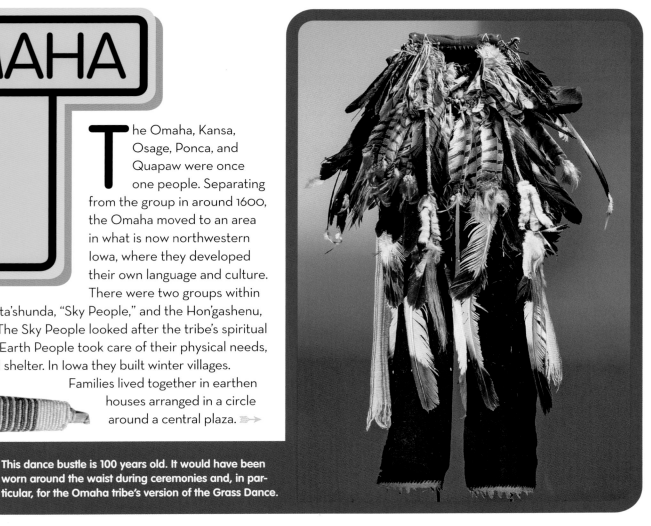

This dance bustle is 100 years old. It would have been worn around the waist during ceremonies and, in particular, for the Omaha tribe's version of the Grass Dance.

The tribe fished in rivers, but also depended on beans and several varieties of corn and other crops. Once they had horses, they could travel farther away to catch buffalo. During the 1700s, the Omaha cultivated a good trading relationship with the French and, later, with the Spanish. When raiding Sioux parties forced them to move into present-day Nebraska, they traded goods from a large village they established, called Ton-wa-tonga. Their relationship with the Europeans led to a devastating smallpox epidemic, which killed many members of the tribe.

From 1831 to 1854, the Omaha signed treaties ceding their lands to the U.S. government. The last treaty assigned a reservation for the tribe in Thurston County, Nebraska. Today, the Omaha Nation manages a farm and a recreation and hunting ground on its reservation lands. ☞

Omaha member Neal Sheridan poses in his Men's Fancy Dance outfit. His feather bustles have long fringes that flow freely during the fast-paced dance.

PEOPLE OF THE HORSE

Wild horses lived in ancient North America, but died out more than 8,000 years ago. In the early 1500s, the Spanish reintroduced them to Mexico, bringing them from Europe. When the Pueblos chased the Spanish out of New Mexico in 1680, they released their horses into the wild by the thousands. The Comanche and other tribes eventually started to capture and domesticate these wild horses. The horse became as much a part of Plains life as the buffalo. It became easier for mounted hunters to chase and capture prey. The horse made traveling better, too, since horses could carry heavy burdens. Within a short time, the horse became part of the war culture on the Plains, as parties of mounted warriors raided other tribes. Although the days of the great horse culture are over, a number of tribes, such as the Nez Perce in the Great Basin region, continue to breed horses. Several of today's breeds have Native ancestry. These include the Nakota and the American Quarter Horse.

OSAGE

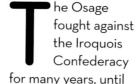

(oh-SAGE)

LANGUAGE GROUP:
Siouan

GREETING:
Hawé

THANK YOU:
Wéewiṇa

LOCATION PRECONTACT:
Arkansas, Kansas,
Nebraska, Oklahoma

LOCATION TODAY:
Oklahoma

The Osage fought against the Iroquois Confederacy for many years, until finally moving west from the Ohio River Valley. Breaking away from a larger group that included the Ponca, Kansa, Omaha, and Quapaw, the Osage settled over parts of present-day Arkansas, Kansas, Nebraska, and Oklahoma. The tribe lived a seminomadic, mostly agricultural life. They planted and harvested crops in the land surrounding their villages and, once or twice a year, headed onto the Plains to hunt buffalo. Each village had a war chief and a peace chief. Inside their villages, they built pole-framed longhouses with hide or woven-mat coverings. The tribe had horses and harvested a wood called Osage orange (after the tribe), which was ideal for making bows.

The Osage tribe formed a strong relationship with French traders, exchanging furs for guns and other European goods. When the French fought the Algonquian tribes to the east, Osage warriors joined them, and in 1725, the French brought some Osage chiefs and warriors to Paris. The tribe was less welcoming to the Spanish, who arrived in the mid-1700s and whom they saw as a threat to the French. The Spanish had to employ French traders as go-betweens with the tribe.

After the Revolutionary War, the new U.S. government sought to extend its control in the West. The Osage signed three treaties in 1808, 1818, and 1825, ceding much of their land. The treaty signed in 1825 allocated a site in Kansas for the tribe, but the terrible conditions there deprived the tribe of its traditional food sources and medicines. The Drum Creek Treaty of 1868 brought further land losses and, in 1870, the Osage sold their

When the U.S. government divided Osage land into allotments, Chief Bigheart (pictured) retained rights to whatever lay beneath the surface. When oil was later found on the land, the Osage were able to claim it.

MARIA TALLCHIEF

The first Native American prima ballerina, Maria Tallchief, was born on the Osage Reservation in Oklahoma in 1925. When she was eight years old, her family moved to California, where she and her sister both learned to dance. Maria Tallchief became the prima ballerina of the New York Ballet in 1947 and, in 1999, the government awarded her the prestigious National Medal of Arts for her work mentoring children and young adults.

land in Kansas to buy land in Oklahoma, where they could make a new start. In 1897, oil was found on the Osage Reservation. Although this led to a huge upsurge in the Osage economy, many tribal members were cheated out of money and land during the boom. Today, the tribe oversees the resources on its land and its other businesses. Among the ancient traditions still upheld by the tribe today is the I'n L'on Schka Dance, which involves the coming together of three drums—one from each of three families—each played by an eldest son. The event is marked by drumming, dancing, and singing of songs passed down through the generations.

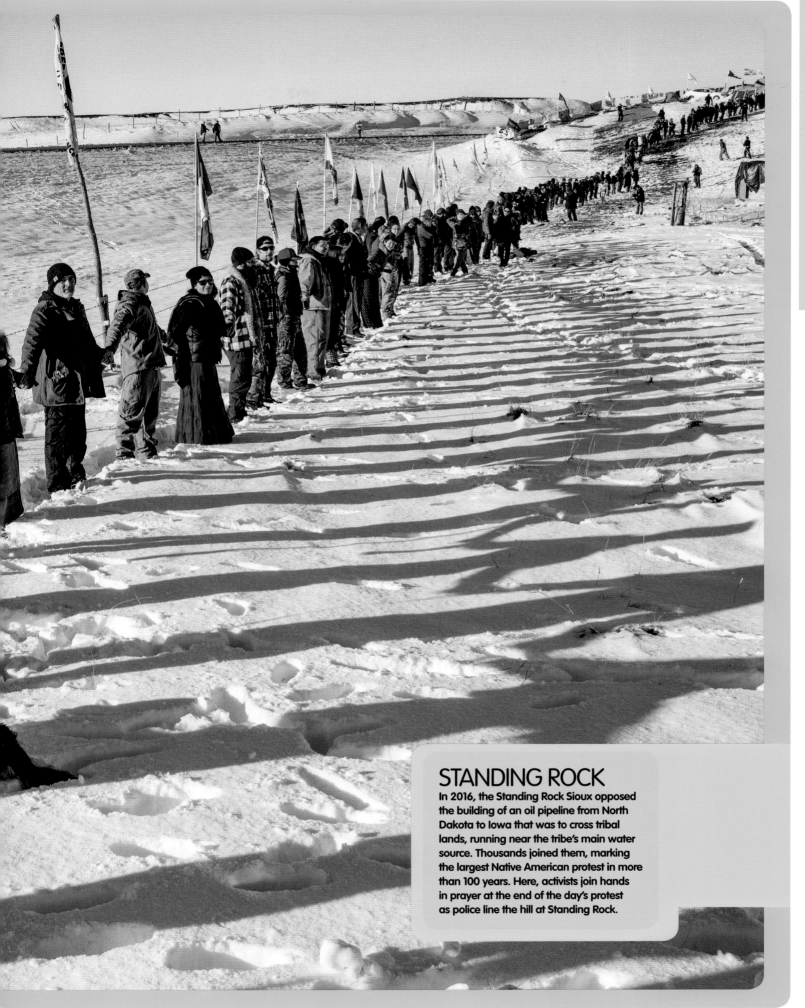

STANDING ROCK

In 2016, the Standing Rock Sioux opposed the building of an oil pipeline from North Dakota to Iowa that was to cross tribal lands, running near the tribe's main water source. Thousands joined them, marking the largest Native American protest in more than 100 years. Here, activists join hands in prayer at the end of the day's protest as police line the hill at Standing Rock.

OTOE-MISSOURIA

(oh-TOE-mi-ZOAR-ee-ah)

LANGUAGE GROUP:
Siouan

GREETING:
Aha (f); *Aho* (m)

THANK YOU:
Warigroxi

LOCATION PRECONTACT:
Missouri, Iowa, Minnesota

LOCATION TODAY:
Oklahoma

The Otoe-Missouria existed originally as two separate tribes in the Great Lakes area. The Otoe lived on the present-day border of Minnesota and Iowa, while the Missouria were based in present-day Missouri. The Otoe moved farther south into Nebraska, where they adapted to a life on the Plains and began trading with the French. Meanwhile, the Missouria farmed, hunted, and traded along the Platte River. The two tribes lived separately until the early 1800s. By this time, the Missouria had suffered many attacks by the Sac and Fox tribes, including one ambush that killed many people. Soon after this, smallpox broke out in Missouria villages. Some survivors moved to Osage and Kaw villages, but most decided to join the Otoe tribe. Settling in permanent villages, the tribes built earthen lodges and followed the seasons for planting crops and harvesting. The men made two buffalo-hunting trips a year.

American settlers began moving onto Otoe-Missouria land in the 1800s. Under pressure from the U.S. government, the Otoe-Missouria signed their first treaty in 1830. Another treaty, in 1854, assigned a reservation for the tribe on the Big Blue River, on the Kansas–Nebraska border. Having lost both their land and their way of life, the Otoe-Missouria struggled to survive. They were expected to farm instead of hunt, and government support and supplies did not arrive as promised. In 1881, the tribe split into two groups: the Quaker band, who had converted to the Quaker religion, and the Coyote band, who continued to follow traditional spiritual practices. The Quaker band sold land in order to buy a reservation in Oklahoma, where the Coyote band later joined them. The two bands are now reunited as the Otoe-Missouria Tribe, and gained official tribal status in 1984.

This coat style emerged among Plains tribes in the 1890s. The decorations represent tribal traditions, such as performing the Buffalo Dance.

Otoe tribal members stand in front of a tepee. The men wear roach-style headdresses. The woman is dressed in white buckskin and wears a warbonnet-style headdress.

PAWNEE

(PAW-nee)

LANGUAGE GROUP:
Caddoan

GREETING:
Kee ka <oos

THANK YOU:
I<i way too <a hay

LOCATION PRECONTACT:
Nebraska, Kansas

LOCATION TODAY:
Oklahoma

Chief Sharitarish was a member of the Chaui band of Pawnee peoples. He was one of a line of Pawnee chiefs who inherited the position through family lines. His head is shaved and his face painted red, to give the appearance of wearing a mask.

Four separate bands made up the Pawnee Nation on the central Plains: Chaui, "grand"; Kitkehahki, or "republican"; Pitahawirata, "noisy"; and Skidi, "wolf." The Pawnee tribe numbered about 12,000 people, divided into bands that lived in their own villages across large parts of present-day Nebraska and Kansas. In their villages, the Pawnee lived in large family groups in earthen lodges. They grew corn and other crops. In fall, after the harvest, village groups moved across the Plains to hunt, traveling far once they had acquired horses. As in other Plains tribes, Pawnee women decorated buffalo-skin clothing with porcupine quills. They also made pottery from clay they took from riverbeds and scratched decorations into the surface using tools made from animal bones.

Despite their large population, the Pawnee had to defend their lands against attacks from other tribes, such as the Lakota Sioux. They were friendly to all Europeans and traded with the Spanish, French, and British. Following the Revolutionary War and the Louisiana Purchase, American settlers started moving into the West, encroaching on Pawnee territory. Between 1818 and 1875, the Pawnee signed a number of treaties that ceded most of their land to the U.S. government. In spite of this, the Pawnee remained friendly toward the United States, even acting as scouts for the U.S. Army during the Civil War and in later wars against the Sioux.

After the last treaty, in 1875, the U.S. government assigned a small reservation for the Pawnee in Nebraska. By then the tribe was much smaller and an easy target for the Lakota Sioux, who continued to attack. In 1875, the Pawnee moved to Oklahoma, where the four bands still live together. At the Pawnee Indian Museum State Historic Site in Kansas stands a reconstructed village from the 1700s. In 2016, the Oklahoma Military Hall of Fame inducted the Pawnee code talkers for their help during World War II. These servicemen had used their native language to send secret, coded information. 🖎

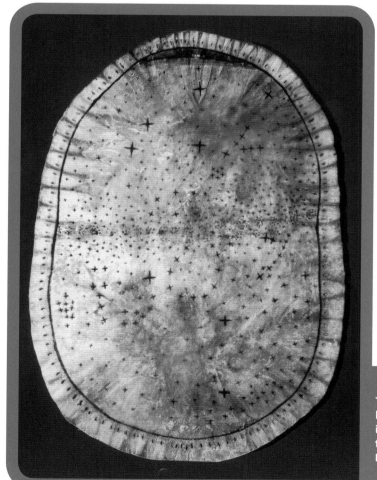

The painted marks on this Pawnee buckskin sky chart represent stars in the night sky. Among them are the North Star and those of the Big and Little Dippers.

💡 IN THE KNOW

The Pawnee and other Plains tribes had medicine bundles for their important ceremonies. They contained sacred objects that might include animal bones, a stone pipe, and/or feathers. Each item had special significance when used during a ritual.

PEORIA

(pee-OR-ria)

LANGUAGE GROUP:
Algonquian

LANGUAGE:
Currently being revived; no dictionary or word lists available

LOCATION PRECONTACT:
Illinois

LOCATION TODAY:
Oklahoma

The ancestors of the Peoria belonged to the Illinois Confederacy, which also included the Kaskaskia, Wea, Piankeshaw, and Tamaroa tribes. By the 1600s, having migrated from the coast of the Atlantic Ocean to the southern Great Lakes, the Peoria were living in present-day Illinois.

French explorers met the tribe in the 1670s and named them Peoria, for the tribal name *piwarea*. It means "he comes carrying a pack on his back," and probably relates to packs the tribe carried when traveling to hunt buffalo. This early meeting with the Europeans led to a long trading relationship.

After 1763, the British took control of the French forts and some Peoria moved to present-day Missouri. Others stayed where they were, but in 1832, the tribe signed the Treaty of Lewisville, giving up lands in Illinois and Missouri to the U.S. government. After the treaty, the Peoria moved to a reservation in Kansas

with their cousins, the Kaskaskia, Piankeshaw, and Wea tribes, who also became known as the Peoria. In 1867, the tribe signed another treaty, agreeing to move to Indian Territory in present-day Oklahoma. The tribe bought land there and settled in the northeast of the territory.

After regaining their tribal status in 1978, the Peoria Tribe of Native Americans focused on strengthening its identity and culture. Today, the Peoria own a golf course and other businesses and are working to revive their language. 🖎

This Peoria hair ornament has decorative metal studs and was probably once part of a dance outfit.

A Peoria man offers a European settler the calumet, or peace pipe. Such pipes were used at meetings or ceremonies. It was believed that all participants would speak truthfully and that the smoke would carry any bad thoughts away.

MODERN CELEBRATIONS

Powwows are modern celebrations of culture, history, and spirituality. The word "powwow" may come from the Narragansett words *pau wau*, meaning "gathering of spiritual leaders."

The first powwows were deeply religious events and may have roots in the Omaha tribe's Grass Dance, performed by warriors after a victory. Warriors wore headdresses and belts of grasses as they danced and sang. The dance evolved, or changed, over time and spread across the Plains. Gradually, tribes added more dances and ceremonies. Today, tribes across North America hold powwows. Women and children now participate in these annual events, which welcome non-Native visitors and include feasting, games, and honoring ceremonies. Men wear their finest ceremonial regalia to compete in the Men's Fancy Dance, while women dance the Jingle Dance, wearing dresses adorned with metal cones. Tribes also perform the Grass Dance, among many other types of dances.

PLAINS CREE

(CREE, to rhyme with see)

LANGUAGE GROUP:
Algonquian

GREETING:
Tânisi

THANK YOU:
Kitatamihin

LOCATION PRECONTACT:
Montana, North Dakota; Alberta, Saskatchewan, Manitoba (Canada)

LOCATION TODAY:
Montana, North Dakota (U.S.); British Columbia, Alberta, Saskatchewan, Manitoba (Canada)

The Plains Cree are related to several other Cree tribes, including the Cree of subarctic Canada. They all used to belong to one group, living in the subarctic region. Over time, the Plains Cree split off from this main group and migrated west, settling in hundreds of villages across what is now central Canada and the northern United States. Plains Cree people who moved to northern Minnesota increased their power and territory by joining with the Assiniboine and Ojibwe. Gradually, the tribe lost its woodland hunter-gatherer lifestyle and adapted to the environment of the Plains. The Plains Cree roamed over such a large territory that they did not have a central government under one leader. Instead, they chose war chiefs and had a society of the bravest warriors, called ➤

The motifs, or symbols, at the center of this Plains Cree shield may symbolize the sun and the moon. Plains warriors often painted their shields with images representing the spirits they believed would guide them to victory during war.

strips for drying. Plains people, including the Cree, made pemmican, a high-energy mixture of dried meat, berries, and animal fat that was very nutritious and lasted a long time.

Because the Cree were so scattered, some bands avoided disease, settlers, and land takeovers for many years. However, this changed in the late 1800s, when the buffalo were almost wiped out, endangering the Cree way of life. Many Cree eventually settled on or off reserves in Canada. In the United States, the Cree were forced to move with the Ojibwe to the Turtle Mountain Reservation in North Dakota, where Cree people still live today. At the same time, many Cree remained landless in Montana. Today, the Rocky Boy Reservation in Montana is home to a community of Cree and Chippewa people.

okichitatawak, "worthy young men." Their war chiefs usually earned their high positions in tribal society by being the best hunters and decision-makers.

Like other Plains tribes, the Cree used horses for covering large distances and the buffalo became their main source of food. It was customary to eat the more perishable parts of the buffalo first—heart, tongue, and kidneys. The shoulder was also prized and eaten first. The rest of the meat would be cut into

PONCA

(PONG-kah)

LANGUAGE GROUP:
Siouan

GREETING:
Hó

THANK YOU:
Hó

LOCATION PRECONTACT:
Kentucky, Indiana, Nebraska

LOCATION TODAY:
Oklahoma, Nebraska

The Ponca, Omaha, Kansa, Osage, and Quapaw tribes all share common ancestors. The five tribes separated around 1600 and moved into several different areas. The Ponca settled close to their cousins, the Omaha, along the Upper Missouri River.

Living in earthen lodges, the Ponca farmed the fertile banks of the river, growing crops of squash, corn, beans, pumpkins, and tobacco. Twice a year, members of the tribe traveled onto the Plains to hunt buffalo together. Culturally, the Ponca were similar to the Omaha, in that they had hereditary chiefs and operated a clan system passed down through a father. Among their celebrations and ceremonies was the Sacred Pipe Ceremony, still practiced today in order to create a link between the earthly and spiritual worlds. Among their crafts were pottery pieces and willow or rush baskets. The tribe was traditionally small, numbering only about 800 people; larger tribes, especially the Sioux, took advantage of this and frequently raided the Ponca, stealing the few supplies they had.

CHIEF STANDING BEAR

In 1878, Chief Standing Bear and a small group of tribal members returned to Nebraska to bury the chief's son in his homeland. The U.S. Army arrested Standing Bear for leaving the reservation in Oklahoma without permission—at the time, Native peoples had to request permission to do so. Standing Bear argued against his unfair arrest. He took legal action against the government of the United States and won—not on the battlefield but in the courtroom. The event marked the first time a Native person was accorded the equal rights of all Americans in a court of law.

"Rabbit" is a contemporary sculpture by Dan SaSuWeh Jones of the Ponca tribe. The plaque features Rabbit, a hero or trickster character in some Ponca stories. The plaque represents major stages in Rabbit's life from birth to old age.

Like other tribes along the Missouri River, the Ponca engaged in the fur trade in the 1700s. They also experienced the smallpox epidemics that took many lives. When the explorers Lewis and Clark met the Ponca in 1804, they estimated that the tribe numbered just 200 people.

Still facing pressure from Sioux raids, the Ponca signed their first treaty with the U.S. government in 1817. Although this was an agreement of friendship and peace, subsequent treaties in 1825, 1858, and 1865 took away Ponca land. The government agreed to provide a reservation for the Ponca on the Niobrara River, which runs through present-day Nebraska and Wyoming, a site the tribe chose for themselves. This became a problem, however, when the government signed the Treaty of Fort Laramie with the Sioux in 1868: This treaty reassigned the land given to the Ponca to the Sioux.

The government decided that the Ponca should move to present-day Oklahoma rather than face a fight with the Sioux. Despite this, for almost 10 years, the Ponca held on in Nebraska. Finally, in 1877, the U.S. Army forced the tribe to leave for Oklahoma. After Chief Standing Bear's protest, the government assigned a reservation in Nebraska. Some Ponca moved there and others stayed in Oklahoma. ☞

QUAPAW

(QUAW-paw)

LANGUAGE GROUP:
Siouan

GREETING:
Hawé

THANK YOU:
Kaniké

LOCATION PRECONTACT:
Arkansas

LOCATION TODAY:
Oklahoma

In about 1200, the Quapaw moved to present-day Arkansas from the Ohio River Valley. For about 300 years, this small tribe enjoyed a rich life there. They lived in villages along the Mississippi River, near the Arkansas River—their name comes from a word meaning "downstream people." In this area, they developed a successful farming culture. They also forged good trading relationships with other tribes, such as the Chickasaw and the Tunica, on the opposite bank of the Mississippi River.

Like other Mississippi tribes, the Quapaw lived in palisaded, or fenced-in, villages where they built mounds in which to bury important members of the tribe, and for their temples.

The tribe was known for its pottery, particularly animal-shaped and head-shaped pots. Once the Quapaw acquired horses, they hunted buffalo on the Plains. Like many tribes of the Plains—and other regions—the Quapaw followed a clan system that continues to operate today. Within society there are Sky People, whose clans include the Fish and the Turtle, and Earth People, whose clans include the Serpent, the Elk, the Crawfish, and the Wolf. Each clan has its own responsibilities, with children inheriting their father's clan. ➤

This Quapaw ceramic bottle is at least 400 years old. The interwoven swirls of red and white are said to represent opposites—dark and light, for example, or earth and sky.

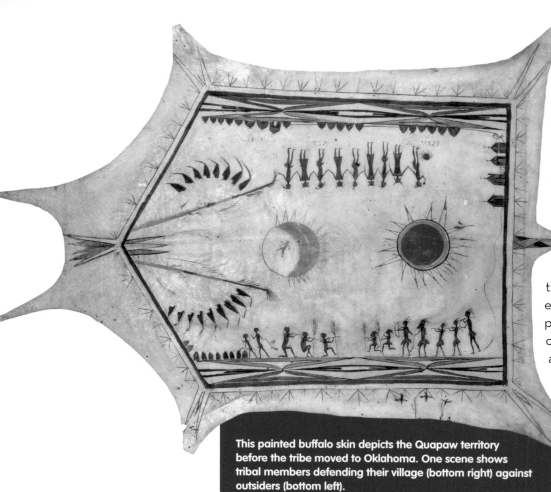

This painted buffalo skin depicts the Quapaw territory before the tribe moved to Oklahoma. One scene shows tribal members defending their village (bottom right) against outsiders (bottom left).

The Spanish, who met the Quapaw in the mid-1500s, disturbed this settled life by bringing disease to the tribe. Although many died, the tribe managed to survive and gradually became strong again. Over a century later, they welcomed French traders and missionaries and formed a special bond with them. Many Quapaw converted to Catholicism.

After signing treaties in the 1800s, the Quapaw ceded their lands in Arkansas to the U.S. government and moved to a reservation in present-day Oklahoma. The tribe now owns a cattle company, raising cattle and buffalo, as well as gaming and tourism facilities. Elders have passed down the oral history of the tribe and there are regular language lessons for children. In addition, an online resource includes a Quapaw dictionary and historical accounts of tribal life. 🖝

SAC & FOX

(SACK and FOX)

LANGUAGE GROUP:
Algonquian

GREETING:
Ahô! (Sac)

THANK YOU:
Kewâwiyâmene! (Sac)

LOCATION PRECONTACT:
Wisconsin

LOCATION TODAY:
Iowa, Kansas, Nebraska, Oklahoma; Mexico

Originally, the Sac and Fox tribes were related to, but independent from, tribes from the Northeast. The Sac, who called themselves Osa'kiwug, "people of the yellow earth," lived in present-day Wisconsin. They followed a seminomadic lifestyle. In the summer, they lived in bark-covered wigwams in villages and fished in local rivers. In winter, they went out hunting on the prairies of the Mississippi Valley, where they built temporary, reed-covered wigwams on their campgrounds for shelter. The Fox, who called themselves Meshkwa Kihug, "people of the red earth," came from an area around present-day Green Bay, Wisconsin.

The French called the Meshkwa Kihug "Fox," after one of the tribe's most

Chief Keokuk was a member of the Sac tribe who rose to his position through merit rather than inheritance. He holds an impressive coup stick as evidence of this.

KEOKUK
CHIEF OF THE SACS & FOXES

These Sac and Fox moccasins date from the 1880s. They are made from deerskin and are almost completely covered in tiny glass beads. The design features colorful abstract motifs as well as geometric patterning.

powerful clans, which lived along the Fox River, a route for French traders. The French were close to the Ojibwe tribe, who were enemies of the Fox, and in 1690, a long war began between the Fox and the French, who were aided by the Ojibwe and Dakota Sioux. The French and their allies attacked again and again, reducing the Fox population from 20,000 to just 500 by 1734. The tribe had no option but to unite with the Sac for protection.

The Sac and Fox signed a treaty with the U.S. government in 1825, but they intended to keep hold of most of their lands. However, after the Black Hawk Rebellion in 1832, the U.S. government forced the tribe to cede even more land than they originally agreed to and to move west. In 1842, some Sac and Fox people agreed to live on a reservation in Kansas, while others returned to Iowa or moved to Mexico, to live with other tribes. In 1867 the government moved the Kansas community to a new reservation in Oklahoma. The tribe now lives in communities in Oklahoma, Iowa, and elsewhere. Besides holding an annual powwow, tribal members on the Sac and Fox Reservation in Oklahoma continue to observe ancient traditions, holding ceremonies to celebrate clan feasts, the naming of newborn babies, and funerals. They also have an extensive online Sac dictionary. ✐

THE WINTER COUNT

Plains tribes found several ways to record their histories using picture symbols. For example, they made rock drawings and carvings, some of which are thousands of years old. One special recording device was the Winter Count, a type of calendar made on a buffalo hide. For the Sioux, a year began with the first snowfall and ended with the next snow. Their word for this was *waniyetu*, which translates as "a winter."

Pictures and symbols on the Winter Count told the stories of events that happened throughout the year and included such things as war victories, droughts, and the appearance of shooting stars. Scenes from a buffalo hunt are pictured here. People recognized the year on a Winter Count from events that it pictured. One person, the keeper, stored the Winter Counts. Eventually, tribes kept records on cloth and then paper.

SHAWNEE

(shaw-NEE)

LANGUAGE GROUP:
Algonquian

GREETING:
Hatito (Eastern)

THANK YOU:
Niyaawe (Eastern)

LOCATION PRECONTACT:
Ohio, Kentucky, Indiana

LOCATION TODAY:
Oklahoma

Three bands of the Shawnee tribe live in Oklahoma today: the Eastern Shawnee, the Loyal Shawnee, and the Absentee Shawnee. Another band, the Shawnee Nation United Remnant Band, lives in Ohio, but does not have federal tribal status. These separate communities developed after years of attempted takeover from settlers and other tribes, as well as war and treaties.

Originally, the Shawnee tribe lived in two major bands on either side of the Appalachian Mountains, from Tennessee to South Carolina. The men traveled long distances to hunt, while the women grew crops. They lived in wigwams—circular shelters made from wooden poles covered with birchbark or hides. As English settlers moved into their territory in the late 1600s, the Shawnee moved north into the Ohio Valley and Pennsylvania.

In the 1700s, desperate to protect their lands and their people, the Shawnee became involved in the struggle for control over North America. Many Shawnee warriors joined the French to fight against the British in the French and Indian War (1754–1763). Later, they fought with the British in the Revolutionary War, hoping their loyalty would help save their homelands if the British won. When the British lost the war, the Shawnee joined

TECUMSEH

Born around 1768, the Shawnee chief Tecumseh grew up amidst the warfare of the Ohio Valley region in the late 1700s. His father was killed in battle during the French and Indian War. From the early 1800s, Tecumseh was horrified to see tribes giving up their land to the Americans. He worked with his brother, Tenskwatawa, to persuade tribes to join them in taking a stand against the Americans. He led a large rebellion against western expansion in the early 1800s but, despite some victories, American troops defeated the rebels at the Battle of Tippecanoe in 1811, burning the Shawnee village of Prophetstown. Tecumseh joined the British to fight, but died at the Battle of the Thames in 1813.

other tribes to defend the Ohio Valley against the Americans, who wanted to settle on their lands. In 1791, Chief Bluejacket led his warriors to victory at the Battle of the Wabash, but the U.S. Army defeated the Shawnee and others that same year.

The Treaty of Greenville in 1795 ceded much of Ohio to the U.S. government. Some Shawnee fled to live with other tribes. In 1831, the remaining Ohio Shawnee signed another treaty with the U.S. government and agreed to move to a reservation in Oklahoma. Two other Shawnee communities also moved to Oklahoma. These groups went on to become the Eastern Shawnee and Absentee Shawnee tribes.

This village scene shows the female members of the Shawnee tribe performing the Pigeon Dance as the men look on. The pigeon was a clan animal to some tribes and dances were performed in its honor.

SIOUX

(SOO)

LANGUAGE GROUP:
Siouan

GREETING:
Ho-ko-dah (Dakota)

THANK YOU:
Pe-dah-mah-yeh (Dakota)

LOCATION PRECONTACT:
Minnesota, Wisconsin, Iowa, North Dakota, South Dakota

LOCATION TODAY:
Minnesota, Montana, Nebraska, North Dakota, South Dakota (U.S.); Alberta, Manitoba, Saskatchewan (Canada)

French fur trappers began using the word Sioux after hearing a longer, but similar, Ojibwe word, *nadouessioux*, which means "little snake," or "enemy." A large tribal group, the Sioux had three major groups: the Dakota in the east, the central Nakota, and the Lakota to the west. Each of these groups had a number of bands. The Lakota were the largest group, and by the end of the 1700s, had divided into seven bands extending into present-day Nebraska, North Dakota, South Dakota, Montana, and Wyoming. Since the Sioux lived over such a wide area, their lifestyles varied. The eastern Sioux depended on fishing, farming, and harvesting wild rice, while the western Sioux hunted. Once the Lakota started using horses, they commanded their vast territory with ease, raiding other tribes and hunting buffalo across the western Plains. As in other tribal communities, responsibilities were divided between the men and the women. Men made tools and weapons and took part in hunting, while women foraged for wild plants, such as prairie turnips, and did most of the cooking and sewing. Children might be given tasks that included fetching firewood or looking after the tribe's dogs.

During the 1700s, the eastern Sioux traded with the French and then the British, leading them to support the British in the Revolutionary War, in the hope of maintaining their trading relationship. They did the same in the War of 1812, leading some Sioux to move north to Canada, which the British still controlled. The Sioux who remained faced some of the most violent

LEGENDARY SIOUX LEADERS

Chiefs Sitting Bull (ca. 1831–1890, left) and Crazy Horse (ca. 1840–1877, right) were famous Sioux leaders during the late 1800s. Sitting Bull was chief of the Dakota Sioux. He killed his first buffalo at the age of 10 and joined his first war party aged 14. He was a great leader who rallied the Sioux to take a stand against American takeover of their lands. Crazy Horse was a legendary warrior and leader of the Lakota Sioux. He joined forces with Sitting Bull and Cheyenne tribes in their defense of the Black Hills to defeat U.S. general George Armstrong Custer and his men at the Battle of the Little Bighorn. Crazy Horse was originally named Curly for his wavy hair, but took his father's name on proving himself in battle. In 1877, Crazy Horse was forced to surrender to federal troops. He was later killed in prison amid rumors that he planned to escape.

conflicts of the century, including the U.S.–Dakota War of 1862, Red Cloud's War (1866–1868), and the Battle of the Little Bighorn (1876). After these wars, treaties and removal acts confined the Sioux to reservation land. The Sioux tribe's fight for its lands and freedom ended on December 29, 1890, when U.S. troops invaded and killed hundreds of Sioux warriors, women, and children at Wounded Knee Creek on the Lakota Pine Ridge Indian Reservation.

Today, there are Sioux communities in many U.S. states and in Canada. Reservations on the Plains include the Yankton Reservation, Standing Rock Reservation, Lower Brule Indian Reservation, and Crow Creek Reservation. Besides the large expanses of wild territory, there are numerous attractions that include monuments, museums, and trails dedicated to the tribe's cultural history. They still celebrate the traditions of their ancestors.

This Sioux man's "scalp" shirt is made from hide and has painted and beaded decorative panels. The sleeves are fringed with human hair, possibly enemy scalp locks taken as trophies in warfare.

BATTLE FOR THE BLACK HILLS

The Black Hills in South Dakota are sacred to the Lakota Sioux. In 1868, the Treaty of Fort Laramie recognized the hills as part of the Sioux Reservation. According to the treaty, white people could not trespass on this land. In 1874, General George Custer led an expedition to the hills and prospectors discovered gold. This led to the Battle of the Little Bighorn in 1876 that pitched the Sioux, Cheyenne, and Arapaho against the U.S. Army. In spite of a tribal victory, the U.S. government claimed the area back from the Sioux in 1877 and authorized mining in the Black Hills. Since that time, the U.S. has acknowledged that the taking of the hills was unlawful, but has yet to agree to return the land to Native Americans.

TONKAWA

(TONG-kuh-wah)

LANGUAGE GROUP:
  Isolate

LANGUAGE:
  Currently dormant; last known speaker died in the 1960s

LOCATION PRECONTACT:
  Oklahoma, Texas

LOCATION TODAY:
  Oklahoma

The Tonkawa may once have numbered 5,000 people at the height of their strength. By the 1700s, the tribe had acquired horses and used them to hunt buffalo and other game across its homelands in Texas and Oklahoma. They also gathered pecan nuts, acorns, roots, seeds, and fruit, and caught fish. Traveling much of the time, the Tonkawa made small shelters from branches and shrubbery. Among the crafts of the Tonkawa were clay pots and woven baskets. They also made rattles from gourds and drums with deerskin stretched over a hoop. The Tonkawa spoke a language that was not related to other native languages, and so it is unclear where the tribe originated. They were fierce warriors and raided Apache villages. The Apache fought back with raids of their own and since the Tonkawa were the smaller tribe, the Apache took over their hunting grounds.

By the mid-1700s, diseases introduced by Spanish missionaries were taking their toll on the Tonkawa, too. When

This colorized photograph of Tonkawa warrior chief John Williams shows him holding a feather fan. Feathers often represented a warrior's success in battle—the more feathers, the greater the warrior.

Tonkawa chief Grant Richards sits at the center of this group of prominent Tonkawa people. His wife, Winnie, stands top left. The photograph was taken in 1898.

American settlers began arriving in Texas in the 1800s, the Tonkawa were friendly. The Americans created two reservations near the Brazos River, in west Texas, to which the Tonkawa moved in 1855. By the time the Civil War started, in 1861, Native tribes took sides, choosing either to support the Union (North) or the Confederacy (South). The Tonkawa warriors fought for the Confederacy, and after the war, their role brought revenge from tribes who had fought alongside the Union. Raiding warriors attacked Tonkawa communities, cutting their population in half.

The survivors stayed in Texas until the 1880s, but the U.S. government forced them to move to Oklahoma in 1884. Today, the Tonkawa Reservation consists of 1,000 acres (400 ha) of land in the northern part of the state. Sadly, the Tonkawa language is no longer used, as the last Tonkawa speaker died in the 1960s. Today, there are various efforts to revive the language using several online resources, which include language booklets, language lessons, and traditional stories passed down through the generations.

WICHITA

(WIH-chih-taw)

LANGUAGE GROUP:
Caddoan

GREETING:
E:si:rasi:c?a:k?a

THANK YOU:
Not available

LOCATION PRECONTACT:
Kansas, Oklahoma, Texas

LOCATION TODAY:
Oklahoma

The Wichita lived on the southern Plains in what became the states of Kansas, Oklahoma, and Texas. The people call themselves Kitikiti'sh, which means "raccoon eyes," because of the tattoos on the men's faces around their eyes. The name Wichita now refers to the entire tribe, but it is also the name of one of the four major bands; the others are the Taovaya, Tawakoni, and Waco. Communities of Wichita lived in villages across their territory. Their homes were quite different from those of other Plains tribes, and had beehive-shaped wooden frames, which were then covered entirely in grass. The tribe grew large crops of corn, beans, and squash, and hunted buffalo, deer, and small game. Typically, the men made large-scale hunting trips in fall and winter.

When the Spanish explorer Francisco Vázquez de Coronado met the Wichita in 1541, they had successful trading relationships with neighboring tribes. In time, the Wichita expanded this network to include the Spanish and, later, the French. They soon had access to many European goods,

A Wichita chief dressed in tribal regalia attends a powwow. His tribe takes turns with the Pawnee tribe to host the annual event.

such as tools, which they either kept for themselves or traded with other tribes. Their contact with the Europeans brought diseases and warfare, decreasing the population by thousands.

After the 1830s, the U.S. government sent many tribes living east of Wichita territory to present-day Oklahoma. White settlers soon moved in, setting up homesteads on the Wichita's ancestral lands. Over the following decades, the Wichita were forced to move to a reservation in Texas, then back to Kansas, and, finally, to a reservation in Oklahoma, where they have stayed since 1872. Together with the Pawnee, they work hard to keep their heritage alive, including holding classes on language and native crafts, such as basket weaving. Every year, the two tribes camp together to honor their histories and cultures. The 10-day pow-wow includes a pipe ceremony, shared meals, and songs.

The Wichita's beehive-shaped houses were often very large—up to 20 feet (6 m) tall—and housed up to eight or ten people. Extending from the top of each house, four poles represented the four world quarters, or gods, of the Wichita religion.

ANIMAL MOTIFS

Plains tribes value everything in the natural world, but pay special tribute to certain animals. Eagle and buffalo motifs are particularly important in ceremonies, storytelling, and pictographs. The eagle symbolizes power and bravery and a spiritual connection with the sky. It was a great honor for a warrior to receive an eagle feather and only the most courageous warriors earned them for their bravery in warfare. The buffalo represents survival, and the Plains people embrace the animal as one of their own. They used to use its skull in religious ceremonies, and featured buffalo motifs on their war shields. The Plains people believe the buffalo kept warriors safe. Pictured here is the Buffalo Dance, performed in thanksgiving to the buffalo for its role in tribal well-being.

WYANDOTTE

(WHY-an-dot)

LANGUAGE GROUP:
Iroquoian

GREETING:
Kweh

THANK YOU:
Tižameh

LOCATION PRECONTACT:
Ontario, Quebec (Canada)

LOCATION TODAY:
Oklahoma

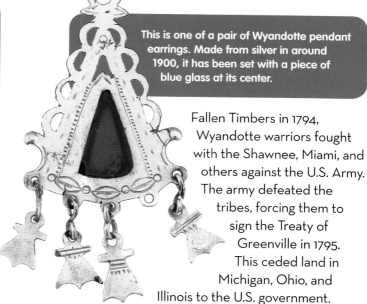

This is one of a pair of Wyandotte pendant earrings. Made from silver in around 1900, it has been set with a piece of blue glass at its center.

The Wyandotte ancestors lived in the woodlands of the Northeast, in present-day Ontario and Quebec, Canada. In the mid-1600s, the Iroquois Confederacy attacked people from the Wendat, or Huron, Confederacy, along with the Attignawantan and the Khionontateronon tribes. The powerful Iroquois wanted to expand their territory and control the fur trade. Their aggression forced their victims to flee and join forces to become the Wyandotte tribe. The tribe first went to Mackinac Island, Michigan (Wyandotte means "island dweller"). From there, the tribe moved close to the French fort at present-day Detroit. Other tribal members moved into Wisconsin and to the Ohio Valley. In their new lands, the Wyandotte continued to hunt and fish as they had always done, but also started growing corn, squash, sunflowers, and tobacco. They built longhouses with wooden frames covered in bark—often elm—and made birchbark canoes for navigating rivers and streams. They used hooks made from animal bone to catch fish and snares for bears and beavers. They also traded with other tribes and French colonists.

The Wyandotte began to lose their new lands in the late 1700s. At the Battle of Fallen Timbers in 1794, Wyandotte warriors fought with the Shawnee, Miami, and others against the U.S. Army. The army defeated the tribes, forcing them to sign the Treaty of Greenville in 1795. This ceded land in Michigan, Ohio, and Illinois to the U.S. government.

By 1842, the Wyandotte were landless and forced to move to Kansas, where they bought some land from the Lenape tribe. After white settlers began to move into the area, another treaty in 1855 took away the Wyandotte's tribal status and its land following the U.S. government's "termination" policy. Some tribal members volunteered to move to Oklahoma to live among other tribes. The Oklahoma Wyandotte eventually received money to buy land, and the government officially recognized this group as the Wyandotte Tribe of Oklahoma in 1937.

From the late 1800s, many Native children were forced to attend boarding school to adopt white American ways of living. They included the four Wyandotte boys pictured here.

IN THE KNOW

According to Wyandotte origin stories, the world was created on the back of a giant turtle. Every summer, at the celebration called "Gathering of Little Turtles," Wyandotte children learn about their tribe's past, arts, sports, and language.

COYOTE AND THE TURKEYS

Coyote had been hunting for several days. His stomach was empty and he was very hungry. As he walked, he heard a flock of turkeys in the distance.

Coyote thought, "At last I might catch something to eat." He crouched low to sneak up on the turkeys and did his best to blend in with the brown dirt.

As hungry as he was, he knew he had to use his trickery not to scare them away. Looking at the turkeys, he thought, "I know what I'll do." He ran back to his den to grab his drum, drumstick, and a sack. Upon returning, he saw the turkeys were still eating. He saw turkeys of all sizes. He knew exactly what he would do. Coyote went a little way from the flock and started singing. Instead of being frightened by the Coyote, the turkeys were curious: Why was Coyote singing? The turkeys watched and listened, but were very careful. Some flew away, but most stayed.

The turkeys that stayed decided they liked his singing and started walking toward him, slowly and carefully. Meanwhile, Coyote sang with his eyes closed, but he opened them slightly to see if the turkeys were still there. The curious turkeys couldn't stand it any longer. They had to know why Coyote was singing. "Brother, why are you singing?" they asked. "I am singing because of you beautiful turkeys," Coyote said. "Your feathers are bright and pretty, and you have caused me to sing," Coyote said. "You should dance to show off your feathers; I'll sing for you." "He's right," the turkeys said, "we do have beautiful feathers."

Coyote smiled; his plan was working. "Before I start singing," said Coyote, "let the big fat turkeys dance closest to me, the medium-size turkeys dance behind them, and the skinny ones dance in an outer circle." The turkeys all agreed and were anxious to dance. Coyote started singing again; he sang one song and started on the next. "This song is special," said Coyote. "To hear it, everyone must have their eyes closed. If you open your eyes, your eyes will turn red."

The turkeys didn't question Coyote, but closed their eyes tightly and began to dance, spreading their tail feathers. Coyote continued to sing and slowly brought out his sack. Then he grabbed the biggest and fattest turkeys closest to him and stuffed them into it. He sang louder so the others couldn't hear what he was doing. In the outer circle, one skinny turkey heard the strange sound and wondered if he should open his eyes. Once again he heard it. And again. Finally, the skinny turkey opened his eyes just a little bit. He saw what Coyote was doing.

"Run, brothers!" shouted the skinny turkey. "He's going to eat us!" Hearing their skinny brother, the dancing turkeys flew away and lived. Still, Coyote's plan had worked and he had caught some of the turkeys. He wasn't hungry for a while. From that day on, the turkeys had red eyes.

Dan SaSuWeh Jones, Ponca

This story plays on the cleverness of Coyote and the vanity of the turkeys. Coyote was lying about their beauty, but the turkeys were proud to spread their wings and forgot to be cautious.

A Navajo woman feeds her sheep in Monument Valley Navajo Tribal Park on the Arizona–Utah border. The Navajo acquired sheep from the Spanish in the mid-1600s, and have bred them ever since. Besides meat and milk, the sheep provide wool for weaving rugs and blankets.

THE SOUTHWEST

Dry deserts, vast canyons, mountains, and deep river valleys make up the landscape of the American Southwest. For thousands of years, people have grown food and built communities in this terrain. Descending from three ancient civilizations, most people settled in the parts of the Southwest that became New Mexico, Arizona, Texas, and northern Mexico. This harsh but beautiful setting is home to some of North America's most vibrant cultures.

THE STORY OF **THE SOUTHWESTERN PEOPLE**

Most southwestern tribes can trace their ancestry back to one of three ancient civilizations: the ancient Pueblo, the Mogollon, and the Hohokam. Adopting the simplest of lifestyles in their desert habitat, the people of each civilization made the most of the natural resources around them. The ancient Pueblo were master builders, who constructed their city at Chaco Canyon, New Mexico, out of sandstone blocks; the Mogollon were expert craftspeople who used clay to make striking pottery; and the Hohokam harnessed water by digging elaborate canal systems. The Hohokam adapted so well to life in the desert that their communities survived for many centuries.

The three ancient groups were succeeded by the Hopi, Zuni, and Pima tribes, who created societies rich in art, spirituality, and tradition. A fourth group of the Southwest, the Athabascans, migrated here from the far north. Their descendants became the Navajo and Apache—two of the area's most powerful tribes. The Navajo and Apache were nomadic and hunted elk, deer, and other animals across a wide territory.

The Arrival of Outsiders

Until the 1500s, the various cultures of the Southwest thrived. Tribes sometimes clashed and raided one another's villages, but they also traded with each other so that everyone had what they needed. The arrival of Spanish settlers brought change and influenced the ways in which the southwestern people lived. Tribes acquired horses, began raising sheep and cattle, and grew crops of wheat and fruit such as apricots and peaches. The Spanish established religious settlements, or missions. They built churches and introduced the people of the Southwest to Catholicism—sometimes by force. Some southwestern people were even taken by the Spanish to be used as slaves.

Native Resistance

The Pueblo people suffered most from the Spanish takeover. In 1680, they banded together to revolt. They burned the Spanish missions and forced the Europeans to leave. Twelve years later, the Spanish returned. To avoid a repeat of their defeat in 1680, the Spanish now offered the Pueblo land grants. Other tribes, such as the Havasupai, lived in rugged areas that did not interest the Spanish, so they were left in peace.

Mexico gained its independence from Spain in 1821. While most southwestern people continued to follow their traditional ways of living, the Apache began to resent the Mexican invasion of their hunting grounds. From 1835, the Apaches waged war on Mexico, killing thousands in fierce attacks and destroying more than 100 Mexican settlements.

New Borders and the Reservation Era

Following Mexico's defeat in the Mexican–American War, the 1848 Treaty of Guadalupe Hidalgo created a new border between the southern United States and Mexico. The treaty did not take account of the tribal homelands that straddled the border—of the Cocopah tribe, for example. When the U.S. government bought more land from Mexico in the Gadsden Purchase of 1854, the Tohono O'odham tribe also found its territory divided between the two countries. Further difficulties came with the California gold rush in 1849, when settlers, mining companies, and U.S. soldiers invaded ancestral homelands. By the end of the century, most tribal members had moved onto reservations.

The Southwest Today

A number of southwestern tribes managed to keep hold of at least some areas of their Native lands. This was largely because the land was too rugged for settlers. Today, the Navajo have the largest reservation in the United States, covering parts of southern Utah, Colorado, New Mexico, and Arizona. Their culture is expressed in their world-famous arts. Southwest tribes with less land have also kept their traditions and languages alive. Since 1922, tribal members from across the Southwest have gathered annually in Gallup, New Mexico, to celebrate their cultures with rodeos, dances, and parades.

Kachina dolls, such as this Zuni bull, forge a link between humans and the spirit world. Some 250 types of kachina dolls existed, representing different aspects of tribal life.

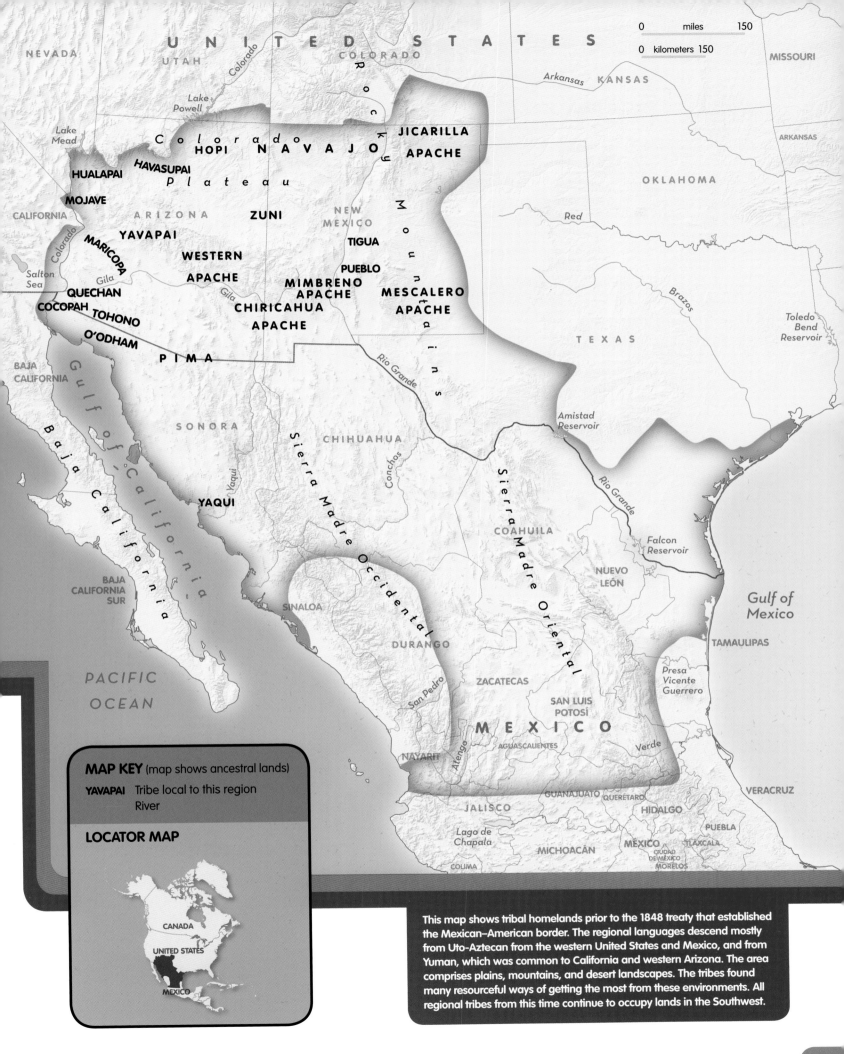

UNITED STATES

NEVADA

UTAH

COLORADO

Lake Powell

Colorado

Arkansas

KANSAS

MISSOURI

Lake Mead

Colorado

Plateau

HOPI

NAVAJO

JICARILLA
APACHE

ARKANSAS

HUALAPAI

HAVASUPAI

MOJAVE

CALIFORNIA

ARIZONA

ZUNI

NEW
MEXICO

OKLAHOMA

Red

YAVAPAI

MARICOPA

WESTERN
APACHE

TIGUA

Salton
Sea

Gila

PUEBLO

QUECHAN

MIMBRENO
APACHE

MESCALERO
APACHE

Gila

COCOPAH

TOHONO
O'ODHAM

CHIRICAHUA
APACHE

Brazos

PIMA

Rio Grande

Toledo
Bend
Reservoir

BAJA
CALIFORNIA

TEXAS

Gulf of California

SONORA

CHIHUAHUA

Conchos

Amistad
Reservoir

Yaqui

Baja California

Rio Grande

Falcon
Reservoir

YAQUI

Sierra Madre Occidental

COAHUILA

Sierra Madre Oriental

NUEVO
LEÓN

BAJA
CALIFORNIA
SUR

SINALOA

Gulf of
Mexico

PACIFIC
OCEAN

DURANGO

ZACATECAS

San Pedro

SAN LUIS
POTOSÍ

Presa
Vicente
Guerrero

TAMAULIPAS

NAYARIT

Atengo

Verde

MEXICO

AGUASCALIENTES

GUANAJUATO

QUERÉTARO

VERACRUZ

JALISCO

HIDALGO

Lago de
Chapala

MICHOACÁN

MÉXICO

PUEBLA

CIUDAD
DE MÉXICO

TLAXCALA

COLIMA

MORELOS

miles

0   150

kilometers

0   150

MAP KEY (map shows ancestral lands)

YAVAPAI   Tribe local to this region
            River

LOCATOR MAP

CANADA

UNITED STATES

MEXICO

This map shows tribal homelands prior to the 1848 treaty that established the Mexican–American border. The regional languages descend mostly from Uto-Aztecan from the western United States and Mexico, and from Yuman, which was common to California and western Arizona. The area comprises plains, mountains, and desert landscapes. The tribes found many resourceful ways of getting the most from these environments. All regional tribes from this time continue to occupy lands in the Southwest.

153

TIME LINE OF THE SOUTHWEST

N ations in the Southwest were thriving by the time the Spanish arrived in the 1500s. Over the next centuries, many fought for their freedom against Spanish, Mexican, and U.S. military forces. By the end of the 1800s, these tribes lived on reservations, many of which were on ancestral tribal lands. In the 1900s, several tribes won court cases to address the harsh mistreatment they received in the past.

100 C.E.
Ancient cultures emerge. The ancient Pueblo, Hohokam, and Mogollon cultures evolved from two civilizations that had lived in the Southwest for millennia. An ancient Pueblan settlement at Mesa Verde, Colorado, is pictured here.

ca. 1150
The village of Oraibi, Arizona, founded. The Hopi have lived in Oraibi since it was first founded.

1536
The first Spanish explorers arrive. Alvar Núñez Cabeza de Vaca and others went in search of gold, beginning the Spanish invasion of the Southwest.

1680
Pueblo Revolt. The Pueblo people rebelled against the Spanish after suffering slavery, war, and disease under European occupation. They forced the Spanish out.

1692
Spanish reconquest. The Spanish returned to Pueblo territory, led by Don Diego de Vargas.

1700
Hopi resistance. The Hopi destroyed Awatovi, their own village, which had been taken over by the Spanish. The tribe remained defiant against the Spanish for decades.

1821
Mexico gains independence from Spain. The Mexicans took over Spain's colonies, but faced resistance from the Apache and the Comanche. Pictured is an Apache chief.

1848

Treaty of Guadalupe Hidalgo. With Mexico's defeat in the Mexican–American War, this treaty created the border between the southern United States and Mexico.

1848–1855

California gold rush. The discovery of gold in 1848 brought 300,000 people into California. Many traveled through the tribal lands of the Southwest. Pictured is a Californian gold-mining town.

1854

Gadsden Purchase. The United States bought land from Mexico for $10 million. The land became part of present-day Arizona and New Mexico.

1864–1866

Navajo Long Walk. The U.S. Army forced the Navajo to march to the Bosque Redondo Reservation in New Mexico. By 1866, 9,000 Navajo had been forced onto the reservation. Hundreds died on the journey.

1886

Geronimo surrenders. The famous Apache leader fought for many years against the Spanish, Mexican, and U.S. armies. The Apache finally surrendered at Skeleton Canyon, Arizona, ending the wars of the Southwest.

1942

Navajo code talkers recruited. In March, the U.S. Marine Corps recruited Navajo men to use their language as a secret code in WWII.

1948

Native Americans given voting rights in Arizona and New Mexico. Native Americans gained U.S. citizenship in 1924, but not voting rights. In 1948, Miguel Trujillo, a former Marine and member of Isleta Pueblo, sued New Mexico for not allowing him to vote. Later that year, New Mexico and Arizona extended voting rights to Native peoples.

1961

National Indian Youth Council (NIYC) established in Gallup, New Mexico. Now based in Albuquerque, the organization aims to support education and rights, and to improve the lives of American Indians.

1968

Navajo Community College opens in Tsaile, Arizona. Now called Diné College, this educational institution was the first of its kind to be tribally owned. Pictured are three Navajo students from the early years.

1975

Havasupai regain acres of homeland in the Grand Canyon. In 1880, after decades of requests from the tribe, the U.S. government created a small reservation of 185,000 acres (75,000 ha) for the tribe.

2004

Arizona Water Settlement Act. The act, signed by President George W. Bush, addressed water rights for Arizona tribes, enabling them to meet the needs of their reservation.

2014

Navajo win settlement. The Navajo Nation sued the U.S. government in 2006, for mismanaging money and resources that it had been looking after on their behalf. The government agreed to pay the Navajo Nation $554 million—the largest settlement ever made with one tribe.

APACHE

(uh-PA-chee)

LANGUAGE GROUP:
Athabascan

GREETING:
Dáanzho (Jicarilla)

THANK YOU:
Iheedn (Jicarilla)

LOCATION PRECONTACT:
Arizona, New Mexico, Colorado, Oklahoma, Texas; Mexico

LOCATION TODAY:
Oklahoma, Arizona, New Mexico

The Apache moved into the Southwest from the north between the late 1200s and the 1500s. Their Athabascan language ties them to the Na-Dené people of the Arctic regions of Canada. When they moved south, the Apache tribe spread across the Southwest, dividing into six major groups: the Chiricahua, Jicarilla, Lipan, Mescalero, Plains Apache, and Western Apache.

All the Apache groups lived a nomadic life as they moved across present-day Arizona and New Mexico. They slept in wickiups—small domed huts with a timber frame and a grass or reed-mat covering for the roof. They hunted bears, deer, buffalo, and beavers and gathered cactus fruits and other wild plants. They wasted nothing—making clothes from hides, tools from animal bones, and blankets from woven yucca, a type of shrub. When the Apache acquired horses, they were able to use them to hunt and trade farther than their traditional region. Fearless warriors, they raided other tribes—as well as Spanish and Mexican settlements—for food, cattle, horses, and other supplies. The Spanish never managed to control the Apache, nor to convert them to Christianity. When Mexico gained its independence from Spain in 1821, the Mexican government wanted to take over Apache land. The Apache fiercely protected their territory, fighting back against Mexican troops and attacking Mexican settlements.

Following Mexico's defeat in the Mexican–American War, the U.S. government claimed ownership of the tribe's vast territory. When discussing the Treaty of Guadalupe Hidalgo,

The Apache made a type of fiddle from a yucca stalk, which they decorated and strung with just one or two strings. Along with various types of drums, it was played at important ceremonies.

RESISTANCE

Southwestern tribes fought against the Spanish, the Mexicans, and the U.S. government as each group invaded their lands. The Hopi took part in the Pueblo Revolt of 1680, and would not convert to Spanish ways of life when the Europeans returned in 1700 and 1740. In the 1800s, the Apache fought against the Mexicans, with great losses on both sides. In 1835, the Mexicans offered a bounty, or reward, for anyone who captured and brought them an Apache fighter. By the 1860s, white settlers had invaded Apache and Navajo lands, and prospectors had taken farmland, looking for gold. Despite resistance, the U.S. Army forced the tribes onto reservations. Some Apache, under a warrior by the name of Geronimo, rebelled again in 1885—they are pictured right, returning from a raid. Despite being forced to surrender, southwestern tribes managed to hold on to parts of their homelands.

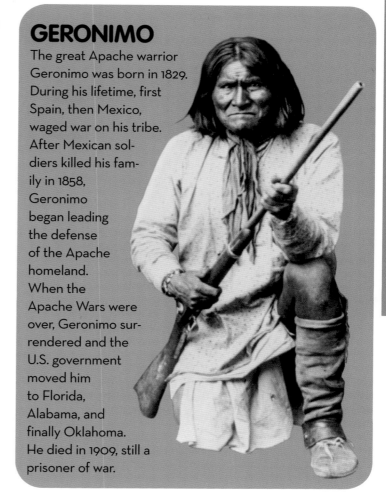

Armbands are often worn by the men of the Apache tribe during tribal ceremonies, such as the Crown Dance, for which they also wear elaborate masks.

which ended the war, the U.S. government excluded Apache members from the meeting to ensure that the tribe could not resist the terms of the treaty. The resulting battles between the Apache and U.S. troops lasted almost 40 years in what became known as the Apache Wars. Over time, the U.S. government pushed the surviving Apache onto reservations. The tribe rebelled again in 1885, but was forced to surrender in 1886.

Today, the Apache live on reservations in Arizona, New Mexico, and Oklahoma, and in communities across the United States. Among the ceremonies still practiced is one that celebrates puberty in girls, marking their growth from childhood to womanhood. The event runs up to four days and involves feasting and dancing as well as centuries-old blessings and rituals. The girl wears the same buckskin dress for the duration of the event and for as many as four days after. ☞

GERONIMO

The great Apache warrior Geronimo was born in 1829. During his lifetime, first Spain, then Mexico, waged war on his tribe. After Mexican soldiers killed his family in 1858, Geronimo began leading the defense of the Apache homeland. When the Apache Wars were over, Geronimo surrendered and the U.S. government moved him to Florida, Alabama, and finally Oklahoma. He died in 1909, still a prisoner of war.

DRESSING FOR THE SEASONS

Some tribes in the Southwest, including the Apache and the Navajo, made buckskin clothing, such as the Apache girl's shirt pictured. They colored their clothes and added beadwork. In the mid-1800s, tribes made clothes using cotton, velvet, or blankets that came from trading with the Europeans. The Pueblos, and other tribes living in very hot areas, wore little clothing, although the women had cotton dresses called *mantas* that tied at the shoulder. Once the Spanish had introduced sheep, southwestern tribes made woolen clothing—for example, the Navajo women wove dresses and ponchos. For several tribes, the yucca plant, which could be used to make a linen-like fabric, provided material for sandals, belts, and

skirts. Tribes such as the Cocopah used willow bark to make women's skirts and men's breechcloths—a rectangular stretch of material fitted between the legs and tied with a belt. In cooler weather, tribal people wore leggings woven from yucca and wrapped themselves in yucca blankets.

COCOPAH

(ko-ko-PAH)

LANGUAGE GROUP:
Yuman

GREETING:
ʔáwka

THANK YOU:
Maʔím muxác

LOCATION PRECONTACT:
Arizona, California; Mexico

LOCATION TODAY:
Arizona (U.S); Mexico

Native tribes played a team game, called shinny, that was not unlike field hockey. It involved striking a ball using a long stick that was curved at one end, as in this Cocopah example.

The Cocopah, the "river people," were once farmers who worked on thousands of acres along the Colorado River's rich delta, where they took advantage of the fertile land of its flood plain. Many families shared large, earthen homes, thatched with arrowweed and built partly underground.

The Cocopah used the natural resources around them. They grew vegetables, hunted small game, fished, and foraged for wild seeds and fruit. The women made skirts from willow bark and grass, while the men wore breechcloths. Today, visitors to a museum on the West Cocopah Reservation can see how the tribe used to live. There are examples of traditional clothing, footwear, and musical instruments made from gourds, as well as pieces of modern-day beadwork. Outside the museum is a traditional thatched dwelling.

Contact with the Spanish in the mid-1500s led to the tribe's first experience of deadly disease. After this, the people kept to themselves, leading a mainly peaceful, settled life for nearly 300 years. This peace shattered in the 1800s when great change came to the Southwest. In 1848, the Treaty of Guadalupe Hidalgo gave the U.S. government control over a large territory that included present-day Arizona and California. A new border agreed between the U.S. and Mexico straddled Cocopah lands.

A year after the treaty, the California gold rush brought thousands of prospectors and settlers west in the hope of making a fortune. The U.S. government worried that the Cocopah would revolt, as tribes had elsewhere, but their fears proved unfounded. Some Cocopah moved away, but others stayed in their homes. When steamboats were introduced on local rivers in the late 1800s, many Cocopah men found work as pilots or guides.

In 1917, the government assigned three areas of land in Arizona to the Cocopah. A number of families lived here—still inhabiting their traditional

IN THE KNOW

A flood plain is an area of flat land by the side of a river. During a seasonal flood, the water spreads fertile soil across the plain. Every year, the Cocopah took advantage of the spring floods to plant their many crops.

A Cocopah elder waves burning sage over a dry marsh that was once part of the Colorado River Delta and teeming with fish. She holds her ceremony in the hope of restoring at least some water to an area drained by drought and irrigation.

arrowweed-thatched homes until the 1960s. At this time they built their first tribal building. Other tribal members live in Mexico, where they are known as the Cucapa people.

Today, the tribe living in Arizona owns and manages businesses, such as golf courses and a speedway, alongside its museum celebrating Cocopah history and culture. Elders continue to teach tribal traditions to the younger generation. This includes documenting their language, which until now has been oral and not written. ☞

HAVASUPAI

(ha-vah-SOO-pie)

LANGUAGE GROUP:
Yuman

LANGUAGE:
Limited number of words in current use; no dictionary available

LOCATION PRECONTACT:
Arizona

LOCATION TODAY:
Arizona

For thousands of years, the Havasupai have lived in the Grand Canyon region of present-day Arizona. The tribe calls itself Havasuw 'Baaja, or "people of the blue-green water," for the intensely blue water of the Cataract Canyon in which they made their home.

Three Havasupai boys sit on a horse at Truxton Canyon Boarding School. Established on the Walapai Reservation in 1901, the school was attended by Walapai and Havasupai students. It closed in 1937.

In the spring and summer, the Havasupai farmed the land in the canyon bed and slept in simple, thatched homes. They irrigated the dry land with water from the river and grew crops of melons, sunflowers, corn, and beans. In winter, they migrated some 400 miles (645 km) southwest to the Coconino Plateau to hunt deer, bighorn sheep, and other animals. Women and children sometimes took part in the hunt, stamping their feet on the ground to drive rabbits from their burrows.

The Spanish did not try to colonize the Havasupai or convert them to Christianity, as the tribe's villages were too remote. The Havasupai lived peacefully until the mid-1800s, when prospectors discovered silver in the Grand Canyon and miners and settlers swarmed into the area, encroaching on the Havasupai homelands. The U.S. government gave Havasupai land to the mining companies and settlers.

In 1880, the government created a small reservation for the Havasupai, which was made even smaller, to 518 acres (210 ha), two years later. This did not include any silver fields or the Coconino Plateau, so the Havasupai were forced to survive by farming a small area in the canyon. They also continued to hunt game. In 1919, the Grand Canyon National Park

opened, and by 1940, the National Park Service had stopped the tribe from hunting on the plateau. Over the following years, the Havasupai fought for the return of their homelands. In 1975, the government established 160,000 acres (65,000 ha) as reservation land. Another 95,000 acres (38,500 ha) of the national park is now available for the tribe's use. Today, the Havasupai live in Supai Village in Havasu Canyon, Arizona, where they continue to use their language. They also run the tribe's campsite and lodge, with many working as guides for tourists to the Grand Canyon.

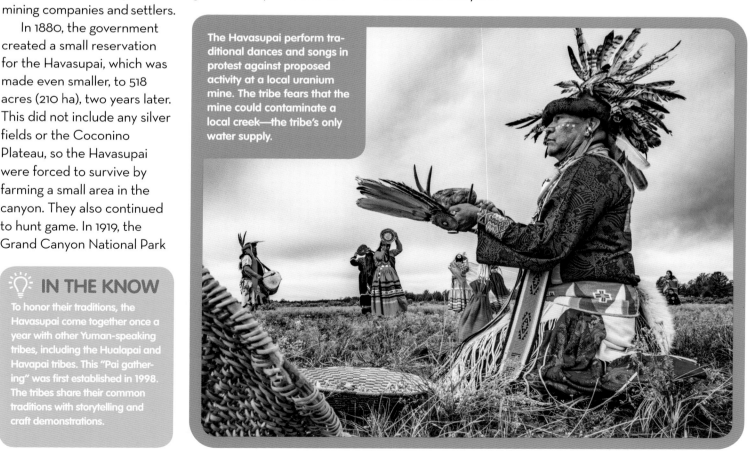

The Havasupai perform traditional dances and songs in protest against proposed activity at a local uranium mine. The tribe fears that the mine could contaminate a local creek—the tribe's only water supply.

IN THE KNOW

To honor their traditions, the Havasupai come together once a year with other Yuman-speaking tribes, including the Hualapai and Havapai tribes. This "Pai gathering" was first established in 1998. The tribes share their common traditions with storytelling and craft demonstrations.

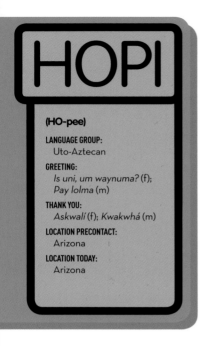
HOPI

(HO-pee)

LANGUAGE GROUP:
Uto-Aztecan

GREETING:
Is uni, um waynuma? (f);
Pay lolma (m)

THANK YOU:
Askwalí (f); *Kwakwhá* (m)

LOCATION PRECONTACT:
Arizona

LOCATION TODAY:
Arizona

The Hopi have lived in northeastern Arizona since 1150. Their village Oraibi is one of the oldest communities in the United States. Their ancestors, the ancient Pueblo, lived in this dry, desert area for many thousands of years. Today, as in ancient times, Hopi villages sit on three mesas, or flat-topped hills, and the tribe farms in the valley below. Early Hopi houses were four or five stories high and made from stone covered with plaster. Even today, some Hopi people live in these traditional homes, with some villagers choosing to do so without electricity or running water. Other Hopi live in modern homes on the reservation, or live off the reservation.

With a long history of farming, the Hopi traditionally grew corn, beans, and squash, using various "dry farming" methods that are still practiced today. These included planting crops in narrow valleys that had access to floodwater, or using rainwater and melted snow, which they carried in buckets to smaller plots near the villages. In the past, the tribe also mined coal for fuel. The Hopi ground corn into flour to make paper-thin feast bread called *piki*, baked on a flat, heated stone. Among the crafts made by the Hopi women were clay bowls, which they decorated with geometric designs.

Most Hopi resisted Spanish attempts to convert them to Christianity, and in 1680 the Hopi fought against the Europeans in the Pueblo Revolt. They also destroyed Awatovi, the one Hopi village that contained a Spanish mission. This ended contact with Europeans until the mid-1800s, although the Hopi still had to defend themselves against Navajo raids. From the 1850s, the U.S. government became interested in taking over Hopi land. Although the government created a reservation for the tribe in 1882, the Hopi lost a lot of that land through the Dawes Act of 1887, which allowed the parceling up of Native land. Some parcels were allotted to tribal members, but many were given to white settlers.

In addition to Oraibi, there are another 12 villages on the Hopi Reservation—an area that is surrounded by the much larger Navajo reservation. Over time, the Hopi have held on to their traditions and beliefs. Today, tribal members on and off the reservation gather for celebrations and dances, such as the Bean Dance, performed in the hope of a good harvest, the Snake Dance that honors past ancestors, and the Flute Ceremony, a ritual that seeks to bring rain. ☛

Hopi basketmaker Fermina Banyacya sits weaving outside her home. The Hopi continue to make pottery and baskets using the methods of their ancestors, sometimes selling them from their homes as souvenirs.

IN THE KNOW

Over the centuries, the Hopi people have grown different types of corn to suit the arid climate of their land. These include white, red, yellow, blue, and speckled varieties. The Hopi follow a number of rituals and ceremonies when it comes to planting and harvesting corn.

Holding a rattle in one hand and a pine bough in the other, this 1960s–1980s silver Hopi pin represents the mudhead *kachina* doll (see Spirit Dolls, opposite).

SPIRIT DOLLS

Kachina dolls are small figures given to children to teach them about the Hopi religion. Craftsmen carve the dolls from cottonwood, before painting them and decorating them with feathers. For the Hopi, the kachinas represent spirits—mainly ancestors, but also animals, plants, and other aspects of nature. The tribe's religion centers on these kachinas. In January or February, people visit the Hopi pueblos and stay there until midsummer. During this time, they take part in several ceremonies dressed as kachinas and wearing masks. They come to bring forth rain every year so the crops will grow.

The best-known kachina is *koyemsi*, the mudhead kachina, so named because the dancer's mask is made from mud. The character is typically clown-like, drumming, dancing, and joking with the audience during ceremonies. Other kachinas include a rainbow, which represents peace and harmony; a buffalo, which can kill evil thoughts; and a wolf, representing the hunt.

HUALAPAI

(WAH-luh-pie)

LANGUAGE GROUP:
Yuman

LANGUAGE:
Currently limited in use; no dictionary of terms available

LOCATION PRECONTACT:
Arizona

LOCATION TODAY:
Arizona

Like their close relatives, the Havasupai, the Hualapai have made their home in the Grand Canyon for thousands of years. Their name means "people of the tall pine," and relates to the piñon pine trees that grow on their traditional lands. Inhabiting less fertile land, the Hualapai hunted more than they farmed, and foraged for wild plants, including pine nuts. They also traded with nearby tribes, such as the Hopi. Due to the warm, dry climate in their region, the Hualapai needed only basic shelter for most of the year. In cooler months, they wrapped themselves in rabbit-skin coats and blankets and slept in domed, pole-framed huts covered with earth and grass. Spanish explorers probably came across the Hualapai in the 1500s, but later conquistadors never tried to colonize the Grand Canyon area, because they found the dry land too difficult to settle on. After the Mexican–American War, white settlers began moving into Hualapai territory, and prospectors searched for valuable metals. When they discovered silver, the miners hired Hualapai to work in the mines.

Faced with the idea of losing their land, the Hualapai rebelled against the settlers. Both sides mounted attacks. ➡

Many Native tribes celebrate a major event with a dance ceremony. Here, members of the Hualapai tribe prepare for the opening of the Grand Canyon Skywalk.

When two Hualapai chiefs were killed, the tribe raided white settlements in revenge. The U.S. Army took action. Battles followed, and the Hualapai surrendered in 1868. In 1874, the U.S. government forced the Hualapai to share the Colorado River Reservation with other tribes, but the Hualapai were unhappy there. Many escaped and returned to their homelands, while others fled to Mexico. In 1883, the government assigned a reservation of nearly one million acres (400,000 ha) in Arizona for the Hualapai. Most of the tribe still live there, supporting their economy with tourist attractions that include hunting expeditions and river rafting. The tribe's cultural center holds classes on traditional cradleboard making and pottery. ✐

MARICOPA

(MA-ree-COH-pah)

LANGUAGE GROUP:
Yuman

LANGUAGE:
Currently dormant; no record of last known speaker

LOCATION PRECONTACT:
Arizona

LOCATION TODAY:
Arizona

A Maricopa woman named Yellow Feather balances a basket with a woven geometric pattern on her head. The photograph was taken in 1898.

The Maricopa people are close relatives of the Cocopah, a neighboring tribe in what is now southwestern Arizona. In their own language, the Maricopa call themselves Xalychidom Piipaash, "people who live toward the water."

The Maricopa lived in the Colorado River Valley until the 1600s, when they moved down the Gila River. There, they became close to the Pima tribe. Like the Pima, the Maricopa built villages and farmed along the river, constructing many miles of canals to water their crops of corn, melons, beans, and tobacco. The men in the tribe also fished and hunted small game. Families lived in small, flat-roofed, pole-framed houses, covered in grass. Among its crafts, the tribe produced striking pottery that included bowls and animal effigies decorated with geometric designs and colored using natural plant dyes. Their friendship with the Pima was important because the two tribes

YELLOW FEATHER
MARICOPA

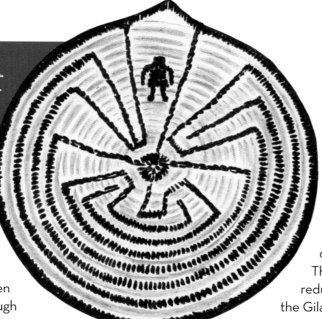

The Great Seal of the Salt River Pima-Maricopa community symbolizes life's journey as a maze. Its center represents a person's achievement of dreams and goals. The design often appeared in basketry.

helped each other defend their villages from raids by the Apache and Yavapai tribes.

During the mid-1800s, the U.S. government encouraged people from the eastern United States to settle in the West. The Maricopa were friendly toward the newcomers and even offered them food as they passed through their lands. When demand for land in the Southwest grew toward the end of the 1800s, the government forced the Maricopa and Pima tribes to move to the Salt River and Gila River Reservations.

In spite of the dry, hot climate, the Maricopa were very successful farmers, drawing water from their local rivers. In 1862, the tribe grew more than a million pounds (450,000 kg) of wheat, some of which they sold. In 1824, a new dam on the Gila River cut the water supply to the area downstream of the dam, where the tribe farmed. Their water supply was again reduced when canals were dug on the Gila River in the late 1800s, forcing the tribe to give up farming. It was not until the 1930s that the tribe could farm again, using water from the San Carlos Lake—a reservoir created on their land by damming the Gila River. Today, the Maricopa and Pima share a tribal government, but each group remains proud of its own history and traditions. In 2004, they opened the Huhugam Heritage Center to showcase tribal art and culture. Huhugam is the name of the Pima tribe's ancestors. 🖎

CHACO CANYON

Between 900 and 1150, the ancient Pueblo, ancestors of the Pueblo and Hopi people, built hundreds of sandstone buildings in Chaco Canyon, New Mexico. The Hopi name for this extraordinary place is Yupkoyvi, which means "the place beyond the horizon." Within a nine-mile (14.5-km) stretch of the canyon in the high desert, the ancient Pueblo constructed large underground spaces called *kivas*. These kivas were used for religious ceremonies. They also built multistory buildings with hundreds of rooms. These buildings became known as "great houses." The largest of all was Pueblo Bonito. It covered the equivalent of 2⅓ football fields and contained more than 600 rooms as well as dozens of kivas.

Chaco Canyon was an important gathering place for trade, ceremonies, and political meetings. A few thousand people may have lived here at one time. A drought may have forced people to move from Chaco Canyon and migrate to other places in the Southwest.

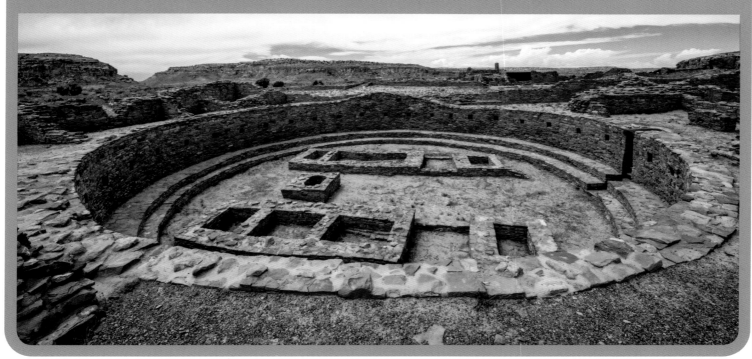

MOJAVE

(mo-HAH-vee)

LANGUAGE GROUP:
Yuman

GREETING:
Kwichkamaduum

THANK YOU:
Kukyee

LOCATION PRECONTACT:
Arizona, California

LOCATION TODAY:
Arizona, California

The Mojave ancestors may have moved south and east from the Mojave Desert area as early as 1150 C.E., to live along the Colorado River, taking advantage of its floodplain. Every year melting snow in the mountains caused the Colorado River to flood, creating fertile soil for agriculture. The tribe used its new territory to farm, but the men also hunted across the region for small game, such as rabbits. There was little rainfall, but the annual river flood enabled the tribe to grow corn, pumpkin, and other crops. Women also harvested roots and berries from the wild. The temperature soared in summer and tribal people wore little more than breechcloths for the men and aprons for the women. Both wore sandals. The men made robes and blankets from rabbit skins to keep the people warm in colder months.

There were at least three bands of Mojave, divided into 22 clans. Although the bands lived in scattered settlements across their territory, they came together in times of war.

IN THE KNOW

Both Mojave men and women had tattooed chins. They often painted their bodies as well, for ceremonies and warfare.

Most warriors were men who had "great dreams," or visions, which they believed gave them special powers in battle. The Mojave became close allies of the Quechan, and fought alongside them in battles against the Pima and Maricopa. The Mojave were friendly toward the first European visitors—Juan de Oñate in 1604 and Father Garcés in 1776—because they did not try to invade Mojave land. This changed in the 1820s, when white trappers and traders started crossing into Mojave land, forcing the tribe to defend its territory.

In 1857, the Mojave and Quechan lost a major battle against the Maricopa and Pima, leaving the Mojave tribe much weaker. The following year, angry that white trespassers continued to cross their lands, the tribe attacked a settlers' wagon train, prompting the U.S. Army to send troops to protect settlers, miners, and others from more Mojave attacks. In 1859, the troops built Fort Mojave and stayed there until 1890, defending the newcomers. In 1865, the Army moved many Mojave people to the Colorado River Reservation.

In 1870, the U.S. government created Fort Mojave Reservation, 42,000 acres (17,000 ha) spread across Arizona, California, and Nevada, where members of the tribe still live today. The Mojave also share the Colorado River Reservation with Navajo, Hopi, and Chemehuevi people. ✎

This photograph, taken in 1887, shows four Mojave chiefs in American-style clothing rather than their Native dress. Second from the left is Rowdy, a Yuma tribal member, acting as interpreter—presumably between the Mojave and the American photographer, Edgar Alexander Mearns (1856–1916).

CODE TALKERS

The first American Indian code talkers served during World War I, at the suggestion of Mose Bellmard, a member of the Kaw Nation of the Great Plains. Code talking was a way of using tribal language to make secret communications. During World War II, the Marine Corps recruited more than 400 Navajo men as code talkers. With the first 29 Navajos recruited, the Marine Corps founded a code-talking school. The code talkers developed a special code that assigned a Navajo word for each letter of the English alphabet, and then they trained the new recruits. Code talkers had to memorize the code and learned how to set up, operate, and fix communications equipment. The Navajo served in the Pacific against Japan, while code talkers from other tribes went to Europe and North Africa.

NAVAJO

(NA-vuh-ho)

LANGUAGE GROUP:
Athabascan (Na-Dené)

GREETING:
Yá'át'ééh

THANK YOU:
'ahéhee'

LOCATION PRECONTACT:
Arizona, New Mexico, Utah, Colorado

LOCATION TODAY:
Arizona, New Mexico, Utah

The Navajo tribe is the largest in the United States, with more than 300,000 members. They call themselves Diné, which means "people" in their language. Their southwestern homeland, Dinétah, is a vast area bordered by four mountains—Mount Blanca, Mount Taylor, the San Francisco Peaks, and Mount Hesperus. These mountains are sacred to the tribe.

Like the Apache, the Navajo tribe speaks an Athabascan language, and originally moved south from Canada. In the Southwest, they lived across a wide area including present-day northern Arizona, New Mexico, Utah, and Colorado. Traditionally, they were nomadic hunters, who raided the Pueblo and Hopi tribes for food and slaves. They also learned skills such as farming and weaving from these tribes.

Spanish colonists introduced horses, sheep, goats, and other animals to the Southwest and, over time, the Navajo became ranching people. They lived in homes called *hogans*, six-sided dwellings, which they made from wooden poles, bark, and packed mud. The doors always faced east toward the rising sun to welcome the sun's warmth. As the Navajo settled into their new life as ranchers, they also developed their arts and crafts. Navajo artists created beautiful turquoise and silver jewelry, baskets, and colorful woven rugs.

During the 1700s and early 1800s, the Navajo continued to raid other tribes, as well as Mexican and Spanish settlements. Tribal leaders such as Manuelito led Navajo attacks in response to the Treaty of Guadalupe Hidalgo, which failed to recognize tribal lands that straddled the new border between Mexico and the United States. The U.S. troops fought back, destroying tribal farms, homes, and ➡

This woven saddle blanket is more than 100 years old. The chevron pattern is typical of Navajo designs, as are the bright colors of the wool.

Eugene Joe, pictured here with his family, is a traditional Navajo medicine man and sand artist. In the distance is Shiprock—a sacred geological site that is featured in stories of Navajo history.

MANUELITO

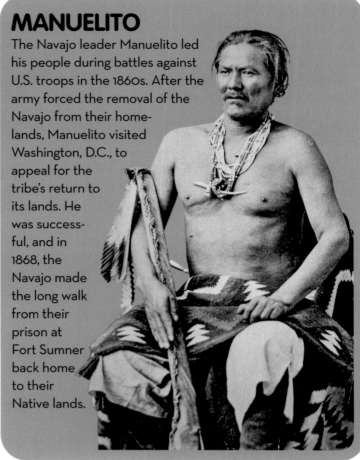

The Navajo leader Manuelito led his people during battles against U.S. troops in the 1860s. After the army forced the removal of the Navajo from their homelands, Manuelito visited Washington, D.C., to appeal for the tribe's return to its lands. He was successful, and in 1868, the Navajo made the long walk from their prison at Fort Sumner back home to their Native lands.

livestock. The Navajo were forced to surrender. About 9,000 Navajo began what they call Hwéeldi, known in English as the "Long Walk," to their imprisonment at Fort Sumner, in Bosque Redondo, New Mexico. Hundreds died on the 18-day, 300-mile (480-km) journey. Many more died at Bosque Redondo, where supplies were scarce and the crops failed to grow. In 1868, the government assigned the Navajo a reservation in their homelands. Many Navajo live there today, on land bordered by the four sacred mountains to the north, east, south, and west.

PIMA

(PEE-mah)

LANGUAGE GROUP:
Uto-Aztecan

GREETING:
Hoin

THANK YOU:
Ab ho'ige'ith

LOCATION PRECONTACT:
Arizona; Mexico

LOCATION TODAY:
Arizona

For centuries, the Pima lived in the Gila and Salt River valleys, near present-day Phoenix, Arizona, and northern Sonora, Mexico. The Spanish, who met them in the 1500s, called the tribe Pima, but the name they call themselves, Akimel O'odham, means "river people." Tribal history traces them back to the Hohokam people who originally inhabited this land. Like their ancestors, the Pima farmed in the dry, hot climate by digging miles of canals between the river and their crops. They produced good harvests of corn, squash, and beans, which kept the Pima communities fed. The Spanish introduced the Pima to wheat, which they grew and traded as well. The tribe gained a reputation for farming, and also for

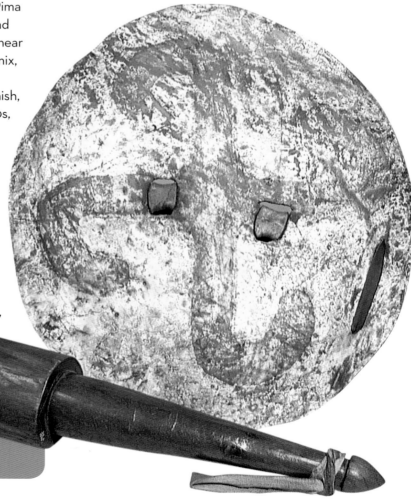

This wooden shield and club date from around 1840 and are typical of the kinds of weapons the Pima used to defend themselves around that time.

A Pima mother attends to her baby, swaddled on a cradle-board. In the distance is their home—a dome-shaped hut made from pliable poles and covered with grass.

weaving beautiful watertight baskets. Many featured the mazelike pattern that is seen on the Great Seal of the Salt River Pima–Maricopa community (pictured on p. 163).

After the 1854 Gadsden Purchase, a deal through which the U.S. bought Mexican land in the Southwest, the United States took control of Pima territory. White settlers moved to the area to farm, and in 1859 the U.S. government transferred most Pima to the Gila River Indian Reservation, along with the Maricopa. Settlers directed river water to their farms, making water on the reservation scarce. In 1879, the government established a second reservation for the Pima and Maricopa farther north, on the Salt River, but the tribes were still short of water. For many years, Pima chiefs appealed to the government to restore their water rights. In 2004, the Arizona Water Settlement Act was passed. It provides the tribe with enough water to meet the basic needs of their reservation. Today, the Pima-Maricopa Irrigation Project hopes to bring back the tribe's farming traditions—in the 1870s, the Pima were producing three million pounds (1.4 millon kg) of wheat a year. Today they farm 12,000 acres-worth (5,000 ha) of cotton, melons, potatoes, onions, broccoli, and carrots. 🖎

IN THE KNOW

Ira Hayes, a Pima tribal member, served in the U.S. Marine Corps during World War II. Hayes was one of the six men to raise the American flag after capturing the island of Iwo Jima from the Japanese in 1945.

THE *HORNO* OVEN

The *horno* is a beehive-shaped, outdoor oven made from adobe (dried clay) or dried clay bricks covered with mud. The horno, which means "oven" in Spanish, came to the Southwest region with Spanish settlers. They themselves had based the design on a North African version. The Spanish also introduced wheat, and the Pueblo began baking bread in the horno. They make a wood fire in the oven, scrape out the ash that is left, and leave the bread to bake in the remaining heat. Bread is a very important part of the Pueblo diet, especially for feasts. Women can bake dozens of loaves at a time in a large horno.

THE TAOS PUEBLO

(village) is the only living Native American community that is both a World Heritage Site and a National Historic Landmark. The Taos lived in these adobe and stone houses between 1000 and 1450 c.e., and the homes are still inhabited today—with no running water or electricity. With a population of around 150 people, this site is the oldest continuously inhabited place in the United States.

PUEBLO

(poo-EB-low)

LANGUAGE GROUP:
Various

GREETING:
Guw'aadzi (Laguna)

THANK YOU:
Dawaa'e (Laguna)

LOCATION PRECONTACT:
New Mexico

LOCATION TODAY:
New Mexico

The word pueblo is Spanish for "village," but it also refers to a group of southwestern people and the type of homes they built. The Pueblo people, who include the Hopi and Zuni tribes, descend from the ancient Pueblo, who lived in villages in the Four Corners area—the point at which the modern states of Colorado, New Mexico, Utah, and Arizona meet. The Pueblo made their homes from adobe—a mix of clay, straw, and water. Often several stories high, these houses contained many rooms. Large groups of people lived in the Pueblo villages and grew corn, beans, and squash on nearby farms. They could grow crops in even the driest areas, using dry farming methods designed to collect and conserve what little rainwater fell. Some Pueblo still maintain traditional homes and continue to farm.

When the Spanish introduced them to tobacco and peaches, the Pueblo began growing these, too. The Spanish demanded a percentage of the Pueblos' crops and labor, and took over their villages. They built churches and tried to erase Pueblo religions, while converting them to Catholicism.

Although the Pueblo people were successful in driving the Spanish out in 1680, during the Pueblo Revolt, their lands came under Spanish rule again 12 years later, and remained so until 1821. Although now the Spanish did not force people to convert to Catholicism, they established church communities that continue to practice today.

There are 19 Pueblo communities: Acoma, Cochiti, Laguna, Isleta, Santo Domingo, Santa Ana, San Felipe, Santa Clara, San Ildefonso, Picuris, Nambe, Pojoaque, Taos, Jemez, Ohkay Owingeh, Zia, Sandia, Zuni, and Tesuque. Of all the tribes of North America, the Pueblo may be the ones whose lives most closely represent the lives of their ancestors. The different communities have similar beliefs and traditions, but each has its own history and identity. They make pottery and baskets using traditional methods, hold traditional dances, speak their native languages, and protect their ancestral cultures. Some Pueblo ranch and farm, and others work in nearby cities. ✐

A member of the Taos Pueblo stands in front of stone houses that look much the same as they did centuries ago. Over the years, the Taos have kept their pueblos intact by re-plastering the walls with thick layers of mud.

PUEBLO REVOLT

Pueblo tribes suffered under the Spanish mission system from the late 1500s onward. The Europeans enforced slavery and new religions and customs, and brought diseases that killed more than 15,000 Pueblo people. By 1680, the Pueblo resolved to fight. They enlisted the help of 46 communities, including members of the Hopi and Zuni tribes. To coordinate events, one member carried a knotted cord from one community to the next (pictured here in a reenactment). Each knot signified a day, counting down to the start of the rebellion. Under the leadership of Popé, a medicine man from the Tewa tribe, the Pueblos attacked Santa Fe. They destroyed Spanish churches and settlements, killed hundreds of Spaniards, and pushed the survivors into Mexico. It was a huge victory for the Pueblo people. The Spanish stayed away for 12 years, and never succeeded in taking the Pueblos' tribal lands.

QUECHAN

(kwuh-TSAN)

LANGUAGE GROUP:
Yuman

LANGUAGE:
Currently limited in use; no dictionary of terms available

LOCATION PRECONTACT:
Arizona, California

LOCATION TODAY:
Arizona, California

For thousands of years, the Quechan people lived along the section of the Colorado River that now forms the border between Arizona and California. They farmed the river valley, using the yearly floods to water their crops of corn, beans, squash, and sunflowers. Women combined wild greens with the beans, corn, and squash to make delicious stews. The men caught fish, and hunted rabbits and other small animals. Like other tribes of the Southwest, the Quechan wore few clothes, particularly in the summer months. Women wore skirts made from bark, but men rarely wore anything. Instead, the men painted their bodies. Blankets and animal hides kept the people warm in winter. Men wore their hair long and in braids, while women tended to have shorter hair, worn loose.

The Quechan traded with other tribes—such as the Hopi, who sold them blankets—but the Pima and Maricopa were their enemies. War was part of Quechan life, and they waged war or raids, depending on their needs. The Quechan tribe also controlled an important crossing on the Colorado River, which brought them into conflict with the Spanish when they built settlements there. When Spanish missionaries tried to convert the tribe to Catholicism, and settlers stole their food and livestock, the Quechan revolted. In 1781 the tribe attacked the settlements and drove the Spanish settlers away.

The Quechan returned to their traditional way of life, but this was disrupted again by the gold rush of 1849. ➡️

This Quechan female figure carries a baby. Made from pottery, she wears a headband and has tattoos on her chin.

For a while, the Quechan kept control of their river crossing, charging settlers and others to cross by ferry. Eventually this led to more clashes. In 1850, the U.S. Army built Fort Yuma on the Colorado River to protect the settlers, and by 1853, the government had taken control of the Quechan lands.

In 1884, the government established a reservation for the Quechan, although the tribe went on to lose many acres of this land to white settlers in the following years. After years of court trials, the government finally returned 25,000 acres (10,000 ha) to the Quechan people in 1978.

Today, the Quechan population totals over 3,200 members. The tribe does not have a written language and there are only around 200 people who can speak it fluently. Largely an agricultural community, the tribe leases thousands of acres of its

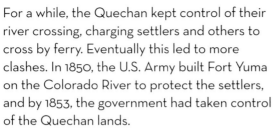

This yellow-brown Quechan water jar has four spouts and is painted with a red geometric pattern. The handle features the figure of a head, decorated with bead earrings and a choker. The jar is around 130 years old.

In Quechan ancestral history, the first people came down to Earth from a sacred mountain. The Quechan name, Kwatsáan, means "those who descended."

reservation to both Native and non-Native farmers, for whom they then work.

In 1996 Quechan elder Preston J. Arrow-Weed founded the Ah-Mut Pipa Foundation (named for the Quechan god, Ah-Mut) on the Fort Yuma Reservation, home to today's Quechan tribe. The organization hosts cultural events—films, talks, and walks—centering on the tribe's history and culture. ☛

TIGUA

(TEE-wah)

LANGUAGE GROUP:
Tanoan

LANGUAGE:
Currently limited in use; no dictionary of terms available

LOCATION PRECONTACT:
New Mexico

LOCATION TODAY:
Texas

The Tigua tribe, also known as the Ysleta del Sur Pueblo, is the oldest community in Texas, and the only one of Pueblo descent. During the Pueblo Revolt in 1680, Pueblo people seized the area that is now Santa Fe, New Mexico, from the Spanish. The Spanish governor Antonio de Otermin escaped with some of his people and fled to Isleta Pueblo.

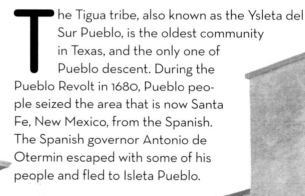

La Misión de la Ysleta del Sur, pictured here, in 1936, was built by the Tigua peoples in 1682. It is thought to be the first mission to have been established in what is now the state of Texas.

As part of an ongoing community garden project, members of the Tigua tribe teach their youth how to grow corn, squash, and beans using modern methods.

Christi de la Ysleta. In their new home, they built canals to water their corn, wheat, and other crops, and raised cattle and horses. In the early days of Spanish and Mexican rule, Tigua men worked as scouts and guides, helping to defend the territory against raiding tribes.

In 1751, the Spanish king gave the tribe a small area of land around what is now El Paso, Texas, but in the 1800s, the Tigua lost most of it to white settlers. In 1854, the state of Texas recognized the Tigua rights to the land, but the city of El Paso grew around the small pueblo, or village, and the tribe struggled to survive on the shrinking area of farmland. Today, the Ysleta del Sur pueblo is about 530 acres (210 ha). The tribe runs an entertainment center and other businesses, and many tribal members work in the city of El Paso. Though the Spanish converted the Tigua to Catholicism, the tribe keeps many of its ancestral customs, including ceremonies at which a Sacred Drum is played. The tribe's most prized relic, the drum is thought to date back as far as 1680. ✐

The Isleta people did not fight in the Pueblo Revolt, but when Otermin arrived, he found the Spanish had burned the pueblo down in an attempt to gain control. Many tribal people had fled, leaving just 385 remaining. Otermin captured them and took them to the area of modern-day El Paso, Texas. Building a new community in El Paso, these people became the Tigua, and called their settlement Ysleta del Sur ("People of the South").

Prepared to embrace some Spanish customs, the Tigua converted to Catholicism and built a church, La Misión de Corpus

TOHONO O'ODHAM

(TOHN-oh AUTH-um)

LANGUAGE GROUP:
Uto-Aztecan

GREETING:
'I 'att hu dada (we have arrived); *Heu'u dada 'amt* (yes, you have arrived)

LOCATION PRECONTACT:
Arizona

LOCATION TODAY:
Arizona (U.S.); Mexico

The homeland of the Tohono O'odham, "desert people," is the Sonoran Desert in what is now Arizona and Mexico. They probably descend from the ancient Hohokam people who once inhabited southern Arizona and northern Mexico. The Tohono O'odham grew some of their food, but they also gathered wild plants and hunted small desert animals. In the winter, the tribe split into family groups and moved to mountain homes, where people had access to water from natural springs. They wore clothes and sandals made from leather and cotton, and used a range of plant materials—yucca, willow, and bear grass among them—to weave coiled baskets for storing and transporting food.

When Spanish settlers arrived in the Southwest, they brought horses, cattle, and new plants. They also built missions, or religious settlements. Many Tohono O'odham people became Catholic. The 1800s brought conflict when miners, ranchers, and others moved into Tohono O'odham territory.

Taken in 1900, this photograph shows a Tohono O'odham basketmaker working on a new round basket. Beside her are several she has already made.

Between 1840 and 1843, the tribe fought to defend their land against Mexican encroachment, but the tribe was unsuccessful. The situation became more complicated in 1854, when the Gadsden Purchase split their territory between Mexico and the United States.

To compensate the tribe, the U.S. government created the first reservation for the Tohono O'odham in 1874, a second ⟫

This illustration shows two Tohono O'odham women harvesting organ pipe cactus fruit. It was printed in a land survey that set out to establish the border between the United States and Mexico in 1857.

in 1882, and a third in 1917. Today, the tribe lives on 2.8 million acres (1.1 million ha) across the three American reservations. (There are another nine Tohono O'odham communities in Mexico, but the border patrols between the United States and Mexico make it difficult for tribal members to travel between the two countries.)

In summer, tribal members work on their farms, planting tepary beans, a traditional food, as well as corn, watermelon, and squash. They also harvest wild desert fruit, such as prickly pear. The tribe's traditions remain an important part of its identity. Singing forms a regular part of reservation life, accompanying planting, healing, dancing, and ceremonies. In this way, the language of the songs and the stories they tell are passed from the elders to the younger generation. Every fall, hundreds of Tohono O'odham people in the United States travel 55 miles (88 km) on foot, to Magdalena de Kino, Mexico, to join their relatives for the Festival of St. Francis—a Catholic tradition honoring St. Francis of Assisi, who gave up a life of luxury to become a Catholic. The intention is for tribal members to take time to reflect on events in their own lives.

IN THE KNOW

The Tonoho O'odham kept calendar sticks that recorded important ceremonies and significant weather events—for example, snow or summer rain. Each stick was divided into segments for each month and carved with symbols to represent the events.

YAQUI

(YAH-kee)

LANGUAGE GROUP:
Uto-Aztecan

GREETING:
Aman ne tevote em yevihnewi

THANK YOU:
Liohbwana

LOCATION PRECONTACT:
Arizona; Mexico

LOCATION TODAY:
Arizona (U.S.); Mexico

The Yaqui inhabited a large area of what is now northwestern Mexico. They lived in small villages along the Yaqui River, in houses built from wooden poles and covered with earth and grass. The tribe dug ditches to catch floodwater to grow crops of corn and cotton. They also collected wild food that grew around them, such as cactus fruit, and caught sea bass in the Gulf of California.

The Yaqui stopped Spanish explorers from crossing their territory in the 1500s, but made peace with them when they returned in 1617. The Spanish established missions and brought new foods, such as wheat and pomegranates. They also introduced cattle and sheep to the Yaqui. The tribe adopted these new things, but they came at a price. The Yaqui were forced to work for the Spanish and to adopt the Catholic religion. Through the decades, the Spanish became more demanding. They created larger Yaqui towns with Catholic churches, and wanted more land and workers. In 1740, the Yaqui rebelled. The Spanish responded by killing at least 5,000 Yaqui people and forcing many others to flee north.

JUAN BANDERAS

During the Yaqui Wars, Juan Banderas (pictured) led his people to defend their lands and rights, joining forces with other tribes, including the Pima. Initial conflict with the Mexicans in 1827 ended with Yaqui defeat, primarily because they had bows and arrows, while the Mexicans had guns. Armed with better weaponry in 1833, Banderas and his followers still could not defeat the Mexicans, and were forced to surrender.

Three young children of the Yaqui tribe play on a canoe made from cattail, a tall marsh plant with long, flat leaves. Two of the children wear traditional grass skirts and the third has a deer-hide apron.

Once Mexico had won independence from Spain, the Yaqui tribe wanted its freedom, too. A Yaqui revolt against the Mexican authorities began in 1825 and lasted eight years. After the Mexican forces had defeated the rebels, many Yaqui moved north to the United States. Those who remained settled in ancestral land along the Yaqui River, where their descendants continue to lead traditional farming lives.

In 1964, the U.S. government gave the Pascua Yaqui Tribe of Arizona a small reservation and officially recognized the tribe in 1978. Yaqui culture has since merged ancestral tradition with that of Catholicism introduced by the Spanish. The tribe has a number of societies, including the Kohtumbre Ya'ura, which focuses on rituals associated with Lent, and the Oficio Achalim, which keeps the Yaqui in touch with ancestral beliefs. ✎

YAVAPAI

(YAV-uh-pie)

LANGUAGE GROUP:
Yuman

GREETING:
M'hahjik'gah

THANK YOU:
Honniiguhm

LOCATION PRECONTACT:
Arizona

LOCATION TODAY:
Arizona (U.S.); Mexico

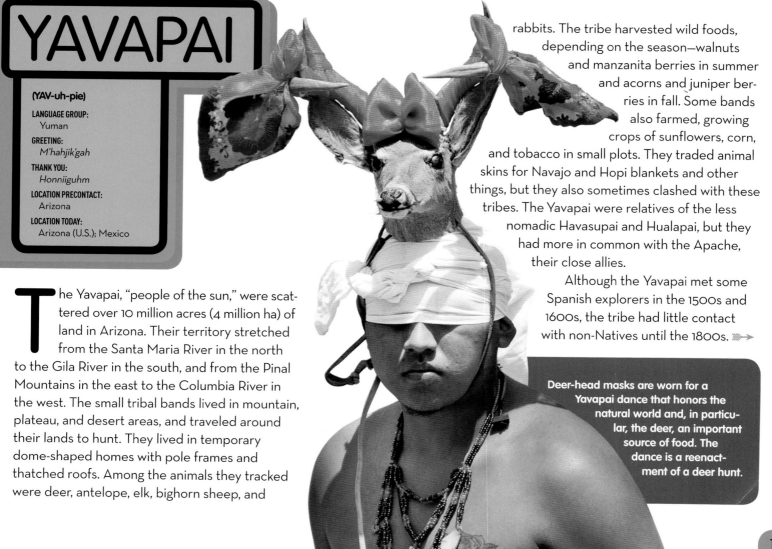

The Yavapai, "people of the sun," were scattered over 10 million acres (4 million ha) of land in Arizona. Their territory stretched from the Santa Maria River in the north to the Gila River in the south, and from the Pinal Mountains in the east to the Columbia River in the west. The small tribal bands lived in mountain, plateau, and desert areas, and traveled around their lands to hunt. They lived in temporary dome-shaped homes with pole frames and thatched roofs. Among the animals they tracked were deer, antelope, elk, bighorn sheep, and rabbits. The tribe harvested wild foods, depending on the season—walnuts and manzanita berries in summer and acorns and juniper berries in fall. Some bands also farmed, growing crops of sunflowers, corn, and tobacco in small plots. They traded animal skins for Navajo and Hopi blankets and other things, but they also sometimes clashed with these tribes. The Yavapai were relatives of the less nomadic Havasupai and Hualapai, but they had more in common with the Apache, their close allies.

Although the Yavapai met some Spanish explorers in the 1500s and 1600s, the tribe had little contact with non-Natives until the 1800s. ➤

Deer-head masks are worn for a Yavapai dance that honors the natural world and, in particular, the deer, an important source of food. The dance is a reenactment of a deer hunt.

This Yavapai basket bowl dates from around 1920 and is made from dried yucca root and willow. The decorative design was probably painted on after weaving and features animal motifs.

VIOLA JIMULLA

Viola Jimulla was the first female chief of a Native American tribe. Born in 1878, she married Sam Jimulla, a Yavapai chief at the Prescott Indian Reservation. After Sam's death in 1940, Viola became chief, guiding her people until her own death in 1966. In 1986, Viola Jimulla was inducted into the Arizona Women's Hall of Fame. Her granddaughter, Patricia McGee, later became the Yavapai tribal president from the 1970s to the 1990s.

Starting in 1863, tensions mounted with the California gold rush, when prospectors found gold on Yavapai land. Miners poured into this part of Arizona.

The U.S. government sent the army to move the Yavapai to a reservation at Rio Verde, Arizona. The bands were scattered over a wide area, so this took some time, but 10 years after the discovery of gold, most Yavapai were living on the Rio Verde Reservation. In the winter of 1875, U.S. soldiers forced 1,500 Apache and Yavapai to march to San Carlos, Arizona, almost 200 miles (320 km) away. Nearly half the people died on the long, cold march.

Finally, in the 1900s, the government established reservations for the Yavapai at Fort McDowell, Prescott, Arizona, and Camp Verde, Arizona. Apache survivors of the forced march also moved to Camp Verde and the two tribes became the Yavapai-Apache Nation. In the 1970s, the Fort McDowell band protested against the building of the Orme Dam, which was set to flood their lands and force them to move again. The government agreed to stop the project in 1981, a victory that is celebrated annually with a powwow.

THE ART OF JEWELRY

Many tribal people used beads, shells, stones, and wood as jewelry. After the mid-1800s, the Navajo, Zuni, and Hopi perfected the art of silver jewelry-making. A Navajo man named Atsidi Sani was one of the first jewelry makers. He also taught his sons the art of working with silver. Sani and his sons created intricate hand-hammered or cast pieces. The Navajo "squash blossom" necklace, with a crescent shape at the bottom, became a trademark of the tribe.

The Hopi started to make silver jewelry in the late 1800s. In the 1900s, the tribe became famous for pieces that used two layers of silver. Meanwhile, the Zuni tribe mastered the art of lapidary, or working with stones and gems. They set turquoise pieces into the silver, creating stunning rings and bracelets (shown here). Today, several tribes still make fine silver and turquoise jewelry for themselves, and to sell as souvenirs to visitors to their reservations.

ZUNI

(ZOO-nee)

LANGUAGE GROUP:
Isolate

GREETING:
Keshhi

THANK YOU:
Elahkwa

LOCATION PRECONTACT:
New Mexico

LOCATION TODAY:
New Mexico

The Zuni people have lived in the Southwest for about 7,000 years, originally building pueblos along the Zuni River in present-day New Mexico. Like other Pueblo communities, the Zuni built stone houses and plastered the walls with mud. Several stories high, they contained many interconnected rooms. The landscape bears witness to their occupation and is dotted with abandoned ancient settlements. Today, most Zuni still live in, or near, the main village of the Zuni Pueblo, a settlement built around 1000 C.E. Their reservation in New Mexico covers 450,000 acres (180,000 ha).

The Zuni were excellent farmers, who began farming new crops and raising animals introduced by the Spanish. They began to grow wheat and raise sheep, chickens, and cattle.

Typical of the Zuni style of pottery, this water jar is decorated with an abstract geometric pattern, painted in black, white, and red. It dates from around 1880.

The Spanish also had a religious influence: In the late 1500s, they built missions in some of the Zuni villages, and tried to force the Zuni to give up their own beliefs and convert to Catholicism. The Zuni resisted and joined the Pueblo Revolt in 1680. After this, the Zuni moved to Corn Mesa—a high mountain that was a sacred place away from conflict. They stayed there for 12 years before moving to live at Halona Idiwan'a, or "the Middle Place." Situated about 150 miles (240 km) west of Albuquerque, New Mexico, this village became the Zuni Pueblo, the tribe's present home.

Today, Zuni people keep their ancestors' traditions alive. Children learn their language at school and the tribe holds many social and religious ceremonies. These include the Sha'lak'o, a dance performed on the winter solstice, asking for blessings on the year to come. Visitors can learn about Zuni culture and history at Zuni's A:shiwi A:wan Museum and Heritage Center. The Zuni people still farm, but they also make beautiful jewelry, pottery, and other arts. ✐

This young Zuni is dressed for the tribe's Comanche dance, originally performed to mimic the Comanches before warring with them. He wears a braided headband decorated on either side with upright eagle feathers.

💡 IN THE KNOW

The Zuni language is unique to the tribe and unlike any other. Linguists use the word "isolate" to describe this. It is not clearly related to any other known native language.

HOW THE STARS CAME TO BE

Coyote is a main character in several American Indian stories relating to the night sky. According to one Navajo story, Coyote is responsible for creating the Milky Way, seen here.

When Mother Earth was born, everything was blank and empty. Then out of all directions came animals of many different varieties. She asked them to be her caretakers. She told them that soon Brother Moon would arrive with an important job for them.

On the third night, Brother Moon arrived. All the animals gathered to hear him. "We must make Mother Earth beautiful," he said. "During four days and nights, each of you will have a job to perform, so that on the fifth day Mother Earth will awaken with limbs made of trees; seeds for nourishment; and ponds, lakes, and rivers with water to quench all thirst." The animals agreed. Then Brother Moon told the birds to drop seeds in all directions so that grass, flowers, and herbs would grow. Next, he asked the badger to dig and dig, to create lakes and ponds. While this creation was happening, lazy Coyote watched. He sat back as the badger tossed dirt into piles that would rise into great mountains; as beavers built dams of wood to divert the waters that would form the rivers; and as buffalo, deer, and antelope trampled the seeds to plant them deep into the ground.

On the fourth night, Coyote thought, "When creation is finished, everybody will be recognized for their good deeds, except me." He finally asked Brother Moon, "What can I do to be important?" Brother Moon replied, "Oh no, you are too lazy and clumsy." Coyote begged, "Please, let me do something." At last Brother Moon gave in: "Okay, Coyote, I have one last task. Take this jar to the South Pole; when you arrive, Polar Bear will meet you and take the jar." Coyote did a dance of joy. Brother Moon said, "Whatever you do, do not open the jar. Only Polar Bear can open it."

During Coyote's journey south all the animals stopped to watch him. "Look, Coyote is actually doing something," said Magpie. Coyote's ego began to grow; he held his head high and hummed a song. "Let them see me," he thought. "I, too, will be important once I complete my task."

His head held high as he neared his destination, Coyote stumbled on a rock. The jar flew into the air and he raced to catch it. But it hit the ground, and the lid broke into pieces. Bright, shiny objects flew out. Coyote tried to catch them, but they were too fast; they flew straight up into the heavens. As they rose up, Coyote began to weep, for he had ruined the sheer blackness of the night. He returned home with his head down, knowing that he would be remembered for ruining the heavens.

To this day Coyote howls as he looks up into the sky because he sees his mistake. On full moon nights, his howls are even stronger because Brother Moon reminds him of it. Little does Coyote know that he created something beautiful for all of us. This is how the stars came to be.

**Cristopher R. Velarde,
Jicarilla Apache/Santa Clara Pueblo**

A Native American Vietnam War veteran sits alongside his granddaughter on the Fort Hall Indian Reservation in Idaho.

THE GREAT BASIN AND PLATEAU

Soaring mountains, river valleys, deserts, forests, and plains make up the Great Basin and Plateau region. This was—and remains—a territory rich in animal and plant life. Native women gathered wild root vegetables, seeds, nuts, and berries, while men hunted buffalo, deer, and bighorn sheep, as well as smaller prey—rabbits, waterfowl, and sage grouse. They fished for salmon and trout in the Fraser, Columbia, Snake, and Colorado Rivers and several large lakes.

THE STORY OF **THE GREAT BASIN AND PLATEAU PEOPLE**

The people of the Great Basin and Plateau shared their homelands for countless generations and some still share these lands today. They used the natural resources that the Earth gave them and thrived, even in the driest deserts and coldest mountains. Each tribe had spiritual beliefs that honored their plant and animal neighbors in different seasons. Each also had rules that governed both where and how much tribal members hunted, gathered, and fished, making sure that the tribes had the same amount of resources available to them every year.

Natural Resources

In 1680, Pueblo tribes of the Southwest rebelled against the Spanish, releasing thousands of Spanish horses into the wild. Captured by people in the Great Basin and Plateau, the horses allowed tribes to travel farther and to transport heavy loads. Some began using horses to hunt big game and to trade goods over greater distances. Horses were also valuable for trade, and tribes such as the Cayuse became richer and more powerful as they owned and domesticated more wild horses.

Some tribes depended on the buffalo as one of their main foods, and lived in tepees covered in buffalo hides. The wild plants and roots gathered by the women were used as food, but also to make medicines and tools. Women cleaned, dried, and stored many foods, to feed their families through winter. When the men brought home meat and fish, the women cleaned and dried these, too. Of particular importance to tribes of this region was the camas root. Tasting a little like baked sweet potato when cooked, the root was a good source of carbohydrates. When dried, it was ground into flour to make bread.

Seasonal Ceremonies

Winters in some parts of this territory could be very cold and harsh and summers were often scorching hot. But the tribes of the Great Basin and Plateau welcomed the seasons and celebrated them with ceremonies. In spring, feasts were held to celebrate the first greens and root vegetables to sprout and the return of the salmon. In fall, celebrations rejoiced in the harvest of berries and pine nuts, and in the arrival of migrating waterfowl.

Trade and the Arrival of Settlers

The central location of the Great Basin and Plateau region allowed the tribes living there to develop a thriving trade network. The Pend d'Oreille, Umatilla, and many others traded with tribes from the Northwest Coast, California, and the Plains regions. People of the Great Basin and Plateau exchanged their hides, roots, dried fish, baskets, and furs for shell beads, oils, and other products of the coastal tribes. They passed these on to Plains tribes, receiving buffalo robes in return.

Once European fur traders arrived in the Great Basin and Plateau region, many tribes also started trading with them. Sadly, the Europeans introduced fatal diseases to the tribes, such as smallpox, measles, and influenza. They also opened the way for more settlers to head West. The opening of the Oregon Trail from Missouri in the east to Oregon in the west changed the tribal homelands forever. It brought thousands of white settlers to the region. The settlers pushed Native tribes off their lands, often by force.

During the mid-1800s, the U.S. government signed many treaties with numerous tribes. Several treaties established reservations for Native people, often in places far away from a tribe's ancestral land. Tribes with different languages and cultures found themselves living side by side on lands that rarely supported hunting, fishing, or gathering. Where the land was relatively flat and fertile, some became ranchers, but many had to find work in towns and cities for their income. More recently, some tribes have opened golf courses, resorts, and other businesses on their reservation lands; others have become energy providers, operating wind and solar farms.

New ways of living have not replaced ancestral traditions and family ties. Annual events are held to honor ancient beliefs. Most importantly, the people of the Great Basin and Plateau region have kept their promise to be guardians of the land. Their mission is always to respect and protect the lakes, rivers, animals, and plants that nourished their ancestors so that generations to come can flourish.

These hide leggings and matching moccasins, from around 1910, belonged to a Shoshone woman. They are decorated with colorful beaded floral motifs.

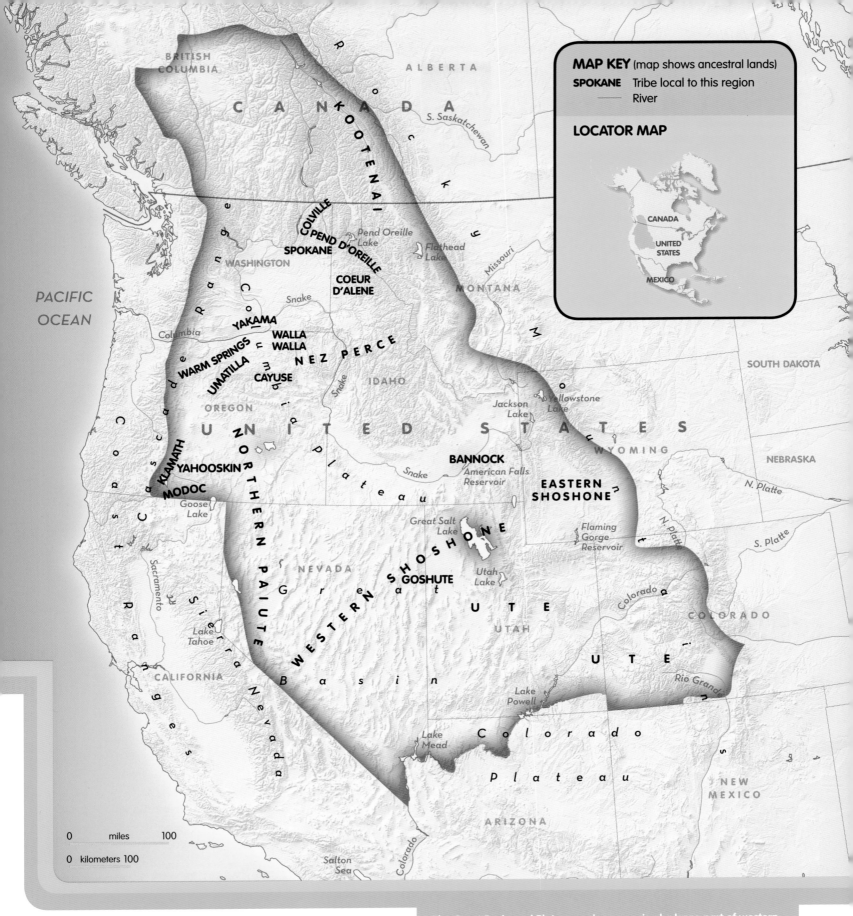

MAP KEY (map shows ancestral lands)
SPOKANE Tribe local to this region
——— River

LOCATOR MAP

PACIFIC OCEAN

BRITISH COLUMBIA

CANADA

ALBERTA

S. Saskatchewan

WASHINGTON

COLVILLE
PEND D'OREILLE
SPOKANE
COEUR D'ALENE

Pend Oreille Lake

Flathead Lake

MONTANA

Missouri

YAKAMA
WALLA WALLA
WARM SPRINGS
UMATILLA
CAYUSE

NEZ PERCE

OREGON

Snake

IDAHO

Columbia

Jackson Lake

Yellowstone Lake

SOUTH DAKOTA

UNITED STATES

KLAMATH
YAHOOSKIN
MODOC

NORTHERN PAIUTE

Plateau

BANNOCK

Snake

American Falls Reservoir

EASTERN SHOSHONE

WYOMING

NEBRASKA

N. Platte

Goose Lake

Great Salt Lake

Flaming Gorge Reservoir

N. Platte

WESTERN SHOSHONE

GOSHUTE

Utah Lake

UTE

NEVADA

Great Basin

UTAH

Colorado

COLORADO

S. Platte

Lake Tahoe

CALIFORNIA

Sierra Nevada

Coast Ranges

Cascade Range

Sacramento

Lake Powell

UTE

Rio Grande

Lake Mead

Colorado Plateau

Colorado

NEW MEXICO

ARIZONA

Salton Sea

Colorado

CANADA
UNITED STATES
MEXICO

0 miles 100
0 kilometers 100

The Great Basin and Plateau region comprised a large part of western North America. Many tribes lived here before contact with Europeans, most of them speaking languages with roots in Uto-Aztecan, Salishan, and Penutian. The only tribe to have lost its ancestral lands since this time is the Modoc tribe, which was forced to move to Oklahoma. The Goshute and Yahooskin are offshoots of the Western Shoshone and Northern Paiute tribes.

The first people to live in the Great Basin and Plateau region left behind amazing artifacts about their lives that give us many clues as to how the tribes lived. Some of their descendants were among the first tribal people to obtain horses. The mid-1800s brought waves of settlers to the area, leading to disease and war. Many tribes fought for recognition, land rights, and land protection throughout the 1900s, and some still do.

12,500 B.C.E.

People living in the region. Excavations of the Paisley Caves, in Oregon, prove that people lived in this area for many thousands of years.

600–1300 C.E.

The Fremont Culture develops. The Fremont people lived along the Fremont River Valley in present-day Utah. These people were hunter-gatherers but also grew crops of corn, beans, and squash. Archaeologists have uncovered rock etchings (pictured) and paintings of animals such as deer and bighorn sheep.

1300

People speaking Numic languages spread through the Great Basin. Numic languages evolved from the Uto-Aztecan family of Native languages (see p. 153). Today's Shoshone, Paiute, and Ute tribes all speak languages with Numic roots.

1600s–1750

Great Basin and Plateau tribes own horses. The Southern Ute and Eastern Shoshone tribes captured horses that once belonged to Spanish explorers. Pictured is a Shoshone robe depicting horses used in battle.

1805–1806

Lewis and Clark expedition. Meriwether Lewis and William Clark met the Nez Perce, Shoshone, and many other tribes in the northern Great Basin and Plateau region. Sacagawea, a Shoshone woman, traveled with them to reassure tribes that they came in peace.

1847–1855

Cayuse War. When missionaries and settlers arrived in Cayuse territory, they brought diseases with them, igniting the Cayuse War.

1847

Mormons arrive in the valley of the Great Salt Lake. The Mormon settlers took over tribal lands, causing conflict.

1860

Pyramid Lake War, Nevada. In 1860, thousands of settlers arrived in Nevada hoping to find gold and silver. This led to unrest between the settlers and the Paiute, Shoshone, and Bannock tribes. War broke out between volunteer militia and tribal warriors, with losses on both sides. Raids and attacks continued into August, followed by a ceasefire.

1842–1860s

Oregon Trail established and California gold rush begins. The Oregon Trail was a 2,000-mile (3,200-km), east-west wagon route from the Missouri River to Oregon that settlers used to move west. When gold was discovered at Sutter's Mill, California, in 1848, 300,000 people streamed into California seeking their fortunes. Many traveled across the Great Basin and Plateau region.

1855

Walla Walla Treaty. In June, the U.S. government signed a treaty with the Cayuse, Umatilla, and Walla Walla tribes. The treaty forced tribes to cede more than 6.4 million acres (2.6 million ha) of land.

1860–1863

Gold discovered. Prospectors found gold deposits in the Great Basin and Plateau region, including in areas that are now Montana and Nevada. This brought thousands of miners, settlers, and others west and onto tribal lands.

1863

Bear River Massacre. The U.S. Army's Third Volunteer soldiers attacked a group of Shoshone at their winter camp on Bear River. The soldiers killed almost 500 Shoshone men, women, and children. The attacking army lost 23 soldiers.

1877

Nez Perce War. Chief Joseph (pictured) led Nez Perce warriors to fight against the U.S. Army. The U.S. government sent the Army to force the tribe to relocate to a small reservation. During the four battles, the Army killed more than 150 Nez Perce people. On October 5, 1877, the Nez Perce surrendered.

1890

Ghost Dance movement begins. A peaceful dance movement evolved in the hope of bringing a brighter future. The U.S. government believed the movement was a threat, and banned it. Pictured is an Arapaho Ghost Dance dress.

1975

Indian Self Determination and Education Assistance Act. The act allowed tribal governments to work with the federal government in running their own schools. Native Americans could now teach their languages and traditions more freely.

1983

Superfund cleanup sites named. The government established a program for cleaning polluted land. In 1983, a silver, lead, and zinc mine at Coeur d'Alene and a uranium mine at Spokane Reservation became cleanup sites.

2001

Coeur d'Alene win land rights battle. When Idaho became a state in 1890, it assumed ownership of Lake Coeur d'Alene. The lake had been included in the Coeur d'Alene Reservation in 1873. In 1889, the tribe sold two-thirds of the lake to the state, but Congress failed to complete the sale. For years, the Coeur d'Alene insisted the sale should be honored—Idaho should keep two-thirds of the lake and return one-third to the tribe. In June 2001, the U.S. Supreme Court finally decided in favor of the tribe and its claim to the southern third of the lake.

BANNOCK

(BAN-uck)

LANGUAGE GROUP:
Uto-Aztecan

GREETING:
Tsaangu beaichehku

THANK YOU:
AisheN

LOCATION PRECONTACT:
Oregon, Idaho

LOCATION TODAY:
Idaho

In the 1600s, the Bannock separated from their Northern Paiute relatives in present-day Oregon and traveled east into what is now southern Idaho, to live among the Northern Shoshone. The Bannock lived in villages in the winter, and moved around the large territory with their Shoshone neighbors in the warmer months. Bannock men hunted pronghorn and bighorn sheep, and fished in the many rivers. The women gathered wild berries, roots, and seeds—making sure to store some for the winter. In the 1700s, the tribe acquired horses. This allowed them to hunt buffalo over much larger distances, including into present-day Wyoming.

Tribal people knew their land well, and the Bannock traveled across the rugged territory using trails and river routes. By the early 1800s, fur traders and American trappers, explorers, and traders also began traveling these Native trails and the land around them. In 1834, Fort Hall in present-day Idaho became a stop for settlers traveling along the Oregon Trail. The trail ran through Bannock and Shoshone territory and tribal members could only watch as homesteaders started claiming more and more land. To the east, settlers were killing large numbers of buffalo, while the pigs they introduced to the land ate the camas roots that were a staple for the people of the Great Basin and Plateau region.

This Bannock necklace is 100 years old. Glass beads are threaded onto strips of leather, along with turquoise stones and charms.

In 1868, the Treaty of Fort Bridger created the Fort Hall Reservation for the Shoshone and the Bannock tribes. The Bannock people tried to continue their traditional hunting and gathering on lands off the reservation, but found many of their resources had been used up by white settlers. In 1878, friction between the Bannock and the settlers grew, resulting in warfare, but the U.S. Army forced the Bannock to surrender within months. The tribe lost much of its land in the following years.

Today, the Bannock tribe shares the Fort Hall Reservation with the Shoshone as the Shoshone-Bannock Tribe. They have a common government and several businesses, and use some of their land for potato crops. In 1966, they brought bison back to the area, and today the herd has 300 to 400 animals. As caretakers of their land, the Bannock and Shoshone work with U.S. and state government agencies to protect and restore endangered species to the rivers and streams. Begun in 1964, the Shoshone-Bannock Indian Festival is hosted by the reservation each summer. This four-day event celebrates the tribes' ancestral culture. Visitors can expect to see traditional dancing and singing competitions, as well as a parade, a rodeo, and dramatic Indian Relay races—on horseback.

This Shoshone-Bannock cowboy father stands with his traditionally dressed daughter and his horse, which is covered in beaded regalia. The same floral motif is on the girl's dress and boots, and also on the horse's blanket and bridle.

IN THE KNOW

In 2015, Fort Hall became the first Purple Heart Reservation. The Purple Heart honors a person's military service. At Fort Hall, so many tribal members received Purple Hearts for wounds inflicted while serving in the U.S. Armed Forces that the honor was given to the whole community.

THE ART OF BEADWORK

The women of the Great Basin and Plateau tribes perfected the art of beading. Their intricate work appeared on clothing, cradleboards, bags, and even horse tack. Early people used beads made from shells, seeds, bones, porcupine quills, and other materials. European traders introduced various different sizes of glass beads—small, bright, colorful pony beads and tiny seed beads became very popular. Many beadwork designs featured geometric shapes and floral motifs. From the late 1800s onward, artists began to create animals, people, and other more realistic images. Beadwork is not just a historical art form. Today's Native artists, such as Jamie Okuma, produce amazing high-fashion pieces, such as jewelry, cuffs, and shoes (pictured). Okuma, who is part Shoshone, has exhibited her art around the United States and in Europe. The Smithsonian National Museum of the American Indian in Washington, D.C., also holds several of her pieces in its collections.

CAYUSE

(KY-yoose)

LANGUAGE GROUP:
Isolate

LANGUAGE:
Dormant; last fluent speakers thought to have died in the 1930s

LOCATION PRECONTACT:
Oregon, Washington

LOCATION TODAY:
Oregon

The Cayuse were a small tribe of nomadic hunters who lived in present-day Oregon and Washington. They hunted deer and elk, using their skins for clothing, and fished for salmon. Their homes were similar to Plains tepees, but were longer and were covered with woven reed mats instead of animal hides. Whenever the tribe moved camp, they took the mats with them, but built new homes from wooden poles they took from trees at the next location.

By the early 1700s, the Cayuse had horses and became expert trainers and breeders, occupying large grazing lands near the Blue Mountains. Horses made the Cayuse wealthy and allowed the tribe to travel farther to hunt buffalo and to trade woven mats for buffalo hides with tribes from the Plains and for *wampum* (shell beads) with tribes from the Northwest coast.

While the Cayuse welcomed the fur traders, and the Lewis and Clark expedition as it passed through Cayuse territory in 1805, things changed when the missionaries arrived. In 1836, ➡️

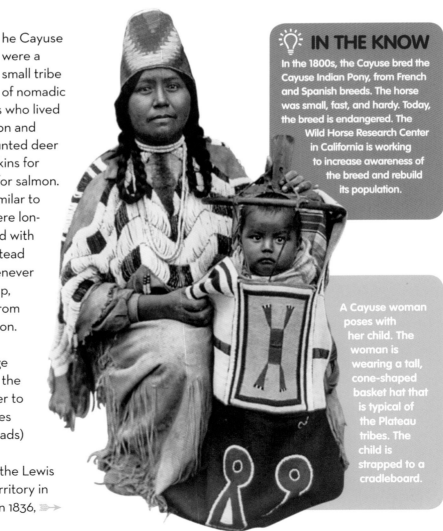

💡 IN THE KNOW

In the 1800s, the Cayuse bred the Cayuse Indian Pony, from French and Spanish breeds. The horse was small, fast, and hardy. Today, the breed is endangered. The Wild Horse Research Center in California is working to increase awareness of the breed and rebuild its population.

A Cayuse woman poses with her child. The woman is wearing a tall, cone-shaped basket hat that is typical of the Plateau tribes. The child is strapped to a cradleboard.

An exhibit of Native Cayuse riding on horseback at the Tamástslikt Cultural Institute in Oregon. The institute is dedicated to showcasing and preserving the history and culture of the Cayuse, Umatilla, and Walla Walla tribes.

Dr. Marcus Whitman, a Methodist, established a mission—a religious outpost—on Cayuse land, and settlers soon followed. The Cayuse became angry at the changes the newcomers introduced, and with the diseases they brought with them. A measles outbreak in 1847 was devastating, wiping out hundreds of people. Later that year, angry that the missionaries had failed to stop the measles epidemic, a group of Native peoples, with Cayuse among them, attacked and killed Whitman, his wife, and 12 others. This event triggered the Cayuse War and the fighting continued for eight years before the tribe surrendered.

In 1855, the U.S. government moved the Cayuse, Umatilla, and Walla Walla tribes to the Umatilla Reservation in Oregon and Washington. Settlers planted wheat crops on the ancestral land that the Cayuse had used to graze their horses. Still living on the reservation, the three tribes use their land for farming, fishing, and logging. They also run a resort that has a tribal museum—the Tamástslikt Cultural Institute. The Cayuse hold regular ceremonies and celebrations that involve singing and drumming. In this way, and in practicing the basket-weaving and beading traditions of their ancestors, they keep the Cayuse culture alive.

GAMBLING GAMES

When tribal people gathered together to feast, socialize, and relax, they also spent time playing games. Most of these games were competitive, and some were games of chance. Gambling was an important part of these games. From the hoop and pole game played by men to the dice games women enjoyed, everyone participated. (A set of four large bone dice are pictured here.) Even children played simple gambling games. People bet their possessions on the outcome of a game, such as blankets or tools. In this way, gambling spread possessions and wealth among tribal members, making sure everyone had their share. It was also a way to teach moral lessons. People learned to lose and win gracefully.

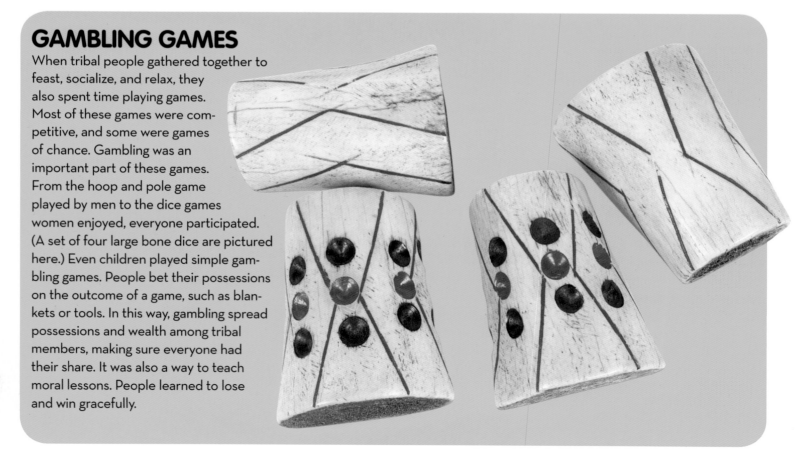

COEUR D'ALENE

(CORE duh-len)

LANGUAGE GROUP:
Salishan

GREETING:
A

THANK YOU:
Lim lemt.sh

LOCATION PRECONTACT:
Idaho, Washington, Montana

LOCATION TODAY:
Idaho

French fur traders gave the people the name Coeur d'Alene, meaning "heart of the awl," but the Coeur d'Alene call themselves Schitsu'umsh, which means "those who were found here." The Coeur d'Alene people lived in winter villages along the Spokane and Coeur d'Alene Rivers, and around Coeur d'Alene Lake in present-day Idaho, Washington, and Montana. Their homes were cone-shaped structures made from pole frames covered in bark or woven mats. The tribe fished using traps and nets, and gathered wild foods, such as camas root and huckleberry. They hunted deer using finely crafted bows made from sinew (animal tendon) and bark from the bitter cherry tree. They made arrows using wood from serviceberry shrubs.

Traditional ways of living began to change for the Coeur d'Alene with the arrival of European missionaries in the 1840s. The missionaries converted many tribal members to Catholicism, and persuaded people to farm more and hunt less. In the 1860s, prospectors and mining companies arrived in Coeur d'Alene territory. Over the next decade, the mining and timber industries grew and demanded more land. Homesteaders and mine workers also wanted land, and so the U.S. government took territory from the Coeur d'Alene. In 1873, the government reduced the tribe's territory to just 600,000 acres (245,000 ha), and in 1894, took more land to build the Washington and Idaho Railway. Today, the Coeur d'Alene reservation in Idaho measures just 345,000 acres (140,000 ha). Tribal members run a logging industry and a 6,000-acre (2,400-ha) farm where they grow crops of wheat and canola.

In 2001, the Coeur d'Alene won a historic U.S. Supreme Court case granting them the right to reclaim part of the Coeur d'Alene Lake, which had been heavily polluted over the decades by millions of tons of waste from lead, silver, and zinc mining. The Supreme Court recognized the tribe's sovereignty over the lake. The tribe is now working with environmental groups to bring the surrounding area back to health. This effort is part of the much wider Superfund program established by the U.S. government in 1983 to undo the years of environmental damage. ✐

A dancer participates in the Coeur d'Alene's Julyamsh Powwow. All dance competitors take part in the Grand Entry, the show's opening event, before competing in their own categories.

IN THE KNOW

The Coeur d'Alene use online resources to keep their language alive. Their website includes a large section on language, where people can familiarize themselves with words and phrases using a wide variety of lessons, songs, stories, and games.

SEASONAL RITUALS

Rituals have always been central to Native culture. Performed widely today, many are deeply spiritual, connecting the people to the land, animals, and plants that sustain them. For tribes in the Great Basin and Plateau region, salmon has long been an important food and First Salmon ceremonies honor the tradition of the salmon returning to local rivers in the spring. Other spring ceremonies welcome the first berries and roots. The Winter Ceremony calls upon guardian spirits to help bring animals for hunting and plentiful foods for gathering. Families once celebrated a boy's first hunting or fishing success or a girl's first root harvesting. Ceremonies vary from tribe to tribe, but most include some kind of dancing and singing. Large feasts are also part of ceremonial rites. Pictured here, Shoshone elders conduct a ground-blessing ceremony. They perform a "smudging" ritual—fanning white sage smoke with eagle wings—to purify the land before building begins.

COLVILLE

(COAL-vill)

LANGUAGE GROUP:
  Various

GREETING:
  Sta! (Okanagan)

THANK YOU:
  Limt (Okanagan)

LOCATION PRECONTACT:
  Washington, Oregon;
  British Columbia (Canada)

LOCATION TODAY:
  Nevada, Utah

In 1825, the Hudson's Bay Company established Fort Colville, near Kettle Falls, in present-day Washington. It became an important trading center for the West, drawing many tribes into the area to trade beaver, fox, mink, and other furs. These tribes became known as Les Chaudières, or "the Kettles," and, later, were called the Confederated Tribes of the Colville Reservation. The 12 different tribes of the confederation are the Wenatchee, Colville, Entiate, Chelan, Okanagan, Nespelem, San Poil, Lakes, Moses-Columbia, Palus, Methow, and a group of Nez Perce—all with different languages. Before the 1840s, the people were nomadic, using the waterways of northwestern Washington to fish—mostly salmon and trout. They hunted mountain goat, sheep, moose, and elk, and gathered wild berries and other plants across the Plateau. These tribes also traveled to join others for feasting and trading; they brought thousands of pelts to the trading post at Fort Colville every year.

JOE FEDDERSEN

Artist Joe Feddersen is an Okanagan tribal member of the Colville Confederated Tribes. He creates different types of art, including glass dishes, paintings, and even baskets. He is known for using interesting geometric patterns like the ones seen in the painting below. Feddersen is inspired by the landscape of the Great Basin and Plateau region and his art has been displayed in different museums, including the Museum of the American Indian in Washington, D.C. This painting is called "Grandmother's Mountain." The mountains are made by laying one sheet of paper over another. Feddersen has drawn a grandmother figure and fishes over the top.

Taken in 1900, this photograph shows how people on the Colville Indian Reservation used a fishing weir to catch fish. The centuries-old design of woven branches stopped the fish from swimming upstream.

In the 1840s, missionaries arrived and converted many tribal members to Catholicism. Further change came in 1846, with the establishment of the U.S.–Canadian border. Some members of the Colville Confederation moved to Canada, while others opted to stay in the U.S. In 1872, President Ulysses S. Grant established a reservation for those who stayed. Although the 12 tribes were separate, the U.S. government consolidated all of them on one reservation. Initially, 10 tribes moved to the reservation, and were followed by the Nez Perce and Palus a few years later. On the reservation, people fished for salmon, as they always had, until the government built the Grand Coulee Dam, which flooded salmon runs and farmland. In 1938, the Colville Confederated Tribes created its own elected government called a tribal council. The tribal council helps to protect the land and the languages of its 12 tribes. Every year, the community hosts events that celebrate the cultures and traditions of its many groups. These include a Traditional Powwow and a Junior Rodeo, both in April, and a First Salmon ceremony in May. ✐

GOSHUTE

(GO-shoot)

LANGUAGE GROUP:
Uto-Aztecan

LANGUAGE:
Currently dormant; no record of last known speaker

LOCATION PRECONTACT:
Nevada, Utah

LOCATION TODAY:
Nevada, Utah

The Goshute, one of the Western Shoshone bands, live in the northern semidesert area southwest of the Great Salt Lake in Utah. The tribe's name comes from a word that means "ashes," or "dust." Another Western Shoshone band, the Timbisha, also lived in a dry place—Death Valley, California. The Goshute and Timbisha knew and respected their land. Fortunately, both had mountains nearby where there was food to be hunted and gathered. The Goshute gathered food such as wild onions and pine nuts and hunted small game, including rabbits. Families moved often, to avoid taking too many of the land's resources at one time. In the winter, the Goshute built wickiups (brush shelters). For centuries, the Goshute lived peacefully because no one was eager to take their land. ➥

The Goshute and the Timbisha developed strong survival skills for living in harsh desert habitats like Death Valley (pictured).

Pictured is one of very few Goshute families currently living on the tribe's Skull Valley Reservation, in Utah. The land here is very dry and natural resources are limited.

In 1855, the life of the Goshute changed with the arrival of the first Mormons. Settling in Goshute territory, ranchers and farmers took over the best land—that is, land that was relatively flat and suitable for grazing animals. The farmers claimed the scarce water sources for themselves, while their livestock grazed over areas that the Goshute used for gathering seeds and roots. Desperate for food, the Goshute launched raids and attacks to push the settlers off their lands. The U.S. Army intervened to defend the settlers, launching an attack in 1860 that killed many of the Goshute people. In 1863, the Goshute surrendered and signed the Treaty of Ruby Valley, as did several other Western Shoshone bands. The treaty allowed travelers to pass through tribal territory. The Goshute were unwilling to move, but having lost vital hunting and gathering lands, the tribe struggled to survive. The government created the Skull Valley Reservation in 1912 and the Deep Creek Reservation in 1914, and the Goshute eventually moved to these two reservations.

Today, the Goshute tribe numbers around 500 people living on the two reservations. Members of the tribe continue to practice the arts, celebrations, traditions, and language of their ancestors. They also work hard to improve the health of their lands and people. ✐

FASHIONS FROM NATURE

For many centuries, the people of the Great Basin and Plateau used plant fibers in their clothing, shredding and pounding bark and tule (a type of water plant known as a bulrush) to soften them. They used these materials to make aprons, breechcloths, and skirts. In the colder months, rabbit-fur blankets provided warmth. From the 1800s, once people had regular contact with tribes from the Plains, most also wore deerskin clothing. Depending on the weather, men wore loose, deerskin poncho shirts (pictured), leggings, and breechcloths. Women wore deerskin dresses or skirts. Women added fringes and decorated garments with colorful beaded designs. When the tribes acquired cloth from the Europeans, they started using that to make clothes instead, and decorated it with their distinctive beadwork.

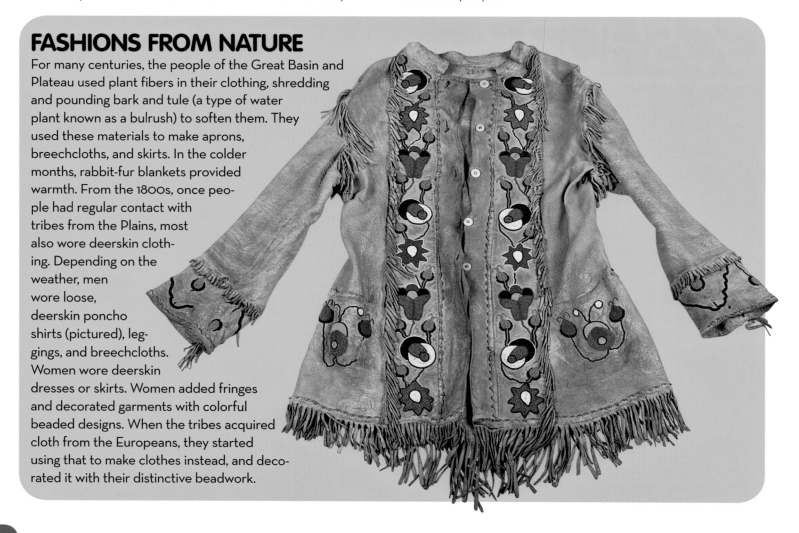

KLAMATH

(CLAM-uth)

LANGUAGE GROUP:
Plateau Penutian

GREETING:
Waq lis ?i

THANK YOU:
Sepk'eec'a

LOCATION PRECONTACT:
Oregon

LOCATION TODAY:
Oregon, Oklahoma

For thousands of years, the Klamath lived in what is now southern Oregon, with their relatives, the Modoc, living nearby. The Klamath lands were rich in fish and small game, and many wild plants. The tribe used dugout canoes to travel and fish along the rivers, and they gathered tule for making mats and baskets. The Klamath used wild wocus—a type of water lily—grinding the flower seeds to make flour. Moving according to the seasons, in winter, the tribe relied on the food the people gathered in warmer months. Their homelands were far away from most white settlements, so the Klamath did not meet any outsiders until 1826, when a Hudson's Bay fur trader named Peter Skene Ogden met the tribe and began trading with it. He also wrote about meeting the Klamath people.

As white settlers moved into the area, they cut the Klamath off from the land's natural resources. In 1864, the Klamath, Modoc, and Yahooskin tribes signed a treaty with the U.S. government that ceded 19.5 million acres (7.9 million ha) of land. The treaty also assigned a reservation for the three tribes, who became ranchers. The Klamath tribe had even greater success with the timber industry. In 1870, the tribe opened a sawmill, and within a short time, was selling large amounts of lumber to the growing Oregon community and the railroad companies. The Klamath tribe became one of the richest in the country.

In 1954, as part of its "termination" policy, the U.S. government took away the Klamath's tribal status and the financial support the tribe had been receiving. The tribe had to sell land to pay taxes and maintain tribal operations. It spent years fighting for its sovereignty and treaty rights. In 1986, the Klamath regained their status and were able to rebuild their community. The tribe still makes money from the lumber industry and farmland. Beginning in 1981, the tribe began holding a Restoration Celebration to honor both their past and future; events include a rodeo and a powwow. ✎

> Once an animal had been killed, very little of it went to waste. This beaded and fringed bag uses the hide from a deer's head.

💡 IN THE KNOW

The people of the Klamath tribe created fine tule basketry trays, containers, and figures. The women wore woven basketry caps and moccasins made of tule before switching to animal hides.

> Klamath people built round, pole-framed houses in summer, and covered them with mats (pictured). Winter homes were built partly underground.

KOOTENAI

(KOOT-nay)

LANGUAGE GROUP:
Isolate

LANGUAGE:
Limited number of
words in current use;
no dictionary available

LOCATION PRECONTACT:
Montana, Idaho, Washington

LOCATION TODAY:
Montana, Idaho (U.S.);
British Columbia (Canada)

In the air, birds were often out of range for a hunter's bow and arrow. Kootenai hunters used decoys made with real feathers—in this example, goose feathers—to attract waterfowl to the surface of a lake, where they were easy to target.

More than 14,000 years ago, the ancestors of the Kootenai were living in present-day Montana, Idaho, and Washington in the U.S. and in British Columbia, Canada, their territory including both the Rocky Mountains and the valley of the Kootenai River. The Upper Kootenai, who lived near the headwaters of the Columbia River, hunted more than they fished. They used bows and arrows—later, guns—to kill elk, caribou, and big game. The Lower Kootenai band depended on fishing in the Kootenai River, which was full of trout, sturgeon, and other large fish. They used spears and basket traps to catch fish. Both bands traveled around their homelands by canoe in the summer and used snowshoes in the winter. Once the tribe had horses, which were traded with other Native tribes, some of the Lower Kootenai hunters joined the Upper Kootenai to hunt buffalo on the Plains. During the year, the bands came together for ceremonies, such as the Jump Dance, a New Year's celebration lasting three nights.

Fur traders and missionaries brought great change to the Kootenai. Many died and others suffered from smallpox epidemics after their first contact with white settlers in 1792. Fur traders also made ancient tensions between the Kootenai and the Blackfeet worse. The Kootenai had often trespassed on Blackfeet territory to hunt buffalo and now they competed for trade. Missionaries converted many Kootenai to Christianity.

In 1855, the Kootenai signed the Hellgate Treaty, which ceded much of their land to the U.S. government. They lost more land during the Plateau gold rushes in the early 1860s. The Hellgate Treaty required the Kootenai to move to the Flathead Reservation in Montana, with the Salish and Pend d'Oreille. A small group of Kootenai moved to the Colville Reservation in present-day Washington, where they remain to this day. Another small community makes up the Kootenai Tribe of Idaho. Other Kootenai live in British Columbia, Canada. The tribe no longer holds as many ceremonies as its ancestors once did, but honors its culture through annual powwows.

IN THE KNOW

In 1974, the Kootenai Tribe of Idaho numbered just 67 members. They declared war on the United States to draw attention to their need to build housing and to improve their highway. There was no violence, but the declaration forced the government to award the tribe grants to do the work.

The Kootenai tribe made lightweight pine and birchbark canoes to travel in. The hull of the boat pictured here turns up at the prow (the front of the canoe) and at the stern (the back of the canoe).

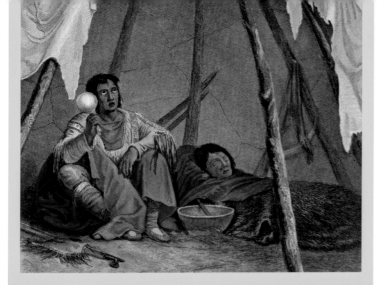

SPIRITUAL LEADERS

Spiritual leaders were important members of the Great Basin and Plateau tribes. People believed that spirit beings called on certain people to be spiritual leaders, and worked through them to help heal and teach the people of the tribe. Curing ceremonies involved singing sacred songs. Many believed that evil spirits caused illness by putting something inside a person that only a spiritual leader could remove. Spiritual leaders also predicted the future, relying on the spirits to tell them about events yet to come.

In the 1990s, the Nez Perce tribe began a breeding program to revive its traditional horse culture. Among the horses they breed are the Appaloosa and the Nez Perce horse. The horse pictured above is an Appaloosa.

NEZ PERCE

(nez PURSE)

LANGUAGE GROUP:
Plateau Penutian

GREETING:
Hó·

THANK YOU:
Qe?ciyéẃyeẃ

LOCATION PRECONTACT:
Idaho, Washington, Oregon

LOCATION TODAY:
Idaho, Washington

The largest tribe inhabiting the Plateau region, the Nez Perce numbered as many as 6,000 people living on 17 million acres (7 million ha) of land. Seminomadic, they lived by the seasons. In spring and summer, they stayed in the valleys along the Snake and Salmon Rivers, in present-day Idaho, Washington, and Oregon. In fall, they moved to higher ground where they harvested crops and hunted game. In their winter villages, they built large, earth-covered, pole-framed pit houses that slept several families. In summer, when traveling the land looking for food, they built temporary lean-to-type shelters using poles draped with woven mats. As in other tribes, family relationships were very important to the Nez Perce. At a young age, children helped their families to fish, gather fruit, and dig roots; young children also learned to ride horses with the adults, many of whom were expert riders. The Nez Perce bred horses, which they traded with other Native tribes.

This beaded Nez Perce horse mask dates from around 1865 and would probably have been worn by a horse during warfare. Tribes continue the tradition of making masks for their horses. These days, they use them for parades and memorial processions.

When the explorers Lewis and Clark met the Nez Perce in 1805, and again in 1806, the tribe offered food and help to them. A translator for the expedition gave the tribe a French name, Nez Percé—meaning "pierced nose"—but the tribe calls itself Nimi'ipuu, which means "real people." A few years after meeting Lewis and Clark, the tribe became very involved in ⇒

the booming fur trade. This contact with white people brought deadly diseases, such as smallpox and tuberculosis. The years that followed brought more hardships for the tribe. Waves of settlers came through Nez Perce territory with the opening of the Oregon Trail, and the U.S. government put pressure on the tribe to give up its land. In 1855, the tribe agreed to cede millions of acres, but kept a large area for hunting and fishing.

In 1860, prospectors found gold on the land still held by the Nez Perce, and thousands of settlers moved into their territory to claim their fortune. Three years later, Nez Perce leaders signed a treaty giving up almost all of their remaining homelands, leaving a small area in Idaho, which became their reservation. One group, led by Chief Joseph among others, refused to go and this led to the Nez Perce War in 1877. After defeating the Nez Perce, the U.S. Army took away the tribe's horses, killed many of the tribal members, and sent most of the surviving Nez Perce to Oklahoma. Some took refuge in Canada or at the Colville Reservation in Washington.

Over time, most tribal people returned to the Plateau region. Today, many Nez Perce live on the small Nez Perce Reservation in Idaho. Other Nez Perce live elsewhere, but they all gather together for powwows, ceremonies, and tribal festivals to celebrate and keep their ancient traditions alive. The tribe has revived its horse culture with a new breeding program that includes teaching the art to young tribal members. ✐

CHIEF JOSEPH

In 1871, Chief Joseph was elected by his people to succeed his father in leading his tribe. Born Hin-mah-too-yah-lat-kekt, his Native name means "Thunder Rolling Down a Mountain." Although he was not a war chief, he is famous for his success during the Nez Perce War of 1877, when the tribe tried to seek refuge from the U.S. Army in Canada. Chief Joseph surrendered rather than risk the lives of his followers when the army finally blocked his escape route. He said, "My heart is sick and sad ... I will fight no more forever." Chief Joseph lived the rest of his life on the Colville Reservation with just a few other Nez Perce people.

PAIUTE

(PIE-yoot)

LANGUAGE GROUP:
Uto-Aztecan

GREETING:
Maik'w

THANK YOU:
Not available

LOCATION PRECONTACT:
Arizona, California, Nevada, Idaho, Utah, Oregon

LOCATION TODAY:
Arizona, California, Nevada, Idaho, Utah, Oregon

Before the 1800s, the Paiute were seminomadic people who lived across a large area of the western Great Basin and Plateau. The landscape varied from mountains, lakes, marshes, and rivers to deserts and plains, and so ways of life differed, too. The tribe was one of the largest in the region, and was divided into three major groups, based on their languages: Northern, Southern, and Owens Valley. Each had several bands, lived in a different environment, and had its own government. These divisions continue to exist today, although some bands now live together on reservations. When the Paiute lived freely across their vast territory, they were hunters and gatherers; some bands also fished in large lakes, including Pyramid Lake and Walker Lake. A few bands, such as the Owens Valley, grew root crops or traded crops including corn, beans, and squash with their Southwest neighbors. People near marshes made life-like duck decoys to lure waterfowl. Wherever they lived, the Paiute

learned to use the wild plants and animals available for food, clothing, medicine, and other necessities.

The first non-Natives to meet the Northern Paiute were fur traders and trappers. These first contacts were peaceful, but European diseases killed many Natives. To the south, the Spanish and Mexicans captured members of the Southern Paiute for the slave trade. From the 1840s, white settlers began making their way west along the Oregon Trail. In the years that followed, gold rushes in California and other western territories brought thousands more to Paiute lands. When Mormons settled in southern Utah and Nevada, the Southern Paiute faced problems that included the spread of disease and the loss of lands best suited to their farming lifestyle. During the 1860s, the Pyramid Lake War, Owens Valley Indian War, and other conflicts over territory brought more devastation to the Paiute people. Over the next 40 years, the U.S. government began moving the Paiute to reservations. Some, like the Chemehuevi, a Southern Paiute band, now have their own reservation, while the Duck Valley and Fallon reservations include both Paiute and Shoshone members. Paiute tribal members also live on small reservations called "colonies" in towns and cities across the western United States.

Through more than 200 years of great change, the Paiute have held on to the teachings of their ancestors. Ceremonies and festivals held throughout the year include the Walker River Pine Nut Festival, on the third weekend in September, in celebration of the pine-nut harvest. Such events offer a chance for tribal members to gather and celebrate Paiute culture. The Pyramid Lake Paiute Tribe of Nevada has a tribal museum and visitor center next to its world-class fishery; the Las Vegas (Southern) Paiute Tribe owns and operates three golf courses; and there are others who own and operate different types of businesses. The money from these businesses supports tribal health centers, a police force, and other community services. 🖋

Owens Valley, in eastern California, is a sacred site for the Paiute tribe. Many rock faces in this region feature petroglyphs, or rock carvings, made by spiritual leaders of the tribe. They represent a leader's spiritual journey.

THE ART OF BASKETRY

Traditionally, baskets were useful items for carrying or holding things. Tribal people stored water in bottle-shaped baskets and cooked food using hot stones in others. They also made large baskets for gathering berries and nuts and cradle baskets to carry babies. Some people, such as the Paiute, wore basket hats. Tribal people coiled, twined, or braided plant fibers such as willow, redbud, and fern into baskets and bowls (pictured). Some were so tightly coiled they were watertight. Many incorporated geometric patterns in their designs. Young girls learned the techniques by watching elders. Today, people continue to learn from elders and organizations that have preserved the art.

SARAH WINNEMUCCA

Sarah Winnemucca, writer, teacher, and speaker, was the daughter of a Northern Paiute chief. She fought for the rights of her people and published *Life Among the Paiutes: Their Wrongs and Claims* in 1883—the first book published in English by a Native woman. Winnemucca built a school for teaching the tribal language, but it was closed down when the U.S. government insisted that Native children should learn in English-only classrooms. Today, several Paiute tribes have language programs. Winnemucca's statue is in the U.S. Capitol in Washington, D.C., as one of two representing the state of Nevada.

DID YOU KNOW?

THE NEZ PERCE once owned the largest herd of horses in North America. They were among the best breeders, raising strong, fast horses that could endure the difficult life on the Plateau. Other tribes prized the horses, and the Nez Perce became a wealthy tribe from trading them. The Nez Perce are particularly famous for breeding the Appaloosa, a beautiful, spotted horse.

PEND D'OREILLE

(pawn duh-RAY)

LANGUAGE GROUP:
Salishan

LANGUAGE:
Currently dormant; no record of last known speaker

LOCATION PRECONTACT:
Washington, Idaho, Montana; British Columbia (Canada)

LOCATION TODAY:
Montana, Washington

When French traders met a tribe of people who wore shell earrings, they called them Pend d'Oreille, "hang from the ears." The tribe's original name is Q'lispé, or Kalispel, meaning "camas people," because the camas root was an important part of their traditional diet. The Pend d'Oreille homeland was a large territory covering parts of present-day Washington, Idaho, Montana, and southern British Columbia, Canada. The area included a vital trade route that used the Pend Oreille River as a link to the Columbia River and to the West. The Lower Pend d'Oreille tribe lived along this river, while the Upper Pend d'Oreille lived along the Clark Fork River to the east. Both groups built their winter villages near the water, erecting cone-shaped houses from poles that they covered with branches or bark. In spring, the tribe moved to fish, hunt game, and

The camas root, which played such an important part in the diet of Great Basin and Plateau tribes, is actually a bulb.

gather wild plants. The tribe wore clothes that they made from animal skins and decorated with porcupine quills. They made tools for hunting, digging, and cooking from stone, animal bones, and wood. Once the Pend d'Oreille had horses, families traveled to the Plains in summer to hunt buffalo—today, the tribe owns a herd of around 200 buffalo.

The Pend d'Oreille had very limited contact with non-Natives until 1844, when Jesuit missionaries began living and working with the Pend d'Oreille people. Less than 10 years later, the Upper Pend d'Oreille signed a treaty with the U.S. government that ceded their lands. The government moved the Upper Pend d'Oreille to a reservation occupied by the Flathead tribe in Montana. The Lower Pend d'Oreille did not sign any treaties. During the next decades, many settlers moved west to establish homesteads on Lower Pend d'Oreille land, and the tribe lost more of its hunting, gathering, and village land. In 1914, the government assigned the tribe a small reservation now known as the Kalispel Indian Reservation, in Washington. In the years that followed, the Pend d'Oreille fought the U.S. government for payment for land losses and won. In 2012, the federal government also awarded the Pend d'Oreille a grant to help save the trout population that has been affected by dams on the Pend Oreille River. The tribe has depended on the trout as a food source for many centuries.

This portrait shows a young Pend d'Oreille woman in 1910. She has white accent marks painted on her hair, probably to make her more attractive. Her blanket dress is decorated with elk teeth.

IN THE KNOW

Like the Kootenai, the Pend d'Oreille used a specially shaped canoe for fishing and gathering food. The canoe's prow was turned up at the front, making it easy to move through the reeds.

THE HAND GAME

One of the most popular games among tribal people is the hand game. It is a guessing and gambling game that can be played with any number of people. Rules vary from tribe to tribe. Those in the Great Basin play a four-bone version of the game, with two plain animal bones (representing O) and two bones with a central black band (representing X). A pair of bones—an O and an X—is given to each of two players on one team and the other team has to guess the position of the plain bones in their hands. The bones can be to the left (OX OX), to the right (XO XO), inside (XO OX), or outside (OX XO). Hand gestures are used for each designation. When the guessing team guesses correctly, they get the bones and it is then their turn to hold the bones. The game is played by most Great Basin tribes at tribal gatherings. Several tribes, including the Shoshone, hold competitions.

SALISH

(SEH-lish)

LANGUAGE GROUP:
Salishan

GREETING:
ʔa

THANK YOU:
Lémlmtš

LOCATION PRECONTACT:
Idaho, Montana, Washington; British Columbia (Canada)

LOCATION TODAY:
Idaho, Montana, Washington (U.S.); British Columbia (Canada)

Native to the Plateau, the Salish, sometimes called the Interior Salish, lived in present-day Washington, Idaho, and Montana, and in British Columbia, Canada. Their relatives, the Coast Salish, were native to the Pacific Northwest. The two groups were in contact with each other and traded goods. The Interior Salish were seminomadic, occupying villages through winter and traveling to temporary camps in summer. They fished salmon in the Columbia and Fraser Rivers, hunted in the mountainous territory, and gathered roots, berries, and plants in the foothills. In their villages, they built cone-shaped pit houses that had pole frames draped with bark or woven mats. The women made blankets, mats, and baskets with colorful, geometric designs. From the 1700s, the tribe had horses that they used for hunting buffalo on the Plains. This caused trouble with the Blackfeet, who resented other tribes invading their hunting grounds. The Blackfeet started raiding the Salish and the ⇒

This Salish headdress is 100 years old and probably belonged to an important member of the tribe. Besides the eagle feathers are peacock feathers, ermine fur, glass beads, and silk ribbon.

This pair of Salish moccasins, from the Flathead Reservation in Montana, dates from around 1880. Made from animal hide, the foot section of each moccasin has been stitched with tiny glass seed beads in bright colors.

Salish retaliated. Raids between the two tribes lasted for years.

The California gold rush of 1849 brought white settlers to Salish lands. Within a few years, the U.S. government decided to take Salish land themselves, to gain access to the minerals and resources found there. The Bitterroot band of the Salish tribe signed the Hellgate Treaty in 1855, which ceded their homelands to the government, and the tribe moved onto the Flathead Reservation with the Upper Kalispel and many Kootenai people. Although the Kootenai and Salish had different traditions and completely unrelated languages, the tribes became today's Confederated Salish and Kootenai Tribes. Other Salish people live on the Colville Reservation and in British Columbia, Canada.

The Salish on the Flathead Reservation are still deeply involved with the land and animals around them. As part of their commitment to protecting animals on their land, Highway 93, which goes through the reservation, has 41 wildlife crossings, two underpasses, and fencing to prevent animals from being hit by vehicles. In 2015, the confederated tribes took control of the former Kerr Dam, in Montana, and its hydroelectric power, buying it from the company that owned it. Now called the Séliš Ksanka Q'lispé Dam, it is the first tribally owned dam in the United States.

SHOSHONE

(show-SHOW-nee)

LANGUAGE GROUP:
Uto-Aztecan

GREETING:
Tsaangu beaichehku

THANK YOU:
AisheN

LOCATION PRECONTACT:
California, Idaho, Nevada, Utah, Wyoming

LOCATION TODAY:
California, Idaho, Nevada, Utah, Wyoming

The Shoshone lived across such a vast area of the Great Basin and Plateau region that their territory ranged from scorching desert to lush valleys. The people adopted different ways of living depending on their environments. Their homelands included territory in present-day California, Idaho, Nevada, Utah, and Wyoming.

The Shoshone's three major bands—the Western, Northern, and Eastern Shoshone—lived in different areas. Another smaller group of Shoshone split from their relatives to move to the southern Plains. This band grew in numbers and became the powerful Comanche tribe. The Eastern Shoshone stayed around the Wind River Valley in Wyoming and adopted some of the ways of Plains tribes—especially once they had horses. They used tepees and, while previously they would have tracked small game animals and foraged for roots, nuts, and seeds, they now hunted for buffalo. Northern Shoshone groups

This leather saddle was made by members of the Shoshone tribe on the Fort Hall Reservation, which they share with the Bannock tribe. The Shoshone acquired horses earlier than many other tribes.

lived around the Snake River in present-day Idaho, and traveled for yearly buffalo hunts. The Western Shoshone moved across the varied landscapes of southern Idaho, northern and eastern Utah, eastern Nevada, and southern California. All groups were seminomadic, moving with the seasons to make sure their communities had enough food.

In the 1800s, fur trappers and traders started using Shoshone lands and hunting their animals. The California gold rush of 1849 brought thousands of gold seekers across the area and homesteaders who stayed permanently. The 1860s brought another wave of people when prospectors discovered gold on the Plateau. The Mormons arrived in the late 1840s and settled in Utah, Idaho, and Wyoming. The new settlers took over large areas for farms and allowed livestock to graze over Shoshone gathering lands. This slowly destroyed the Shoshone's traditional way of life, limiting the supply of natural resources and reducing the territory over which the Natives could hunt.

Today, the Shoshone live on a number of reservations, including the Wind River Reservation in Wyoming—shared with the Arapaho—and Duck Valley in Nevada and Idaho, shared with Paiute. There are also several smaller reservations (known as colonies) near towns and cities. Dancing, music, storytelling, language, and craft traditions are still an important part of life for this tribe. The Shoshone people honor their ancestors by continuing their respectful relationship with the land and animals around them. 🖎

HOVIA EDWARDS

Hovia Edwards, of Shoshone-Navajo-Okanagan heritage, learned to play the Native American flute at a young age. Her father, a flute maker, taught her how to play. Even her name comes from a Shoshone word meaning "song." Hovia recorded her first album when she was just 14 years old, and at 18, she played the flute during the opening ceremony of the 2002 Olympics in Salt Lake City, Utah. Hovia was nominated for a Grammy award in 1998.

THE BEAR RIVER MASSACRE

On the morning of January 29, 1863, the U.S. Army attacked and killed hundreds of Shoshone people in Idaho, including many women and children. This became known as the Bear River Massacre and counts as one of the worst U.S. military attacks ever on tribal people. Leading up to the event, conflicts erupted between the Shoshone and the Mormon settlers who had moved onto their lands. Desperate and hungry, the Shoshone raided Mormon farms for food. The U.S. Army came to put a stop to the raids. They stormed the Shoshone winter camp early in the morning, firing their guns and pushing people into the ice-cold river. Shoshone warriors returned fire, killing about 23 soldiers. After the four-hour attack, the soldiers took the few surviving women and children as captives. Today, members of the Shoshone visit the site, bringing gifts with which to decorate a prayer tree in memory of the lives lost.

SPOKANE

(spoke-ANN)

LANGUAGE GROUP:
Salishan

GREETING:
A.

THANK YOU:
Lemlmtš

LOCATION PRECONTACT:
Washington

LOCATION TODAY:
Idaho, Montana, Washington

The Spokane lived on the Northern Plateau around what are now the Spokane and Columbia Rivers in Washington. The tribe divided its homelands among the three major bands: the Lower, Upper, and Middle Spokane. Each had its own chief. The Spokane were expert fishermen who depended on the salmon that filled their rivers. In the winter, communities settled in villages, where they built large rectangular houses that could accommodate several families. During the summer, they moved from place to place to hunt and forage across the open plain. Here, they lived in lightweight tepees. The Spokane Falls was a traditional summer gathering place for large groups, and games were a favorite pastime for children and adults. They showed off their skills at running, weight lifting, and other competitions. In the summer, the women also gathered food, much of which was dried and stored to use later in the year. They gathered as many as 130 different plants using a digging stick. This tool was a wooden stick with either one sharpened end or a short length of bone or antler attached to the top and perpendicular to the stick.

When settlers and mining companies arrived in Spokane territory, they took away traditional gathering, hunting, and fishing lands. In 1858, the Spokane, with the Coeur d'Alene and Palus tribes, fought the U.S. Army to defend their lands. At the Battle of Four Lakes, U.S. troops destroyed Spokane crops and horses, and forced the tribe to

When a Spokane girl was old enough, she received her own "digging stick" for gathering plants. The first camas root the girl dug up was a prize that she kept in a bag. From that time on, she always wore the bag when digging.

Red, yellow, and black are the dominant colors of the traditional regalia that this Spokane man is wearing. Even his forehead bears a red stripe. He is attending the tribal Labor Day Powwow on the Spokane Reservation in Wellpinit, eastern Washington.

surrender. The Spokane tried to continue hunting and gathering, but they found it impossible to provide sufficient food with so little land available to them. In 1881, the U.S. government created the Spokane Reservation. Most Lower Spokane moved there, while the remaining people later moved to the Coeur d'Alene, Colville, and Flathead Reservations. In 2014, the Spokane Reservation celebrated its 100th annual powwow, held every Labor Day weekend. A year later, Carol Evans became the first woman to lead the Spokane tribal council. She oversees the tribe's efforts to keep its language and culture alive. The tribe is working to bring salmon back to its rivers, a fish that was so important to their ancestors. They also publish a monthly community paper, *The Rawhide Press.*

UMATILLA

(um-uh-TILL-uh)

LANGUAGE GROUP:
Plateau Penutian

GREETING:
Niix máycqi

THANK YOU:
Qayciyáwyaw

LOCATION PRECONTACT:
Oregon, Washington

LOCATION TODAY:
Oregon

The Umatilla are close relatives of the Nez Perce, Walla Walla, Palus, and Yakama, who also made their home on the Plateau. The tribe lived on both sides of the Columbia River and the Umatilla River in present-day Oregon and Washington. They stayed close to the river in the winter, but moved around at other times of the year, gathering plants and hunting. Huckleberries were a favorite fruit, but the tribe also gathered camas root and many other plants.

The Columbia River system provided salmon and trout, while the Umatilla hunting grounds were full of deer, mountain sheep, and rabbits. The river was also a trade route, and before European fur traders arrived, the Umatilla were already skilled traders. When they began to use horses in the early 1700s, they became expert riders and trainers, too. Horses allowed them to travel farther to trade and hunt buffalo on the Plains.

The Umatilla still keep horses today, though their grazing lands are much smaller. The opening of the Oregon Trail and the gold rushes of the mid-1800s brought thousands to settle on Umatilla land. In 1855, the Umatilla, Cayuse, and Walla Walla tribes signed the Walla Walla Treaty, which ceded tribal lands and created a reservation in Oregon. The Umatilla still live on this reservation and rent much of their farmland to outsiders. In 2016, the Confederated Tribes of the Umatilla Indian Reservation, as the three tribes are now known, won a historic land claims settlement with the U.S. government. The government admitted to using lands without paying and promised $20 million to the tribe.

IN THE KNOW

The Umatilla are one of the sponsors of the annual Pendleton Round-Up, held every year since 1910. It is one of the country's largest rodeos. During the festivities, the Umatilla Reservation hosts a tribal village with 300 tepees. A spectacular Wild West show also takes place.

This Umatilla deer-hide bag dates from the early 1900s. The beaded front panel depicts a scene in which an Umatilla man holding a spear stands with his horse and a bird flies overhead.

A Native woman sits in front of her reed-mat tepee, wearing traditional clothes. Her name is Edna Kash-kash. This is one of several thousands of images taken by Major Lee Moorhouse at the Umatilla Reservation in the early 1910s.

THE GHOST DANCE

By the late 1800s, most tribes lived on reservations. During this time, missionaries and government workers forced tribes to adopt the English language and Christian religions. They tried to force an end to tribal customs and beliefs. With their traditional livelihoods taken away, people had to adjust to new ways of living.

In 1890, a Paiute tribal member, Wovoka, began a spiritual movement to give people hope for the future. Wovoka had experienced a dream in which spirits told him that the tribal people would regain their world from the whites. The Ghost Dance—depicted here, painted on buckskin—became an expression of Wovoka's dream. If everyone practiced the dance, he said, the world would renew itself for them. The Ghost Dance was a secret movement that caught on among the tribes of the Great Basin and Plateau region, and spread to the Plains. The U.S. government heard about it and suspected a rebellion. It acted swiftly to outlaw the dance and other ceremonies. Some tribes continued to practice it for a while, but it is not a feature of tribal life today.

UTE

(YOOT)

LANGUAGE GROUP:
Uto-Aztecan

GREETING:
Mike

THANK YOU:
Tŏ/we ŏck

LOCATION PRECONTACT:
Colorado, Utah

LOCATION TODAY:
Colorado, Utah

The state of Utah is named for the Ute tribe, the original people of large parts of Utah and Colorado. The seven Ute bands that were later classified as the Southern, Eastern, and Western Ute lived for countless generations in central Utah and on the Colorado Plateau and surrounding areas, including the Rocky Mountains. The territory provided rich resources for the bands, with a variety of plants, fish, and game. Depending on their location, the tribe had access to different types of foods. The Western Ute, for example, fished in Utah Lake and gathered the pine nuts that grew so well in their territory; Southern Ute could eat the flowers and fruits of prickly pear cactus and other kinds of plants that grew on the Colorado Plateau and farther south. The Southern Ute also made soap from the root of the yucca plant and used fiber from the leaves of the plant to make rope and nets. All had access to deer and bighorn sheep, and some to buffalo.

Once the Spanish introduced horses to the Southern and Eastern Ute in the 1600s, tribal members hunted large buffalo herds of the western Plains more efficiently. Eventually, various Ute bands grew very powerful. They raised and traded horses, which they used to travel farther and carry loads, or to raid other, smaller tribes—some going far into the Southwest and even California. The Ute traded with the Pueblos of New Mexico and with the Spanish. Once the tribe was using horses for travel, they also changed their shelters. Earlier Ute people lived in wickiups made from poles with bark or bulrush coverings. Later, many Ute bands lived in hide-covered tepees. These were much easier to put up and take down as they followed the buffalo herds.

Mormons arrived and began settling on Ute lands in western and central Utah the mid-1800s. The Ute protested by raiding the Mormon settlements. The U.S. government wanted the Ute to stay in one place and farm, but the Ute did not want to change their traditional ways of living. By 1869, the government had moved most Western and Northern Ute onto the Uintah Valley Reservation. Later, two other bands moved to the nearby

Pictured are Ute petroglyphs of bighorn sheep and men on horseback. The carvings are made on rock near Wolfe Ranch in Arches National Park, eastern Utah.

Uintah and Ouray Indian Reservation. Southern Ute were moved to a reservation in southern Colorado around the same time. Today, there are almost 3,000 members of the Ute tribe—half of them living on reservations. The Uintah and Ouray form one reservation in Utah—the second largest in the United States. Some Ute in southeastern Utah live separately on reserved lands but are part of the Mountain Ute Reservation in Colorado. Between them, the Ute oversee about 1.3 million acres (500,000 ha) of land.

This is a portrait of Ute chief Severo, and his family, from the late 1800s. The chief (rear, left) wears an American military jacket, while his family members are dressed in more traditional Native clothing.

WALLA WALLA

(WAH-la WAH-la)

LANGUAGE GROUP:
Isolate

LANGUAGE:
Currently dormant; no dictionary available online or in print

LOCATION PRECONTACT:
Oregon, Washington

LOCATION TODAY:
Oregon

Walla Walla means "many waters," and the name suits a tribe that lived in a land full of rivers and lakes—its people were great fishermen and hunters. They followed a seasonal life cycle, fishing salmon and digging roots in spring and hunting game and gathering berries in summer. The Umatilla, who lived nearby, were close relatives.

The Walla Walla lived in tule-covered longhouses along the Columbia River as well as parts of the Yakima, Walla Walla, and Snake Rivers in Washington and Oregon. This location was ideal for trading with tribes from all directions, especially with Plains and Pacific coastal people. The traditional fishing grounds at Celilo Falls, between modern-day Oregon and Washington, was a trading hub. The Walla Walla became expert traders, learning to deal with many different cultures and languages. The tribal people shared their skills with others in their communities. They elected leaders based on skill and experience—they ➡

This pair of men's leggings is made from hemp and features deer-hide fringes on the outer edges. A geometric pattern covers the front of the leggings, which are also decorated with rabbit fur.

were healers, artists, cooks, and storytellers. Each person was an important part in making the tribe successful.

The Walla Walla met the Lewis and Clark expedition in 1805, and were eager to trade with the explorers. In 1811, a fur-trading post was established at Fort Astoria in Oregon, on the Columbia River, and drew the Walla Walla and other tribes into the fur trade. Other posts followed, but the opening of the Oregon Trail was the first major change for the Walla Walla people. Thousands of settlers made their way west in 1849, drawn by the discovery of gold in California. In 1855, the Walla Walla signed a treaty that ceded their lands and forced them to agree to live on the Umatilla Indian Reservation with the Umatilla and Cayuse tribes. Today, the three tribes are a confederation with a single council. Working with the state of Oregon, the tribe has restored its salmon runs and reintroduced chinook salmon to the Umatilla River after 70 years of extinction.

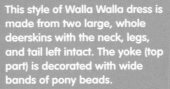

This style of Walla Walla dress is made from two large, whole deerskins with the neck, legs, and tail left intact. The yoke (top part) is decorated with wide bands of pony beads.

WARM SPRINGS

(WARM SPRINGS)

LANGUAGE GROUP:
Various

LANGUAGE:
Currently in limited use; no dictionary available online or in print

LOCATION PRECONTACT:
Oregon

LOCATION TODAY:
Oregon

Warm Springs is a confederation of three tribes: the Tenino, also known as Warm Springs, the Wasco, and the Paiute. They currently live on the Warm Springs Reservation in Oregon. The three tribes spoke different languages and had different cultures, but an 1855 treaty forced them together. The Tenino and Wasco tribes were the first to arrive on the reservation, followed by a band of 38 Paiute, who joined them in 1879. Other Paiute, who no longer had a home elsewhere, came later.

Before moving onto the reservation, the Tenino tribe had been seminomadic, moving with the seasons to fish, hunt, and gather food. From their summer villages along the Columbia River and its tributaries, the men fished for salmon. They built wooden

Two sisters from the Warm Springs Reservation ride the family's horse. The girls are dressed in traditional beaded clothing. Their horse is decorated with similar colors and motifs.

ANIMAL SYMBOLS

Native carvings, ancestral history, and dances frequently include animal motifs or symbols. The stories of tribes in the Great Basin and Plateau tell of Coyote and Wolf ruling the world before humans arrived. Coyote sometimes appears as the younger brother of Wolf, a powerful transformer spirit. Coyote can also be a trickster spirit, so is not entirely trustworthy. For the Shoshone, Wolf is both a trickster and a hero. The thunderbird is another powerful figure. This bird is a very large and powerful creature that is also important to tribes in the Northwest Coast region, the Plains, and Alaska. The beaded shield pictured dates from 2003 and features an eagle. In the past, warriors often painted animals on their shields to represent spirits that might bring a warrior courage or strength in battle. Animals continue to play an important role today.

scaffolding with raised platforms on which to stand over the waterfalls so they could use their long-handled nets to catch the fish that fell over. The Tenino did not speak the same language as the Wasco, but the two tribes were trading partners. The Wasco were also fishermen who lived on the Columbia River, and they traded bear grass, ground salmon, and roots in exchange for game, horses, and clothing. The Paiute who later joined the Tenino and Wasco were hunters who lived on the high plains in southeastern Oregon.

Beginning in the early 1840s, thousands of settlers moved into the West. The U.S. government wanted to make land available for homesteaders, businesses, and railroads. In 1855, the Tenino and Wasco signed a treaty ceding approximately 10 million acres (4 million ha) of their land, keeping only a small area for their new reservation. On the reservation, the tribes began to adapt to their new environment and each other. The Tenino and Wasco continued to fish and gather roots and berries, while the Paiute learned these new ways of life. Every year, they celebrate the gift of these traditional foods with the Root Feast, the Salmon Feast, and the Huckleberry Feast.

Determined to keep their ancient traditions alive, the three tribes opened a museum in 1993, with exhibits of traditional Plateau arts, such as beadwork and baskets, and cultural histories. Efforts to revive the languages of the Tenino, Wasco, and Paiute people are also under way, since very few speakers remain.

The Warm Springs tribe used winnowing baskets to separate grain from its husks. Husks blew away when tossing the basket's contents in the air.

CHIEF NELSON WALLULATUM

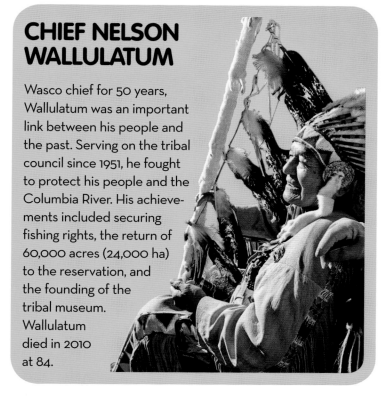

Wasco chief for 50 years, Wallulatum was an important link between his people and the past. Serving on the tribal council since 1951, he fought to protect his people and the Columbia River. His achievements included securing fishing rights, the return of 60,000 acres (24,000 ha) to the reservation, and the founding of the tribal museum. Wallulatum died in 2010 at 84.

YAHOOSKIN

(ya-WHO-skin)

LANGUAGE GROUP:
Uto-Aztecan

LANGUAGE:
Currently dormant;
no dictionary available
online or in print

LOCATION PRECONTACT:
Idaho, Oregon

LOCATION TODAY:
Oregon

Originally a band of the Northern Paiute tribe, the Yahooskin lived close to the border between present-day Idaho and Oregon. They were hunters, gatherers, and fishermen who moved around to find the food they needed. The tribe's first contact with a non-Native was in 1826 with Peter Skene Ogden, a Canadian fur trader. It was not long before more people began to travel into Yahooskin lands to trade and to settle; by the 1840s, they were arriving and settling in large numbers.

In 1864, the Yahooskin, Modoc, and Klamath tribes signed a treaty that ceded 19.5 million acres (7.9 million ha) of land to the U.S. government and forced them to move onto the Klamath Reservation, where they became known as the Klamath Tribes.

On the reservation, the Yahooskin could not travel and hunt as widely as they had done before. Along with the other tribes, they became ranchers, and built a sawmill. In time, the lumber industry brought large profits to the tribe, making them one of the wealthiest in the United States.

In 1954, the Klamath Termination Act stripped the tribes of their official status and they lost much of their reservation land. The act also ended all federal funding to the tribes, resulting in a loss of education, housing, and health services to which non-terminated tribes were entitled. The Klamath Restoration Act of 1986 did not return any land, but did restore the benefits that had been taken. In 1986 the tribes regained their status with the federal government. Today, they share a tribal council and resources, such as housing and child-care programs.

The Yahooskin's tribal ancestors always welcomed the return in the spring of the *c'waam*, or Lost River sucker fish. Today, the tribe honors this in its own Return of the *C'waam* Ceremony. Tribal members gather to release a pair of *c'waam* into the river, and later dance, drum, and feast in celebration.

> **IN THE KNOW**
>
> Early settlers called the Yahooskin the "Snake Indians," because much of their territory was located on the Snake River.

In this picture from the Return of the *C'waam* Ceremony, elder Mary Ann Wright blesses one of the c'waam before the fish is returned to the river. It is traditional for tribal elders to perform this blessing at the ceremony.

YAKAMA

(YEAH-kuh-mah)

LANGUAGE GROUP:
Plateau Penutian

GREETING:
Áay

THANK YOU:
Kw'alanuu shamash

LOCATION PRECONTACT:
Washington

LOCATION TODAY:
Washington

In 1855, 14 tribal groups came together to form the Confederated Tribes and Bands of the Yakama Nation. They were the Palus, Kah-milt-pay, Wenatshapam, Shyiks, Kow-was-say-ee, Li-ay-was, Se-ap-cat, Linquit, Skin-pah, Ochechotes, Klikatat, Pasquouse, Wish-ham, and Yakama. Although their languages are related, each tribe spoke its own dialect. The Yakama tribal homelands in the Columbia River Basin covered 10.8 million acres (4.4 million ha) in present-day Washington. The people lived in the region's hills, mountains, and valleys. They built homes from frames of pine poles hung with tule reeds, and used these shelters through the summer while they gathered roots, chokeberries, and other foods. In the winter, they built more permanent earthen lodges.

A young Yakama child helps to pick huckleberries, which are sacred to his tribe. In the distance stands Mount Adams of the Cascade Mountains.

Yakama men ride on horseback through the rugged Washington terrain, in around 1950. Each is clothed in tribal regalia, complete with an eagle-feather headdress. The leader carries a coup stick.

In the spring, people gathered at Celilo Falls, an important fishing and trading center for the Plateau tribes. They also spent the warmer months fishing for salmon in the rivers. Before returning to their winter villages, tribal members cleaned, dried, and stored food for the long, cold months ahead. After preparing for winter, it was time to celebrate with stick games, horse races, ceremonies, and feasts before settling into their permanent winter homes. These shelters were lodges made from mud, reeds, and grasses. This cycle of life continued until 1855, when the Yakama were forced to sign a treaty with the U.S. government ceding most of their ancestral lands.

The Yakama Nation Treaty of 1855 left 1.4 million acres (570,000 ha) for the Yakama reservation. The same year, prospectors found gold in northeast Washington. White settlers and miners crossed tribal land, resulting in conflict with the Yakama. The U.S. Army stepped in, fighting the Yakama until 1858. U.S. troops killed Yakama warriors, raided and burned villages, and captured and killed hundreds of horses.

Over 150 years later, more than 12,000 Yakama Nation peoples live on, or near, the rolling hills of the Yakama Indian Reservation. The confederation owns modern businesses that include an energy company, a sawmill, and a fruit farm. The Yakama Nation Museum opened in 1980 and is one of the oldest Native American museums in the U.S. Each year in June, the museum and cultural center host Yakama Nation Treaty Day to commemorate and reflect on the signing of the 1855 treaty. The five-day event begins with a parade and features a powwow, a rodeo, and demonstrations of native crafts. ✐

HOW COYOTE CAME BY HIS POWERS

The Great Spirit called all his animals together from all over the Earth. He told them: "I will give you new names, and the Animal World will rule." Along with each new name, each animal will have a new duty to perform.

Excitement grew. Each one desired a great name. Everyone wanted power to rule some tribe, some kingdom of the Animal World.

No one liked Coyote. He boasted too much, and now he bragged about the great name he would choose. He said, "I will have three big names to select from: Grizzly Bear, who will be ruler over all the running, four-footed animals; Eagle, who will lead all the flying birds; Salmon, who will be chief over all the fish."

Coyote's twin brother, Fox, said to him, "Do not be too sure. Maybe no one will have his choice of names. Maybe you will have to retain your own name, Coyote."

Coyote went to his tepee in anger. Coyote's wife, sitting at the side of the doorway, said in a disappointed tone, "Have you no food for the children? They are starving!"

"Eh-ha!" grunted Coyote "I am no common one to be spoken to in that fashion. Do you know that I am going to be a great Chief tomorrow? I shall be Grizzly Bear. I will devour my enemies with ease. I will be a great warrior and Chief."

Before Coyote knew it, he was asleep. He was awakened by his wife when the sun was high in the morning sky.

Coyote jumped up. He hurried to the lodge of the Chief Spirit to be named. Nobody was there, and Coyote thought that he was first. He went into the lodge and spoke, "I am going to be Grizzly Bear!"

The Chief answered, "Grizzly Bear was taken at daybreak!"

The balance of nature relies on the coexistence of the plants and animals Coyote would protect. A deer feeds on plants and fruits. In turn, it is eaten by wolves, grizzly bears, and humans.

Coyote said, "Then I shall be called Eagle!"

The Chief answered Coyote, "Eagle has chosen his name. He flew away long ago."

Coyote then said, "I think that I will be called Salmon."

"Salmon has also been taken. Only Coyote remains. No one wished to steal your name from you."

Poor Coyote sank down sadly, and the heart of the Spirit Chief was touched by the mischief-maker. After a silence the Chief spoke, "You are Coyote! I have chosen you from among all others to be father for all the tribes. You will have power to change yourself into anything when in danger or distress. There are man-eating monsters on the Earth who are destroying the people. The tribes cannot increase and grow as I wish. These monsters must all be destroyed before the new people come. This is your work to do. I have given your twin brother, Fox, power to help you. Now go, Coyote! Do good for the benefit of your people."

—**Mourning Dove, Okanogan, from *Coyote Stories*, University of Nebraska Press**

Crowds gather and some play drums to welcome the canoes as they arrive at the start of an inter-tribal Canoe Journeys celebration hosted by the Lummi tribe. Participants dance, sing, and "potlatch," or feast, for a week with their hosts, before leaving to make their voyage home.

 # THE NORTHWEST COAST

A long, narrow area bordered by the Pacific Ocean to the west and mountain ranges to the east, the Northwest Coast stretches from southern Alaska to Oregon. Many tribes settled in this region, on islands and peninsulas and in river valleys and foothills. For thousands of years, they lived in harmony with the seasons, hunting, fishing, and gathering. Although much has changed, the Northwest Coast is still a region of vibrant Native cultures.

The first people moved to the Pacific Northwest more than 10,000 years ago. Over time, separate communities sprang up along the coast, rivers, and nearby islands. This was a place of plenty—an ocean teeming with fish and sea mammals, tide flats full of clams, and lush forests with towering red cedar trees and woodland animals. The people built large dugout canoes from the red cedar and mastered fishing in the Pacific Ocean. Members of the Makah tribe, in particular, became expert whale and seal hunters. Among other tribes, many caught sea otters, seals, and fish. The large catches fed entire villages and provided valuable oils and furs. Respected and honored by the people of the Northwest Coast, salmon were particularly important. They were central to tribal ceremonies and stories because they were a vital source of food. Many tribes held a First Salmon Ceremony to celebrate the salmon's return to freshwater rivers from the ocean.

Tribal Communities

The abundance of natural resources enabled sophisticated societies to develop and flourish. In winter, the tribes lived in cedar houses large enough for many families to share. Several houses formed a village. Tribes such as the Tlingit and Haida carved spectacular totem poles at the entrances to their homes, declaring and honoring family ties. A hierarchy operated in each village, with upper, middle, and lower classes, as well as slaves from other tribes. On special occasions, such as memorials, marriages, and naming ceremonies, the upper class, or nobles, would hold a potlatch—a gift-giving feast. This was an opportunity for them to share their riches with other classes and feast with guests.

In the spring and summer months, tribes often split into smaller family groups to hunt deer, elk, and other animals, to gather berries, and to dig camas roots. As with the tribes of the Great Basin and Plateau region, the camas root made up a large portion of the northwestern diet. People lived in temporary shelters that could be moved from place to place. In the late fall, tribal members returned to their winter villages. Through the summer months, they dried and stored extra food to help feed the tribe in winter.

Trade and the Arrival of Outsiders

The Northwest tribes were part of a large tribal trading network, which Russian and European fur traders also joined in the 1700s. Coastal tribes traded sea otter, seal, beaver, and mink pelts for cloth, iron, and other goods. In 1794, the Jay Treaty created a boundary line between the United States and Canada, although the tribes that lived along this line refused to recognize the border, since it divided their lands. Within a few years, the governments of both countries set their sights on tribal lands, and Russians set up colonies in Alaska. Settlers crossed tribal lands in the mid-1830s, using the newly opened Oregon Trail that connected the eastern states to those in the West. The search for gold brought even more people to the Northwest. Between 1854 and 1855, the government signed treaties with many tribes of the Northwest Coast, forcing or encouraging them to give up all or most of their lands and settle on reservations. Tribes found they no longer had access to their traditional fishing, hunting, or gathering lands or the ocean. Potlatches and other tribal customs were banned by the American and Canadian governments, who wanted the Native people to adopt more "American" and "Canadian" ways instead of following their own cultures.

Fighting Back

In the 1900s, tribes throughout the region fought legal battles to regain treaty rights and tribal status. These court cases took years to resolve, but many were successful. Tribes expanded their land ownership and revived their languages and arts. Today young tribal members learn and enjoy the traditions of their ancestors—from carving and potlatches to fishing and basket weaving. The First Salmon Ceremony is once again a yearly event.

This mask was made by a member of the Makah tribe in around 1890. The wooden mask is painted with wolflike features and has real wolf fur attached.

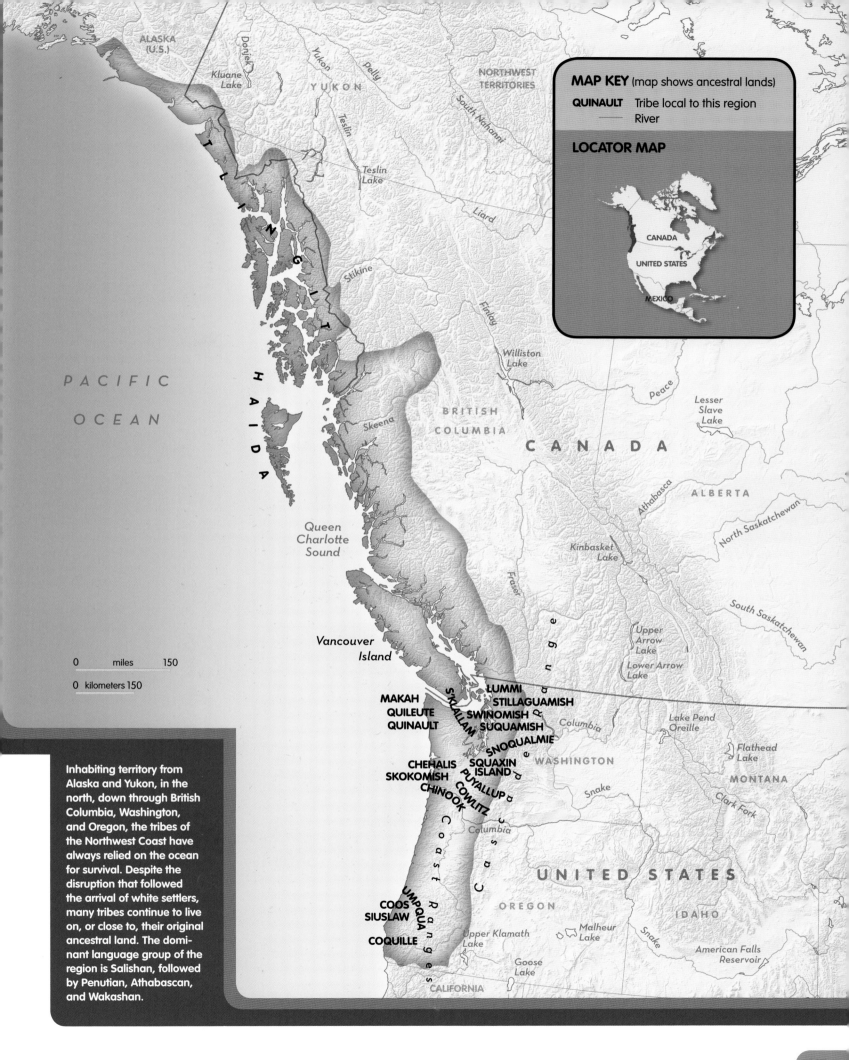

ALASKA
(U.S.)

Donjek

Kluane
Lake

Yukon

Pelly

YUKON

South Nahanni

NORTHWEST
TERRITORIES

Teslin

Teslin
Lake

Liard

MAP KEY (map shows ancestral lands)

QUINAULT   Tribe local to this region
             River

LOCATOR MAP

CANADA

UNITED STATES

MEXICO

T
L
I
N
G
I
T

Stikine

H
A
I
D
A

PACIFIC

OCEAN

Queen
Charlotte
Sound

Skeena

BRITISH

COLUMBIA

Williston
Lake

Finlay

CANADA

Peace

Lesser
Slave
Lake

Athabasca

ALBERTA

North Saskatchewan

South Saskatchewan

Kinbasket
Lake

Upper
Arrow
Lake

Lower Arrow
Lake

Vancouver
Island

Fraser

0   miles   150

0   kilometers 150

MAKAH
QUILEUTE
QUINAULT

S'KALLAM

LUMMI
STILLAGUAMISH
SWINOMISH
SUQUAMISH

SNOQUALMIE

CHEHALIS
SKOKOMISH

SQUAXIN
ISLAND
PUYALLUP
COWLITZ

CHINOOK

Columbia

WASHINGTON

Lake Pend
Oreille

Flathead
Lake

MONTANA

Snake

Clark Fork

Coast Ranges

Columbia

Cascade Range

UNITED   STATES

OREGON

IDAHO

COOS
SIUSLAW

UMPQUA

COQUILLE

Upper Klamath
Lake

Malheur
Lake

Snake

American Falls
Reservoir

Goose
Lake

CALIFORNIA

Inhabiting territory from
Alaska and Yukon, in the
north, down through British
Columbia, Washington,
and Oregon, the tribes of
the Northwest Coast have
always relied on the ocean
for survival. Despite the
disruption that followed
the arrival of white settlers,
many tribes continue to live
on, or close to, their original
ancestral land. The domi-
nant language group of the
region is Salishan, followed
by Penutian, Athabascan,
and Wakashan.

TIME LINE OF THE NORTHWEST COAST

The people of the Northwest Coast lived for thousands of years without outside interference. With the arrival of the Russians in the 1700s, traditional lives began to change. The Lewis and Clark expedition in the early 1800s and the opening of the Oregon Trail encouraged settlers to move west. Gold rushes followed, and the U.S. government began its takeover of tribal lands, moving the tribes to reservations.

3000 B.C.E.

Tribes and villages established. By 3000 B.C.E., people of the Northwest Coast had established tribes and permanent villages. Near their homes, the people had everything they needed. The Pacific Ocean provided whales, seals, and other seafood, while the many rivers teemed with salmon. Building materials came from spruce and red cedar.

1794

Jay Treaty establishes the U.S.-Canada border. After the Revolutionary War, Great Britain and the United States signed the Jay Treaty, creating a boundary between British-controlled Canada and the United States. The invisible border ran through tribal lands. Although the treaty stated that tribal members could cross the border freely, border controls on both sides made this difficult. This is still the case today.

1799

Russians establish a colony at Sitka. After colonizing areas in Alaska, the Russian-American Company built a post near Sitka, in Tlingit territory. The Russians expected the Tlingit to provide free labor. Resenting Russian attempts to control their people, the Tlingit revolted in 1802. They attacked the Russians and their Aleut allies, killing more than 120 people. The Russians then left Sitka.

1804

Battle of Sitka. When the Russians returned to Sitka after a two-year absence, Tlingit warriors attacked the Russians and their Aleut allies, killing many, before running out of ammunition and fleeing. The Russians took over Sitka again and renamed their post New Archangel. Eventually, some Tlingit returned to the area, but conflicts continued.

1805

Lewis and Clark expedition arrives, sighting the Pacific Ocean for the first time. Meriwether Lewis and William Clark met and traded with the Chinook during their travels. Pictured is William Clark's compass.

1836

Oregon Trail brings settlers. Some 400,000 settlers arrived in the Northwest between 1836 and 1869, following the Oregon Trail, which was used by fur trappers and traders.

1850–1899

Gold rushes bring settlers, miners, and prospectors. During the last half of the 19th century, 26 separate gold rushes brought thousands to the Northwest Coast.

1850

Donation Land Act passed by Congress. Congress passed this act to divide lands in Oregon for white settlers. It allowed a person to claim 320 acres (130 ha) of land free of charge, prompting thousands to move into the territory.

1854

Medicine Creek Treaty. Nine tribes and bands, including the Puyallup and Squaxin Island people, ceded 2.5 million acres (1 million ha) of land, although the treaty acknowledged tribal rights to fish. Treaties with the Quinault and Neah Bay tribes, among others, followed in 1855 and 1856, also taking tribal land. Pictured is a member of the Quinault tribe.

1855–1856

Puget Sound War and Rogue River War. White settlers, backed by U.S. troops, fought against Northwest tribes. There were many deaths on both sides, and the tribes moved onto reservations.

1882

Indian Shaker Church founded. John Slocum, a Squaxin, and his wife, Mary, founded the Indian Shaker Church as a blend of Christian and traditional tribal beliefs. The Indian Shaker Church spread among tribes throughout the Northwest. Pictured is an Indian Shaker Church at Tulalip, Washington.

1887

Dawes Act signed. The act split tribal lands into small plots (called allotments) of up to 160 acres (65 ha), for distribution among tribal members. They had to prove they were farming the land and had to live separately from the tribe. Any extra land was sold to white settlers (pictured here, rushing to claim Cherokee land). The act also introduced boarding schools to educate tribal children in white American history and culture.

1960s

Fish Wars protests begin. During the 1960s and 1970s, tribal people in the Northwest Coast region staged "fish-ins." These were protests to highlight the importance of fishing to the tribes and the impact that commercial fishing (pictured) was having on their fishing areas.

1974

Tribes' rights upheld by the Boldt Decision. In the *U.S. v. Washington State* court case, Federal District Judge George Boldt upheld the tribes' rights to fish in their traditional fishing grounds under the terms of the historic treaties signed by the tribes.

2009

Queen Charlotte Islands renamed. The British Columbia provincial government agreed to rename the Queen Charlotte Islands Haida Gwaii in recognition of the Haida people and their ancestors, who traditionally made their homes on the islands.

CHEHALIS

(sh-HAY-lis)

LANGUAGE GROUP:
Salishan

GREETING:
Máya-

THANK YOU:
Náxʷłqʷulati

LOCATION PRECONTACT:
Washington

LOCATION TODAY:
Washington (U.S.); British Columbia (Canada)

Chehalis people live in both the United States and Canada. The Upper Chehalis and Lower Chehalis are two of four groups that live in the United States. Both traditionally lived near water; the Lower Chehalis near the ocean, on which they depended for seafood, seals, and fish, and the Upper Chehalis on inland rivers, which they fished and used as trade routes. Chehalis comes from a word that means "sand." The Upper Chehalis gathered camas roots and other wild plants. Both groups lived in longhouses built of cedar wood.

Unlike many tribes in the Northwest and elsewhere, the Chehalis never signed a treaty with the U.S. government. Even so, the government created a reservation for the tribe in 1864, at the confluence of the Chehalis and Black Rivers in present-day Washington. Many Chehalis preferred to stay in their homelands. A second reservation was created in 1866 on Willapa Bay for the Lower Chehalis, Chinooks, and several other tribes, but they received little help from the government. Those who stayed on their ancestral land lost some of it to homesteaders. In 1906, the Chehalis in Washington State began a land-claim lawsuit to get back their lands. It wasn't until 1962 that they received just 90 cents per acre (0.4 ha) for some of the land they had lost.

In recent years, Chehalis on and off the reservation have developed programs to protect their language and traditions. They gather for tribal ceremonies, storytelling, and arts activities, and care for the water and land that surrounds them. They still fish in the Chehalis River, just as their ancestors did hundreds of years ago.

Every year, the Chehalis join other regional tribes to take part in the intertribal Canoe Journeys, a celebration of Northwest culture and tradition. With a different destination each year, the canoe journey is made in oceangoing canoes—some made traditionally from cedar wood. The distance changes each year and can take as long as one month to complete. On arrival, participants spend several days sharing tribal songs, stories, and dances. The first Canoe Journey, called the Paddle to Seattle, was held in 1989. ✐

HAZEL PETE

When she was five years old, Hazel Pete began to weave baskets. Her grandmother taught her the traditional way. Hazel went on to become one of the tribe's master weavers and to teach the craft to others in her tribe. She passed on her knowledge of weaving to younger generations as well, showing them how to weave clothing from cedar bark and to make mats from cattail—a tall marsh plant.

A salmon swims up the Chehalis River to spawn. Members of the Chehalis tribe fish for salmon in spring. They eat the first fish they catch in a feast to celebrate the harvest time.

CHINOOK

(CHIN-ook)

LANGUAGE GROUP:
Chinookan

GREETING:
Nah sikhs

THANK YOU:
Mahsie

LOCATION PRECONTACT:
Oregon, Washington

LOCATION TODAY:
Oregon, Washington

This contemporary basket with lid was made in 2003. The grasses and raffia have been dyed red, black, and white to create a repeating geometric pattern.

The Chinook, a group of 16 different bands, inhabited the Columbia River Delta, in present-day Oregon and Washington. They spoke Chinookan languages, which have their origins in Penutian (see p. 217). In winter, they lived in villages, but in summer they camped, gathering food such as clams, hunting elk and small game, and fishing for salmon in the Columbia River. A strict class system governed Chinook society, and children were forbidden from playing with anyone of a different class.

The Chinook were expert craftspeople who made dugout canoes with a decorated prow and stern. The largest of these, which were up to 50 feet (15 m) long, could handle ocean currents, while a smaller-size canoe was ideal for paddling to trading posts along the Columbia River. Trade with other tribes was very important to the Chinook. When the Chinook began to trade with Europeans, they developed a language to communicate with them. This language, known as Chinook Jargon, is a mix of English and words from the Chinookan and other tribal languages—a simplified language that is easy to understand.

Other tribes in the area also adopted Chinook Jargon.

In the 1850s, the U.S. government signed treaties with the coastal tribes and many moved to reservations. The government failed to ratify any treaties it discussed with the Chinook, and so the tribe did not receive reservation land or support. Some Chinook people settled on reservations allocated to other tribes as a result. Today, five tribes make up the Chinook Nation. They have a tribal office in Washington, but they do not have their own reservation or federal status.

Tribal members keep the Chinook history and customs alive with storytelling gatherings and ceremonies, including the First Salmon Ceremony, which they hold in June—other tribes celebrate this festival at different times of the year. A 2015 documentary, *Promised Land*, told the story of the Chinook and Duwamish tribes' fight with the U.S. government for official status and rights. ☞

☀ IN THE KNOW

The Plateau band of Chinook flattened their heads as a status symbol. Higher-class members of the tribe pressed a board to their babies' foreheads every day to mold their skulls. These people became known as the Flatheads.

When a member of the tribe died, the Chinook custom was to place the body in a canoe and hoist it into the branches of a tree, out of reach of animals.

THE ART OF THE CANOE

Tribes in the Northwest Coast region depended heavily on the ocean and inland rivers for food, travel, war, and trade. They built five different kinds of canoes for these purposes. Four of these were large, oceangoing canoes. The fifth was smaller and used for river travel. Master builders carved canoes from towering red cedar or spruce trees. Once they felled, or cut, the timber, builders shaped it, hollowed it out,

and carved it. Some canoes could be up to 50 feet (15 m) long and might carry as many as 30 people.

A canoe's high, curved prows were practical as well as being works of art. They featured carved and painted tribal designs. For tribes such as the Haida, these spectacular canoes became valuable trade items. Many tribes still practice this art today.

COOS, UMPQUA, SIUSLAW

(COOS, UMP-quaw, sy-OOS-lah)

LANGUAGE GROUP:
Coos, Isolate, Penutian

LANGUAGE:
Currently being revived; no dictionary or word lists available

LOCATION PRECONTACT:
Oregon

LOCATION TODAY:
Oregon

Originally, the Coos, Lower Umpqua, and Siuslaw lived along the coast of Oregon—the Coos around what is now Coos Bay, Oregon, and the Lower Umpqua and Siuslaw to the north. In winter, the tribes lived in longhouses made of cedar on the river estuaries; in the summer, they moved inland to hunt and gather. The three tribes lived well off both the land and sea. Salmon, shellfish, wild berries, and onions were plentiful. They also gathered seafood, shells, and other goods to trade with tribes inland. Throughout the year, the Coos, Siuslaw, and Umpqua held ceremonies—for example, for the naming of a newborn child—with feasting, games, and dancing.

The tribes lived peacefully most of the time, and did not encounter British and American

traders until the late 1700s, when they arrived by ship. Fur traders came to the region in the 1820s, and in the early 1850s miners and settlers flocked to the coastal areas of Oregon, bringing destruction and disease. In 1853, the Cow Creek Umpqua band signed a government treaty promising a reservation in return for land, but the reservation was never created. Two years later, in 1855, the Rogue River War broke out as northwestern tribes resisted relocation by the government.

While some of the Cow Creek Umpqua were forced to move to the Grand Ronde Reservation with other tribes, others went into hiding inland. Eventually, these Cow Creek Umpqua returned to their territory. The Cow Creek Umpqua were not formally

The decorative design on this Coos deerskin bag features rows of tiny seed beads in red, white, and blue. They radiate out from a central star motif.

recognized as a tribe by the U.S. government until 1982.

The Coos and Siuslaw signed a treaty in 1855 that ceded all their land to the U.S. government. The government never delivered the rights promised in the treaty, and in 1860, members of the Coos and Lower Umpqua were forced to march 60 miles (96 km) north to the Coast Indian Reservation in Yachats, Oregon. Many died of hunger and disease on the way, and more died after they arrived. The government moved the tribes again in 1876—not to a reservation of their own, but to the Siletz Reservation. In 1941, the government assigned a tiny parcel of land, just over six acres (2.4 ha), for the Coos, Lower Umpqua, and Siuslaw in Coos Bay, Oregon.

In spite of their difficult history, the confederated tribes of the Coos, Lower Umpqua, and Siuslaw have rebuilt their community. They now own businesses in real estate and golf and run the charitable Three Rivers Foundation, which offers grants for improvements to local health, cultural, and education programs. They promote their traditions through regular classes in traditional crafts and hosting annual events, such as the Salmon Ceremony, which they hold in August.

This Coos dress and moccasins are made from rush, a type of marsh plant. The dress has a braided belt. Red beads, shells, and deer hooves are stitched on as decoration. The moccasins are made from braided rushes.

COQUILLE

(ko-KWELL)

LANGUAGE GROUP:
Athabascan

LANGUAGE:
Currently being revived; no dictionary or word lists available

LOCATION PRECONTACT:
Oregon

LOCATION TODAY:
Oregon

For thousands of years, the Coquille—a group of 11 tribes—have lived in southwestern Oregon, around what are now the Coquille River, the Coos River, and Coos Bay. Their ancestors were a band of people called the Mishikhwutmetunne, "people living on the stream called mishi." The Coquille hunted deer and small game and gathered acorns and berries. When French fur trappers met them in the 1800s, they called the tribe Coquille, meaning "shell." Like other northwestern people, the tribe ate mussels, clams, and other seafood, and used seashells in art and jewelry.

When prospectors discovered gold in Oregon in the early 1850s, miners migrated to Coquille territory. Settlers flocked there soon after and claimed Coquille lands as their own. Mining and livestock polluted tribal hunting and fishing grounds, and conflict between the Coquille and the settlers turned violent. In one massacre, a volunteer army group killed many Lower Coquille members.

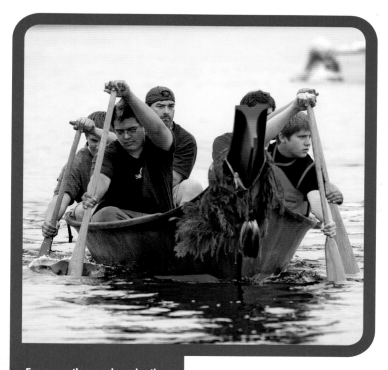

For more than a decade, the Coquille tribe has hosted an annual event—the Mill Luck Salmon Celebration. Among the festival's popular features are cultural demonstrations and intertribal canoe races (pictured).

Taken in 1922, this image shows Coquille women and children dressed in more typically "American"-looking clothes, while still living a traditional Native life.

In 1855, the Coquille signed a treaty ceding their lands in return for their own reservation and government services. However, in 1856, the Rogue River War erupted between several tribes and the U.S. Army and local militias. The Coquille lost warriors and many of their villages were destroyed, forcing many Coquille onto reservations with other tribes. In 1954, the U.S. government terminated the status of the Coquille tribe. Children were sent to government boarding schools, where they were expected to assimilate with white Americans rather than practice their own traditions, and the Coquille language virtually disappeared. Yet more than 30 years later, in 1989, the Coquille regained its official tribal status. Today, the Coquille tribe runs successful forestry, energy, and other businesses. In 2015, the tribe bought 3,200 acres (1,300 ha) of forestland in the Siskiyou National Forest, Oregon. They named it Sek-wet-se—their ancestors' tribal name for the Rogue River, which runs through the park. The tribe is dedicated to reviving the traditions of their ancestors and meet weekly to dance, drum, and sing together. They continue to gather the camas root and to collect clams and mussels.

MONEY FROM THE OCEAN

Dentalia (left) are rare tooth-shaped ocean mollusks that became highly valuable in the trading networks of the Pacific Northwest and south into California. The west coast of Vancouver Island, Canada, was a particularly good source of the shells, but they were not easy to harvest. Tribes collected the shells from the ocean floor using brushes attached to long spears. Once they had collected the shells, people used them as money. A tribe that wanted to buy a canoe, for example, would offer dentalia as payment.

People also used dentalia for decoration on clothing, as on the Vancouver Island hat pictured at right. Owning dentalia meant a person was wealthy and of a higher class in society. A rich family's baby might have dentalia wrapped around his or her ankles.

COWLITZ

(COW-litts)

LANGUAGE GROUP:
Salishan, Sahaptin

GREETING:
Not available

THANK YOU:
Naxʷłqʷul'as

LOCATION PRECONTACT:
Washington

LOCATION TODAY:
Washington

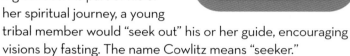

Cowlitz elder Kaktsamah. This 1913 portrait is one of hundreds taken by Edward S. Curtis for his book, *The North American Indian.*

Before settlers arrived in the Northwest, the Upper and Lower Cowlitz homelands covered more than two million acres (800,000 ha) of what is now western Washington. Both groups lived inland along the Cowlitz and Lewis Rivers. The larger band, the Lower Cowlitz, also called the Kawlic, lived in 30 villages west of their Upper Cowlitz relatives and spoke a Salishan language. The Upper Cowlitz, also known as the Taidnapam, adapted the Sahaptin language from the Penutian language. In winter, the Lower and Upper Cowlitz lived by the rivers in large, plank houses shared by up to 15 families. Inside these houses, each family had its own section, with bunk beds spread with furs.

During the spring and summer months, the Cowlitz moved to temporary camps to gather and hunt, spreading over a wide area. The Cowlitz were excellent businesspeople, with a wide trade network. In addition to furs, hides, and fish, Cowlitz baskets were valuable trade items. The watertight baskets made of red cedar root and bark were strong and beautifully designed.

In Cowlitz tradition, it was important for young tribal members to find their spiritual guides—guardians who also helped with hunting, healing, felling trees, and shaping canoes. As part of his or her spiritual journey, a young tribal member would "seek out" his or her guide, encouraging visions by fasting. The name Cowlitz means "seeker."

The Cowlitz had good relationships with many neighboring tribes, and most meetings with early fur traders and trappers were friendly. Contact with the Europeans brought influenza, which almost wiped out the entire tribe. Those who could fled to the coast to avoid infection. By the 1850s, after 20 years of white settlement on their land, the Cowlitz returning from the coast formed a much smaller tribe, having lost as many as three-quarters to disease. Tribal leaders discussed treaty negotiations with the U.S. government, but refused to sign their land away. The Cowlitz remained on their land, but without a designated reservation, and received no government support in return for those areas occupied by white settlers.

In the 1900s, the tribe began negotiations to regain the land lost to white settlers, clashing with both state and federal authorities over their rights. In 2002, the government granted the Cowlitz official tribal status and in 2015, it established a small reservation for the tribe in southwestern Washington. Many of today's tribal members live on this reservation, or in parts of western Washington, and follow the religious, marital, child-rearing, and hunting traditions of their ancestors. Twice a year, several groups meet at Cowlitz Prairie, in Lewis County, to share their knowledge with younger generations.

A scene from the banks of the Cowlitz River. Members of the Cowlitz tribe were buried beside the river. They were placed in canoes (pictured) along with their favorite possessions.

IN THE KNOW

During the Cowlitz First Salmon Ceremony, tribal members gather by the river one morning in early June. They await a canoe bearing a salmon caught earlier that day. They sing and drum in thanks to the salmon for providing the food they need to survive.

GRAND RONDE

(grand RAWND)

LANGUAGE GROUP:
Various

GREETING:
Kloshe konaway

THANK YOU:
Máh-sie

LOCATION PRECONTACT:
Oregon, California

LOCATION TODAY:
Oregon

In the 1850s, the U.S. government moved more than 20 tribes from western Oregon and Northern California to the 60,000 acre (24,000 ha) Grand Ronde Reservation. They became known as the Grand Ronde tribe. At first, the people spoke so many languages and dialects that it was difficult for them to understand each other. Over time, many of the original languages were no longer used and people communicated using Cinuk Wawa (Chinook Jargon), a simplified language that is a mix of English and words from tribal languages.

The tribes had differences in social structure and religious practices, but they all shared a bond with nature. Traditionally, they hunted, fished, and gathered, and they held ceremonies to honor the animals and land that fed them. Most tribes lived in plank homes where families shared food and storytelling.

The land on the reservation was not very fertile, but the government expected the people to farm. Tribal religions were banned and a Christian church was built. In 1901, the government seized another 28,000 acres (11,000 ha) of land. In 1954, under its "termination" policy, the government canceled the tribe's legal status, forcing members to leave the reservation to look for work and places to live elsewhere. Yet the people of the Grand Ronde did not give up hope. They fought to regain their rights, and in 1983, the government restored their status and returned almost 10,000 acres (4,000 ha) of land. The tribe has worked hard to revive its traditions—in building a traditional plank house on its land, for example. Cinuk Wawa is taught in school and the tribe has published a language dictionary. ✒

IN THE KNOW

The 1950s "termination" policy removed many rights. It stated that historic treaties were no longer legal and that reservation land and their resources, such as timber, pasture, and water, did not belong to the tribes. Tribes lost their tribal status and had to pay taxes on their land.

Members from the Grand Ronde tribe perform on "A Day to Celebrate," held at the Oregon State Capitol in Salem in May 2015. The event marks the beginning of American Indian Week, an annual cultural gathering of Oregon's tribes.

HAIDA

(HIGH-dah)

LANGUAGE GROUP:
Isolate

GREETING:
Gasán uu dáng gíidang?

THANK YOU:
Háw'aa

LOCATION PRECONTACT:
Alaska; British Columbia (Canada)

LOCATION TODAY:
Alaska; British Columbia (Canada)

Most Haida still live on Haida Gwaii, or the Queen Charlotte Islands, off the coast of British Columbia, Canada. Some live farther north, on Prince of Wales Island, Alaska. Their ancestors lived in villages and made large, expertly carved canoes from the cedar trees that grew on the islands. Using these canoes, they trawled the surrounding water for halibut and other saltwater fish using V-shaped hooks baited with octopus. They lived far from other tribes, so they traveled long distances to trade their valuable canoes, fish, and other food. They did most of their trading for blankets woven from mountain goat fleeces made by the Tlingit tribe.

In Haida society, children belong to the clan of their mother. Each large family group has a male chief who is expected to hold regular feasts, such as potlatches, as part of his duties. In their villages, the Haida build homes shared by many families of the same clan. Outside each house stands a towering totem pole decorated with the family crest. The Haida also carve crests on dishes used for feasts and paint crests on their faces.

The first recorded contact between the Haida and European settlers took place in the late 1700s. The Europeans traded iron and cloth for sea otter pelts, and introduced the Haida to potatoes. By 1925 the tribe was producing large potato crops. When the sea otter population declined, from around 1834, fur traders went back to the mainland, forcing the Haida to travel farther to trade. In 1862, contact with the Europeans brought devastating disease to the tribes and thousands died. By 1915, the Haida had declined from a precontact population of 7,000 to just 588 people.

Today, the largest Haida populations live on the Masset and Skidegate reserves on Graham Island and in the Native Village of Hydraburg, in Alaska. The people live in modern houses, but uphold many traditions, from carving and weaving to speaking their native language. In 1981, the Haida village of Ninstints, British Columbia, became a UNESCO World Heritage site. It contains the remains of Haida plank houses and several memorial totem poles. 🖝

🔆 IN THE KNOW

The Haida tribe built some of the region's largest gabled houses—that is, houses with sloping roofs. As well as placing totem poles outside, the craftsmen sometimes carved figures into the posts that supported a house's roof. These figures were said to watch for danger.

Haida clans belong to one of two main groups: the Raven or the Eagle. Carved representations of these birds are featured on the totem poles that stand outside tribal family homes. (A raven is pictured.)

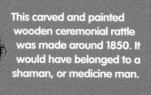

This carved and painted wooden ceremonial rattle was made around 1850. It would have belonged to a shaman, or medicine man.

Lummi fishermen perch on the rigs that tower above their boats and wait for their nets to fill. This "reefnet" fishing involves suspending a net in the water between two canoes. Salmon are trapped on their migratory journey from the ocean to the rivers.

LUMMI

(LUH-mee)

LANGUAGE GROUP:
Salishan

GREETING:
Not available

THANK YOU:
Hekh

LOCATION PRECONTACT:
Washington

LOCATION TODAY:
Washington

Originally, the Lummi lived on the San Juan Islands and the nearby mainland of northwest Washington. The Lummi call themselves Lhaqu'temish, "people of the sea," reflecting the importance of fishing and the ocean to their culture and identity. The salmon was paramount, and the tribe traditionally held feasts and ceremonies to celebrate it, but they also caught crabs, shrimp, birds, and sea mammals. Since they lived near or by water, the Lummi built red cedar canoes to travel and to fish, moving from place to place with the seasons. They also made rope and baskets from red cedar wood.

In 1855, the Lummi and several other tribes in the Puget Sound area signed the Treaty of Point Elliott. They agreed to give up most of their territory to the United States government and settle on a small section of land that became their reservation. The treaty allowed the Lummi to fish in their traditional places, but this did not stop others from fishing there, too. By the late 1800s, the salmon industry had become big business, pushing the Lummi out of their fishing areas. In 1974, the Supreme Court recognized this problem and ruled that the Lummi could fish for salmon again as their treaty agreement stated.

Today, the Lummi work to protect the precious natural resources of their homelands, including helping to clean up salmon habitats. In 1973, the tribe founded the Lummi School of Aquaculture to train younger tribal members in the fishing industry. Now called the Northwest Indian College, with its main campus on the Lummi Indian Reservation, this is the only accredited tribal college in the northwestern United States. 🖋

💡 IN THE KNOW

The Lummi presented *Huli Ta Tum Uhw: The Earth Is Alive* at the 2015 UN climate change conference in Paris, France. The film, by a Lummi producer, explained ancestral teachings about caring for the environment.

Lummi artist Melissa Bob depicts Native life before and after the colonial years. Before (top), the land is green and forested with a dynamic "living" life-line in red. After (bottom), the land has become gray and overdeveloped, and its red life-line is flatlining, signifying death.

THE WHALE HUNT

Whaling was an honorable and highly skilled tradition. Tribes performed ceremonies before and after a whale hunt, thanking the whale for its gift to their people. Almost all of the whale had a use: The blubber and flesh were eaten fresh, while the stomach and intestines were dried for use as storage vessels for whale oil. Bones were used to make tools. The Makah captured gray and humpback whales. To do so, they learned their migration patterns, so they would know exactly when the whales were passing their stretch of coast. Using harpoons, hunters struck a whale in just the right place while it was swimming close by. Attached to the harpoon rope, buoys made from seal skins slowed the whale down as it tried to escape, tiring it out. Once it was exhausted, tribal members could get close enough to the animal to spear and kill it. They towed it back to land (pictured below), where they cut it up on the shore to share with the rest of the tribe. Native tribes need to apply for a special license to hunt whales today.

MAKAH

(muh-KAH)

LANGUAGE GROUP:
Wakashan

GREETING:
Ɂux̌uɁaƛa·k

THANK YOU:
Ɂu·šu·yakšɁalica

LOCATION PRECONTACT:
Washington

LOCATION TODAY:
Washington

The Makah call themselves Qwih-dich-chuh-ahtx, "people of the Cape." The tribe has inhabited the northwestern tip, or cape, of present-day Washington for at least 4,000 years. Their ancestral lands, stretching from the Lyre River to Cape Johnson, Washington, were rich in natural resources. They felled red cedar to make homes, canoes, and carvings, and used a wide variety of plants for food, weaving, and medicine. In winter, the tribe lived in five main villages on the shores of the Pacific Ocean and the Strait of Juan de Fuca, then moved to summer villages close to their whaling and fishing grounds.

In the fall, when various types of salmon returned to freshwater rivers to spawn, some families moved to fishing camps for the season. Salmon and halibut were important to the tribe, but, more than any other Northwest Coast tribe, the Makah were also expert whalers, and hunted the gray and humpback whales. Only men of high rank could be harpoonsmen, but everyone in the village shared the meat and oil from a successful hunt. Makahs were also the greatest traders on what is now the Washington coast and could communicate in several languages. They had strong family values and a rich social life, expressed in song, dance, storytelling, competitions, and games.

In the 1780s, Europeans and Americans arrived in Makah territory. Within 60 years, smallpox epidemics and other diseases had wiped out large numbers of the Makah population. The Makah signed the Treaty of Neah Bay in 1855. The treaty ceded more than 300,000 acres (120,000 ha) of land to the U.S. government but allowed the tribe to continue hunting whales and to fish. However, overhunting by the U.S. whaling industry caused gray whales to become almost extinct in the early 1900s. The Makah stopped hunting whales in the 1920s.

By the early 1990s, the gray whale population had recovered because of the conservation efforts made to prevent its extinction, and the Makah campaigned to revive their ancient tradition. In 1999, a group of Makah hunted the tribe's first whale in 70 years, under a special license, although environmentalists oppose plans to restore Makah whale-hunting rights permanently. Many Makah people still rely on ocean fish ➡➤

DALE JOHNSON

Dale Johnson was a chairman of the Makah Tribal Council and helped create today's successful Makah fishing industry. For many years, Johnson also skippered a war canoe that took part in races against other tribes during the Makah Days celebration. The sport originated in the Northwest Coast region some 150 years ago.

and mammals for food. They also work in the fishing and lumber industries. The Makah tribe welcomes everyone to its event-packed Makah Days celebration, held around August 26 each year. The tribe has also made good use of the spectacular landscape of their territory. Visitors can walk the Cape Flattery Trail (at the northwest tip of the state), head to stunning ocean beaches to swim or fish, and visit the world-renowned Makah Museum to see traditional artifacts from Ozette village. ✑

This is a Makah Thunderbird mask. In Makah ancestry, the thunderbird hunts whales and showed the Makah how to hunt them, too.

MUCKLESHOOT

(MAH-col-shoot)

LANGUAGE GROUP:
Lushootseed

GREETING:
ʔəy'-d-ágʷəl

THANK YOU:
Ckʷálidxʷ

LOCATION PRECONTACT:
Washington

LOCATION TODAY:
Washington

The name Muckleshoot is not a tribal name for one group. It comes from the Native name for the prairie land of the reservation with the same name and refers to various coastal Salish tribes (known collectively as the Coast Salish) who came together in the mid-1800s. These tribes were the Stkamish, Smulkamish, Yilalkoamish, Duwuamish,

Snoqualmie, Tulalip, Suquamish, and Tkwakwamish—all Salish-speaking people who had lived in the Northwest Coast region for thousands of years. Their homelands stretched along parts of Puget Sound and inland to the western edges of the Cascade Mountains. The land and the ocean provided everything they needed—salmon, seals, shellfish, cedar, berries, and much more—and they lived according to the seasons, moving from winter villages to summer camps to fish, hunt, and gather. The tribal women wore skirts, dresses, and capes made from cedar bark, and wove coiled baskets with geometric patterns.

In the mid-1800s, Coast Salish tribes signed the Point Elliott and Medicine Creek treaties with the U.S. government. These promised a reservation, where the tribes could live together, as well as traditional fishing, hunting, and gathering rights. When negotiations failed, the Puget Sound Indian War (1855–1856) erupted between white settlers and the tribes of the area.

This wooden handle has been carved to look like a duck. It was once the handle of an ax-like tool used by the Muckleshoot for cutting large pieces of timber.

💡 IN THE KNOW

The Muckleshoot language was converted from an oral form to a written form in the 1960s and 1970s and this has helped to keep the language alive. The alphabet has 41 letters—some sounds do not exist in English.

After the war, tribal members from the different bands settled on the Muckleshoot Reservation. Gradually, Muckleshoot became the name for everyone there. With access to fewer resources, life was difficult on the reservation and the Muckleshoot struggled, especially to fish in their traditional places.

In 1974, the U.S. Supreme Court reinstated the Muckleshoot's right to fish in traditional tribal fishing locations. Since then, members have worked to keep many more ancestral traditions alive, with annual ceremonies and gatherings including the First Salmon Ceremony, which celebrates the return of the salmon from the ocean. Once the community has welcomed the salmon, the Muckleshoot people share in eating it. They then return the fish's bones to the river and ask its spirit to tell the living salmon of their kindness. ✍

Muckleshoot members celebrate the opening of the Evergreen Point Floating Bridge with music. Connecting the cities of Seattle and Bellevue, Washington, it is the longest floating bridge in the world.

PUYALLUP

(pyoo-AH-lup)

LANGUAGE GROUP:
Salishan

GREETING:
Haʔł sləx̌il

THANK YOU:
Hiskʷuʔ

LOCATION PRECONTACT:
Washington

LOCATION TODAY:
Washington

Canoes have long been part of tribal life for the Puyallup. In 2018, the tribe hosted the intertribal Canoe Journeys. They called the event Power Paddle to Puyallup.

The Puyallup are a southern Coast Salish people from the Puget Sound area of Washington. Their language is a dialect of Lushootseed, which is part of the Salish language. They call themselves the S'Puyalupubsh, a word meaning "generous and welcoming behavior to all people who enter our lands."

The Puyallup lived in villages along the shores of Puget Sound, on the islands, along the riverbanks, and in the foothills of Mount Tacoma. They built permanent homes using planks they cut from tall cedar trees. The houses were often close to the water's edge and the Puyallup mostly traveled around their land by river, in dugout canoes.

The land and ocean fed the Puyallup well. They were expert fishermen, who caught salmon and steelhead trout. Puyallup women gathered shellfish, berries, and plants. Like other Northwest Coast tribes, the Puyallup held many ceremonies, including potlatches. The Puyallup's relatives, the Nisqually, also spoke a Lushootseed dialect and lived in a similar way.

The Puyallup first met European explorers in 1792, but settlers did not move into the area until the 1830s. Over the next 20 years, the Puyallup lost more and more of their traditional lands. In 1854, the Medicine Creek Treaty assigned a reservation for the Puyallup, Nisqually, and Squaxin tribes. Although the Puyallup had never been farmers, they began growing ➤

CHIEF LESCHI

Chief Leschi of the Nisqually tribe represented the Puyallup at the Medicine Creek Treaty Council. Leschi was unhappy with the Medicine Creek Treaty, which ceded the Nisqually's and Puyallup's richest lands in return for only a small reservation. His protests led to the Puget Sound War (1855–1856). The U.S. Army defeated the tribe and then arrested, tried, and hanged Leschi for murder. In 2004, a court declared Leschi innocent. The Nisqually honor the chief on January 27 each year, the day of his birth.

wheat and other crops on the reservation in order to survive. In 1887, the U.S. government introduced the Dawes Act—an allotment policy by which tribal members received small parcels of land, while the rest was sold off to settlers.

In the 1900s, the tribe began a long fight for their lost rights and homelands. Eventually, a 1990 land-claim settlement brought much needed money to the tribe, which they have put toward developing law enforcement, education, welfare, and other services on their reservation. Today, the Puyallup own businesses in the Puget Sound area. They also promote their culture. The tribe hosts its own channel on YouTube with films of events on the reservation. The Puyallup powwow takes place in September and the Lushootseed Language Institute at the University of Washington teaches and promotes the Lushootseed language.

QUILEUTE

(KWILL-ee-oot)

LANGUAGE GROUP:
Chimakuan

GREETING:
Ayásocha (how are you?)

RESPONSE:
Hachli (I am well)

LOCATION PRECONTACT:
Washington

LOCATION TODAY:
Washington

There is evidence of Quileute presence in western Washington since the end of the last ice age, 10,000 years ago, making it one of the oldest tribes in the Northwest Coast region. According to tribal creation stories, a figure named Kwati changed wolves into the Quileute people. The Quileute lived along the Quillayute River and controlled the territory south of the Makah tribe, who were both their trading partners and their rivals. The tribe was very close to their other neighbors, the Hoh, and many Quileute married Hoh people.

Quileute society was divided into three broad groups—the wolf (warriors); the fishermen, the hunters, and the whale hunters; and the weathermen. People were inducted as members of these societies during winter ceremonies that included dancing and singing. They made waterfront plank houses and canoes from red cedar, which was plentiful, and like other coastal tribes, the Quileute depended on mammals and ocean fish for

David Hudson is the Quileute's traditional tribal chief. Here, he is pictured at age 11 in the late 1960s. He wears a carved and painted Thunderbird mask. David inherited the position at just three years of age, from his grandfather.

A Quileute tribal member performs a paddle dance at the Seattle Art Museum for the opening of the exhibit "Behind the Scenes: The Real Story of Quileute Wolves." The exhibition focused on the role the wolf plays in the tribe's culture.

TOWERING TOTEM POLES

Totem poles are tall, carved, and painted cedar posts. Tribes of the Northwest Coast made these poles to represent their family histories, status, and rights. Some were house posts that supported the home and symbolized the heritage of the family living in it. Others were mortuary poles to honor the deaths of chiefs or other important people. The figures and crests carved on the poles were often animals or supernatural beings associated with the family clan and its ancestors. The Thunderbird (pictured), Raven, and Bear are all common crests used on totem poles. Early poles had simple carvings, but became more detailed after carvers obtained metal tools from white traders. Tribes continue the tradition of carving totem poles today for museums, parks, and modern-day potlatches, or feasts.

food. The Quileute used their sturdy canoes to hunt whale and seal, trading the animals' valuable oils with other tribes. The tribe also bred dogs with long, wool-like hair specifically to weave blankets from their hair.

The Quinault Treaty of 1855 and the Treaty of Olympia in 1856 ceded Quileute land to the U.S. government and proposed that the tribe should join the Quinault on a reservation. The Quileute refused, however, and did not move until 1889, when a reservation was provided at La Push, in present-day Clallum County, Washington.

Today, the Quileute oversee fishing, hunting, and gathering on their land, making sure the land is protected and not overused. The tribe also owns a resort and marina, and welcomes visitors from all over the world. A tribal school teaches the Quileute language and heritage. 🖝

IN THE KNOW
Stephenie Meyer's Twilight novels are set in the town of Forks, Washington, not far from La Push. Fictional Quileute characters and the Quileute wolf origin story are featured in the novels and in movies that were based on the books.

233

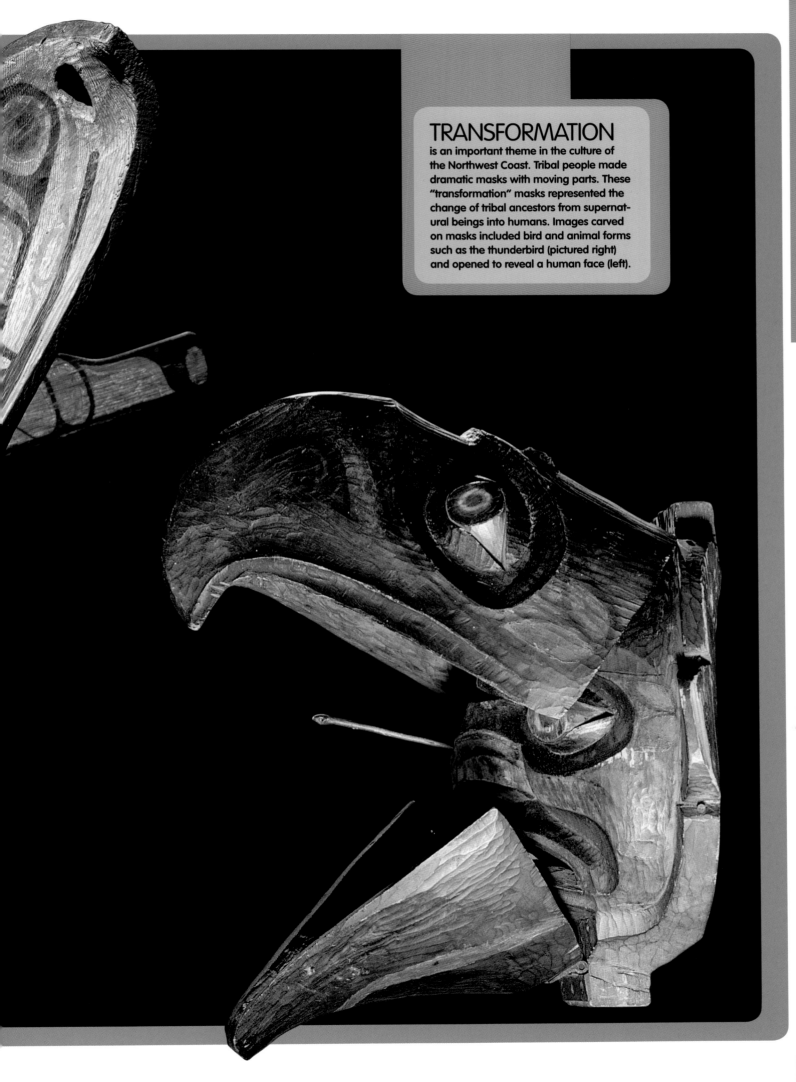

TRANSFORMATION

is an important theme in the culture of the Northwest Coast. Tribal people made dramatic masks with moving parts. These "transformation" masks represented the change of tribal ancestors from supernatural beings into humans. Images carved on masks included bird and animal forms such as the thunderbird (pictured right) and opened to reveal a human face (left).

QUINAULT

(kwih-NAWLT)

LANGUAGE GROUP:
Salishan

GREETING:
Oonugwito

THANK YOU:
Siqwil

LOCATION PRECONTACT:
Washington

LOCATION TODAY:
Washington

The Quinault are known as the "canoe people" or "people of the cedar tree." They shared many characteristics with the Hoh, the two tribes having split from one another hundreds of years ago. It was common for Quinault and Hoh people to marry one another.

For many centuries the Quinault lived in western present-day Washington state, at the mouth of what is now the Quinault River. The tribe depended on the ocean and rivers for most of its food. People hunted whales and other sea mammals, but they prized the salmon above all else. One day between December and March, Quinault fishermen would catch their first salmon of the season, which would be shared by everyone in the village and celebrated at the tribe's First Salmon Ceremony. Quinault territory also included forests inhabited by deer, bears, and other animals. The tribe hunted these animals for food and clothing and cut down red cedar trees to build houses and dugout canoes. The Quinault built large, sturdy canoes with high sides for fishing or traveling in the ocean and smaller ones to use on rivers.

This young Quinault boy is James Black—his tribal name is Tow Wah Us. He is wearing a traditional carved cedar mask at an event held by the Quinault tribe on the Olympic Peninsula, Washington.

JOSEPH BURTON DELACRUZ

The Quinault leader Joseph Burton DeLaCruz was an activist. He served two terms as president of the National Congress of American Indians, and campaigned for the rights of indigenous people in Canada and South America as well as in the United States. He battled with the government over such issues as fishing and logging rights, and once famously blocked a bridge with his truck to prevent loggers from entering the Quinault reservation, which has suffered from extensive logging in the past (pictured).

The Quinault were hostile toward the Spanish when they arrived in 1775, and resisted the influence of other European settlers who began arriving on their lands in the 1800s. The tribe did not want to be part of this rapidly changing culture. By the mid-1800s, the U.S. government wanted the land along the Northwest Coast for settlement, logging, and mining, and began issuing treaties. The Quinault, Quileute, and Hoh tribes signed the Quinault River Treaty in 1855, giving up most of their lands. Later treaties established the Quinault Reservation in return for more land for the U.S. government.

Since the 1970s, the Quinault have worked to reforest land destroyed by logging, and on rebuilding native fish populations. Today, most live on a small reservation on part of their homelands, along with some Hoh people (most Hoh live on their own reservation). The Quinault run businesses such as the Quinault Beach Resort and Casino. Others live in communities outside the reservation. 🖋

S'KLALLAM

(SKLAH-lum)

LANGUAGE GROUP:
Salishan

GREETING:
Sxʷaʔníŋ' cxʷ?

THANK YOU:
Háʔnəŋ cn

LOCATION PRECONTACT:
Washington; British Columbia (Canada)

LOCATION TODAY:
Washington (U.S.); British Columbia (Canada)

The S'klallam, originally a large tribe with as many as 30 villages in what is today western Washington and Vancouver Island, Canada, call themselves Nux Sklai Yem, or "strong people." The tribe has kept its identity and traditions through years of change. Their traditional homelands included ocean shores, river valleys, and mountains. The S'klallam people fished throughout the year, catching salmon in the rivers and halibut or cod in the ocean. They also hunted whales, elk, and deer; harvested clams; and gathered plants and berries. S'klallam women wove beautiful blankets and shawls from wool that they obtained from mountain goats and using hair from dogs. They used cedar bark to weave robes and skirts. The S'klallam traded and socialized with their Salish-speaking neighbors. The most important homes in each village—those of the highest-ranking families in the tribe—had a carved totem pole outside the entrance that told the family's story.

Fur traders and trappers were the first non-Natives to arrive in S'klallam territory, but settlers soon followed. By the mid-1800s, many tribal members had died from smallpox and measles, introduced by the newcomers. In 1855, the year in which many Northwest Coast tribes signed treaties, the S'klallam signed the Treaty of Point No Point with the U.S. government. This began a gradual split of the S'klallam bands into separate communities. While the Lower Elwha, Port Gamble, and Scia'new bands agreed to move to reservations, the Jamestown band raised the funds to buy a strip of ancestral land. In accordance with the government's "termination" policy, the Jamestown band lost its official status in 1954, because it refused to leave its ancestral land and move to a reservation. It did not regain its status until 1981.

Today, most S'klallam people live on three reservations in Washington—the Lower Elwha Reservation, the Port Gamble Reservation, and the Jamestown Reservation—and the Scia'new First Nation Reserve on Vancouver Island. They work in various businesses, including tribal-owned sawmills, resorts, and fish hatcheries (places where people raise fish from eggs). Special programs keep the arts and S'klallam language alive for future generations, and every year, the S'klallam take part in the intertribal Canoe Journeys event. 🖋

IN THE KNOW

In 2003, a construction project unearthed the 2,700-year-old S'klallam village Tse-whit-zen. Construction was halted to allow archaeologists and tribal members to excavate the site. They found human bones, the remains of longhouses, and thousands of native artifacts.

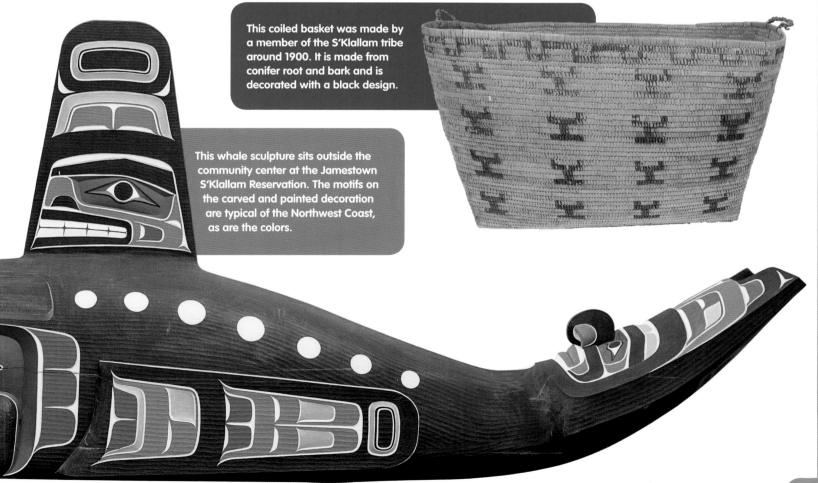

This coiled basket was made by a member of the S'Klallam tribe around 1900. It is made from conifer root and bark and is decorated with a black design.

This whale sculpture sits outside the community center at the Jamestown S'Klallam Reservation. The motifs on the carved and painted decoration are typical of the Northwest Coast, as are the colors.

SKOKOMISH

(SKA-com-ish)

LANGUAGE GROUP:
Salishan

LANGUAGE:
Currently dormant;
no record of last
known speaker

LOCATION PRECONTACT:
Washington

LOCATION TODAY:
Washington

The Skokomish tribe was the largest of nine Twana tribes whose homelands were in the Puget Sound area of western Washington. Their neighbors were the Chinook to the south and the Chehalis to the north. The Skokomish, meaning "big river people," depended mostly on fishing. They lived in permanent villages near the Skokomish River but moved to seasonal camps in spring to hunt and gather. Seafood, plants, and game were plentiful, but salmon was their most important resource. Society was divided into upper and lower classes, and slaves. The richest man in the village was usually the leader, responsible for holding feasts such as potlatches. Family relationships were important and people from different villages often married.

The tribe's seasonal lifestyle continued until the 1840s, when white settlers arrived around Puget Sound. Missionaries came to the area to convert the tribal people to Christianity. White

This photograph of a Skokomish man named Lahkeudup was taken by Edward S. Curtis in 1912. The man is wrapped in a woven shawl, possibly made from cattail, a tall marsh plant.

SPINNING AND WEAVING

Women in the Northwest created stunning blankets, cloaks, and skirts using mountain goat wool, cedar bark, spruce root, and dog hair. Coast Salish people kept woolly dogs especially for their hair. Spinners prepared yarn by softening and straightening the fibers. They rolled the wool on their thighs to create yarn, or used a spindle whorl. This simple tool used a weighted disk attached to a spindle, or wooden stick, that was pointed at one end, to spin yarn. Weavers had looms, and used their fingers to weave the yarn in and out. Tribal chiefs owned what they called Chilkat robes—ceremonial wraps made from mountain goat wool. Weaving is a craft that is still practiced today. Pictured below, a member of the Tlingit weaves in the Chilkat style.

IN THE KNOW

Both men and women used canoes, but their paddles differed. Men's paddles were longer and narrow near the end. Women's paddles were wider at the end and shorter overall. Longer paddles tend to suit taller people.

In the summer, Skokomish people built simple houses close to the river so they could fish. The timber-framed houses were covered with reed mats and the family's canoe sat on the riverbank outside.

settlements eventually pushed the Skokomish people off their lands and away from their traditional ways of life into other types of jobs, such as logging and picking flowers of the hop plant (hops) for making beer. In the 1900s, the Skokomish lost some of their tribal lands to a business developer, and in 1926 and 1930 the city of Tacoma built two dams, destroying more Skokomish land and drastically reducing the salmon and other fish populations. The creation of Potlatch State Park in 1960 took away more of the tribe's land, this time along the shore.

The loss of access to their most important resources was devastating to the Skokomish tribe and they fought back. In 1965, the tribe won a land claims award of almost $375,000, with which they invested in a fish-processing plant and housing. Further success followed in 1974, when a historic court case, known as the Boldt Decision, restored the tribe's long-lost fishing rights. Since then, the Skokomish tribe has reintroduced a number of traditions to younger generations, including basketry, carving, and naming ceremonies of newborn children. ✎

SNOQUALMIE

(sno-KWALL-mee)

LANGUAGE GROUP:
Salishan

LANGUAGE:
Currently limited in use; no dictionary available

LOCATION PRECONTACT:
Washington

LOCATION TODAY:
Washington

The Snoqualmie are Coast Salish people who, like the S'klallam and many other tribes, made western Washington their home. Their name means "people of Moon," a reference to an old Salish creation story about Moon the Transformer, a figure who created everything. For thousands of years, the Snoqualmie fished, gathered, and hunted in the Puget Sound area, which was rich in salmon, deer, nuts, berries, and other foods. The large tribe lived in longhouses in villages throughout their tribal lands.

Faced with European settlers coming onto their lands, Snoqualmie chief Patkanim decided that the tribe would be safer if his people were more welcoming to white settlers than other tribes in the area. Instead of fighting the settlers, some Snoqualmie acted as scouts for the U.S. government; others fought alongside the settlers against other tribes. In 1855, believing the government would give them a reservation that would protect their hunting, fishing, and other rights, Chief Patkanim signed the Treaty of Point Elliott. The treaty promises were not kept, however. Instead, the Snoqualmie people were expected to live with other tribes on the Tulalip Reservation, about 60 miles (97 km) north. Some tribal members moved to the reservation, while others stayed where they were. ➠

On January 22, 1914, at the Tulalip Reservation, members of the Snoqualmie tribe joined others from the Swinomish, Suquamish, and Lummi tribes to celebrate the 59th anniversary of the signing of the Treaty of Point Elliott.

Snoqualmie Falls is sacred to the Snoqualmie tribe, and is considered the place of their creation. Tribal members believe in the Sacred Spirit of Snoqualmie Falls. They sometimes gather together at the falls to pray for this spirit and for the survival of their people.

In 1953, the U.S. government withdrew tribal status from the Snoqualmie as part of its "termination" policy. This marked the start of a long court battle between the tribe and the U.S. government. In October 1999, the Snoqualmie finally regained their tribal status, but they still did not have any land of their own. Eventually, in 2006, the government gave them a small area of land southwest of the city of Snoqualmie and the Snoqualmie River to establish a reservation.

Today, some 500 members of the Snoqualmie tribe live on the reservation. The youth learn about their heritage. The tribe takes part in an annual intertribal Canoe Journeys celebration, which honors the tribal history of the Puget Sound. The Snoqualmie are making efforts to revive their language, which is endangered because only a few speakers remain. Tribal members are finding ways to link the language with activities such as carving and intertribal Canoe Journeys, during which participants learn words and phrases associated with the activities they take part in.

SQUAXIN ISLAND

(SKWAK-sin Island)

LANGUAGE GROUP:
Salishan

LANGUAGE:
Currently limited in use; no dictionary available

LOCATION PRECONTACT:
Washington

LOCATION TODAY:
Washington

The people of the Squaxin bands are Lushootseed-speaking Coast Salish. The bands came together with the signing of the Treaty of Medicine Creek in 1854, which ceded more than two million acres (810,000 ha) of their homelands to the U.S. government.

Before 1854, the Squaxin, or "people of the water," lived peacefully along the many bountiful waterways of the southern Puget Sound. They carved red cedar canoes and fished, hunted, and gathered. Following waterways and trading routes, they traveled across the Cascade Mountains, into the Columbia River Basin, and elsewhere to hunt for prey, to fish, and to trade goods with other tribes.

The Treaty of Medicine Creek confined tribal territory to the tiny Squaxin Island Reservation on Squaxin Island. Hundreds of tribal members were held prisoner here during the Puget Sound War of 1855–1856. After the war, the U.S. government set up Indian agent headquarters on Squaxin Island. Indian agents were white Americans who acted as go-betweens for the government, to create smooth relationships with Native tribes throughout the country.

The Squaxin tried to make the island home, but farming was difficult and many people left to find work on the mainland. In the 1880s, the Squaxin began attending the Indian Shaker Church, founded by Squaxin tribal member John Slocum as a blend of Christian and traditional tribal beliefs. He built his first church on Church Point on Hammersley Inlet on the mainland. In the late 1880s, the government gave away this important site to a ship's captain, possibly in an attempt to curb the influence of the Indian Shaker Church.

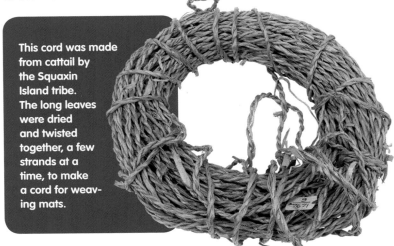

This cord was made from cattail by the Squaxin Island tribe. The long leaves were dried and twisted together, a few strands at a time, to make a cord for weaving mats.

POTLATCH FEASTS

In many Northwest Coast tribes, wealthy families held feasts, called potlatches, to honor a birth, death, and other life events. Once invited, entire tribes arrived to eat, sing, dance, and observe ceremonies. Hosts gave generous gifts to their guests, including blankets and carved posts, which could not be declined. Often, recipients were expected to return a gift with interest at a later date. This caused problems if the value of the gift exceeded the recipient's wealth—his tribe might be obliged to cover the debt. In this way, hosts were able to increase their wealth and status in society. A potlatch might also celebrate the passing of certain rights from one generation to the next, such as access to particular hunting or fishing grounds. The U.S. and Canadian governments banned potlatches in the late 1800s, when they tried to force tribes to give up their culture. The U.S. dropped the ban in 1934 and Canada did the same in 1951. Pictured is a potlatch on Vancouver Island, Canada.

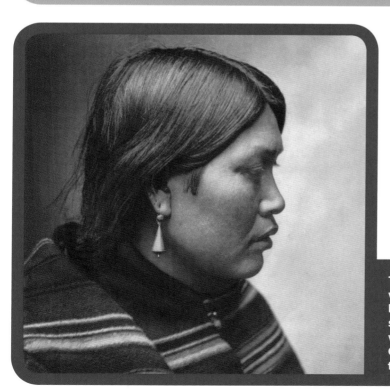

The Squaxin did not get it back until they bought the land from the U.S. government in 1995.

Although people no longer live on the island, it is a very important spiritual place for the Squaxin people, who go there to fish, hunt, and camp. Squaxin tribal members now live on the mainland, on land they purchased in the southern part of Puget Sound. A tribal council manages the Squaxin Island Tribe's government, businesses, and community. In nearby Shelton, the tribe opened the Squaxin Island Museum, a center for tribal history, arts, and events. 🖋

This photograph is of a Squaxin woman wrapped in a striped blanket and wearing cone-shaped pendant earrings. It was taken in 1912 by Edward S. Curtis, who made many portraits of Native Americans.

💡 IN THE KNOW

It was not uncommon for Squaxin Island people to live for 100 years. Many attribute this to their diet at the time. Today, seeing a decline in age of all Northwest tribal populations, the Traditional Foods of Puget Sound Project aims to increase access to such foods as the camas root, berries, fresh fish, and shellfish, to help tribal people return to a healthier way of life.

STILLAGUAMISH

(still-AG-wa-mish)

LANGUAGE GROUP:
Lushootseed

GREETING:
ʔi

THANK YOU:
Tʼigʷicid

LOCATION PRECONTACT:
Washington

LOCATION TODAY:
Washington

Before the 1850s, the ancestors of the Stillaguamish lived along the Stillaguamish River in northwestern Washington. The tribe, then known as the Stoluckwamish River Tribe, was large and wealthy, with many villages. They held potlatches and other feasts to give thanks for the salmon, deer, and wild plants that abounded in the area. The Stillaguamish used cedar and grasses to make canoes, baskets, and clothing. They also traded with other tribes, and with the settlers who arrived in the 1800s. The Europeans introduced the Stillaguamish to potatoes, which the tribe began to grow in addition to the foods they hunted and gathered.

The Stillaguamish worked with the settlers, helping them to clear lands for their crops. But the settlers and the U.S. government wanted more land, and in the 1855 Treaty of Point Elliott the Stillaguamish ceded their land in exchange for reservations, payments, and fishing and hunting rights. The Stillaguamish did not receive their own reservation; instead, they were expected to move to the Tulalip Reservation, 20 miles (32 km) to the south. Many did this, but others stayed where they were or returned to the Stillaguamish River. In 1870, the tribe lost its official status.

The following years were difficult for the Stillaguamish. The community had no central council or government, and by 1920, the tribal population had fallen to just 29 people. In 1970, the Stillaguamish received money for some of the land they had lost, and in 1974, they gained the fishing rights promised in the 1855 treaty. This followed the Boldt Decision, which affirmed the fishing rights of all tribes in the state of Washington. Finally,

ESTHER ROSS

Esther Ross was born in California in 1904, to a Norwegian father and a Stillaguamish mother. As a child, she listened to the ancestral stories of both her parents. Esther's great-grandfather had been a chief of the Stillaguamish tribe and her mother recounted tales of how the tribe had been forced to leave its ancestral lands. Esther was so taken with the stories she heard that she returned to her Stillaguamish roots in the 1920s and went on to lead the fight for tribal recognition, which was finally granted in 1979.

in February 1979, the U.S. government granted the Stillaguamish federal recognition. With around 500 members, the tribe remains small today, but has its own government and reservation lands. Stillaguamish businesses include salmon hatcheries, a buffalo herd, and a hotel and entertainment center. The Stillaguamish River is still central to the tribe's heritage and members work hard to continue their long-standing relationship with nature.

Each year the tribe holds a Festival of the River, a celebration of the salmon, which aims to show visitors how they can make the environment a healthier place for people, fish, and wildlife.

Several salmon species spawn in the Stillaguamish River at Arlington, Washington, including the chinook (pictured), pink, and sockeye salmon.

SUQUAMISH

(su-KWAH-mish)

LANGUAGE GROUP:
Salishan

LANGUAGE:
Currently limited in use; no dictionary available

LOCATION PRECONTACT:
Washington

LOCATION TODAY:
Washington

The ancestors of today's Suquamish people lived in small villages around Washington's Puget Sound, an area rich in seafood, plants, and animal life. Their name refers to their homelands and comes from a phrase in the Lushootseed language meaning "people of the clear salt water." The Suquamish caught salmon and cod, clams, and water birds in and around the waters of the sound and in the region's many rivers. On the land, they hunted elk and deer, dug up roots, and gathered berries. During winter, the tribe lived in wooden longhouses shared by related families, but in the summer, family groups split up to go hunting and gathering. In these warmer months, people lived in shelters made from wooden poles covered with woven mats.

This eagle is carved at the top of a memorial pole commemorating the life of a former Suquamish chairman. To Native people, the eagle represents a link between Earth and god.

Suquamish women were expert weavers. They made baskets from coiled cedar roots and blankets from mountain goat wool or hair from dogs that they bred specifically for their hair. Like other tribes in the area, the Suquamish held potlatch feasts, when wealthy tribal hosts shared good food and gave away blankets and baskets.

Early fur traders traded cloth and items made from iron with the Suquamish. However, the tribe's relationship with Europeans deteriorated in the 1840s and 1850s. During this time, the Oregon Donation Land Claim Act allowed settlers to claim tribal lands. In 1855, the Suquamish signed the Treaty of Point Elliott, which ceded their lands, and that of many neighboring tribes, to the U.S. government. The treaty promised land at the Port Madison Reservation, along with fishing and hunting rights, education, and other services, not all of which were granted. Most, but not all, Suquamish moved to the reservation, where Indian agents and missionaries expected them to adopt a new language, religion, and lifestyle. The tribe lost more land through the Dawes Act of 1887, which split tribal lands into small plots for individual tribal members. The Suquamish people are still trying to get these lands back.

Today, the Suquamish people practice many of their ancestors' traditions. Every spring, they gather cedar for weaving into baskets, mats, and other items. In 1985, the Suquamish founded a museum to celebrate their rich tribal history.

This colorized photograph of Kikisoblu, eldest daughter of Suquamish chief Seattle, was made in 1906. She was named Angeline by Catherine Maynard, the second wife of David Maynard, founder of Seattle.

IN THE KNOW

Seattle is named for Suquamish chief Seattle, who befriended the city's founder, David Maynard. He was a charismatic leader and fearsome warrior. At 6 feet (1.8 m) tall, he was much taller than other Native people of the region and was known by Hudson's Bay Company traders as Le Gros (the big one).

SWINOMISH

(SWIN-a-mish)

LANGUAGE GROUP:
Lushootseed

GREETING:
ʔi

THANK YOU:
Tʼigʷicid

LOCATION PRECONTACT:
Washington

LOCATION TODAY:
Washington

In 1855, the Swinomish, Kikiallus, Lower Skagit, and Samish tribes ceded their lands in the Treaty of Point Elliott. These four Coast Salish tribes moved to a reservation on Fidalgo Island, Washington, and eventually became the Swinomish Indian Tribal Community. This was a major change for the tribes, whose ancestors had lived in the area for many thousands of years.

The original Swinomish and the other Coast Salish tribes depended on salmon for their survival, but they also hunted and gathered. They lived in villages in the colder months and moved from place to place in the spring and summer, depending on what was growing where and on seasonal animal habits. Explorers met the Swinomish as early as the 1500s, but the tribe continued with their traditional life until the Treaty of Point Elliott forced them from their lands.

The Samish lived in a similar way to the Swinomish tribe, but were often raided by the Haida and Tsimshian. The Samish also caught smallpox from contact with non-Natives; from a population of some 2,000 members, only 150 people were left by the time the treaty was signed. Some moved to the Lummi Indian Reservation and others joined the Swinomish at their reservation. Moving to the reservation did not guarantee the Swinomish tribe's future. The Dawes Act of 1887, introducing the U.S. government's allotment policy, led to the loss of more land. A few years later, the government banned traditions such as spirit dancing and feasts, forcing the tribe to hold these celebrations and events in secret.

The Swinomish Indian Tribal Community was determined to change its fortunes. In 1936, the tribe created a senate and established a constitution. In 2004, the Swinomish regained more than 1,000 acres (400 ha) of its lost land, and the tribe now runs a fishing company, catching salmon and shellfish. Every year, the Swinomish gather for a Treaty Day Celebration, in memory of the Point Elliot Treaty of 1855. They also take part in the annual intertribal Canoe Journeys to honor their traditions. 🖋

IN THE KNOW

Nisqually tribal member Billy Frank, Jr., (1931–2014) spent his life campaigning to secure fishing rights for Native peoples, including during the Fish Wars protests of the 1960s and 1970s. For his lifelong fight for tribal rights and environmental sustainability, President Obama awarded him the Presidential Medal of Freedom, the highest civilian honor in the United States.

This canoe bailer is carved from a section of cedar bark and bound with leather. Canoe bailers are used to scoop water out of canoes.

Members of the Swinomish tribe carry a dugout canoe to the water's edge, sometime around the end of the 19th century. Impressively long, the dugout canoe is made from a hollowed-out cedar tree and can accommodate at least 11 oarsmen.

TLINGIT

(KLIN-kit)

LANGUAGE GROUP:
Athabascan

GREETING:
Sh tug·a xat ditee ixw siteeni

THANK YOU:
GunalchÈesh

LOCATION PRECONTACT:
Alaska; British Columbia (Canada)

LOCATION TODAY:
Alaska (U.S.); British Columbia (Canada)

The Tlingit people are part of a large tribe that once included people living by the Pacific Ocean as well as others who lived inland. Tlingit territory stretched from northern British Columbia to parts of southern Alaska and the Yukon Territory. The Tlingit regularly met and traded with their neighbors, the Haida and Tsimshian, although the three tribes also raided one another's villages from time to time, taking items that were in short supply, such as the Chilkat robes for which the Tlingit were known. The Tlingit people were fishermen, woodcarvers, and weavers. They thrived in their northern home for more than 11,000 years.

Family was, and still is, very important to the Tlingit people. Tribal members belong to one of two main groups, Raven or Eagle, each of which divides into many clans. Children belong to their mother's clan. Huge totem poles carved with the symbols of a clan were placed outside their plank longhouses. More than 40 family members would have lived in such houses.

Their peaceful lives changed drastically in the 1780s when Russians set up colonies in Alaska. By 1867, the Russian-American Company, which was set up in order to establish Russian settlements in Alaska, and to trade with Natives, had 14 forts in North America. Its capital and major port was New Archangel (present-day Sitka, Alaska) in Tlingit territory. The Russians expected the Tlingit to work for them, marry them, and convert to their religion.

In 1802, the Tlingit destroyed New Archangel, but the Russians returned and set up another colony. After some time, the Tlingit began trading with the Russians. This contact brought disease, the worst of which manifested in a smallpox epidemic in 1862 that killed many Tlingit people.

In the 20th century, the Tlingit lost much of their land to mining and logging companies, but after years of claims, the Tlingit and other Alaskan people regained some of their tribal lands in 1971. Today, many Tlingit live in First Nations communities in Canada and in Alaskan villages. Others live in towns and cities. Tlingit, Haida, and Tsimshian people gather twice a year for Celebration, a five-day event with storytelling and traditional art workshops, dancing, and feasting. ☞

ELIZABETH PERATROVICH

Born into the Tlingit tribe in 1911, Elizabeth Peratrovich was adopted at a young age and raised in Petersburg, Alaska. Once married, she and her husband moved to Juneau, and discovered that segregation—a system of separating people from one another because of race—was common in 1940s Alaska. Peratrovich was compelled to campaign for the rights of Native people, fighting against segregation. It was with her help that the Alaska Anti-Discrimination Bill became law on February 16, 1945, banning segregation. In 1989, the Alaskan government made February 16 Elizabeth Peratrovich Day.

A group of Tlingit tribal members from Chilkat Indian village, Klukwan, Alaska, in "button" blankets. Such garments are typically worn at ceremonies and potlatches.

THE THUNDERBIRD AND THE WHALE

In some stories, the whale is a monstrous creature that must be subdued by the thunderbird. When they fight, the thunderbird lifts the whale from the ocean, so starting the whaling tradition.

Once, a long time ago, there was a famine, no food. There was absolutely nothing. The people became very poor.

Also, it was wintertime and the weather got very bad out on the ocean. The people couldn't go fishing because of a fierce storm. They tried to hunt on land, but there was absolutely nothing in the forest. For some reason, the tide did not get low, and they couldn't even get food from the beach. They were unable to get any food at all! The people's food boxes were almost getting empty, and it was not so long before all the food was gone. The people all became very hungry.

Now there was one young man who went to the mountain. He was going to pray because the people were all dying from their own hunger. This young man began to pray. He had just started when he began to hear a strange sound in the sky. Here was a big Thunderbird! Whenever the bird spread his wings, the sky thundered! It got very dark when he spread his wings. Then, when the Thunderbird began to look around, he had lightning coming from his eyes. The Thunderbird even had a lightning serpent belt—and these lightning serpents were flashing lightning.

The Thunderbird dived down toward the water, and then with him, coming out of the water, in his talons, was a big whale! The man was astonished, this young man who had been praying. The Thunderbird carried the whale toward the houses where the people lived. The man ran ahead to tell them that they finally had food. "We will live now! We will live!" the man said. "All of you bring your knives; we will slice this whale!" said the man. They were all happy because they had food. That's all.

Helma Swan Ward, Makah

This is Sky Rock, so-called because it is covered in petroglyphs that face the sky. It is thought that ancestors of the Paiute tribe made them. The petroglyphs lie atop an enormous boulder in the Volcanic Tablelands—an area of small hills and canyons north of Bishop, California, U.S.A.

CALIFORNIA

California is a land of extremes—from rainy, northern redwood forests to scorching southern deserts. Among its many features are the snow-capped Sierra Nevada Mountains, the lush farmlands of the Central Valley, the Mojave Desert, and a Pacific Ocean coastline with rocky shores in the north and long stretches of sandy beaches in the south. With such a wide range of habitats, it is no wonder Native peoples found many places in which to live and thrive.

THE STORY OF **THE CALIFORNIA PEOPLE**

Of all the regions of North America, California was particularly plentiful in resources, and supported a diverse range of lifestyles for thousands of years. In the north, the Tolowa built canoes and dwellings from giant redwood trees; in the south, the Cahuilla used the agave plant for food, and to make clothes, nets, and sandals. Coastal tribes, such as the Chumash, caught whales and sea lions from the ocean, while inland, people hunted deer and fished for salmon. Women fashioned jewelry from abalone shells and became highly skilled basketmakers, designing containers that were both decorative and useful. Tribes shared among themselves, and many were part of a vast trading network in which tribal members traveled by foot or by river to exchange their locally sourced goods with members of other tribes.

The Mission Years

There was little contact between early European explorers and California tribes. The first major changes came in the late 1700s, when Spanish colonists arrived in the West. Between 1769 and 1823, the Spanish built 21 missions—religious settlements— in California, many of them on tribal land. Their cattle and horses grazed on the land, eating the vegetation that played such a large role in the diets of the tribal people. Native people had long depended on hunting, fishing, and gathering, but were now forced to run ranches and farms on their ancestral land, working for the Spanish. The Spanish banned tribal celebrations and languages, causing people to practice their cultural traditions in secret to keep them alive. Native people who lived on the land taken by the Spanish were known as "Mission Indians" and had very little power to resist the Spanish military. Many lost their lives trying or perished from diseases the Spanish brought with them.

The Gold Rush

The Oregon Trail—a 2,000-mile (3,200-km), east-west wagon route from the Missouri River to Oregon—was established in the 1830s, bringing the first U.S. settlers to the West. In 1848, gold was discovered at Sutter's Mill on the South Fork American River in Coloma, California, unleashing a wave of migration from the eastern states, Europe, and Asia. The gold rush endangered tribal resources. Prospectors and miners established camps wherever there was a possibility of finding gold, and settlers moved onto tribal lands to start farms and ranches. The farms and mines destroyed traditional gathering lands and polluted the rivers. Settlers also hunted here, diminishing the supply of deer and other game.

Conflicts soon erupted. Following many losses for the Native people, the U.S. government stepped in to control the situation and pushed most of them onto reservations and rancherias—smaller settlements, named for the Spanish word *ranchería*—which were mission villages.

In the 1850s California tribes signed 18 treaties with the U.S. government. The treaties promised rancheria or reservation land, but California officials and settlers were opposed to the agreements, leading Congress never to make them official. In the decades that followed, when Native people tried to return to the lands that the prospectors had overtaken, they found them occupied by American settlers. Many remained landless until the late 1880s, when reservations were finally established on their ancestral homelands, while others had no option but to return to the rancherias they had left.

California Native Americans Today

More than 100 federally recognized tribes and many other Native communities live in California today, each with its own vibrant culture and identity. Classes, books, and apps have revived languages across the state. From their families, young people learn the dances and ceremonies that united their ancestors. The many different tribes of the California region are united by a common cause: to protect and restore their lands for generations to come. There is greater awareness than ever of the need to harness water resources, protect salmon runs, grow sustainable forests, and support other vital environmental causes in California.

Woven from willow, this Pomo basket was made in the 1950s. It is decorated with quail, duck, and woodpecker feathers and strings of shell beads.

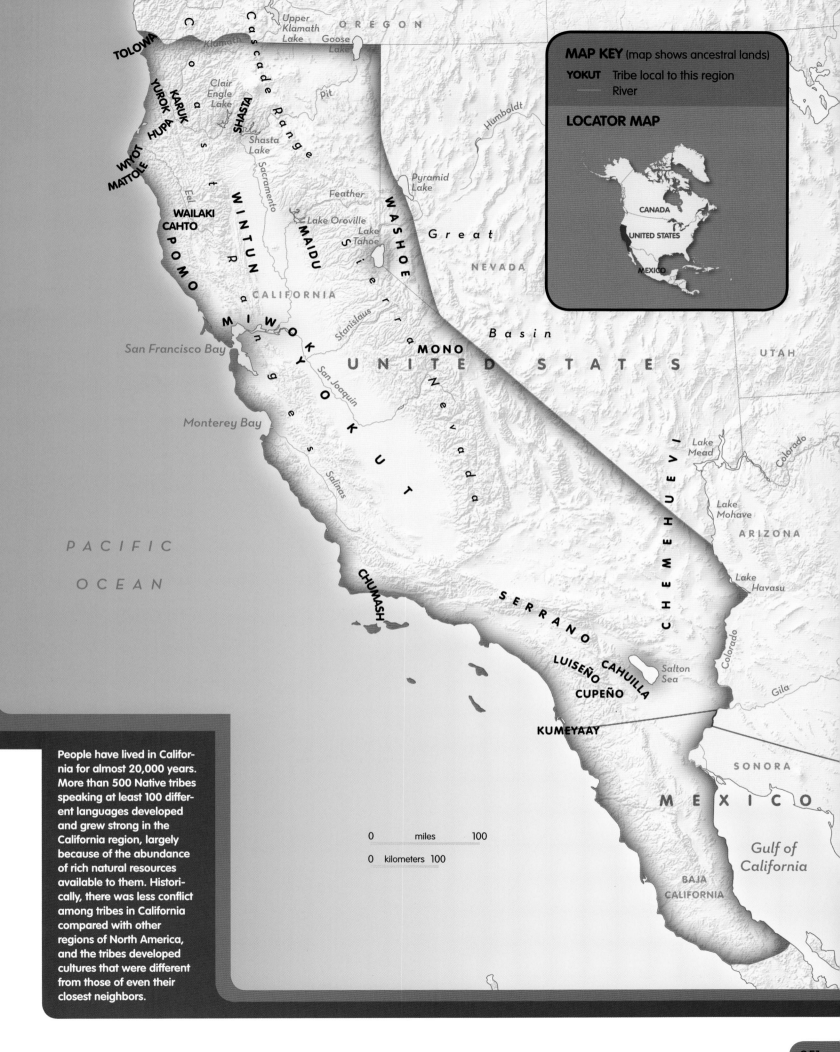

TOLOWA

Klamath

Upper
Klamath
Lake

Goose
Lake

OREGON

Cascade Range

Pit

C
o
a
s
t

Clair
Engle
Lake

SHASTA

Shasta
Lake

YUROK

KARUK

HUPA

WIYOT

MATTOLE

Eel

Sacramento

R
a
n
g
e
s

WINTUN

Feather

Lake Oroville

MAIDU

WASHOE

Pyramid
Lake

Humboldt

Great

NEVADA

WAILAKI

CAHTO

POMO

MIWOK

San Francisco Bay

CALIFORNIA

Stanislaus

Lake
Tahoe

S
i
e
r
r
a

San Joaquin

YOKUT

N
e
v
a
d
a

MONO

Basin

UNITED STATES

UTAH

Monterey Bay

Salinas

PACIFIC

OCEAN

CHUMASH

SERRANO

CAHUILLA

LUISEÑO

CUPEÑO

C
H
E
M
E
H
U
E
V
I

Lake
Mead

Colorado

ARIZONA

Lake
Mohave

Lake
Havasu

Salton
Sea

Colorado

Gila

KUMEYAAY

SONORA

M E X I C O

Gulf of
California

BAJA
CALIFORNIA

People have lived in California for almost 20,000 years. More than 500 Native tribes speaking at least 100 different languages developed and grew strong in the California region, largely because of the abundance of rich natural resources available to them. Historically, there was less conflict among tribes in California compared with other regions of North America, and the tribes developed cultures that were different from those of even their closest neighbors.

0   miles   100

0   kilometers   100

There were an estimated 310,000 Native people in California before Europeans arrived. By the early 1900s, this figure had dropped to 20,000. In those 200 years, the tribes of California endured the Spanish mission system and the spread of disease, and U.S. expansion. Miners and settlers threatened and sometimes killed tribal people and drove them from their lands. California Natives fought for federal recognition during the 20th century and, today, the state has more federally recognized tribes than any other.

17,000 B.C.E.
People already living in California. Archaeologists have found evidence, including stone tools, that shows people lived in California many thousands of years ago.

3000 B.C.E.
People live in large settlements along the coast. Archaeological evidence shows that these early people ate more than 20 different kinds of shellfish.

1769
The first Spanish mission is established. On July 16, 1769, the Spanish founded the San Diego de Alcalá mission on Kumeyaay land. The tribe rebelled many times, weakening the mission. In 1775, the Spanish rebuilt the mission near the Kumeyaay village of Kosa'aay. This is now Old Town San Diego. Some Kumeyaay became Mission Indians, working as laborers for the Spanish. The Spanish built another 20 missions in California.

1812–1841
Russians establish Fort Ross. The Russians built a fur-trading post, Fort Ross, in Pomo territory near Bodega Bay in northern California. The Russians used the Pomo as farmhands and brought disease, including a measles epidemic in 1828, which killed many Pomo people.

1821
Mexico gains independence from Spain. Pictured are celebrations of the event in Mexico City. The mission system continued in Mexico until 1834. Many tribes worked for Mexican ranchers.

1842
John Frémont expeditions begin. Frémont led four major expeditions in the West and worked closely with Kit Carson. Frémont and Carson opened the way for westward expansion into California. Their reports encouraged people to move there from the East, many of them settling on tribal lands.

1846–1848
Mexican–American War starts as a conflict over control of Texas. The war ended with the Treaty of Guadalupe Hidalgo, through which the United States acquired lands from the Mexicans that included present-day California.

1848
Gold discovered at Sutter's Mill. After the discovery of gold, thousands made their way west. Settlers and miners made their homes, camped, and mined on tribal lands. The mining and farming activity destroyed hunting and fishing grounds and pushed tribes out of their homelands.

1850
Act for the Government and Protection of Indians is passed. The act allowed the unfair arrests and unpaid labor of Native peoples. A white rancher could keep Natives in enslavement until they had paid off a fine. The act encouraged the kidnapping, slavery, and illegal sale of thousands of people.

1850s
Treaties signed with California tribes. The U.S. government signed 18 treaties with California tribes, setting aside 8.5 million acres (3.5 million ha) for reservations. State officials and white settlers opposed the treaties, and the U.S. Congress failed to ratify any of them. This left many tribes with promises, but no land.

1855

Klamath and Salmon Indian War. The Klamath tribes rebelled against mining activity on their lands. The U.S. Army and miners overwhelmed tribal warriors (pictured) and forced them to surrender. The Klamath people refused to leave their homelands and they live there still.

1887

Dawes Act passed. The act required the government to divide tribal land into parcels that were allotted to individual Native peoples. Those who accepted gained U.S. citizenship.

1872–1873

Modoc War. Kintpuash, also known as Captain Jack, led his tribe to fight the U.S. Army in northern California. The Modoc refused to return to the reservation with the Klamath in Oregon. Modoc warriors held off the U.S. troops for five months. The U.S. Army captured and hanged the leaders, including Kintpuash, in June 1873. The Modoc people were then removed and sent to Oklahoma, where many of them live today. A pole (pictured) marks the spot where the Modoc people made their last resistance, and serves as a memory of the people who died there.

1891

Act for the Relief of Mission Indians passed. With the act, the U.S. government agreed to establish 32 small reservations in southern California.

1934

Indian Reorganization Act passed. The act allowed tribes to manage their own affairs. More than 150 tribes wrote constitutions that formalized tribal government. The act still serves as the basis of federal laws concerning the tribes today.

1952

Urban Indian Relocation Program begins. This U.S. government program encouraged tribal people to leave their reservations and work in cities. In California, large numbers of tribal people went to work in Los Angeles and Oakland.

1958

California Rancheria Act passed. The act terminated, or ended, the federal status of 41 rancherias. The tribes lost recognition and lands. The Inter-Tribal Council of California formed in 1968. Among its goals, it worked to promote and protect tribal governments, fight for land rights, and preserve cultures. In 1979, some of the tribes united to sue the government over the termination.

1969

Native students take over Alcatraz (pictured). On November 20, 1969, 80 Native American students protested at the abandoned Alcatraz prison in San Francisco Bay. The students wanted to raise awareness of broken treaty promises and to build a Native American college, spiritual center, and museum. Their occupation of the island lasted about 19 months.

1987

California v. Cabazon Band of Mission Indians court ruling. The Cabazon and Morongo bands of Mission Indians went to court to win the right to run a gambling business on their reservation. The U.S. Supreme Court ruled in their favor. This ruling opened the door to other tribal gambling businesses around the country. Many California Native Americans run casinos (pictured), including the Chumash, Karuk, Mattole, and Pit River tribes.

1992

California Indian Basketweavers' Association (CIBA) forms. CIBA was created in order to preserve, promote, and continue California's basket-weaving tradition. Members hold gatherings each year. Also in 1992, the Advocates for Indigenous California Language Survival (AICLS) was formed. Its mission is to help California Native communities and individuals keep their languages alive. The board of directors is all Native.

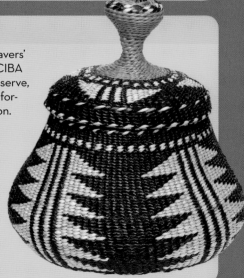

CAHTO

(CAH-toh)

LANGUAGE GROUP:
Athabascan

LANGUAGE:
Currently being revived; no dictionary or word list available

LOCATION PRECONTACT:
California

LOCATION TODAY:
California

The Cahto refer to themselves as *djilbi*, which is their word for the most important lake and village in their ancestral homeland. In fact, the Cahto name comes from a Northern Pomo word meaning "lake." Before Europeans arrived in the West, the tribe lived in about 50 villages in northern California. Fir, pine, and redwood trees grew in their territory, which was mountainous in places and criss-crossed with many small rivers. Each community had at least one head-man, or chief. Many members of the tribe—both men and women—had tattooed lines on their faces, arms, and legs, possibly as a means of identifying the tribe or because they were considered beautiful. Typically, they wore clothing made from tanned deer skin.

The larger villages had a dance house that was used for tribal ceremonies—Cahto people still use these dance houses today. One of the most important Cahto dances was the Acorn Dance. Performed in winter, the dance involved praying for a good harvest—acorns were a staple food and the entire tribe took part in gathering them. Once the acorns were collected, Cahto women used them to make soup and bread. In addition to nuts, the Cahto ate grasshoppers, bees, caterpillars, and

This photograph from around 1924 shows a woman from the Cahto tribe. Both men and women in the tribe wore their hair long. Sometimes they covered it with a hairnet made of iris fibers, a plant with long, broad leaves.

other insects. Cahto men hunted deer, raccoons, and other animals, and caught salmon in the rivers using large nets. Once a year, the Cahto walked to the coast to gather seaweed and fish; today, it has become a tradition for tribal members to retrace the steps of their ancestors on an annual trek.

By the mid-1800s, the U.S. government had forced many tribes onto reservations—including one at Round Valley, to which a small group of Cahto were moved. In the early 1900s, missionaries bought some land for other Cahto to live on, but this rancheria, or reservation, was small. Following European settlement, the Cahto could no longer hunt and gather on their homelands, so many turned to work off the rancheria, either on settlers' ranches or in the timber industry. Language and cultural practices became hard for the Cahto to maintain. Today, there are very few Cahto speakers left, but the tribe is working to revive its language. While a number of them remain at Round Valley, the majority of tribal members are living at the Laytonville Rancheria in northern Mendocino County. In 2013, the tribe adopted a flag that features a bear claw—one of the Cahto's most important spirit beings—as well as a lake symbol to represent their ancestral lands.

Today, the Cahto are one of several tribes working to restore Eel River, once a major source of salmon. Since 1906, the diversion of water to other areas has reduced its fish populations.

IN THE KNOW

The Cahto tribe made small beads from magnesite, a stone found in northern California. They heated the beads in a fire, turning them a pink color, and polished them. The beads, used for trading, were considered more valuable than shell money.

EARLY ISLANDERS

Archaeologists have collected evidence that people started living on the Channel Islands off the mainland of southern California from 8,000 to 11,000 years ago. The ancient Tongva tribe lived on the most southern of the Channel Islands. The Tongva also had villages in and around what is now Los Angeles, and traded with the Chumash (depicted here), who also lived on the islands. The Chumash built some 21 villages and developed a sophisticated society. People traveled to and from the mainland to buy what they needed. The name Chumash comes from the word "Michumash," which means "makers of shell bead money." The money was made from giant clam shells, which the Chumash broke into pieces. They rounded each piece and punched a hole in it, for threading on to strings. When the Spanish took control, they brought disease and drew on the islands' natural resources. The Chumash found it difficult to survive. By the 1820s, what small populations remained had moved to the mainland.

W Langdon Kihn '46

CAHUILLA

(kaw-WEE-ah)

LANGUAGE GROUP:
Uto-Aztecan

GREETING:
Meyaxwhen

THANK YOU:
Ac'ama

LOCATION PRECONTACT:
California

LOCATION TODAY:
California

Southern California, south of the San Bernardino Mountains, has been home to the Cahuilla for thousands of years. The Cahuilla, whose name means "masters" or "powerful ones," dominated three territories: the San Gorgonio Pass and Palm Springs area, the San Jacinto and Santa Rosa Mountains, and the Coachella Valley desert. Across these homelands, the Cahuilla had several villages where family groups gathered for ceremonies including songs and dances. The hot springs were also a traditional gathering place for the tribe to bathe and to heal members when sick.

For food, the Cahuilla ate mesquite beans, dates, pine nuts and other wild plants—as well as rabbit, deer, and reptiles. Some bands grew corn, melon, and squash, and used the agave plant for food, but also to make sandals, slings, and nets. For other items, the tribe belonged to a large trading network. They met with neighboring tribes to exchange the riches of their lands for shell beads, which were used as money.

The Cahuilla escaped invasion and disease until the mid-1800s, but when it came, it was devastating. White settlement, the railroad, measles, and smallpox each took their ⟫

💡 IN THE KNOW

Members of the Cahuilla tribe belonged to one of two groups, represented by animal totems, depending on their ancestry. They were either Coyotes or Wildcats.

This "Salt Grass Lady" was made as a toy for a child on the Agua Caliente Cahuilla Reservation in the 1990s. It is made from grass, pine needles, raffia, and wool cloth.

This desert house dates from around 1924. Tribal members used structures like this for ceremonies. A simple wooden frame is covered in a thick layer of grass to keep the interior cool in summer. The frame extends from the doorway to create a sheltered enclosure for a fire.

toll on the tribe. The California gold rush led the tribe to cede its lands and move onto reservations. Fortunately, unlike many other tribes, the Cahuilla still oversee the lands of their ancestors today. Part of the Agua Caliente Reservation lies within the Palm Springs city limits and the Cahuilla community oversees a group of canyons known as the Indian Canyons of Palm, Tahquitz, Andreas, and Murray. These canyons are home to

Cahuilla cave paintings, trails, and other ancient remains. The vibrant Cahuilla culture continues to be celebrated on the Agua Caliente Reservation and elsewhere; elders speak the language of their ancestors and the tribe's songs and ceremonies remain an important part of tribal life. In 1965 the Malki Museum was founded to exhibit Cahuilla arts and crafts. It was the first museum in California founded and run by American Indians. ✏

SONG CYCLES

Among southern California tribes, song cycles are a series of songs sung at ceremonies. They often combine ancestral dreams and stories. Long ago, there were many different song cycles, each telling a different story. Some had as many as 300 pieces. The men sang, using gourds filled with palm seeds to keep the rhythm. At the same time, women danced the story of the song. Tribes lost many song cycle traditions through the Spanish mission years, although some, called Bird Songs, have survived. Originating with the Kumeyaay tribe, Bird Songs were intended as instruction to children on leaving home and used bird metaphors, such as leaving the nest. For the Cahuilla, the Bird Songs cycle tells their creation story. Southern California tribes continue to sing at ceremonies today. Pictured are the White Rose Singers from Sherman Indian High School—an off-reservation school for Native Americans in Riverside, southern California. They are singing in celebration of the agave plant, a longtime staple for the Cahuilla and Kumeyaay tribes.

CHEMEHUEVI

(che-meh-WAY-vee)

LANGUAGE GROUP:
Uto-Aztecan

LANGUAGE:
In limited use; last known record of fluent speakers dates from the 1970s

LOCATION PRECONTACT:
California

LOCATION TODAY:
California

The ancestors of the Chemehuevi were the Southern Paiute who lived across a large area in the high deserts of Arizona, California, and Nevada. Sometime before the 1800s, the Chemehuevi split from the Paiute and moved to what is now known as the Chemehuevi Valley and the Mojave Desert, south of Las Vegas, Nevada. This was a hot, dry place to live, but the Chemehuevi gathered mesquite beans and other available plants, and hunted small animals including snakes and lizards. Large game was scarce.

The Colorado River provided fresh fish and made the land surrounding the river fertile for growing crops. Even so, food could be lacking at times, so the Chemehuevi dried and stored whatever they could—sometimes in baskets or pots, which they hid in caves. Preparation and survival skills were important to the tribe, so both boys and girls learned to make and use weapons and tools for hunting and the preparation of food.

At the start of the gold rush, thousands of people moved west in a very short time, creating a huge demand for mining and settlement land. The U.S. government pressured the Chemehuevi to move and, in 1865, the Colorado River Reservation was created for the Chemehuevi and Mojave people. While half of the tribe moved to this reservation, the rest tried to continue their traditional way of life by the river. This became more difficult as settlers and Indian agents (who interacted with Natives on behalf of the U.S. government) forced them to relocate. In 1907, the government created the Chemehuevi Valley Reservation on part of their land, but this was flooded in 1940 by the creation of the Parker Dam. More members moved to the Colorado River Reservation after this. The government withdrew the tribe's legal status in the 1950s, in accordance with its "termination" policy, and did not reinstate it until 1970, along with payment for the land lost to the flood. Today, the tribe is strong and proud of its long history. The Chemehuevi Cultural Center offers language classes and exhibits, and oversees projects to preserve the Chemehuevi traditions for generations to come.

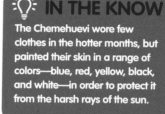

IN THE KNOW

The Chemehuevi wore few clothes in the hotter months, but painted their skin in a range of colors—blue, red, yellow, black, and white—in order to protect it from the harsh rays of the sun.

The illustration shows three Chemehuevi people from the Colorado River region in the late 1850s. The men wear footwear and hold hunting weapons. The woman (left) is barefoot. All three of them wear their hair loose.

CHUMASH

(CHOO-mahsh)

LANGUAGE GROUP:
Isolate

GREETING:
Hatyu (Northern Chumash)

THANK YOU:
Au (Northern Chumash)

LOCATION PRECONTACT:
California

LOCATION TODAY:
California

The Chumash occupied beautiful coastal and inland areas of south-western California, from San Luis Obispo to Los Angeles, and the nearby Channel Islands of Santa Cruz, Santa Rosa, and San Miguel. This large tribe was made up of coastal and island bands.

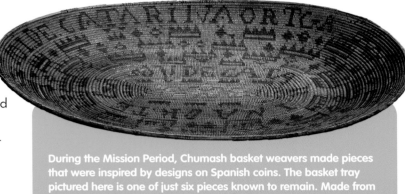

During the **Mission Period,** Chumash basket weavers made pieces that were inspired by designs on Spanish coins. The basket tray pictured here is one of just six pieces known to remain. Made from juncus rush, it bears a Spanish inscription.

Traditionally, Chumash people lived in villages, where they built homes called *'aps* from willow branches covered with mats made from tule (a type of water plant). Some of the homes were huge—big enough for 50 people to live in, with hanging mats creating walls for privacy. A typical village also contained storehouses for food, a gaming area, a place for ceremonies, and a sweathouse. Operating much like a modern-day sauna, the sweathouse was a hut in which water was poured over hot stones to create a steam atmosphere. Tribal members came here for ceremonial or cleansing sweating.

The tribe had many local resources: plant materials for weaving baskets and making clothes, a bountiful ocean, and open country in which to hunt. Each village had its own territory for hunting, fishing, and gathering, and the head chief, who could be male or female, controlled the use of that land. The Chumash who lived by the ocean built canoes from local redwood trunks. Society was well structured, with jobs from sweeping floors to lighting the fires assigned to the people. Favorite pastimes were dancing and music. They also loved to play shinny—a game similar to field hockey.

Drawn by the warm, lush Chumash land, the Spanish built their first mission in 1772 at San Luis Obispo. Five more missions were built by 1817. The Spanish pushed the tribe to plant crops and raise livestock. Living near the missions seemed the only option for the tribe, because the missionaries' use of their land led to a loss of much of their natural resources. The Spanish also exposed the Chumash people to deadly diseases, including measles and smallpox. By the time the U.S. government established the Santa Ynez Reservation for the tribe in 1901, very few Chumash people were left.

Today, the Santa Ynez Band of Chumash is the only federally recognized Chumash tribe, although other groups still exist. The band runs a resort that funds cultural programs and language classes. Located on a historic village site, the tribal museum in Thousand Oaks, California, exhibits a Chumash canoe, baskets, and other artifacts. The Chumash have always believed in giving back. They call this generous spirit *amuyich*. In 2005, the tribe established the Ynez Band of Chumash Indians Foundation, a charity that has donated more than $18 million to local organizations, schools, and other groups. ✒

The Chumash still practice the Native ritual of "smudging," which involves administering a sacred blessing through burning the appropriate herbs. The herbs smolder in a "smudge bowl," traditionally made from an abalone shell.

💡 IN THE KNOW

The Chumash were particularly fond of a bulb that came from the amole, or soap plant. They extracted juices from the bulb, which they used as a kind of soap. They also made brushes from the husks and roasted the bulbs for eating.

CAVE ART

Painted Cave is a sandstone cave in the mountains near Santa Barbara, California. This is one of many sites containing rock paintings (such as the one pictured here) by the Chumash people. Painted Cave State Historic Park is the only place where the public can see the art, so that other sites may be preserved. Chumash shamans, or spiritual leaders, painted the images as part of their religious ceremonies, and they are still sacred to the tribe today. They feature human and insect figures as well as motifs such the spoked wheel, which represents spiritual knowledge and power. The Chumash made the paintings using minerals mixed with plant juice or water. Iron oxide created red, for example. Other colors were white, yellow, black, blue, and green.

CUPEÑO

(koo-PANE-yoh)

LANGUAGE GROUP:
Uto-Aztecan

GREETING:
Miyaxwa

THANK YOU:
Ichaam

LOCATION PRECONTACT:
California

LOCATION TODAY:
California

In their native language, the Cupeño call themselves Kuupangaxwichem, which means "people who slept here." The Cupeño name itself has Spanish origins: Before the early 1900s, this tribe lived in two villages, Cupa and Wilakal, in the mountains of south-western California. The Spanish added eño—meaning "of the"—to the village name Cupa, and so the people of both villages became known as the Cupeño. Living far from the ocean, the tribe hunted deer, working together to force a creature into a canyon where they could shoot it with their bows and arrows. They also trapped small animals, such as rabbits and birds. The tribe gathered acorns, cactus fruit, and berries, too.

The Cupeño had little contact with outsiders until 1810, when white settlers began passing through the area. Up to this time, the tribe had used the hot mineral springs near Cupa as a healing place, but these soon became a tourist attraction. Spanish priests set up mission settlements on Cupeño land and allowed their cattle to graze there. In 1840, a Mexican rancher established Rancho San Jose de Valle on 48,000 acres (19,500 ha) of Cupeño territory. Four years later, the ranch was passed to John Warner, an American with Mexican citizenship, and many Cupeño started working on the ranch for little or no pay. In 1851, a revolt led to ➤➤

💡 IN THE KNOW

When the Cupeño first arrived at their reservation in Pala, in 1903, they had been walking for three days. There were no houses for them to live in on the reservation, so the people had to sleep outside. Today, the tribe commemorates the walk in an event known as Cupa Days, held annually on the first weekend in May.

This Cupeño horse saddle blanket is made from twisted and woven yucca fibers. The Spanish introduced horses to the region and many tribal members became skilled horsemen during the course of the 18th century.

Among the many traditions upheld by the members of the Cupeño tribe is that of singing Bird Songs. Here, a group of men use gourd rattles to beat out a steady rhythm as they sing.

the capture and death of Cupeño leader Antonio Garra, as well as the burning of Cupa. The next owner of the ranch, California governor John Downey, did not want the Cupeño to work for him. Instead, he wanted the tribe to leave what had once been their land.

On May 12, 1903, the U.S. government sent an Indian agent and armed men to force the Cupeño from the ranch to a reservation at Pala, 40 miles (64 km) away. Today, the tribe shares this reservation with Luiseño people in a community that is now known as the Pala Band of Mission Indians. Many Cupeño also live in Los Angeles, while several Cupeño descendants live among the Los Coyotes Band of Cahuilla and Cupeño Indians in Warner Springs, California. Although few of them now live on their homelands, Cupeño tribal members have kept a strong sense of identity by continuing to teach their language and their arts. The Los Coyotes Band runs businesses, such as an avocado grove and a resort, and sponsors education, youth, and housing programs to support their tribal members. ✍

MISSION INDIANS

When the Spanish arrived in California, they began a brutal campaign to convert and control the tribes there. They established 21 missions—religious settlements such as the one depicted here—each with a church, farm, and places for carpentry and blacksmith work. There were Spanish soldiers at each mission and, usually, two priests. The Spanish used the tribal people for free or cheap labor on their farms and in the workshops. They also baptized as many as possible into the Catholic Church; these people became the Mission Indians. Tribes including the Kumeyaay, Chumash, and Yokut rebelled, but Spanish soldiers forced them to surrender.

The Mexicans took over from the Spanish in 1821 and ended the mission system in 1834. By this time, many tribal members had died because of disease, starvation, and overwork. Having lost their traditional ways of life, many families depended on work at ranches to survive. In 1891, the U.S. government passed the Act for the Relief of Mission Indians and began establishing reservations for them. Today's bands live on reservations throughout California.

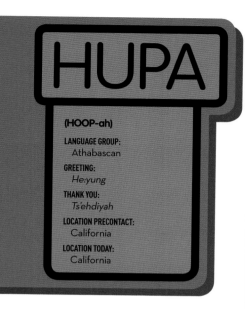

HUPA

(HOOP-ah)

LANGUAGE GROUP:
Athabascan

GREETING:
He:yung

THANK YOU:
Ts'ehdiyah

LOCATION PRECONTACT:
California

LOCATION TODAY:
California

The Hupa migrated to northwestern California from the north about 1,200 years ago. They made their home in the Hoopa Valley, an area of land with thick forests and plentiful wildlife. The tribe fished in the Trinity River for salmon and steelhead trout and hunted deer in the forests. Some animals, such as reptiles, were off limits for religious reasons. Most of the time, Hupa families lived in permanent villages along the river. They used local resources to make their tools, baskets, and clothes—men carved spoons and moneyboxes from elk horns and built their houses using red cedar wood. Families lived together in the wooden houses. All villages had a sweathouse, used for sweating rituals and as a clubhouse for the men of the tribe; when boys were old enough, they joined their fathers and other male relatives in the sweathouse.

The 1849 gold rush brought a wave of prospectors, miners, merchants, and settlers through Hupa land. Prospectors found little gold in the Upper Trinity River and soon moved on, but the settlers stayed. The government established Fort Gaston so that the military could watch over the area and keep the peace. In 1864, Congress recognized Hupa sovereignty and established a reservation in the Hoopa Valley for the tribe. The government paid the white settlers to move, allowing the Hupa to be

A Hupa man stands barefoot and poised with his spear on a rock midstream in the Lake Tahoe region near the Donner Pass in the Sierra Nevada Mountains, California, in 1923.

one of the few tribes to stay on their ancestral land. Gradually, the Hupa began farming and keeping cattle, although they continued to hunt and fish in their traditional ways.

Today, the Hoopa Valley Tribe has one of the largest reservations in California. They work to protect the Trinity River, which is as important to the tribe today as it was to their ancestors hundreds of years ago. Other Hupa people live at Cher-Ae Heights Indian Community and the Elk Valley Rancheria, 60 and 80 miles (95 and 130 km) north, respectively. The tribe continues to hold tribal events and to preserve its culture. One such event, the White Deerskin Dance, is performed in fall, to bring balance to the world. It can last as long as 10 days. In 2016, an app became available to encourage younger generations to keep the Hupa language alive.

This whistle is made from animal bones and bound with animal hide. Hupa dancers taking part in the White Deerskin Dance once held whistles like this in their mouths, blowing them as they moved. Today's whistles are made from plastic.

 IN THE KNOW

The Hupa made glue from the swim bladders of sturgeon fish. They used the glue and sinew (a tendon from an animal) to attach pieces of sharpened rock to the ends of their arrows. The canoes that the Hupa used for fishing were acquired through trade with the Yurok people.

CLOTHING

In southern California, the weather was very warm much of the time—as it is now—so people did not wear much clothing. Many people went barefoot a lot of the time, although the Cahuilla made sandals from deerskin or cactus fibers.

Many southern tribal women wore aprons made from tree bark or plants such as mesquite. Often women decorated their skirts with shells, nuts, seeds, and grasses, as in the Hupa dance skirt pictured here. Pomo women, who lived in northern California, often wore capes over their shoulders and long skirts. In the winter, northern tribal people also wore deerskin or rabbit clothing and shawls.

Patterned basket hats were popular with the men of the Yokut, Hupa, and other tribes. Women and girls wore small, rounded caps.

KARUK

(KAR-uck)

LANGUAGE GROUP:
Hokan

GREETING:
Ayukîi

THANK YOU:
Yootva

LOCATION PRECONTACT:
California

LOCATION TODAY:
California

The Karuk were living along the middle stretch of the Klamath River in northern California by 10,000 B.C.E., according to anthropologists. They built their villages beside the river, where they fished for salmon, or alongside nearby streams. The Karuk were close to their neighbors, the Yurok. The tribes' names translate as "upstream" (*karuk*) and "downstream" (*yurok*).

The Karuk fished for salmon by building platforms along the river and scooping the fish up using dip nets. They hunted various animals in their woodlands—bear, elk, deer, beaver. Deer was a prize catch. Before leaving for a deer hunt, Karuk men prepared carefully by bathing and fasting. For the hunt, they wore masks made from real deer heads, while hunting dogs ran their prey into traps. The tribe gathered acorns, berries, and other plants. Village life was full and lively with regular ceremonies, when the Karuk danced, feasted, and sang for new beginnings and to ensure enough food for the coming season.

Fur traders were probably the first outsiders to meet the Karuk in the early 1800s, but their full traditional lives continued until 1850. That year, a gold rush began on Karuk territory, and miners and settlers built homes all over tribal lands. The U.S. government and the Karuk agreed to a treaty that year, but Congress did not ratify (approve) it. Clashes with the whites led to the deaths of several Karuk people, forcing the survivors to flee their homes for a short time.

NAOMI LANG

In 2002, the ice skater Naomi Lang became the first Native woman to participate in the Winter Olympic Games. Born in 1978, Naomi is a member of the Karuk tribe—her Native name is Maheetahan, which means "Morning Star."

Naomi began ice skating at the age of eight and was ice dancing by the age of 12. She skates with her partner, the Russian Peter Tchernyshev. The couple were U.S. Ice Dance champions five times in a row, from 1999 through 2003. For the Vancouver Winter Olympics, in 2010, Lang dressed in full Native clothing.

Karuk men fish at Ishi Pishi Falls, near Somes Bar, using traditional 12-foot (3.6-m)-long dip nets (pictured). This tribe once fished for salmon from 120 villages on the Klamath and Salmon Rivers.

When they returned, they found their villages had been burned and taken over by the settlers. From this time, the Karuk lived where they could, until the Dawes Act was passed in 1887. The act introduced a policy of allotting parcels of land to tribal members so that more of their territory could be given to white settlers.

For many years, the tribe struggled to find new ways to survive. In 1979, a group of elders finally purchased a small piece of ancestral land, and the U.S. government granted the Karuk tribe legal status. Today, the tribe is one of the largest in California and the Karuk people maintain their deep bond with the land through traditional events—such as the Pick-ya-wih (World Renewal Ceremony), in which tribal members dance to heal the Earth. This dance acknowledges their ongoing relationship with the natural world. The tribe also works hard to protect the Klamath River and the surrounding area. ✒

KUMEYAAY

(KOO-meye)

LANGUAGE GROUP:
Yuman

GREETING:
Haawka

THANK YOU:
'uuhayi'

LOCATION PRECONTACT:
California; Mexico

LOCATION TODAY:
California (U.S.); Mexico

This large tribe, whose presence in Baja California and southern California goes back approximately 12,000 years, currently has 13 federally recognized Kumeyaay bands in California and five Kumeyaay communities in Mexico. The tribe lived in many villages across their vast lands. In their winter villages, people lived in homes called *ewaa*, made from willow branches, leaves, and tule reeds, while in summer and fall, the tribe moved around, making temporary camps wherever needed in order to harvest food. Their territory included coastal areas, mountains, and desert land, so the tribe had many natural resources. The Kumeyaay depended largely on the acorn harvest, but gathered other plants as well, while hunters caught deer, rabbits, and birds. For hunting, and to defend themselves, the Kumeyaay made bows and arrows from willow trees. For bowstrings they used deer ligament, while arrowheads were made of stone or wood. The Kumeyaay were part of a wide trading network, exchanging shells and baskets for honey, mesquite beans, and other items.

In 1769, the Spanish established the San Diego de Alcalá mission and fort on land occupied by the Kumeyaay. In the years that followed, these Kumeyaay rebelled, and in 1775, tribal warriors destroyed the mission. Within a short time of the rebellion, the Europeans put many Kumeyaay to work as ➤➤

This double-spouted Kumeyaay jar is around 100 years old. It was made from coils of clay that were piled one on top of the other and rubbed over to form a smooth surface.

263

ranchers and farmers. The Kumeyaay were forbidden to practice their traditions, but in secret they sang and played games, such as *peon*—a guessing game played with animal bones and sticks. In this way, they kept their traditions alive.

Some Kumeyaay fled to the mountains to avoid living at the mission. When California became a state in 1850, the border between the United States and Mexico divided the Kumeyaay people, making it difficult for families to see each other. The tribe was left without land until 1875, when President Ulysses S. Grant created the Capitan Grande Reservation. Today, the Barona and Viejas bands of the Kumeyaay tribe share ownership of this land, but it is dry and arid, so it remains uninhabited. It is estimated that today the tribe owns 193 square miles (500 sq km) of San Diego County, California. In 2000, the tribe opened the Barona Cultural Center and Museum to honor its history, arts, and language, and plans to create a virtual display of ancestral artifacts online. ✐

The Kumeyaay ground acorns to make meal, which they cooked in water, to eat as mush. Today, you can still see the stone holes they used for grinding the acorns.

GETTING AROUND

Tribes such as the Yurok and Pomo used tule reeds to make canoe-shaped rafts, which they moved through the water using long poles. These, and small dugout canoes, were useful for fishing near the coast and on inland rivers. The Chumash also built strong, ocean-going canoes for traveling, trade, fishing, and visiting their relatives on the Channel Islands.

Master builders constructed the *tomol*, the oldest type of ocean-worthy boat in North America. The tomol was a large, flat-bottomed canoe made from redwood planks and plant fibers (pictured). The planks came from trees that had fallen then drifted along the coast. Builders applied tar to make the boat waterproof. Tomols were 10 to 30 feet (3 to 9 m) long, and could carry at least 12 people. In 2001, Chumash people re-created an age-old tradition when they paddled a newly made tomol from the mainland to Santa Cruz Island.

LUISEÑO

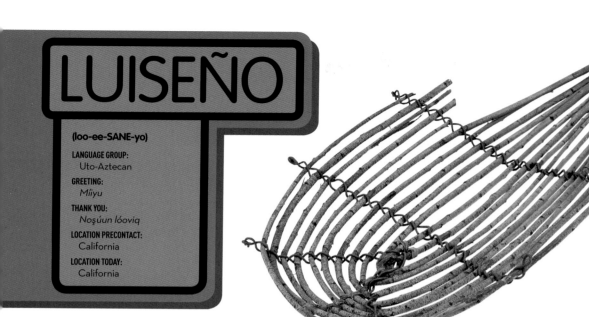

(loo-ee-SANE-yo)

LANGUAGE GROUP:
Uto-Aztecan

GREETING:
Míiyu

THANK YOU:
Noṣúun lóoviq

LOCATION PRECONTACT:
California

LOCATION TODAY:
California

This seed beater is made from bent twigs that are held in place using wire. It once belonged to Luisa Lugo (see below) and it is thought that she made it. Seed beaters were used for brushing seeds straight from a bush and into a basket.

The Luiseño lived in the area between present-day Los Angeles and San Diego Counties, in southern California. The Spanish named the tribe for the mission they founded in 1798, San Luis Rey de Francia, but the people call themselves Payómkawichum, which means "people of the West."

Bands of the Luiseño tribe lived in around 30 villages across their ancestral land, and each community gathered, hunted, and fished in its own area. They built cone-shaped homes called *kíicha*, which they made from the materials they found nearby: willow trees in the valleys, bark in the mountains, and tule (a type of water plant) in waterfront villages. The Luiseño learned how to manage their land while caring for the environment. They used controlled burning to encourage certain plants, such as yucca, to grow. Burning land after a harvest got rid of weeds and reduced the number of pests likely to attack a new crop. The fire also cleared the area so the Luiseño could hunt small game, such as rabbits, more easily. The ocean and inland rivers provided fish, and the Luiseño also collected salt from the ocean salt marshes; seashells and salt were valuable trade items.

When the Spanish arrived in the late 1700s, they disrupted this peaceful life and forced the Luiseño into life at the missions. Over the next few decades, many Luiseño people died from measles, smallpox, and influenza as European diseases swept through the region. The Spanish introduced a new language and religion and forced the Luiseño into slave labor. After the Mexican-American War of 1846–1848, in which the United States gained California from Mexico, the Luiseño tried to return to their lives as villagers and farmers, but found they had lost a vast amount of land to ranchers and settlers. In 1875, President Grant established the first Luiseño Reservation and more followed.

IN THE KNOW

Luiseño rattles set the rhythm in ceremonial dances. The rattles have different meanings. A deer-hoof rattle, for example, is used when someone dies, to help them into the next world.

Luiseño people still learn and speak their language, and continue to make traditional rattles, which are important in ceremonies. Over the decades, the tribe has fought hard for water and land rights to protect its communities.

Luisa Lugo, a Luiseño woman pictured here in 1917, holds the seed beater pictured above. The seeds would have been kept in clay jars, or *ollas*, like the ones at her feet.

DID YOU KNOW?

CALIFORNIA'S COSO

Mountains contain more than 100,000 petroglyphs—images made on rocks by chipping, scratching, rubbing, or chiseling the surface to reveal the lighter-colored stone beneath. Thought to be the work of spiritual leaders, the images feature human figures, coyotes, abstract shapes, and bighorn sheep. They are between 1,000 and 10,000 years old.

MAIDU

(MY-doo)

LANGUAGE GROUP:
Penutian

GREETING:
Hesasika (Mountain Maidu)

THANK YOU:
Héw

LOCATION PRECONTACT:
California

LOCATION TODAY:
California

The Maidu people lived north of present-day Sacramento, California, across many thousands of acres of mountainous terrain. This tribe had three major bands: the Mountain Maidu; the Northwestern Maidu, or Konkow, who lived in the valleys; and the Southern Maidu, or Nisenan, who lived in the foothills.

Around their own village communities, the Maidu hunted, fished, and gathered their favorite foods, which included salmon, eel, acorns, and insects. The various plants and animals had many other uses, too, and the tribe used what they needed for medicine, clothing, and tools. Maidu women were excellent basket weavers, sometimes decorating their creations with feathers and shells.

In spite of many customs that tied them together, language and other differences separated the Maidu groups. The Mountain Maidu, for example, were expert hunters and used dogs to help capture bears, mountain lions, and deer, whereas those in the Northwest didn't eat mountain lion or bear. While the Mountain Maidu built homes that had pole frames covered with brush or bark, the valley-dwelling tribes built large earth-covered homes in pits.

This Maidu pendant is made from abalone shell. The abalone is a large sea snail whose shell has a coating of shimmery mother-of-pearl on the inside that is perfect for making stunning jewelry.

All of the Maidu groups suffered when settlers and miners began invading and settling in their territory. Fur trappers, including the explorer Jedediah Smith and his men, met the Maidu in the late 1820s. Other whites followed. In 1833, an epidemic—probably malaria—swept through the Maidu communities, killing many people. In 1848, a group of Maidu was working with the carpenter James Marshall when he discovered gold at Colomo. This discovery sparked the gold rush, bringing thousands of people to California and onto Maidu land. In the early 1850s, the U.S. government drafted treaties for the California tribes, but Congress never approved them, leaving many with no land or rights. Conflicts between California tribes and white settlers created unrest. Eventually, the Maidu settled on several rancherias and elsewhere.

Today, the Maidu Museum and Historic Site in Roseville celebrates the Maidu past and present. It sits on ancestral land amid boulders carved with petroglyphs, and hosts many events and exhibits historical artifacts alongside modern Maidu artwork. ☞

Maidu artist Frank Day (1902–1976) painted scenes from Maidu ancestral stories. His 1967 "Bear Attacking Mother and Child" takes inspiration from Maidu tales that centered on the very real fear of an attack by a grizzly bear.

💡 IN THE KNOW

The Northwestern Maidu did not name their children until they were at least two or three years old, as they wanted to give their children names that suited their personalities.

REGIONAL DWELLINGS

Many California tribes, especially those who lived by the water, lived in permanent villages. They built their homes from the materials that grew around them. On the coast, the Pomo built homes from slabs of redwood bark. The Miwok, who lived in the mountains, made cone-shaped bark houses (pictured). The Maidu made round earth lodges. The Chumash lived farther south and constructed circular homes using wooden poles for a frame and grass or tule (a type of bulrush) for the roof and walls. All over California, members of the tribe left to go hunting or gathering, depending on the season. They traveled for a few days or weeks at a time throughout the year, harvesting anything from pine nuts to acorns, or hunting deer and trapping fish. In the warm summer months, the tribes built temporary brush huts at their hunting and gathering camps.

MATTOLE

(MATT-oll)

LANGUAGE GROUP:
Athabascan

LANGUAGE:
Currently dormant;
no record of last
known speaker

LOCATION PRECONTACT:
California

LOCATION TODAY:
California

The area that is now Humboldt County, in northwestern California, has been home to the Mattole tribe for centuries. The Mattole were close to the Wailaki and other neighboring tribes, and lived in similar ways. To make their round, single-family homes, the Mattole dug into the ground about two feet (60 cm) to lay the floors and used poles and bark to create walls and a roof. Each home was sturdy, with a fire pit in the center, and kept the family warm and sheltered throughout the winter.

In the summer, the Mattole left their village homes to camp out near hunting and gathering places. Quite often they traveled and camped as single-family groups. Salmon was the most important food for the tribe, and the Bear and Mattole Rivers provided an ample supply of the fish. The tribe also lived close enough to the Pacific Ocean to benefit from all kinds of seafood. Inland, hunters caught animals such as deer and rabbits, which they took back to the village for the women to cook.

The women made clothing and drums from the deer hide and blankets from rabbit skins. Acorns were another regular food resource, though there were not as many oak trees in Mattole territory as in other nearby areas.

The Mattole lost their lands when the Spanish established control in California during the late 1700s and early 1800s. The Mexicans took over in 1821, and California was within American control by 1848, making it impossible for the Mattole to recover their lands. Yet the Mattole and other tribes in the area did not give in without a fight. From 1858, they fought a series of battles against U.S. Army troops and California militia, known as the Bald Hills War. ➤➤

 IN THE KNOW

In many tribes, only women had facial tattoos. The Mattole tribe was unusual because both men and women tattooed their faces. The men traditionally tattooed a small round dot on their foreheads.

JOE DUNCAN

Born around 1850, Joe Duncan was one of very few Mattole to survive contact with the Spanish settlers. He and his son lived near the mouth of the Mattole River and labored as ranch hands. In the 1920s, Joe was interviewed by anthropologists—people who study different aspects of human life. They discovered that Joe was one of the last people to speak the tribe's native language.

The fighting tribes, which included the Hupa and Wiyot as well as the Mattole, had many objections against what the Americans were doing to their lands, including the over-hunting of deer and the establishment of farms. This disturbed the tribes' way of life. By 1864, the war ended in defeat for the tribes. Most tribal people ended up on reservations. The Mattole moved to the Rohnerville Rancheria with some Wiyot and Bear River people, who spoke a different language. The Mattole language gradually fell out of use—some reports say that it has not been spoken since the 1950s. The two groups combined to become the Bear River Band of the Rohnerville Rancheria. Today they run a number of businesses, including the Bear River Recreation Center and the Bear River Casino Resort. ✐

Over the last century, deforestation and logging have damaged the Mattole River and its surrounding territory. The Mattole are working to restore the river.

MIWOK

(MEE-wuck)

LANGUAGE GROUP:
Penutian

GREETING:
Michaksas (Northern)

THANK YOU:
Ka molis (Coast)

LOCATION PRECONTACT:
California

LOCATION TODAY:
California

When the Miwok lived across their large territory in north-central California, it is estimated that the tribe numbered over 10,000 people within four different groups: Coast, Plains and Sierra, Bay, and Lake. Although all the Miwok bands depended on hunting, fishing, and gathering, each group lived in a separate area with its own resources. The Coast Miwok, for example, occupied more than 600 villages along and near the Pacific Ocean in an area north of San Francisco that was full of bays, rivers, and lagoons. Tribal members had many foods available to them, from fish and deer to rabbits and birds. The Coast Miwok also ate clams and used their shells as currency when trading with other tribes. The Plains and Sierra people lived to the southeast in the Yosemite region, where they gathered acorns, berries, and insects for eating. They also fished in the Merced and Stanislaus Rivers. The Bay Miwok, who lived near present-day Walnut Creek, moved around their lands to hunt and gather according to the seasons. The area around Clear Lake was home to the Lake Miwok people, who built special dance houses for their ceremonies.

From the late 1700s to the mid-1800s, the Miwok came under threat when Spanish missionaries rounded up people from several communities in order to convert them to Catholicism. They succeeded in converting some Miwok to Christianity, and brought disease and death to many. The gold rush introduced waves of miners and settlers into Plains and Sierra Miwok territory, but the tribe fought back against the newcomers. The Mariposa Indian War of 1850–1851 ensued, with both sides attacking each other. White troops raided and burned Miwok villages

This Miwok burden basket was made around 1900. Burden baskets were used for carrying heavy loads on the back, their shape helping to distribute the weight.

A group of Miwok men dance at the Gallup Inter-Tribal Indian Ceremonial. The Miwok have a deep respect for the animals around them and sometimes imitate them in their dances.

and forced the surviving Miwok to retreat.

Over time, the Miwok moved onto rancherias, many of which now have federal recognition. The tribe has kept strong ties to the land and the traditions of the people. Today, members come together for language and arts programs, and cultural events such as the Big Time Festival. Hosted by the Federated Indians of Graton Rancheria, it celebrates basketmaking, clam shell beading, and other crafts. The Acorn Festival is held annually by the Tuolumne Band of Me-Wuk Indians on the fourth weekend of September. 🖋

MONO

(MON-oh)

LANGUAGE GROUP:
Uto-Aztecan

GREETING:
Munahoo (North Fork)

THANK YOU:
Mannoho-b̯ (Western)

LOCATION PRECONTACT:
California

LOCATION TODAY:
California

Long ago, the Mono people separated from the Paiute and became a distinct tribe in its own right. Its people settled in the Sierra Nevada area. This group later divided again into two main bands: the Eastern Mono, sometimes called the Owens Valley Paiute, and the Western Mono, also called the Monache or Mono Lake Paiute. Both groups of Mono lived near creeks and rivers in small villages where they built cone-shaped homes covered in bark.

Villages usually featured a sweathouse for the men, a large, open space for dances, and a granary for storing acorns. The floor of the granary, which was made from sticks and mats, was raised up about six feet (1.8 m) above the floor, keeping the acorns off the moist ground and away from animals. Although acorns were important to the tribe, they were not abundant in all the Mono homelands, so the Eastern Mono traded with their relatives in the west to get them. Pine nuts, rabbit, and deer were also favorite foods.

Mono societies included chiefs and messengers. The chiefs were not all-powerful, as in some tribes, but did have several duties, such as making sure that everyone had enough to eat and appointing times for ceremonies. Messengers not only carried messages back and forth to the chief, but also directed dances and ceremonies and kept order in the village. Baskets of food and other items were usually carried by the women of the tribe. They also wore woven hats to cushion the baskets' tumplines. The tumpline was a strap that went across the forehead and under the basket, to support the weight of its load on the back.

The Mono did not have contact with outsiders until the Oregon Trail opened and settlers began to ⟫

Dating from around 1920, this decorative beaded bottle was made by a member of the Lake Mono band. Among the different stitches used are gourd stitch (zigzags) and brick stitch.

head west. Once prospectors discovered gold in California in 1848, thousands of people made their way through Mono territory to seek their fortunes. Settlers, ranchers, and miners spread across Mono land, pushing the tribe out of their villages. In the late 1800s, the Mono people began moving onto rancherias. Today, 11 of these communities have federal recognition, including the North Fork Rancheria, Big Sandy Rancheria of Western Mono, Big Pine Band Paiute Tribe, Cold Springs Rancheria, and the Bridgeport Paiute Indian Community.

The Sierra Mono Museum in the town of North Fork exhibits traditional Mono baskets, games, and tools. It is also a center for history, for learning the Mono language, and for storytelling. Since 1971, the museum has hosted the Indian Fair Days festival—a two-day intertribal event during which visitors can enjoy ancestral traditions that include singing, dancing, and craftmaking. The festival is held annually, on the first weekend of August. ✒

Two Mono women carry baskets, possibly taking part in a game, around 1900. They wear multiple necklaces, beaded belts, and long cloth dresses.

BEAUTIFUL BASKETRY

Basket weaving has been a tradition in California for many centuries, producing some of the finest examples in the world. The Pomo and Washoe tribes are particularly famous for their baskets. Originally, people made strong, watertight baskets that were used for different purposes. The baskets held or cooked food, or people used them in ceremonies and for trade. California basket weavers had a wide variety of materials to choose from, including willow, roots, and grasses. They used different colored plants or dyed them to create patterns in the baskets. The patterns can have meanings, such as the Pomo "Dau," or "Spirit Door," design that allows good spirits to enter the basket. The Pomo were also known for decorating baskets with feathers. Today, some of these baskets are worth thousands of dollars and are on display in museums and in private art collections.

Pictured is a contemporary Pomo basket. Once a year, the California Indian Basketweavers' Association organizes a gathering of artists who come together to share their knowledge, and to preserve their art for future generations.

PIT RIVER

(PIT RIVER)

LANGUAGE GROUP:
Hokan

GREETING:
Izkhadzi

THANK YOU:
Tusi uwi

LOCATION PRECONTACT:
California

LOCATION TODAY:
California

This engraving from 1872 shows the dramatic landscape of the Pit River region. Native Americans camp close to the river with the Sierra Nevada Mountains in the background.

Eleven bands, speaking the Atwamsini and the Atsugewi languages, make up the Pit River tribe of northern and northeastern California. The people call themselves Hewisedawi, which means "those from on top." Their traditional territory included a large expanse of land along what is now called the Pit River, so named because the tribal people caught deer using large pits, or holes. Many made their homes along the river and depended on it for fishing. They also dug roots and camas bulbs, and gathered nuts, plants, and insects to eat. In winter, the Pit River people lived in villages, in earthen homes built partially underground. In warmer weather, they made temporary shelters from poles and tule mats and moved from one place to another, gathering the plants that were in season. The Pit River people wove willow and grasses into beautiful and useful baskets decorated with fern, bark, and other natural items.

During the gold rush, it became impossible for the Pit River people to continue their traditional ways of life in their homelands. Settlers claimed acres of tribal territory, grazing their sheep and cattle on Pit River hunting and gathering grounds. Some Pit River people rebelled, along with neighboring tribes, but the revolts did not stop the settlement. Many were forced to move to the Round Valley Reservation, while others, who wanted to stay close to their homelands, worked as ranch hands and millworkers to survive. Following the Dawes Act of 1887, some Pit River people bought back plots of ancestral land, and in the early 1900s, the U.S. government created seven small rancherias in the area.

The Pit River tribe gained federal recognition in 1976 and now actively protects its lands and sacred places. One such place, Medicine Lake, has had spiritual significance for the tribe for many generations. It has long been used for ceremonies, including vision quests in which tribal members spend time alone in the hope of finding their spiritual guide. Every July, the tribe hosts a gathering at Medicine Lake with a talking circle, in which members sit in a circle and take turns speaking and sharing burdens, storytelling, and other cultural activities.

ISTET WOICHE

Istet Woiche, also known as William Hulsey, was an important member of the Madhesi band of the Pit River tribe that once lived by the Madhesi Valley in northeastern California. Woiche was also the last fluent speaker of the Pit River tribe's language. Having studied tribal history for 25 years, he earned the title Keeper of the Laws, History, and Chronology of the Pit River People. Istet Woiche shared his stories with American naturalist C. Hart Merriam, who published them as a collection of stories titled *Annikadel: The History of the Universe as told by the Achomawi Indians.*

This Pit River breastplate was made from plant fibers, woven on a loom, around 1890. The striking geometric design is made from colorful seed beads, stitched to the surface. The breastplate would have been worn as a decorative addition to an outfit.

CALIFORNIA TREATIES

When the Mexican–American War ended, in 1848, the United States took control of California. The gold rush (pictured) followed later that same year, bringing thousands of settlers to the West. The U.S. government started programs to control the tribes, and sent agents to negotiate treaties. From 1851 to 1852, the agents arranged 18 treaties, but did not take the time to learn about the California tribes and made their agreements with tribal people who may or may not have understood what they were signing. The treaties promised reservations as well as farming equipment to help the tribes survive. Facing fierce protests from the California government and white settlers, who did not want any land going to tribal people, the U.S. Senate rejected the treaties and locked them away. This left the tribes landless until the early 1900s, when the U.S. government established rancherias.

POMO

(POH-moh)

LANGUAGE GROUP:
Hokan

GREETING:
He-en ma-iwa

THANK YOU:
Yah weh

LOCATION PRECONTACT:
California

LOCATION TODAY:
California

The Pomo tribe was large and split into seven different groups with just as many dialects. The tribe's traditional homelands stretched along the coast of northern California and included redwood forests, river valleys, and foothills. Many Pomo made their homes around the ancient Clear Lake and others lived as far east as the Coast Range mountains. Groups of Pomo people lived in separate villages where they were close to many sources of food—ocean fish and seaweed and deer and elk. Many plants were useful for food—including seven types of acorn—and others for clothing, such as tule reeds and shredded redwood bark.

The tribe operated a sophisticated social system, in which men and women of lower rank wore willow or redwood bark clothes, while wealthier people wore skins, especially in the colder weather. Jewelry was also a sign of wealth and status; richer people wore shell necklaces, beaded wristbands, and other decorative pieces. The Pomo had access to many items by trading with far-off relatives and other tribes. The Pomo held trade feasts, to which they invited people from other tribes to trade and socialize. Renowned for their fine basketmaking skills, the Pomo traded their baskets and raw materials, such as salt, for goods brought by their guests.

From the late 1700s, the arrival of Spanish missionaries and Russian fur traders marked a time of great change for

Between the two Pomo rattles above is a "clapper stick," a length of wood that is split at one end. It is played by slapping the split end into the palm of the hand and is used to keep a steady beat.

These Pomo dancers, photographed in 1906, wear "flicker" headdresses. Traditionally made from feathers of a flicker (a type of woodpecker), the style is typical of a number of California tribes.

traditional Pomo culture. The outsiders brought new religions and forced labor to the Pomo. When the Mexican government took over, in 1821, the Mexicans brought disease, raided Pomo villages for slaves, and established ranches in tribal territory. After the gold rush and California statehood, the Pomo faced invasions from settlers and miners. The U.S. government took action, forcing the Pomo onto reservations and allowing white settlers to claim their land. Many Pomo left the reservations and found work on the ranches or elsewhere.

Today, numerous communities of Pomo live in small, separate areas of their ancestral lands and in towns and cities spread across California. Tribal groups sponsor language learning and events, such as Big Time celebrations—events that celebrate ancestral Pomo dancing, games, and food. Pomo baskets are featured in many museum collections, and basketmaking continues to thrive today, as do the traditional arts of dancing, singing, and jewelry-making. ✒

FOOD AND DRINK

Hunters in the California tribes caught rabbits, deer, and other game, using bows and arrows and knives. Fishermen caught salmon in the rivers using large lifting nets. They took the fish home to the women of the tribe, who cooked them over wood fires or smoked them (pictured). Women and children gathered berries, insects, nuts, and roots. They made drinks from elderberries and wild grapes, or pounded nuts and mixed them with water. People also ate insects after drying or roasting them. Seeds and nuts, such as mesquite, acorns, and pine nuts, produced flour for bread or a mush to mix with other flavorings. Tribal people added salt to many of these foods. The salt was gathered from marshes and seaweed. Although California tribes had lots of food available to them, they traded with other tribes for foods that were more scarce in their region.

ROUND VALLEY

(ROUND VALLEY)

LANGUAGE GROUP:
Various

LANGUAGE:
Currently dormant;
no record of last
known speaker

LOCATION PRECONTACT:
California

LOCATION TODAY:
California

Yuki and Pomo members gather outside the office of the Indian Agency on the Nome Lackee Reservation, about 20 miles (32 km) west of present-day Tehama in northern California, in 1900.

In 1854, the U.S. government forced various tribes, including the Yuki and some Pomo, to the Nome Lackee Reservation in northern California. This act removed thousands of tribal people from their homelands and allowed settlers to begin building and farming there. However, the U.S. government soon wanted the reservation, too. In 1863 the government moved the tribes from Nome Lackee to a farm called the Nome Cult Farm. The difficult journey over the mountains took two weeks and was called the Nome Cult Trail, also known as the Koncow Trail of Tears. In 1870, the Nome Cult Farm became the Round Valley Reservation—a site still shared by descendants of the Yuki, Cahto, Wailaki, Pit River, Concow-Maidu, Pomo, and Nomlaki people. These unrelated tribes became the Covelo Indian Community, and eventually, the Round Valley Indian Tribes. Before the 1850s, these California tribes had lived by hunting, gathering, and fishing, and each group had its own language and customs. Over time, the tribes learned to live and work together, and in 1934, the Round Valley community elected a tribal council and wrote a constitution.

Although the reservation is one of the oldest and largest in California, it is remote. Tribal members who live on the reservation have access to a school, community center, and health clinic. The tribe runs a gaming and motel business and some tribal members have ranches and farms on the reservation. Each September, the California Native American Days celebration honors tribal history with a parade, games, dancing, and food—traditional and contemporary. ✐

Members of the Round Valley Indian Tribes retrace the 1863 route of the Nome Cult walk, the forced relocation of their ancestors from Chico, California, to Covelo, California.

💡 IN THE KNOW

Round Valley takes its name from the shape of the area, which is almost completely round and surrounded by mountains and rivers.

SERRANO

(se-RAY-noh)

LANGUAGE GROUP:
Uto-Aztecan

GREETING:
Hamiinat

THANK YOU:
Hakupa' ay

LOCATION PRECONTACT:
California

LOCATION TODAY:
California

The Serrano name comes from the Spanish word for "of the mountains." The Spanish gave this name to the people they met in the mountainous areas east of modern-day Los Angeles and the Mojave Desert. Similarly, the Serrano people call themselves Yuhaviatam, "people of the pines." The Serrano people trace their history back to their settlement of the San Bernardino Mountains. According to a Serrano creation story, a white eagle led the first people to the top of these mountains, and then the tribe spread across the nearby territory, building villages near streams, lakes, and rivers.

Serrano villages included family homes, a sweathouse, granaries to store food, and a structure for ceremonies. The Kika, the religious leader of the village, lived in the ceremonial building. Ceremonies included songs, dancing, and feasting and were held to welcome new babies, mourn the dead, and for other important life events. The tribe lived across a wide area, and its people depended on the food they could hunt or gather near their villages. Those who lived in the foothills of the mountains gathered pine nuts and acorns and hunted deer, mountain sheep, and other animals. The desert Serrano captured small animals, dug yucca roots, and picked cactus fruit for their meals. They also traveled to the foothills to gather nuts. Like their neighboring tribes, the Serrano used the plants and animals around them to make baskets, musical instruments, wall coverings, and blankets. They were not farming people until the Spanish took them into the mission system.

In 1771, the Spanish established the Mission San Gabriel Arcángel and began colonizing the Serrano, by forcing them to work at the missions and follow Catholicism. The Serrano, Cahuilla, and Quechan revolted in 1812, but did not succeed in driving the Spanish out. By the end of the 1800s, the Serrano had two reservations, San Manuel—named after the prominent chief Santos Manuel—and Morongo. Today, the communities support cultural events, such as spring celebrations, Heritage Days, and powwows. The San Manuel tribe runs the Serrano Language Revitalization Program, and has preserved ceremonial songs to ensure children learn their language and the voice of their ancestors. 🖋

IN THE KNOW

Serrano homes were mainly used for sleeping and storage. Tribal members tended to cook their food out in the open and carried out other household chores under the shade of a ramada. This was a simple structure made from poles and a thatched roof with no walls.

To keep warm in winter, members of the Serrano tribe wore blankets made from otter or rabbit fur. This rabbit-fur blanket was made by Maria Johnson of the San Manuel Reservation, San Bernardino County, California, around 1880.

WORLD RENEWAL

Tribes such as the Hupa and the Karuk (pictured) celebrate World Renewal ceremonies. During the ceremony, male dancers move and sing to ensure plentiful food and to prevent disasters, such as earthquakes. The White Deerskin Dance marks the beginning of the ceremony. Dancers carry long blades made from obsidian, a useful rock for making tools. They wear necklaces of dentalia shells and display white deerskins on wooden sticks. Traditionally, white deer were rare and dancers displayed their skins to show the good fortune that had come their way. The Jumping Dance is also important and represents the re-creation of the world. Men carry special baskets and wear woodpecker scalp headbands topped with white feathers. Their movements include jumping at certain points during the dance. With these movements, the dancers seek to remove evil from the world and replace it with good.

SHASTA

(SHASS-tah)

LANGUAGE GROUP:
Hokan

LANGUAGE:
Currently dormant; no record of last known speaker

LOCATION PRECONTACT:
California

LOCATION TODAY:
California

The Shasta lived in northern California and southern Oregon, in approximately 150 small villages near the Shasta, Scott, and Klamath Rivers. Their territory included mountains, rivers, and forests rich in deer, bear, nuts, berries, insects, and fish. They hunted prey using bows and arrows, and made nets, basket traps, and spears for catching fish. In summer, women and children dived to the bottom of the Klamath River to harvest mussels.

In their winter villages, the Shasta lived in pit houses dug partly underground, with a central fire for warmth. The houses had little furniture, and people slept on tule pillows and wrapped up in deerskin blankets. In the warmer weather, the Shasta moved from these homes to summer camps where they made brush huts for shelter. The fall was time for acorn gathering, so the Shasta moved once again and built bark huts in which to sleep.

IN THE KNOW

Shasta women, like other California tribal women, had three wide stripes tattooed on their chins—generally such tattoos were considered a mark of beauty. Both men and women wore body paint and had ear and nose piercings.

This Shasta belt is made from braided horsehair—possibly traded from horse-riding tribes of the Plateau region. It is decorated with thimbles and buttons.

Storytelling was, and remains, a popular and important pastime to the Shasta tribe. For centuries, elders have used stories to pass on valuable lessons and beliefs to the next generation. The Shasta were active traders. Their main trading partners were the Karuk, Yurok, and Hupa, with whom they traded beads and obsidian in exchange for shells, baskets, and other goods.

Fur trappers probably met the Shasta in the early 1800s, but the arrival of miners and settlers in the 1850s marked the beginning of difficult times for the tribe. Once prospectors found gold in Shasta territory, the tribe faced conflict over their lands and violence against their people. Shasta headmen signed a treaty in 1851, but the California government and local people complained, wanting to keep the land for themselves, so Congress never made the agreement official. Driven from their villages, the Shasta tried to survive

The Shasta often received baskets in trade from the Karuk, Hupa, and Yurok. They also made some of their own (pictured)—a hazel, conifer root, and bear grass basket with a star motif.

where and how they could. Shasta warriors fought against the government in the Rogue River War in southern Oregon, but had little success. Many Shasta were moved to the Grand Ronde and Siletz Reservations along with members from a number of other California tribes.

Today, Shasta people live with the Klamath and Karuk people on the Quartz Valley Rancheria in Siskiyou County, California. In order to keep their traditions alive, the reservation runs a five-day culture camp each summer, during which children learn the ways of their ancestors. Traditional food preparation, beading, drum-making, and dancing are among the activities.

TOLOWA

(toh-LAW-wah)

LANGUAGE GROUP:
Athabascan

GREETING:
Dv-laa-ha~

THANK YOU:
Shu'-'aa-shii-nin-la

LOCATION PRECONTACT:
California

LOCATION TODAY:
California

The Tolowa live together, or with members of other tribes, on rancherias such as Elk Valley, near Crescent City, California. Their traditional homelands were much larger, covering a coastal stretch of northern California and southern Oregon. Dense redwood forests and the ocean supplied the tribe with many resources. For much of the year, the Tolowa lived in eight coastal villages. Men hunted sea lions in dugout canoes up to 42 feet (13 m) long. The first sea lion hunt of the year took place in late summer and was an important occasion. Men from each village gathered to start the hunt together. At different times of the year, the Tolowa traveled inland to fish for salmon in the Smith River and to gather acorns.

Men and women lived separately in Tolowa villages. The tribe built redwood or cedar plank homes for the women and children, while adult men and ➡️

LOREN ME'-LASH-NE BOMMELYN

In recent years, Loren Bommelyn has done much to keep Tolowa tradition alive, and to ensure that the tribe's history, crafts, dancing traditions, and language do not disappear with the passing of elders. Learning directly from them, Bommelyn immersed himself in tribal heritage to learn songs, basketmaking, dances, and stories. After graduating from the University of Oregon, he worked with Tolowa Dee-ni' speakers, and helped to develop an alphabet for writing the language. Bommelyn dances, sings, and hosts ceremonies for the Tolowa and, in 2012, the National Endowment for the Arts awarded him with a National Heritage Fellowship, which honors the work of master folk and traditional artists.

279

THE ALCATRAZ TAKEOVER

The Alcatraz prison, on an island in San Francisco Bay, closed in 1963. Six years later, on November 20, 1969, a group of Native American college students (some of them are pictured here) took it over. Calling themselves the Indians of All Tribes, they wanted to repurpose the abandoned buildings as a way to reclaim abandoned federal lands for Native peoples. They also wanted to focus attention on California's unratified treaties, tribal rights, and loss of tribal land. The federal government tried to end the protest, but a sympathetic public sent supplies to the island. That Thanksgiving, there were 400 protestors on the island. In June 1970, President Nixon ended the U.S. tribal "termination" policy and the protestors started to leave. On June 10, 1971, police removed the last 15 people from the island.

teenage boys slept in the village sweathouse. There was much emphasis on spiritual wealth in Tolowa society, which was earned through being a good person.

White settlers began moving onto Tolowa lands in 1850. They brought disease and conflict, and within 50 years, the Tolowa population fell by thousands. Some survivors moved to the Hupa and Siletz Reservations. The Tolowa adopted the Ghost Dance, a ritual among many tribes, through which they hoped to invoke the spirits of their ancestors to bring about the disappearance of the settlers. Some later turned to the Indian Shaker Church—a movement that combined Christianity with Native tradition—to regain some sense of tribal identity and spirit. In 1906, the government passed the Landless California Indians Act, through which it purchased small areas of land for non-reservation Native Americans, including the Tolowa. In 1960, the tribe lost their federal status, after which their lands were allotted to individuals. Following a court case against the government, the Tolowa regained their status in 1983 and continue to revive their language and protect their lands. ✐

The Tolowa use an ancient method to fish for smelts in the ocean surf. Their traditional A-frame nets trap the little fish in the "belly" of the net as the front of the net is raised out of the water. Once caught, the fish are laid out in rows on the beach to dry.

WAILAKI

(why-LAH-kee)

LANGUAGE GROUP:
Athabascan

GREETING:
En-ch'ong

THANK YOU:
Nshong-shaa-nul-la

LOCATION PRECONTACT:
California

LOCATION TODAY:
California

Northern California has been home to the Wailaki for many generations. Traditionally, the tribe lived in about 95 villages along the coast and on the banks of the Eel River. The Pacific Ocean provided plentiful shellfish and seaweed, while the river provided salmon, eels, and trout. The Wailaki moved with the seasons to hunt deer and elk, and to harvest berries, nuts, and camas root. In the winter, they lived in circular homes—wooden or bark-covered houses shared by two or more families. Inside, people bundled up under hide or rabbit-skin blankets.

Everyone in the village shared the chores, and children learned many skills at a young age: Girls learned cooking and basket weaving, while boys trained in hunting and fishing. When they were not working, the Wailaki enjoyed feasts, games, storytelling, and ceremonies. The people ran competitions—boys and girls raced each other and played jump rope, while men competed in archery and spear-throwing games. The women played a game with seashells or flat wooden dice.

In the early 1800s, Wailaki land was taken by the Spanish for missions. In the 1850s, white settlers brought deadly diseases that devastated the Wailaki population. They used tribal gathering lands for farming and grazing their cattle, and pushed the Wailaki from their hunting grounds. In 1858, along with a number of other tribes, the Wailaki rebelled against the U.S. government and fought in what became known as the Bald Hills War. By 1863, the U.S. Army defeated the rebel tribes and forced the people to move to reservations.

Today, the Wailaki live on the Round Valley and other shared reservations. The last fluent native Wailaki speaker died in the 1960s, but the tribe is currently working to revive its language. Since 2014, students at the Round Valley High School can learn Wailaki as part of their core curriculum. ☛

💡 IN THE KNOW

Wailaki healers used as many as 90 different plants in their work. For example, they used lichen to dry up oozing sores, wormwood to treat a stomachache, and elderberry blossoms to calm a fever, and they made a cough syrup from mountain balm.

This 1920s photograph of a Wailaki man wrapped in an animal pelt formed part of Edward S. Curtis's huge catalog of Native portraits.

Hundreds of little clam shells and tiny red, blue, and black seed beads were strung onto thread to make this Wailaki necklace. It is at least 100 years old.

WASHOE

(WAH-show)

LANGUAGE GROUP:
Isolate

GREETING:
Mi·li·gi iŋaw waʔ di hamu aŋawi

THANK YOU:
Not available

LOCATION PRECONTACT:
California

LOCATION TODAY:
California, Nevada

The Washoe homelands once included more than 2.5 million acres (one million ha) of land around Lake Tahoe, running east into Nevada and west into California. This position put the Washoe between the Great Basin region, a dry area, and the forests of California. The tribe lived in different areas but came together for hunts and ceremonies throughout the seasons. In the spring, the Washoe gathered at Lake Tahoe to socialize, play games, and welcome new plant and animal life. The summer brought plentiful fish, which the tribe caught, dried, and smoked. Family groups set up summer camps along nearby rivers where they could fish and gather food. In the fall, the Washoe came together again for the pine nut harvest and ceremony. In winter, families depended on the food they caught or gathered in the warmer months. Storytelling was an important part of life during the quieter winter months, and because knowledge was passed down from generation to generation through the stories that were told.

The discovery of gold in 1848 sparked a large migration of settlers, traders, miners, and merchants from the East to the West. In the following years, some settlers made their homes on Washoe tribal lands. They cleared the pine groves and their cattle grazed on tribal gathering lands. Lake Tahoe and the surrounding rivers were overfished, leaving the Washoe with even less to eat. The Washoe fought back when they could, but in order to survive, many Washoe people started working for ranchers or other settlers. The Washoe eventually settled on the Reno-Sparks Indian Colony Reservation in Nevada, established in 1917, and on small parcels of their ancestral land in California. Like their ancestors, the Washoe people continue to celebrate many traditions throughout the year, including the Pine Nut Festival in August, a three-day event celebrating tribal culture past and present. Events include a cradleboard competition, a tug-of-war, a handgame contest, and a powwow. 🖋

LOUISA KEYSER

Lousia Keyser was a Washoe whose birth name, Dabuda, means "Young Willow." She was also known as Dat so la lee. In keeping with tradition, Louisa learned basketry at a young age. In her lifetime, she made almost 300 stunning, coiled baskets from willow and decorated them with bracken fern and red branches. The traditional *degikup* were useful for holding food, but the Washoe also gave them as gifts during ceremonies. Louisa Keyser's expertly made baskets are now valuable art pieces in museums.

Cave Rock, on the southeastern shore of Lake Tahoe, is known to the Washoe tribe as De'ek wadapush or Standing Gray Rock. It is a sacred place for the Washoe. Once popular with rock climbers, the rock was made off-limits in recent years in order to preserve it.

THE LAST YAHI

The Yahi were a band of southern Yana people who lived along the upper Sacramento River. From the mid-1840s, settlers started living on Yana land, at which time there were about 1,900 Yana altogether. By 1884, following a series of massacres, there were just 35. From 1860 to 1911, one Yahi man hid in the southern Cascade Mountains. After being found, the man (pictured here) ended up at the University of California Museum of Anthropology. The anthropologist Alfred Kroeber named him Ishi, which means "man" in Yana. Ishi was the last survivor of the Yahi tribe. He lived at the university, where he learned English so that he could tell his stories and teach the ways of his culture. At the same time, Ishi was like a living exhibit, because people went to the university to watch him make arrows and perform other traditional tasks. Ishi died in 1916, but in this short time, scientists learned a lot from him about this lost tribe.

WINTUN

(win-TOON)

LANGUAGE GROUP:
Penutian

GREETING:
Hestum

THANK YOU:
Chalaa besken

LOCATION PRECONTACT:
California

LOCATION TODAY:
California

The Wintun, along with their close relatives, the Nomlaki and Patwin, lived in the areas surrounding the Sacramento River—including the river valley, its tributaries, and nearby mountains. Here, the tribe lived in several communities, some with as many as 150 members. Several families shared each Wintun home, which was a round, partially underground shelter that people entered through a hole in the roof. The hole also allowed smoke to escape from the central fire pit inside the home.

Like most California tribes, the Wintun depended on hunting, fishing, and gathering food. Sometimes, men hunted together, using dogs to help drive deer toward a trap or a cliff. Wintun hunters caught brown bears in a similar way, but avoided grizzly bears—animals they feared. The Wintun fished for salmon and trout in the rivers, and women gathered plants. Entire families, including children, helped collect acorns at harvest time. The men shook the trees using sticks or by climbing into the branches, while the women and children picked up the acorns that fell. Acorn soup and bread remain favorite recipes of the tribe to this day. The Wintun were social people and often held feasts and dances, especially after a good harvest. They also traded with the Shasta and other tribes to the north, and exchanged deer hides for dentalia shells and other items. The Russians, who met the Wintun in the early 1800s, traded with them, while the Spanish forced some Wintun people ➤

Marshall McKay (left) is the former chairman and CEO of the Yocha Dehe Wintun Nation. He is dedicated to reviving tribal culture through stories, art, and language. Here, he reads during a visit to the Yocha Dehe preparatory school in Sacramento, California.

into the mission system. Early fur traders brought malaria to the tribe, wiping out much of the population.

The gold rush of 1848 brought settlers and miners into Wintun territory. Wanting to drive the Natives from their land, settlers once poisoned the food they gave to the Wintun, killing over 100 people. Miners burned a Wintun village, killing approximately 300 more. More conflicts followed, and many Wintun people were forced onto reservations. Today, the Wintun live in several communities in California, including the Yocha Dehe Wintun Nation, the Cortina Indian Rancheria, and the Colusa Rancheria. In 2001, the Wintun people were featured in the documentary *In the Light of Reverence*. The film includes Wintun, Hopi, and Lakota elders talking about the spiritual meaning of sacred places such as Mount Shasta in northern California. ✐

The Yocha Dehe Wintun Nation operate a 1,400-acre (570-ha) farm, on which the tribe produces wine, olive oil, and honey, and manages up to 16 crops. Some of the farmland is certified organic.

🔆 IN THE KNOW

Instead of making boats or canoes, the Wintun people built log rafts for crossing streams. The women shredded iris plant fibers, which the men then used to make cords for tying the logs to one another. Supplies—and sometimes children—were placed in large baskets that were then tied to a raft for transporting across a stream.

WIYOT

(WEE-yot)

LANGUAGE GROUP:
Algonquian

GREETING:
He-ba-lo

THANK YOU:
Hou'!

LOCATION PRECONTACT:
California

LOCATION TODAY:
California

The Wiyot have lived in their northern Californian homelands for centuries. Traditionally, they built their villages around Humboldt Bay and near the Eel and Mad Rivers, where plentiful fish, game, and plants were available. Although the Wiyot lived close to the ocean and ate some seafood, they relied more on inland resources. They fished for salmon and hunted deer, elk, and rabbit. As well as providing meat, the animals' hides were useful for clothing, their fur for warm blankets, and their bones for tools. Tribal beliefs banned the eating of the fox, wolf, bear, and skunk, so hunters avoided these animals. Women made baskets and skirts from plant fibers and redwood forests provided lumber for houses and dugout canoes.

The rich and beautiful Wiyot land was very appealing to the settlers who arrived during the gold rush. In 1860, the Wiyot lost their sacred Indian Island in Humboldt Bay to white settlers. During the night of February 26, settlers rowed over to the island and killed at least 100 Wiyot, most of them women, children, and elders. Inland, settlers attacked Wiyot villages on the same night, killing 100 more people. The Wiyot who survived the Indian Island massacre suffered starvation, poverty, and disease. By 1862, the U.S. government had forced the surviving Wiyot people onto reservations. Almost a century later, the government withdrew the Wiyot's legal status, and did not reinstate it for 20 years.

Members of the Wiyot tribe paddle a dugout redwood canoe across Humboldt Bay. In the background is Indian Island, currently in the process of being returned to the Wiyot tribe.

WILDERNESS FIREFIGHTERS

Wildfires are a hazard in California's hot, dry climate, and groups of specially trained firefighters help to combat them. The Hotshots are crews of 20 people that respond to fires in remote areas. California Hotshots include many tribal members from across the state. The U.S. Forest Service also works with tribes, including the Karuk and Hupa, among many others, on fire management and prevention. The agency has tapped into traditional methods, such as controlled fires and thinning forest canopies. Controlled fires help to prevent larger fires and encourage new plants to grow. Thinning the trees—that is, removing whole trees or several branches from the more dense trees—allows rain to come through and keep the ground from drying out.

Today, many Wiyot live off the reservations, but join together for Wiyot Days ceremonies in which ancient traditions, such as the Brush Dance and the Stick Game, are revived. Language and other cultural programs are held to help link the tribe's younger members with their past. In 2014, the Wiyot people held the World Renewal ceremony at Tuluwat on Indian Island for the first time since the massacre of 1860. ☞

This bear mask was made in 1990 by Native American artist Rick Bartow (1946–2016), a member of the Mad River Band of the Wiyot tribe. Made of wood, the mask is decorated with traditional materials, including horsehair, glass beads, shells, animal bone, and raffia.

YOKUT

(YOH-cut)

LANGUAGE GROUP:
Penutian

GREETING:
Mun'ahoo (Chukchansi)

THANK YOU:
Mech gayis (Chukchansi)

LOCATION PRECONTACT:
California

LOCATION TODAY:
California

As many as 50,000 Yokut are estimated once to have lived across the San Joaquin Valley and the Sierra Nevada foothills in central California. Their territory was vast, and the tribe spread into three major groups: the Northern Valley Yokut, Southern Valley Yokut, and Foothill Yokut. At least 60 bands made up these groups, each with its own name, language, and territory. Each area provided different resources that bands could trade with one another. For example, the Northern Valley Yokut had better access to salmon and acorns than their southern relatives did. The Yokut also traded with other tribes to get what they needed, or traveled to find it.

The Yokut lived in permanent villages, but made summer fishing and gathering trips. Their winter homes were made from the materials that were available in their different territories. Northern Yokut people used bark or grass for their houses, while the Southern Valley Yokut built homes made from poles covered in tule mats. Some Foothill Yokut lived in earthen lodges, homes built partly underground. All Yokut tribes shared a belief in spiritual guides represented by animals, such as the Eagle, Cougar, or Bear. The Yokut believed these guides gave them knowledge and strength. When a baby was born, he or she became connected with his or her family guide. Similar to the traditions of many California tribes, the Yokut tattooed girls' chins when they became adults; some Yokut men had tattoos, as well.

From the late 1700s, the Northern Valley Yokut suffered terribly under the Spanish mission system, and then under Mexican rule. Deadly diseases affected them and other groups of Yokut. From 1850, waves of settlers arrived in the San Joaquin Valley, and pushed the Yokut from their lands. The U.S. government moved the Yokut people to a number of different reservations. Today, descendants of several Yokut tribes—including the Choinumni, Tachi, Chukchansi, and Wukchumni—live in various California communities.

Yokut women made large, flat basket trays (t'aiwan) on which they played games of dice. The eight dice (huech) were halved walnut shells that were studded with pieces of seashell for the spots. Women used both hands to scatter the dice across the tray.

Two Yokut women build a house around 1930. Having first made a willow-pole frame, they are now attaching flexible bulrush mats to the exterior.

IN THE KNOW

The Painted Rock site, on the Tule River Reservation, contains pictographs that include a painting of a "Bigfoot" family of tall, hairy people. The paintings, which relate to a Yokut creation story, are 500 to 1,000 years old.

YUROK

CALIFORNIA

(YOOR-ock)

LANGUAGE GROUP:
Algonquian

GREETING:
Hoyeee

THANK YOU:
Wokhlew

LOCATION PRECONTACT:
California

LOCATION TODAY:
California

The Yurok tribe has the largest Native population in California, and many of today's tribal members live on the Yurok Reservation, along a 44-mile (71-km) stretch of the Klamath River. This is their ancestral land. Originally, the Yurok lived in 50 villages along the Klamath River and the northern coast. They built village homes and dugout canoes from redwood, the large tree growing in the forests nearby. When they went out gathering in the summer, they also made simple brush huts in which to shelter. In Yurok society, the wealthiest man was often the leader, and he was responsible for hosting ceremonies. The White Deerskin Dance, an important ritual held before the First Salmon Ceremony in April, guarded the tribe's health and called for an ample supply of game and fish. The Yurok generally had friendly relationships with their neighbors. Tribes met to trade, play games, and socialize with one another.

In 1828, the explorer Jedediah Smith and his group of trappers met the Yurok. The reports of Smith's travels began a movement of settlers to the West. However, it was the gold rush that ignited the major wave of migration, during which many prospectors, miners, and settlers ended up in Yurok territory. At first, the Yurok were helpful and welcoming, but conflicts erupted within a short time as the newcomers took over Yurok land and introduced devastating diseases. The tribe lost three-quarters of its population to war, disease, and starvation.

After the U.S. government forced the Yurok onto reservations, the tribe worked for years to regain some of what it had lost. They have had major successes, including

CHE-NA-WAH-WEITCH-AH-WAH

Lucy Thompson, a member of the Yurok tribe, was born Che-na-wah-Weitch-ah-wah in Pec-Wan Village on the Klamath River in 1856. Later, she married Milton J. Thompson, which is when she took the name Lucy. In 1916, the year that this photo was taken, Lucy wrote *To the American Indian: Reminiscences of a Yurok Woman*, a book of the stories of her people. The book was given the American Book Award many years later, in 1992.

the Klamath Basin Restoration Agreement (2010), which will remove dams on the river and help restore the salmon population. Whether they live on or off the reservation, the Yurok teach their language and celebrate their culture. Today, visitors to the Yurok Reservation can experience traditional ceremonies and storytelling, see exhibits of Yurok baskets and jewelry, and hike through forests of towering redwoods. ✒

Fishermen clean their net while fishing for sturgeon in the Klamath River. Along with the salmon, the sturgeon has been a staple of the Yurok diet for thousands of years.

THE RABBIT AND THE FROG

A long, long time ago there was a rabbit and he made his warren, which is like a hole in the ground. He made it for the wintertime. It was getting cold outside. The rabbit had all his food prepared. He had the walls all padded with leaves and rabbit hair. Rabbit was going to be comfortable throughout the winter.

So Rabbit closed his door. He was getting ready to go to sleep, but he could hear something. The wind was blowing outside. But with it, he heard a low rumble. "What was that?" Rabbit thought. He heard the rumble again. It sounded like a croak. He listened hard and heard it once more, but this time he heard a knock at his door.

Rabbit said, "Who is this?"

The voice replied, "The frog."

"What do you want?" said Rabbit.

"Please let me in," said Frog.

"Get out of here," Rabbit said to him. "Leave me alone. Go back into your pond; that's where you belong."

So Frog went away.

The wind kept blowing and Rabbit again got ready to go to sleep, when he heard the rumbling croak of Frog again.

"Let me in," said Frog.

The Rabbit said, "What do you want?"

"Let me in," Frog said again.

"No, get out of here," Rabbit said.

So Frog went away.

But he came back a third time, and Rabbit heard Frog's rumbling croak again.

"It's cold. Let me in," Frog said.

And the Rabbit thought, "Oh my gosh. He's going to keep me up all wintertime." So Rabbit opened the door and told Frog that he could come in, but that he had to stay in a corner. "Don't you bother me," Rabbit said. "Don't make any noise." Then Rabbit started to get ready to go to sleep.

But Frog started to croak louder and louder. With each croak he grew bigger and bigger. Rabbit said, "Stop it." But

The rabbit is an important animal for California tribal people, having provided meat and fur for many centuries. This story hints at the way in which white settlers encroached on Native territory and on the Natives' access to this resource.

Frog would not stop. He just croaked and grew bigger until Rabbit was pressed against a wall. Frog was so big.

Rabbit said, "Get out of here. There's not enough room for both of us."

"No. You go!" Frog croaked.

So Rabbit had to leave his house because he let Frog in. What is the moral to this story? Be careful who you invite into your territory.

**Stanley Rodriguez,
Iipay Nation of Santa Ysabel**

GLOSSARY

This young Ojibwe girl plays a traditionally made birchbark drum covered with rawhide.

Adobe A mixture of clay, water, and straw made into bricks that are dried in the sun and used for building.

American Revolutionary War (1775–1783) Also known as the American War of Independence, a conflict between Great Britain and its 13 colonies, which declared independence as the United States of America.

Amulet A small object worn for good luck and protection against illness or danger.

Ancestral lands The lands on which American Indian tribes lived before contact with Europeans in the 1500s.

Archipelago A group of small islands in a large body of water.

Awl A small pointed hand tool used for making holes, especially in leather.

Baleen whale A toothless whale with baleen, a flexible, horny material, hanging from its upper jaw; baleen filters food from seawater.

Band A division of a tribe consisting of a group of people who share a common land and culture; one tribe may have several bands.

Boarding school: A private school where students live.

Brush shelter A simple, temporary structure made from nearby materials such as branches and plants; Native people built brush shelters on hunting and fishing trips.

Bypass A road or route passing around a town or village rather than through it.

Calumet A tobacco pipe, smoked and shared during ceremonies.

Captivity Being kept in a prison or other place and not able to leave or be free.

Catholicism The religion of the Roman Catholic Church.

Cede To give control of something, such as land, to another group, such as the government.

Clan A group of people, usually a family.

Colonization Settling and taking control of a place and its indigenous people.

Colonization period The time from 1607 to 1783, during which Europeans settled in what is now the United States.

Confederacy A group of people or states that join together for a political purpose.

Confluence The point at which two rivers or streams meet and become one.

Conquistador The name given to a Spanish soldier and explorer in the 1500s, who conquered, or took control of, American Indian civilizations.

Decimate To destroy a large number or part of something.

Decoy Someone or something used to distract attention or lead to a trap.

Delta An area of low, flat wetland formed when a river empties into other rivers, lakes, or the ocean.

Dentalia Tusk shells used as currency among some American Indian tribes.

Dialect A variation of a language used in a certain area or by a certain group of people.

Diorama A three-dimensional model depicting a scene or event.

Discrimination The unfair or different treatment of a person or people based on the group to which they belong.

Dormant In language, a tongue no longer spoken but still associated with an ethnic group.

Dry farming A method of growing crops without irrigation, using plants that need little rain and conserving existing moisture in the soil.

Effigy A model of a disliked person, made in order to be destroyed as a protest.

Encroachment Gradually moving into an area or taking control of something that belongs to someone or something else.

Epidemic An outbreak of a disease that spreads quickly and affects many people.

Erosion The gradual wearing away of a substance, such as rock, due to natural forces such as water or wind.

Fast, fasting The practice of eating little or no food for a given period of time.

Federal recognition The term used to describe the giving of official status by the United States government, under which land and other rights are protected.

Fertile Land that is able to produce and sustain crops.

Fishing camp A temporary living place for people on summer fishing trips.

Fishing rights For American Indians, the legal right to fish in traditional or ancestral fishing locations.

Flood plain A low, flat area along a river or stream likely to flood.

Forage To search for food or other needs in the wild; food for animals such as cattle.

Forebear An ancestor or member of a family in the past.

Fort A strong, protected building where soldiers live.

Game Animals that are hunted.

Grant A sum of money given by a government or other organization for a particular purpose.

Harvest Gathered and collected plants, such as crops, or animals.

Hereditary Passed down from parents to children.

Hide The skin of an animal.

Hierarchy A system in which people or things are placed at different levels of importance.

Homesteader A person who lives on, and farms, an area of government land in order to own it.

Indian agent A person representing the U.S. government to deal with tribes, especially on reservations.

Inherit To receive something, such as money, from someone who dies.

Interest As in "pay back with interest," an additional amount of money paid on top of a borrowed amount.

Invoke To refer to something or someone, or make use of something, such as a law.

Isolate language A language with no relationship or similarity to another language.

Land claim A legal appeal by a group to recover land promised by treaty or taken away illegally.

Legal status The position of a person or group—their powers, rights, and restrictions—according to the laws of the country in which they live.

Longhouse A long, often large, building used as a traditional home for several people, including by tribes belonging to the Iroquois League.

Medicine bundle A wrapped package of items, such as herbs, used in religious or healing rituals.

Mission A religious, and sometimes military, place or building established by a particular religious group in a country not their own.

Moccasin A flat, soft shoe or slipper made from animal skin.

Mortuary pole Traditionally, a carved pole in which the ashes of a deceased person are placed.

Nation A group of people who share a common history, tradition, language, and government.

Native Village In Alaska, a term used for a reservation or area of land assigned to a tribe of the region.

Negotiate To discuss in order to reach an agreement.

Nomadic Not living in a permanent place; moving from place to place.

Northwest Passage A sea route through the Arctic from the Atlantic Ocean to the Pacific Ocean.

Oblige To force someone to do something, or make them promise to do something.

Palisade A high, wooden fence of pointed stakes.

Paraphernalia The equipment needed for a particular activity.

Parcel of land An area of land that is owned or claimed.

Patriot army The military group that fought against Britain in the American Revolutionary War.

Peninsula A piece of land almost completely surrounded by water but attached to a larger piece of land.

Petroglyph A carving or drawing on a rock.

Pictograph An image that represents an idea or word.

Haida tribal members row a canoe decorated with typical Northwest Coast motifs.

A Sioux man rides across the Pine Ridge Indian Reservation, South Dakota.

Plateau A large, flat area of land higher than the surrounding land.

Potlatch A feast common to tribes of the Northwest Coast, in which it is customary for the host to give gifts to guests.

Prohibit To not allow someone to do something.

GLOSSARY

Prospector A person who searches or mines for precious metals, such as gold.

Raiding party A small military group of people that attacks another group, especially to take prisoners or goods.

Rancheria A small area set aside as tribal land in California.

Ratify To make official by giving formal, usually signed, approval.

Regalia Special clothes and decorations for ceremonies.

Reinstate To return a position, such as a tribal status, that was taken away.

Reparation Something done, given, or paid to make up for damages, injuries, or mistakes made in the past.

Reservation In the United States, an area of land set aside for the use of an American Indian tribe.

Reserve In Canada, an area of land set aside for the use of a First Nation group.

Resin A sticky substance produced from plants or trees used to make other products.

River basin An area of land from which water flows into a river.

Roach A hairpiece made from dyed porcupine or deer hair.

Russian Orthodox A religion founded in Russia.

Seminomadic Having a permanent home for some part of the year as well as moving to temporary camps, usually to hunt, fish, or harvest food.

Shaman A person or religious leader believed to have special powers, especially for healing.

Snare A trap used to capture animals.

Sovereignty A nation's right to govern itself.

Subarctic region The cold-climate area south of the Arctic Circle, including Alaska and northern Canada.

Superfund program A U.S. government program for cleaning polluted land sites.

Sustainable When a source is able to be used without destroying or using it up.

Sustenance Something that keeps someone or something alive, e.g. food.

Tepee A portable, cone-shaped tent; traditionally made from wooden poles and deer hide.

Termination In American–Indian relations, a U.S. government policy that removed official recognition of many tribal nations and their rights to land, aid, and self-government.

Toboggan A long, flat, narrow sled with a curved front, traditionally made of wood.

Trapper A person who captures wild animals for fur.

Travois A sled made from two poles and netting that is placed on dogs to transport loads.

Trawl To catch fish by dragging a large net through the water.

Treaty: A written contract made between two or more groups.

Tribal society A large community of people following the organization, culture, and traditions of tribes.

Tribal status The official position of a tribe assigned and recognized by the federal government.

Tribe A community of one or several family groups who share a common culture.

Tributary A stream that flows into a larger stream or river.

Tule A large grass-like plant found in marshes, also known as bulrush, and dried when used for weaving.

Tumpline A strap or sling passed across the forehead or chest and attached to loads carried on the back.

Vagrant A person who has no job or place to live.

Wampum Small cylindrical beads made from shells and strung together. They were worn as decoration or used as money.

Wampum belt A sash made from shell beads woven into patterns. Such belts were used to record treaties or agreements and American Indian law.

Watershed An area of land that includes an entire river system.

Western expansion The name given to the period during the 1800s when the United States acquired and settled the land west of the Mississippi River to the Pacific Ocean.

Wigwam or wickiup A traditional hut made from a curved, wooden frame covered with mats, hides, or other materials.

These young Inuits from Barrow, Alaska, are dressed in ceremonial parkas.

FEDERALLY RECOGNIZED TRIBES

The tribes profiled in this book are among the 573 Native American tribes federally recognized by the Bureau of Indian Affairs (BIA; https://www.bia.gov) of the United States, as well as those among the more than 600 recognized Inuit and First Nations governments in Canada (http://fnp-ppn.aandc-aadnc.gc.ca/fnp/Main/Search/SearchFN.aspx?lang=eng).

The Arctic and Subarctic
Ahtna
Aleut
Alutiit
Cree
Dena'ina
Eyak
Gwich'in
Holikachuk
Iglulit
Innu
Inupiat
Inuvialuit
James Bay Cree
Oji-Cree
Yup'ik

The Northeast
Cayuga
Kickapoo
Maliseet
Menominee
Micmac
Mohawk
Mohegan
Narragansett
Ojibwe
Oneida
Onondaga
Ottawa
Passamaquoddy
Penobscot

Pequot
Potawatomi
Powhatan
Seneca
Shinnecock
Tuscarora
Wampanoag

The Southeast
Biloxi
Catawba
Cherokee
Chitimacha
Choctaw
Coushatta
Creek
Miccosukee
Seminole
Tunica

The Plains
Alabama
Arapaho
Arikara
Assiniboine
Blackfeet
Caddo
Cheyenne
Chickasaw
Comanche
Crow
Delaware
Gros Ventre
Hidatsa
Ho-Chunk
Iowa
Kaw
Kiowa
Mandan
Miami
Modoc
Omaha
Osage
Otoe-Missouria
Pawnee

Peoria
Plains Cree
Ponca
Quapaw
Sac & Fox
Shawnee
Sioux
Tonkawa
Wichita
Wyandotte

The Southwest
Apache
Cocopah
Havasupai
Hopi
Hualapai
Maricopa
Mojave
Navajo
Pima
Pueblo
Quechan
Tigua
Tohono O'odham
Yaqui
Yavapai
Zuni

The Great Basin and Plateau
Bannock
Cayuse
Coeur d'Alene
Colville
Goshute
Klamath
Kootenai
Nez Perce
Paiute
Pend d'Oreille
Salish
Shoshone
Spokane
Umatilla
Ute

Walla Walla
Warm Springs
Yahooskin
Yakama

The Northwest Coast
Chehalis
Chinook
Coos, Umpqua, Siuslaw
Coquille
Cowlitz
Grand Ronde
Haida
Lummi
Makah
Muckleshoot
Puyallup
Quileute
Quinault
S'klallam
Skokomish
Snoqualmie
Squaxin Island
Stillaguamish
Suquamish
Swinomish
Tlingit

California
Cahto
Cahuilla
Chemehuevi
Chumash
Cupeño
Hupa
Karuk
Kumeyaay
Luiseño
Maidu
Mattole
Miwok
Mono
Pit River
Pomo
Round Valley
Serrano
Shasta
Tolowa
Wailaki
Washoe
Wintun
Wiyot
Yokut
Yurok

RESERVATION AND RESERVE LANDS

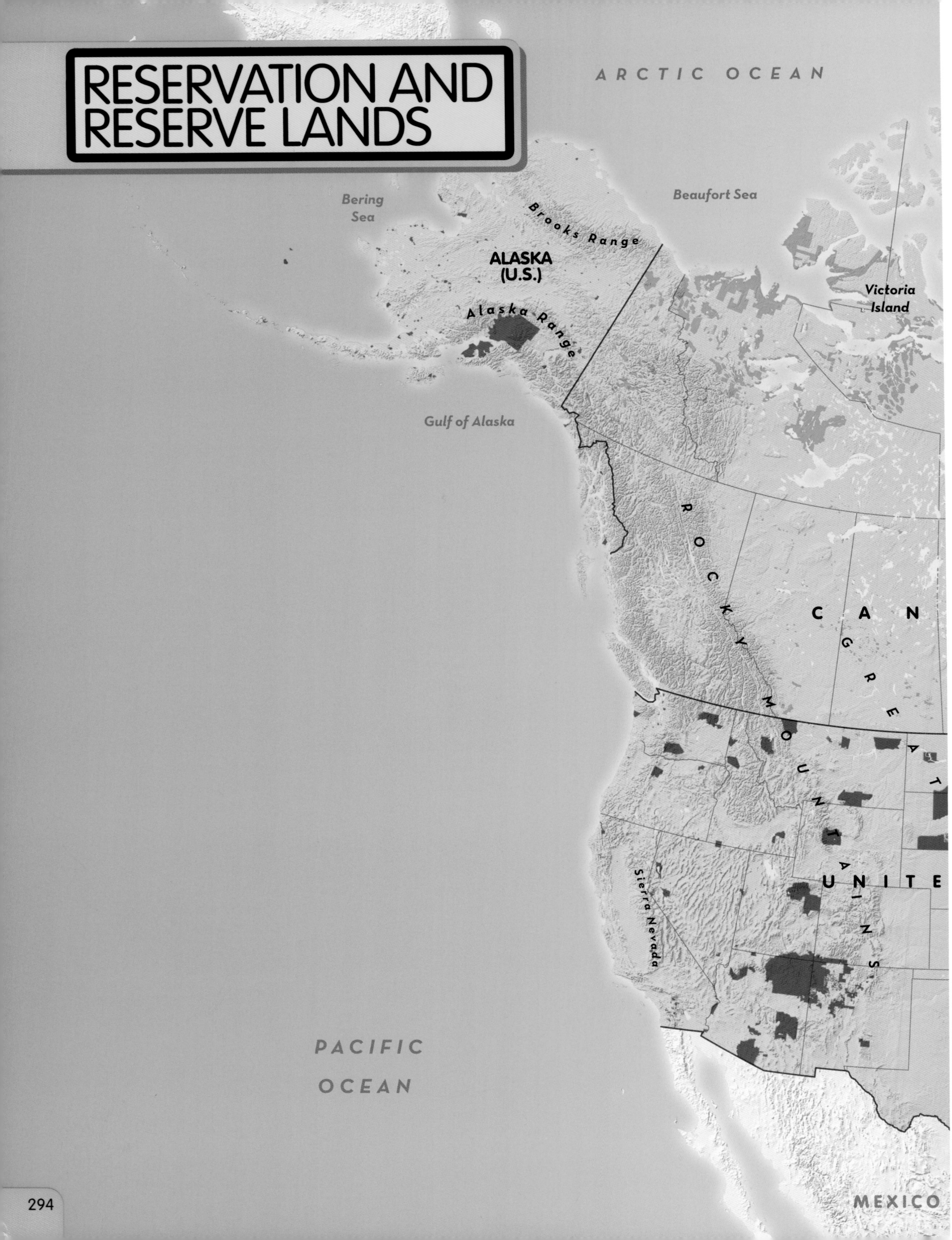

ARCTIC OCEAN

Bering
Sea

Beaufort Sea

Brooks Range

**ALASKA
(U.S.)**

Victoria
Island

Alaska Range

Gulf of Alaska

R
O
C
K
Y

C
A
N

G
R
E
A
T

M
O
U
N
T
A
I
N
S

U
N
I
T
E

Sierra Nevada

PACIFIC

OCEAN

MEXICO

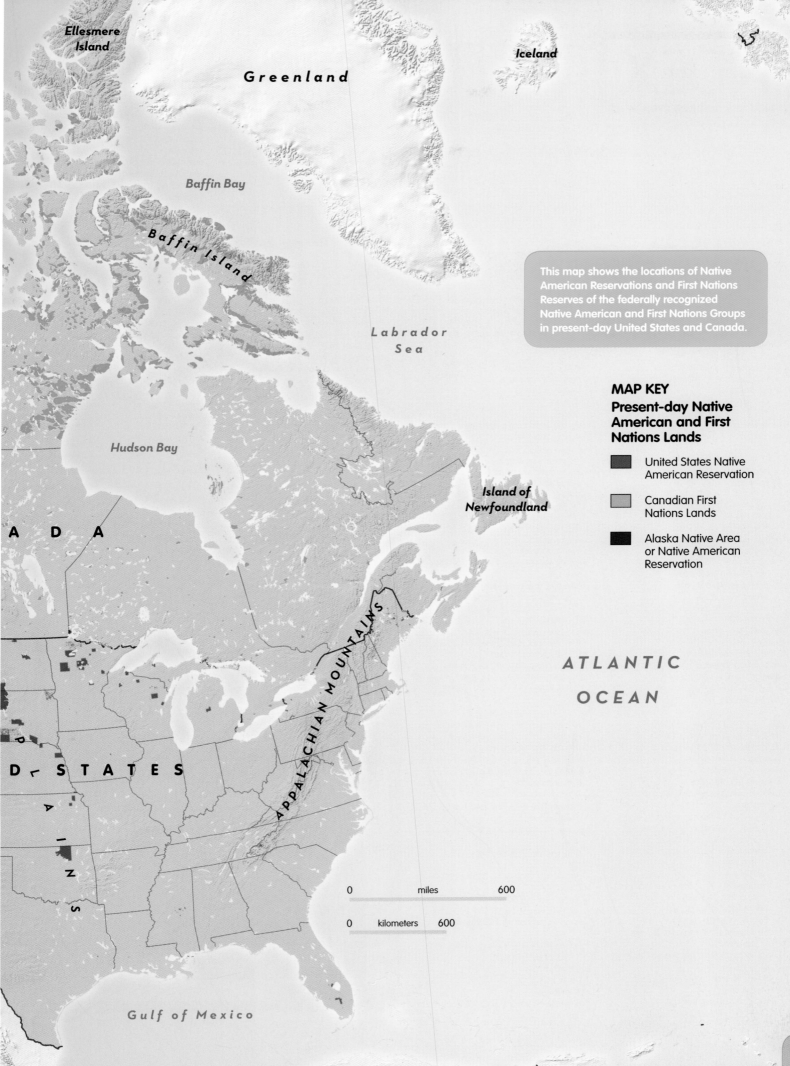

Ellesmere
Island

Greenland

Iceland

Baffin Bay

Baffin Island

Labrador
Sea

Hudson Bay

Island of
Newfoundland

This map shows the locations of Native
American Reservations and First Nations
Reserves of the federally recognized
Native American and First Nations Groups
in present-day United States and Canada.

MAP KEY
**Present-day Native
American and First
Nations Lands**

United States Native
American Reservation

Canadian First
Nations Lands

Alaska Native Area
or Native American
Reservation

A   D   A

ATLANTIC

OCEAN

D   STATES

APPALACHIAN MOUNTAINS

P

A

I

N

S

0   miles   600

0   kilometers   600

Gulf of Mexico

INDEX

Page numbers in **bold** indicate the main page reference for a specific tribe; page numbers in *italic* refer to illustrations.

This Ojibwe man's tunic is decorated with beaded floral patterns and tassels.

This feather bustle is worn by a man taking part in an Oji-Cree powwow.

Birdlike motifs are typical of totem poles carved by members of First Nation tribes.

A Zuni tribal member is dressed for a powwow. He wears a roach and beaded jewelry.

INDEX

Chumash elder Mati Waiya performs a riverside purification, cleansing, and blessing ceremony.

CONSULTANTS

Herman J. Viola, Ph.D., curator emeritus with the National Museum of the American Indian at the Smithsonian Institution, Washington, D.C., and an adopted member of the Crow Nation, is an authority on American Indian history and culture and on the exploration of the American West. His many books include *Warriors in Uniform: The Legacy of American Indian Heroism; Little Bighorn Remembered: The Untold Indian Story of Custer's Last Stand; Warrior Artists: Historic Cheyenne and Kiowa Indian Ledger Art Drawn by Making Medicine and Zotom;* and *It Is a Good Day to Die: Indian Eye Witnesses Tell the Story of the Battle of the Little Bighorn.*

Mert Martens, Ph.D., is an education and social studies curriculum consultant. A social studies teacher for more than 30 years, she is the past president of the National Social Studies Supervisors Association, and a Fulbright Fellow. A graduate of the University of Oklahoma and Oklahoma State University, she is currently active in many state and national education initiatives.

ARCTIC AND SUBARCTIC TRIBES: William Fitzhugh
A former chair of the Department of Anthropology at the Smithsonian Institution's National Museum of Natural History, William Fitzhugh specializes in the peoples and cultures of the circumpolar Arctic, focusing on cross-cultural studies and culture change. He has published widely and organized numerous museum exhibitions on Arctic subjects, including Alaskan Eskimo culture and art, Vikings, and narwhals.

NORTHEAST AND SOUTHEAST TRIBES: Karenne Wood
Karenne Wood is a member of the Monacan Indian Nation and director of the award-winning Virginia Indian Heritage Program at the Virginia Foundation for the Humanities. She is a Ford Fellow in Anthropology at the University of Virginia and focuses on revitalizing indigenous languages and cultural practices. She has been a researcher with the Smithsonian Institution's National Museum of the American Indian and was appointed by the governor of Virginia to the Virginia Council on Indians.

PLAINS AND SOUTHWEST TRIBES: Theresa Lynn (Teri) Fraizer
A member of the Laguna, Hopi, and Chippewa tribes, Teri Fraizer is an award-winning classroom teacher and artist with a master's degree in secondary education and administration. She currently serves as the chief communications officer for McKinley County Schools in Gallup, New Mexico.

GREAT BASIN TRIBES: Catherine (Kay) Fowler
Professor emerita of anthropology at the University of Nevada–Reno, Catherine Fowler has spent her career helping to document and preserve the cultures of the indigenous peoples of the Great Basin. She is a research associate for the Nevada State Museum and the Smithsonian National Museum of Natural History, and an elected member of the U.S. National Academy of Sciences. She has served on the board of trustees for the National Museum of the American Indian.

PLATEAU TRIBES: Anton Treuer
Anton Treuer is professor of Ojibwe at Bemidji State University and author of 14 books. He has a B.A. from Princeton University and an M.A. and Ph.D. from the University of Minnesota. He is editor of the *Oshkaabewis* (pronounced o-shkaah-bay-wis) *Native Journal,* the only academic journal of the Ojibwe language.

NORTHWEST COAST TRIBES: Janine Ledford
Janine Ledford is the executive director of the Makah Cultural and Research Center, a position she has held since 1995. As the director, she oversees the Makah language program, the archives and library, the education department, and curation/exhibits. She is also the Makah tribal historic preservation officer and lives on the Makah Indian Reservation with her four children.

CALIFORNIA TRIBES: Terria Smith
Terria Smith is an enrolled tribal member of the Torres Martinez Desert Cahuilla Indians and is the director of Heyday's California Indian Publishing Program, known as the Berkeley Roundhouse. She is the editor of *News from Native California,* a quarterly magazine "devoted to the vibrant cultures, art, languages, histories, social-justice movements, and stories of California's diverse Indian peoples." She has a master's degree from the University of California Berkeley Graduate School of Journalism.

STORIES EXPERT: Dan SaSuWeh Jones, Ponca Nation
Former chairman of the Ponca Nation of Oklahoma, Dan Jones is an educator and transcriber of the Ponca Myth series (https://sasuweh.com/ponca-myth-series-2/). He was appointed by Oklahoma governor Brad Henry as the vice-chairman of the Oklahoma Indian Affairs Commission. He is a writer, bronze sculptor, and filmmaker, and as a member of the Producers Guild of America, he is active in promoting American Indians in all aspects of film and television.

PHOTO CREDITS

A Cheyenne woman wears silver jewelry set with large turquoise stones.

Museum of the American Indian, Smithsonian Institution (20/8105). Photo by NMAI Photo Services; 186 (LO), Marilyn Angel Wynn/GI; 187 (UP), Jamie Okuma; 187 (LO), LOC, Washington, D.C.; 188 (UP), WorldFoto/ASP; 188 (LO), National Museum of the American Indian, Smithsonian Institution (16/5430). Photo by NMAI Photo Services; 189, Gregory Johnston/SS; 190 (UP), Marilyn Angel Wynn/GI; 190 (LO), National Museum of the American Indian, Smithsonian Institution (26/4326); 191 (UP), Photo by Corbis/Corbis via GI; 191 (LO), Robert Fried/ASP; 192 (UP), Photo by Helen H. Richardson/The Denver Post via GI; 192 (LO), National Museum of the American Indian, Smithsonian Institution (1/2853). Photo by NMAI Photo Services; 193 (UP), National Museum of the American Indian, Smithsonian Institution (1/6681). Photo by NMAI Photo Services; 193 (LO), LOC, Washington, D.C.; 194 (UP), National Museum of the American Indian, Smithsonian Institution (10/7974). Photo by NMAI Photo Services; 194 (LO), LOC, Washington, D.C.; 195 (UP LE), Newberry Library, Chicago, Illinois, U.S.A./BI; 195 (UP RT), mariait/SS; 195 (LO), National Museum of the American Indian, Smithsonian Institution (9/1386). Photo by NMAI Photo Services; 196 (UP), LOC, Washington, D.C.; 196 (LO), NGIC/BI; 197 (UP), National Museum of the American Indian, Smithsonian Institution (14/2136). Photo by NMAI Photo Services; 197 (LO), Transcendental Graphics/GI; 198–199, Spirit Wolf Photography/Nancy Greifenhagen/ASP; 200 (UP), Michael Durham/Minden Pictures/ASP; 200 (LO), LOC, Washington, D.C.; 201 (UP), Universal History Archive/UIG/BI; 201 (LO), National Museum of the American Indian, Smithsonian Institution (14/3536). Photo by NMAI Photo Services; 202 (UP), National Museum of the American Indian, Smithsonian Institution (14/3541). Photo by NMAI Photo Services; 202 (LO), Marilyn Angel Wynn/GI; 203 (UP), Photo by Rudi Williams/American Press Service/U.S. Department of Defense; 203 (LO), Mark A. Wilson (Department of Geology/The College of Wooster)/Wikimedia Commons; 204 (UP), SuperStock/George Ostertag/ASP; 204 (LO), Danita Delimont/ASP; 205 (LE) National Museum of the American Indian, Smithsonian Institution (21/7902). Photo by NMAI Photo Services; 205 (RT), LOC, Washington, D.C.; 206 (UP), Look and Learn/Elgar Collection/BI; 206 (LO), Allison14/Dreamstime; 207 (UP), LOC, Washington, D.C.; 207 (LO), National Museum of the American Indian, Smithsonian Institution (10/8091). Photo by NMAI Photo Services; 208 (UP), National Museum of the American Indian, Smithsonian Institution (1048). Photo by NMAI Photo Services; 208 (LO), Marilyn Angel Wynn/GI; 209 (UP), National Museum of the American Indian, Smithsonian Institution (26/3995). Photo by NMAI Photo Services; 209 (CTR), National Museum of the American Indian, Smithsonian Institution (10/7583). Photo by NMAI Photo Services; 209 (LO), Brendan Smialowski/AFP/GI; 210, Andrew Mariman/Herald and News; 211 (UP), David Hiser/GI; 211 (LO), Superstock/GI; 212 (UP), Peter Kniez/SS; 212 (LO), Steve Collender/SS; 213, Craig Tuttle/GI;

NORTHWEST 214–215, Aurora Photos/ASP; 215 (UP), Joe West/SS; 216, National Museum of the American Indian, Smithsonian Institution (5/5049). Photo by NMAI Photo Services; 217, NG Maps; 218 (UP), Stephanie S. Cordle/AP/SS; 218 (UP CTR LE), Paul S. Wolf/SS; 218 (CTR RT), De Agostini Picture Library/BI; 218 (LO LE), Stephanie S. Cordle/AP/SS; 218 (LO RT), Private Collection/Photo Christie's Images/BI; 219 (UP), LOC, Washington, D.C.; 219 (CTR LE), Courtesy of the Everett Public Library; 219 (LO LE), Robert Cicchetti/SS; 219 (LO RT), MPI/GI; 220 (UP), Courtesy of the family of Hazel Pete/Curtis Du Puis; 220 (LO), Adam Cegledi/SS; 221 (UP), National Museum of the American Indian, Smithsonian Institution (26/2612). Photo by NMAI Photo Services; 221 (LO), Detroit Institute of Arts, USA/ BI; 222 (UP), Michael Wheatley/All Canada Photos/GI; 222 (LO), National Museum of the American Indian, Smithsonian Institution (15/4690). Photo by NMAI Photo Services; 223 (UP), National Museum of the American Indian, Smithsonian

Institution (25/5194). Photo by NMAI Photo Services; 223 (LO), Courtesy of the Coquille Indian Tribe; 224 (UP), Courtesy of the Coquille Indian Tribe; 224 (LO LE), Roberto Nistri/ASP; 224 (LO RT), National Museum of the American Indian, Smithsonian Institution (8608). Photo by NMAI Photo Services; 225 (UP), Edward S. Curtis/NGIC; 225 (LO), Oldtime/ASP; 226, Michelle Alaimo; 227 (UP), Alejandro Barreras/Dreamstime; 227 (LO), National Museum of the American Indian, Smithsonian Institution (1/8027). Photo by NMAI Photo Services; 228–229, David Alan Harvey/NGIC; 228 (LO), National Museum of the American Indian, Smithsonian Institution (26/6058); 229 (RT), Richard Schlect/NGIC; 230 (UP LE), Debbie Preston/Northwest Indian Fisheries Commission; 230 (UP RT), National Museum of the American Indian, Smithsonian Institution (1/9326). Photo by NMAI Photo Services; 230 (LO), National Museum of the American Indian, Smithsonian Institution (10/216). Photo by NMAI Photo Services; 231 (UP), Paul Gordon/ASP; 231 (LO), Elaine Thompson/Associated Press; 232 (UP), Art Collection 3/ASP; 232 (LO), Photo by Corbis/Corbis via GI; 233 (UP), Marcus Donner/Zuma Press/ASP; 233 (LO), Andrea Izzotti/SS; 234, Private Collection/Photo Boltin Picture Library/BI; 235, Centennial Museum, Vancouver, British Columbia, Canada/Werner Forman Archive; 236 (UP), Joel W. Rogers/GI; 236 (LO), Universal Images Group North America LLC/ASP; 237 (LE), Greg Gard/ASP; 237 (RT), National Museum of the American Indian, Smithsonian Institution (5/7843). Photo by NMAI Photo Services; 238 (UP), Edward S. Curtis/NGIC; 238 (LO), Melissa Farlow/NGIC; 239 (UP), LOC, Washington, D.C.; 239 (LO), LOC, Washington, D.C.; 240 (UP), Patrick Tr/SS; 240 (LO), National Museum of the American Indian, Smithsonian Institution (9/7671). Photo by NMAI Photo Services; 241 (UP), Hemis/ASP; 241 (LO), Edward S. Curtis/NGIC; 242 (UP), Derivative image of Esther Ross by Kuo Kang Chen from an original photograph by Jim Leo, The Daily Herald, Everett, WA; 242 (LO), Cristina Mittermeier/GI; 243 (UP), Don Paulson/Jaynes Gallery/DanitaDelimont/ASP; 243 (LO), Transcendental Graphics/GI; 244 (UP), National Museum of the American Indian, Smithsonian Institution (25/5693). Photo by NMAI Photo Services; 244 (LO), PVDE/BI; 245, Blaine Harrington III/ASP; 246 (UP), Johan Swanepoel/SS; 246 (LO), LeshaBu/SS; 247, NaturesMomentsuk/SS;

CALIFORNIA 248–249, JTBaskinphoto/GI; 249 (UP), National Museum of the American Indian, Smithsonian Institution (10/9610). Photo by NMAI Photo Services; 250, National Museum of the American Indian, Smithsonian Institution (26/0). Photo by NMAI Photo Services; 251, NG Maps; 252 (UP), De Agostini Picture Library/G. Dagli Orti/BI; 252 (CTR LE), De Agostini Picture Library/G. Dagli Orti/BI; 252 (CTR RT), Gary Saxe/SS; 252 (LO), Peter Newark American Pictures/BI; 253 (UP LE), J.R. Browne/Wikimedia Commons; 253 (UP RT), David Bacon/ASP; 253 (CTR), Bettmann/GI; 253 (LO LE), Richard Cummins/GI; 253 (LO RT), National Museum of the American Indian, Smithsonian Institution (24/6951). Photo by NMAI Photo Services; 254 (UP), Art Collection 3/ASP; 254 (LO), LatitudeStock/ASP; 255 (UP), W. Langdon Kihn/NGIC; 255 (LO), National Museum of the American Indian, Smithsonian Institution (26/5444). Photo by NMAI Photo Services; 256 (UP), LOC, Washington, D.C.; 256 (LO), David McNew/AFP/GI; 257, LOC, Washington, D.C.; 258 (UP), National Museum of the American Indian, Smithsonian Institution (25/1). Photo by NMAI Photo Services; 258 (LO), George Guajardo/NGIC; 259 (UP), Marek Zuk/ASP; 259 (LO), National Museum of the American Indian, Smithsonian Institution (6/5900). Photo by NMAI Photo Services; 260 (UP), David Ryan/ASP; 260 (LO), Private Collection/BI; 261 (UP), LOC, Washington, D.C.; 261 (LO), National Museum of the American Indian, Smithsonian Institution (1380). Photo by NMAI Photo Services; 262 (UP), NativeStock Pictures/UIG/SS; 262 (LO), Timothy A. Clary/AFP/GI; 263 (UP), Aurora/ASP; 263 (LO), National Museum of the American Indian, Smithsonian Institution

(4/9400). Photo by NMAI Photo Services; 264 (UP), Kent Kobersteen/NGIC; 264 (LO), Spencer Weiner/Los Angeles Times via GI; 265 (UP), National Museum of the American Indian, Smithsonian Institution (7/2255). Photo by NMAI Photo Services; 265 (LO), National Museum of the American Indian, Smithsonian Institution (P01808); 266–267, RGB Ventures/SuperStock/ASP; 268 (UP), Werner Forman/Universal Images Group/GI; 268 (LO), National Museum of the American Indian, Smithsonian Institution (26/2174); 269, jmoor17/iStockphoto; 270 (UP), Gary Crabbe/Enlightened Images/ASP; 270 (LO), National Museum of the American Indian, Smithsonian Institution (19/8179). Photo by NMAI Photo Services; 271 (UP), Charles Mann/ASP; 271 (LO), National Museum of the American Indian, Smithsonian Institution (24/4148). Photo by NMAI Photo Services; 272 (UP), National Museum of the American Indian, Smithsonian Institution (P22102); 272 (LO), National Museum of the American Indian, Smithsonian Institution (23/5700). Photo by NMAI Photo Services; 273 (UP), Gado Images/ASP; 273 (LO), National Museum of the American Indian, Smithsonian Institution (10/9610). Photo by NMAI Photo Services; 274 (UP), Private Collection/BI; 274 (LO), NativeStock Pictures/UIG/SS; 275 (UP), Danita Delimont/ASP; 275 (LO), Macduff Everton/NGIC; 276 (UP), nsf/ASP; 276–277 (LO), U.S. Forest Service; 277 (LO RT), National Museum of the American Indian, Smithsonian Institution (7/2281). Photo by NMAI Photo Services; 278 (UP), David McLain/GI; 278 (LO), National Museum of the American Indian, Smithsonian Institution (3/9299). Photo by NMAI Photo Services;

279 (UP), National Museum of the American Indian, Smithsonian Institution (22/2684). Photo by NMAI Photo Services; 279 (LO), Courtesy of the Department of Veterans Affairs; 280 (UP), Bob Kreisel/ASP; 280 (LO), Suntayea Steinruck; 281 (UP), LOC, Washington, D.C.; 281 (LO), National Museum of the American Indian, Smithsonian Institution (11/3566). Photo by NMAI Photo Services; 282 (LE), LOC, Washington, D.C.; 282 (RT), Kim Karpeles/ASP; 283 (UP), Granger Historical Archive/ASP; 283 (LO), Photo by Hector Amezcua/Sacramento Bee/MCT via GI; 284 (UP), Zuma Press, Inc/ASP; 284–285 (LO), Ben Margot/AP/REX/SS; 285 (UP), David McNew/GI; 285 (LO RT), National Museum of the American Indian, Smithsonian Institution (25/4798). Photo by NMAI Photo Services; 286 (UP), National Museum of the American Indian, Smithsonian Institution (18/4871). Photo by NMAI Photo Services; 286 (LO), Bobbi Onia/Underwood Archives/GI; 287 (UP), Universal History Archive/UIG /BI; 287 (LO), Terray Sylvester/VWPics/ASP; 288 (UP), Khoroshunova Olga/SS; 288 (LO), Chros/SS; 289, Jim Cumming/SS; **END MATTER** 290, Marilyn Angel Wynn/GI; 291 (UP), Design Pics/NGIC; 291 (LO), Aaron Huey/GI; 292, Michael Sewell/GI; 294–295, NG Maps; 296, National Museum of the American Indian, Smithsonian Institution (20/949). Photo by NMAI Photo Services; 297, Emily Riddell/GI; 298, Chase Clausen/SS; 299, Blaine Harrington III/GI; 300, Photo by Al Seib/Los Angeles Times via GI; 302, Blaine Harrington III/GI; 303, Nancy G Western Photography/Nancy Greifenhagen/ASP; 304, sumikophoto/SS

A horseback rider travels the Crazy Horse trail at a camp at Beaver Wall in Nebraska.

Located in Mesa Verde National Park, the ancient Pueblan Cliff Palace is the largest cliff dwelling in North America.

Front Cover Photo:
This Kainai man wears his Fancy Dance outfit. Also known as "bloods," the Kainai were one of the three major bands of the Plains Blackfeet. "Bloods" is thought to refer to the tribe's hands and faces that were stained from the berries they ate. The Fancy Dance originated in the 1920s, a time when Indian religious dances were forbidden. Instead, to keep traditional values alive, tribal members danced wearing their finest regalia, typically bright and full of color. The Fancy Dance is now a popular competition event at powwows.

The publisher wishes to thank the book team: project editor Priyanka Lamichhane; senior designer Callie Broaddus, senior photo editor Sarah J. Mock; production assistants Anne LeongSon and Gus Tello; and Potomac Global Media: publisher Kevin Mulroy; editorial consultant Barbara Brownell Grogan; story consultant Dan C. Jones; and Toucan Books: editorial director Ellen Dupont; editor Anna Southgate; designer Thomas Keenes; picture manager Christine Vincent; picture researchers Matt Propert and Uliana Bazar; picture clearance manager Susannah Jayes; proofreader Robert Sargant; and indexer Marie Lorimer. We gratefully acknowledge the generous support of the Smithsonian National Museum of the American Indian (NMAI) Archive Center.

Since 1888, the National Geographic Society has funded more than 12,000 research, exploration, and preservation projects around the world. The Society receives funds from National Geographic Partners, LLC, funded in part by your purchase. A portion of the proceeds from this book supports this vital work. To learn more, visit natgeo.com/info.

NATIONAL GEOGRAPHIC and Yellow Border Design are trademarks of the National Geographic Society, used under license.

For more information, visit nationalgeographic.com, call 1-800-647-5463, or write to the following address:

National Geographic Partners
1145 17th Street N.W.
Washington, D.C. 20036-4688 U.S.A.

Visit us online at nationalgeographic.com/books

For librarians and teachers: ngchildrensbooks.org

More for kids from National Geographic: natgeokids.com

National Geographic Kids magazine inspires children to explore their world with fun yet educational articles on animals, science, nature, and more. Using fresh storytelling and amazing photography, Nat Geo Kids shows kids ages 6 to 14 the fascinating truth about the world—and why they should care. kids.nationalgeographic.com/subscribe

For information about special discounts for bulk purchases, please contact National Geographic Books Special Sales: specialsales@natgeo.com

For rights or permissions inquiries, please contact National Geographic Books Subsidiary Rights: bookrights@natgeo.com

Library of Congress Cataloging-in-Publication Data

Title: Encyclopedia of the American Indian / By National Geographic Kids.
Other titles: National Geographic kids.
Description: Washington, DC : National Geographic Kids, [2019] | Includes index. | Audience: 8-12 years
Identifiers: LCCN 2018031435| ISBN 9781426334535 (hardcover) | ISBN 9781426334542 (hardcover)
Subjects: LCSH: Indians of North America--Encyclopedias, Juvenile. | LCGFT: Encyclopedias.
Classification: LCC E77.4 .E53 2019 | DDC 970.004/97--dc23
LC record available at https://lccn.loc.gov/2018031435

Printed in China
19/PPS/1